Dunn, Dennis J.
    The Catholic Church and the Soviet
Government, 1939-1949. Boulder : East
European quarterly ; New York :
distributed by Columbia University
Press, 1977.
    viii, 267 p. ; 23 cm. (East European
monographs, no. 30)
    Keston book, no. 10

THE CATHOLIC CHURCH
AND THE SOVIET GOVERNMENT, 1939-1949

DENNIS J. DUNN

EAST EUROPEAN QUARTERLY, BOULDER
DISTRIBUTED BY COLUMBIA UNIVERSITY PRESS
NEW YORK

1977

EAST EUROPEAN MONOGRAPH, NO. XXX

KESTON BOOK NO. 10

Dennis J. Dunn is Associate Professor
of History at Southwest Texas State University

Printed in the United States of America

For Margaret, Denise, and Meg

TABLE OF CONTENTS

PREFACE

The history of World War Two and the embryonic years of the Cold War have been the subjects of an increasing number of scholarly books and studies and justly so. The period between 1939 and 1949 is of supreme importance in understanding contemporary society. World War Two turned the then-existing order topsy turvy and the four years following the war saw the rapid crystallization of new political, social, and economic configurations. The Cold War, initially an antagonistic but fluid relationship between the United States and the Soviet Union, was, by 1949, with the formation of NATO, the Soviet explosion of a nuclear bomb, the Communist conquest of China, the growing success of the Marshall Plan and the Soviets' tightening grip on Eastern Europe, an indomitable, intransigent, and inscrutable corrivalry.

This work attempts to shed more light on this crucial era by examining a heretofore unexplored but extremely important aspect of the period: Soviet-Catholic relations. In the process it seeks to reveal, at least in part, Soviet and Papal motivation in the elaboration of war and postwar policy, Soviet rationale in the formulation of domestic religious policy during and, especially, after the war when the Communists had included in their jurisdiction the Catholic regions of Lithuania, Galicia, and Transcarpathia, and, finally, Soviet and Catholic attitudes in the evolution of governmental policies in those postwar countries, controlled by the USSR, where the Catholic Church was a dominant force.

The preoccupation of the study is preceded by three chapters which provide both historical perspective and background necessary to understand Catholic-Soviet relations during the crucial decade following the beginning of WWII. The major reason, undoubtedly, why this study has not been done to date is that definitive sources have only recently become available with the publication of the Vatican's *Actes et documents du Saint Siege relatifs a la seconde guerre mondiale*. Soviet sources are still sparse, but there is enough to warrant an examination.

This book owes a primary debt of gratitude to Alfred Levin of Kent State University who read the entire manuscript and offered criticism of inestimable value. I am also indebted to Bohdan R. Bociurkiw of Carleton University who read the manuscript and improved it greatly through his perceptive comments and cogent criticisms. I am further obligated to Thomas Bird of Queens College, C.U.N.Y., who read the material on Leopold Braun and the Assumptionists and who offered valuable suggestions. Without the invaluable assistance of the Assumptionist Order, this work would have been incomplete. I thank the Assumptionists for the use of their archives and, in particular, Revs. Patrick Croghan, Georges Bissonnette, Adrien Pepin, and Joseph-Marie Grenier. I should also like to express my appreciation of assistance rendered by Revs. Y. Krajcar and M. Lacko of the Pontifical Institute of Oriental Studies, Rome. My thanks go also to the *Collegium Russicum* for the hospitality of its library. To Michael S. Pap of John Carroll University I am forever indebted for introducing me to Joseph Cardinal Slipyi, Metropolitan of the Ukrainian Uniate Church, and Panas Fedenko of the former Institute For the Study of the USSR in Munich. Both of the latter individuals were of invaluable aid in giving me their impressions of Stalinism and directing me to material. The Organized Research Committee of Southwest Texas State University and the Graduate School of Kent State University have been most generous in providing assistance during the making of this work. The librarians of Kent State University, Biblioteca del Pontificio Instituto Orientale, *Collegium Russicum,* Institute For the Study of the USSR, Franklin D. Roosevelt, Catholic University of America, Library of Congress, John Carroll University, Cleveland Public Library, University of Texas at Austin, and Southwest Texas State University have shown forebearance beyond the call of duty.

A special debt of gratitude goes to my wife, Margaret, who helped proofread the manuscript and provided comfort and encouragement. Of course, I am solely responsible for the general thesis and whatever errors there might be in this work.

San Marcos, Texas

D. J. D.

June 1977

CHAPTER I
THE LEGACY OF THE PAST:
Catholic-Russian Relations to 1917

The Bolshevik *coup d'etat* in November 1917 did not sever all ties to the past and did not mean that continuities between tsars and commissars were non-existent. On the contrary, the Bolsheviks were the heirs of the tsars and, in regard to the Catholic Church, received an inheritance that was distinct and longstanding.

The nature of that legacy can be summarized, at the risk of oversimplification, by the word acrimonious. The wellsprings of such an antagonistic relationship are many and varied and go back, at least, to the 10th century and the state of Kievan Rus. Vladimir, the ruling prince of Kiev, converted, around 988, his people to Byzantine Orthodoxy.[1] The conversion, to be sure, was superficial, but it began a process by which the Eastern Slavs, over the course of many centuries, imbibed the cultural aura of the Byzantine Empire. One of the major characteristics of that emanation was hostility toward the Roman Catholic West. The Byzantine East and the Roman West had been drifting apart for centuries over a multitude of political, cultural, and economic issues. The major divisive factors were papal infallibility and caesaropapism, but it was the religious question of *filioque* which finally precipitated a permanent break between Orthodoxy and western Christianity in 1054.[2] The religious fracture, of course, was evidential of the deeper divisions which, in the course of the 12th and 13th centuries, were reinforced by the crusades, especially the fourth crusade which culminated in the Latin occupation of Constantinople for some fifty years.[3]

Once Orthodoxy became the state religion of Kievan Rus, the cultural antipathy existing between East and West took root in the civilization growing along the banks of the Dnieper River.[4] Although it soon dissipated in the western and southern parts of the country, it took firm root in the north. This anti-western tendency, although certainly mitigated by trade patterns with the West through Novgorod, actually grew in the thirteenth century and continued to flourish in succeeding generations. This was partly due to the fact that the occupants of the north, the Russians, under Mongol occupation from 1240 to 1480, cherished Orthodoxy, with its caesaropapist and anti-western propensities, as a concrete institution of national self-identity and a firm connection with the non-Mongolized world. As the Orthodox culture grew in significance for the Russians, so also did their anti-occidental feeling mature. It was also due to the fact that, as the political stability of Kievan Rus dissipated with its problem of political succession, challenges for control of the Eastern European plain were soon emanating from the Catholic countries of Poland, Lithuania, and Livonia. Alexander Nevsky, the prince of Novgorod, a city which protected the northwestern flank of Kievan Rus, decisively defeated the Teutonic Knights at the Battle of Ice in 1242 and that victory temporarily halted any expansionist moves on the part of the Germans. In the late 1930's, when the Soviet Government recalled Nevsky's victory over the Germans and condemned the anti-Russian role of the Catholic Church throughout history, it was an acknowledgment of a fundamental link with the imperial past.[5] And Stalin's 1919 declaration that the "world has definitely and irrevocably split into two camps" was indicative of more than simply the ideological antagonism existing between the capitalistic west and the socialistic east.[6]

The victory of Nevsky over the Germans, however, did not halt the dissolution of Kievan Rus which was in shambles due to the Mongol invasion and, although Novgorod managed to hold its own against the Mongols by paying tribute and against the Swedes and Knights by force of arms, the remaining western regions of Kievan Rus could not withstand the expand-ing powers of Lithuania and Poland.[7] In the first half of the 14th century, Lithuania pushed eastward and annexed part of Belorussia and Volynia and the Poles conquered Galicia. In the second half of that century Poland annexed the greater part of the Ukraine, including Kiev and Smolensk. In 1385 the Lithuanian ruler, Iagailo, married Jadwiga, the queen of Poland, and thereby established a personal union that not only increased the two states' strength but eventually, in 1569, led to a political union.

While the power and rule of Lithuania and Poland expanded, a Russian successor state, centered around Moscow, emerged in the 14th century. Muscovy, as the new state was eventually called, was forced to struggle against both Mongols and the western Catholic states for control of the plain stretching between Europe and Asia. To abet its expansion and struggle, Muscovy developed early in its history a sense of nationalism. That reality, of course, was not too unusual for expansionist nationalism or to use a more mundane term, imperialism, has been a factor in the history of every major country. But Muscovite imperialism did exhibit two unique traits which were utilized as justifications for expansion and for struggling with any other power which claimed a share of the Eastern European plain, whether it be the Golden Horde, Germany, Lithuania, Poland, Sweden, or Turkey. The first characteristic might be described, for lack of a better word, as pan-Russianism. The Great Russians of Muscovy claimed the right to gather, under their leadership, all Russian lands, whether they were populated by Great Russians, Ukrainians, or Belorussians, and whether they had been originally included in the boundaries of Kievan Rus. The Muscovites justified such an expansion first, in regard to the surrounding autonomous Russian lands, as a natural process of reuniting the eastern Slavic peoples who shared the same religion, a similar language, and common political roots stretching back to Kievan Rus. And secondly the accretion was rationalized, vis-à-vis the Catholic states of Poland and Lithuania, not only as a reunification process but also as a freeing of eastern Slavic peasants suffering from foreign political oppression. This populist rationale can also be detected in the Soviet Union's relations with its Eastern European neighbors. After World War Two, it was partly on such grounds that the Soviets annexed into the Soviet Union the Ukrainian speaking territories of Bukovina, Bessarabia, Ruthenia, the Carpatho-Ukraine, and the Ukrainian-Belorussian regions of pre-1939 eastern Poland.[8] Stalin could never abide the concept of Ukrainian or Belorussian nationalism, indeed, nationalism of any gender other than Great Russian nationalism.[9] To many of his biographers, critics, and contemporaries, he was, despite or maybe because of his Georgian background, a "Great Russian Russifyer."[10]

The second novel characteristic of Muscovite imperialism was the evolvement of a religious-political ideology called Moscow the Third Rome. In the course of the 15th and 16th centuries, the Russians, once they freed themselves from the Mongol Horde and once Byzantium fell to the Turks, proclaimed that God had chosen them, like the Jews of yesteryear, as mankind's religious and political leaders.[11] They maintained that Russian Orthodoxy was the true Christian faith and that all other Christian sects, including Catholicism, were heretical. As the holders of the truth, the Russians assumed a dual obligation of spreading Orthodoxy (an argument for expansion based upon divine calling) and of protecting their sacred trust from such extraneous and infectious diseases as Catholicism, Protestantism, and, much later, liberty, freedom, etc. (a justification for a closed, totalitarian society).[12] Accordingly, Muscovy had not only the right but the duty to "liberate" Orthodox peasants within the borders of Poland-Lithuania from persecution at the hands of heretical Catholics. She also had the moral onus of reclaiming the Ukrainian Uniate Catholics who, from the Russians' point of view, were forced by Polish-Papal pressure to give up their ties to Orthodoxy and accept union with Rome at Brest in 1596.[13] A forced reconversion of the Uniates, however, was important not only because they had been persecuted by heretics but because Uniatism, from the Orthodox vantage point, represented the cultural avant-garde of Polish political incursions into Eastern Europe.[14] And finally the Russians had a divine imperative to move their boundary continuously forward (in all directions) and convert all peoples, including Catholics, Jews, Muslims, Protestants, etc., to Orthodoxy and, thus, integrate these peoples and their lands into the Russian Empire. The Soviet Government did not fail to demonstrate all of these traits of Third Romanism in its postwar dealings with the Orthodox Ukrainians of Bukovina and Bessarabia, with the Uniates of Galicia and Transcarpathia, and with the Latin Catholics of Poland, Lithuania, Czechoslovakia, Hungary, and elsewhere in Soviet-occupied Eastern Europe. Stalin, an ardent Russian nationalist and a former Orthodox seminarian, seemed to have intuitively shared Orthodoxy's inclinations and the chroniclers of his life have not failed to compare him with some of the great promoters of the Orthodox Leviathon, including Ivan the Terrible, Peter the Great, and Nicholas I.[15] It was not, in other words, simply historical caprice or propagandistic expediency that Stalin declared in 1919, in the best tradition of the Orthodox Slavophils, that "Light is coming from the East."[16]

The actual historical contest between the rising state of Muscovy and the West for control of the Eastern European plain needs to be briefly summarized to place the influence of tradition on the Soviet Union and the story of the Soviets' relationship with the Catholic Church in perspective. By the end of the reign of Ivan III (1462-1505), Muscovy had freed itself from the Mongols, annexed Novgorod and Tver, and laid claim to West Russia as a patrimony. By this time, Lithuania was already in decline but it would soon revive through a union with Poland. The Byzantine Empire had fallen in 1452 and Ivan, realizing that this presented him with an opportunity to bolster his right to the western territories, soon launched a number of policies to arrogate for Muscovy the mantle of imperial and religious leadership. Part of the ground work for such a warrant had already been laid by Ivan's father, Vasili II (1425-1462), who rejected the union of the Orthodox and Catholic Church which had been worked out in 1439 at the Council of Florence.[17] Vasili reacted to the Florentine decision by censuring Byzantine Orthodoxy as heretical (for wedding with the heretical Catholics) and by establishing an Autocephalous Russian Orthodix Church under Metropolitan Jonas in 1448. Although Vasili had no intention of making the separation from Byzantine Orthodoxy permanent, his action nonetheless provided a foundation for Russian Orthodoxy to assert for itself the leadership of the Orthodox world. With the political conquest of the

Byzantine Empire, Ivan was presented with an opportunity to lay claim not only to religious leadership but also political leadership. In 1470 Ivan announced that the Patriarch of Constantinople was deprived of any rights over the Russian Orthodox Church. Two years later he married the niece of the last Byzantine emperor, Sophia Paleologus. This marriage had been arranged by the Pope in the hope that Ivan would convert to Roman Catholicism and also would join the Latins in a crusade against the Turks. Ivan revealed a great deal of shrewdness in dealing with the Papacy for he obtained what he desired, namely a firm dynastic link with the last ruling family of the Byzantine Empire, yet he did not accommodate the Pope on either of his designs. The Communists, although also politically acute, were incapable of exploiting for their advantage the Papacy's long sought goal of a reunification of the eastern and western churches because the antireligious theories of Marxism-Leninism obscured their perception of the nature and value of papal influence. This myopia was modified after the German attack in 1941, but then Moscow found it impossible, due to its persecutory past, to convince the Vatican that it was not simply an atheistic addict on an expedient, temporary low.

In 1489 Ivan, continuing to provide a foundation for his claim to imperial legitimacy, proclaimed to Nicholas Poppel, the Jesuit representative of the German Emperor, Frederick III, who with the Pope was again attempting to awe Ivan into an alliance against the Turks by investing him with kingship, that he was sovereign and "invested with power by God" and did "not need investiture by anyone else."[18] Ivan was clearly announcing to Poppel that he was the legitimate successor of the Byzantine Emperor and that the German emperor had no rights or authority over Russia. In 1491 Ivan adopted the double-headed imperial eagle of Byzantium as the state seal of Muscovy and in 1492 Metropolitan Zosimius plainly pinpointed the direction in which Ivan was moving by designating Ivan as the "new Emperor Constantine of the new Constantinople-Moscow."[19]

It was not, however, until the reign of Ivan's son, Vasili III (1505-1533) that the ideology supporting Muscovy as the political and religious successor of Byzantium finally crystalized. In 1510, an Orthodox monk by the name of Philotheus wrote the famous passage in a letter to Vasili: "I say unto thee: take care pious tsar; all the empires of Christendom are united in thine, for two Romes have fallen and the third exists and there will not be a fourth."[20] Vasili, with this ideological base to stand upon, continued the process of vying with Lithuania-Poland for supremacy over the Eurasian plain. In 1514 he managed to annex Smolensk. His son, Ivan IV (1533-1584), pursued the same policy and, in 1558, launched a concerted drive of westward expansion against Livonia. The Livonian Knights, unable to withstand Ivan, quickly placed themselves under the protection of Lithuania which, in turn, united, in 1569 at the Union of Lublin, with Poland. Ivan, now confronted with a formidable coalition (Sweden also joined Lithuania-Poland against Muscovy) and certain defeat, took a page from the political handbook of Ivan III and cleverly pleaded with the Pope to mediate between the Russians and the Catholic Poles who were led by Stephen Batory. The Pope, again hoping this was an opportunity to lay ground for the conversion of Russia to Catholicism, sent the Jesuit, Antonio Possevino, to Batory and Possevino managed to persuade the Poles to sign an armistice with the Muscovites. Ivan was, thus, saved and, like Ivan III, he failed to gratify the Pope's desire for unity. Ivan's reaction was a disappointment to the Pope and no doubt caused him to regret halting Batory but little did he realize how bitter his successors would regret the armistice of 1582 in the 20th century, when the Russians set up a Communist government in Poland.

During the reign of Ivan's feeble-minded son, Theodore (1584-1598), the Catholic Church and the Polish state took an action that was gravely feared in Muscovy. In 1596, at the Union of Brest, the Church created a new rite, the Ukrainian Uniate or Uniate rite, by which Orthodox peoples could accept union with Rome but maintain their own Orthodox liturgy and practices. Under the guiding, political hand of Poland, sizable numbers of Ruthenian Orthodox in Galicia, Belorussia, and the Ukraine converted to the Uniate Catholic Church. The Russian ecclesiastical and political leaders interpreted Brest as a ploy by the west to infiltrate the western borderlands of Muscovy, spread western culture, and hope that it would serve as a primer for Polish-Catholic political incursions into Muscovy itself.[21] The Russians had been aware of the Polish-Papal plans to institute the Uniate rite for some time and in 1589, before the rite was officially established, the Russian Orthodox Church attempted to blunt its development and strengthen Orthodoxy's religious position with the Ruthenian Orthodox peoples by creating a Russian Patriarch. This development, of course, must also be seen as the logical, religious culmination of the ideology of Moscow the Third Rome just as the coronation of Ivan IV in 1547 as "tsar" (caesar or emperor) was its political climax.

During the Time of Troubles (1598-1613), Muscovy was invaded by the Poles and Swedes and lost considerable stretches of real estate in the west, including Smolensk and Seversk to Poland and the entire littoral of the Gulf of Finland to Sweden. But with the advent of the Romanov dynasty, following the Time of Troubles, Poland began to wane and Russia managed not only to recoup its early losses but to increase its western holdings. In 1634, the Poles, preoccupied with a Turkish threat, gave up a small strip of land to Michael Romanov (1613-1645) and, then, in 1667, they ceded

Smolensk, Chernigov, and the entire left bank of the Ukraine to Michael's son, Alexis (1645-1684). In 1654, Alexis, reflecting the populist rationale for expansion, assumed the title of "tsar of all the Great, the Little, and the White Russias." This was in conjunction with Alexis' acceptance of a protectorate over the Ukrainian Cossack state which Bohdan Khmelnytskyi's revolt in 1648 against Poland had produced.[22] With the rule of Peter the Great (1689-1725), Russia definitely emerged as the leading candidate to win control of the Eastern European plain. Peter not only reduced Sweden to an insignificant power but also Poland and initiated a Russian policy of actively interfering in the internal affairs of the Polish state. Poland continued to weaken in the 18th century, but it was not until the advent of Catherine the Great (1762-1796) that the Polish denouement was finally completed. Catherine, working with the Prussians and Austrians, partitioned, in 1772, 1793, and 1795, Poland out of existence. From the point of view of the Catholic Church and the Catholic-Russian relations, the apportionment of Poland was a pregnant event for it was the beginning, in a substantive sense, of the Catholic Church in Russia. In the first partition Russia annexed the White Russian areas of Polotsk, Vitebsk, and Mogilev, in addition to part of Lithuania. By the second partition Russia acquired the White Russian area of Minsk and also right bank Ukraine. In the third partition Russia took not only the last parts of White Russia but Kurland and the remainder of Lithuania-territory which had never been part of Kievan Rus. All told the newly acquired land brought seven Latin dioceses and five Uniate dioceses within the borders of the Russian Empire. The former constituted the dioceses of Livonia, Samogitia, Vilnius (encompassing most of Lithuania), Lutsk (including part of Lithuania and Volyn), Kiev-Zhitomir (embracing most of Volyn and part of Podolia), Mogilev, and Kemenets-Podol'ski.[23] The Uniate dioceses overlapped the Latin episcopates and included Brest-Litovsk, Pinsk, Lutsk, Polotsk, and Kiev (whose bishop was called metropolitan).[24] For centuries the Russians had been inimical to the Catholic Church but never had they actually confronted the institution directly. However, their pre-partition attitude was a premonition of what could be expected in the event of contiguous encounter and, true to history, Catherine launched a vigorous policy of persecution against the Latin and Uniate Catholics populating the western borderlands of her empire. Her policy was predicated first upon a desire to russify the former Polish subjects whose Catholicism, she correctly feared, harbored seeds of Polish nationalism, to erase what she deemed to be a suprastate loyalty to a foreign center, the Vatican, to reclaim the harbingers of the Polish-Catholic *drang nach Osten*, the Uniates, and, finally, to bring the truth, Orthodoxy, to the Latin Catholics whom she, like her predecessors and successors, considered to be heretics.

The Soviet Government needless to say, exhibited similar, motivating attitudes in its relations with the Latin Catholics of Eastern Europe, especially Lithuania, and the Uniates of Ruthenia and the Carpatho-Ukraine.

Catherine's actions toward the Latins were mainly administrative: she suppressed the dioceses of Lutsk, Kiev, Kamenets-Podol'ski, and the title of the diocese of Vilnius.[25] But her measures against the Uniates harkened back to Nero. That pattern of operation, however, was quite consistent from Catherine to Stalin; the Uniates were always considered a primary target for persecution and the Latins only a secondary quarry. Shortly after the first partition, Orthodox pastors began to be nominated for Uniate rite parishes and a systematic campaign to close Uniate parishes and monasteries was inaugurated.[26] Simultaneously, to undermine the economic base of the Uniate Church, the Russian Government confiscated some of its monastic and episcopal properties.[27] In 1794 it was made a crime to be a member of the Greek rite Church.[28] After the second and third partitions, Catherine amplified her attack to realize the expunction of the Uniate Church. Forced conversions to Orthodoxy, the closure of parishes and monasteries drastically increased, and, in September, 1795, Catherine abolished the metropolitan see of Kiev and the dioceses of Pinsk, Brest-Litovsk, and Lutsk.[29] All told, by the end of Catherine's reign, the Uniate Church lost 9,000 of 11,000 parishes, 145 monasteries, and more than 8,000,000 people. Only 1,500 churches remained in Union with a total congregation of approximately 2,000,000.[30]

Under Paul I (1796-1801) both the Latin and Uniate rites in Russia enjoyed a respite and, indeed, a recovery. Paul was quite unique among Russian rulers in his attitude toward Catholics and, no doubt, this was attributable to his mental derangement. Determined to reverse many of Catherine's policies for personal reasons best known to Paul, the son of Catherine the Great allowed the Latin Catholics to reorganize their hierarchical structure. The Latin archbishop of Mogilev, Stanislas Siestrzencewicz, was accordingly named head of the Latin hierarchy as well as president of a new administrative department of Roman Catholic Affairs.[31] Paul also enlarged the jurisdiction of the archbishop of Mogilev to include the dioceses of Lutsk, Samogitia, Vilnius, Kamenets-Podol'ski, as well as a new diocese at Minsk. Finally, the Russian tsar permitted the new head of the Latin Catholic Church, the archbishop of Mogilev, to name three auxiliary bishops to help him administer Catholic affairs.[32]

The Uniate Catholic Church fared even better than the Latin Church under Paul. He revivified two Uniate bishoprics, Brest and Lutsk, so that, at the beginning of the 19th century, the Uniates had three dioceses, including Polotsk, and three bishops.[33] Paul did not, however, re-establish the metropolitinate of Kiev, due primarily to the ojbections of both the Holy Synod and Bishop Siestrzencewicz who, imprudently and shortsightedly, wanted control of not only the Latin Church but also the Uniate Church.[34] However, Siestrzencewicz was not given any authority over the Uniate Church, except in his capacity as the head of the department of Roman Catholic affairs to which, for administrative purposes, the Uniate Church was subordinated.[35]

Under Alexander I (1801-1825) the Latin and Uniate Churches experienced, as befitted the liberal-conservative syndrome of Alexander's personality, mixed blessings. The Latin Church received the basic organization it was to maintain until the Communists came to power. Alexander superseded the Roman Catholic department with a Roman Catholic Ecclesiastical College, under the presidency of Siestrzencewicz, which was charged with handling the affairs of the Catholic Church in Russia. As of 1801, such a task encompassed the administration of six dioceses, 1,710 secular priests, 3,094 male religious in 318 monasteries and religious houses, 569 religious women in 80 convents, 845 churches, and 1,639,854 faithful over fourteen years of age.[36] But the Ecclesiastical College was firmly under the control of the autocratic government and, like the Orthodox Church, laymen, responsible to the government, were placed on its governing board. This arrangement permitted Alexander not only to curb Rome's relations with the Church in Russia but also to interfere in such politically insignificant matters as matrimonial problems, monastic elections, etc.[37] That reality, plus the fact that Alexander constituted the measure without the Vatican's approval, reflected the traditional penchant of the tsars to rub out foreign influences within their country and to maintain autocratic control over all institutions within their jurisdiction. These attitudes, of course, were not missing in the Communits' governmental make-up. Once they occupied Eastern Europe, they, like Alexander, attempted to remove and retard Rome's authority in the dominantly Catholic countires of Lithuania and Czechoslovakia by creating a series of national "Catholic Churches" under Moscow's authority.[38]

Under Alexander, the Uniate Church, ironically, was buffeted more by the Latin Catholic leader, Archbishop Siestrzencewicz, than the Russian government. Siestrzencewicz, in his capacity as head of the Ecclesiastical College, on which the Uniates were not represented until the creation of an Eastern Catholic department in 1804, attempted to forcibly convert the Uniates to the Latin rite and succeeded only in weakening the internal structure of the Uniate Church and in alienating many Uniates.[39] Alexander, no doubt, did not object to Siestrzencewicz's debilitating policy, but he himself, aside from whittling the monastic clergy from 768 to 666 and the monasteries from 94 to 78, demonstrated a tolerant attitude toward the Uniates. In 1806 he created the post of "Metropolitan of the Uniate Church in Russia" and in 1809 he established Vilnius as a new Uniate diocese.[40] Both of these actions were carried out without the sanction of the Papacy, and thus, did create some canonical confusion but canonical consternation was a vast improvement over violent extirpation. And, despite Siestrzencewicz's efforts, the Uniates actually underwent, between 1804 and 1825, an increase in lay priests and faithful, the latter stretching from 1,398,478 to 1,427,559, and the former from 1,681 to 1,985.[41]

Under Nicholas I (1825-1855) the reprieve the Latins and Uniates experienced under Paul and Alexander was revoked and persecution à la Catherine the Great returned with vigor. Nicholas I was a dedicated ideologue of autocracy and Orthodoxy. His reign has been aptly summarized by the phrase "Autocracy, Nationality, and Orthodoxy," for he was determined to support and expand autocratic government, the Russian nationality, and the Orthodox religion.[42] More so than any other Russian ruler, with the possible exceptions of Stalin and Ivan the Terrible, Nicholas resolved to suppress any and all threats, real or imagined, to his regime and erect a uniform "Orthodox-Russified" populace which, he judged, would be easier to control and more likely to bear his rule since he was the leader of both the Russian state and the Orthodox Church. He particularly felt threatened by the force of nationalism released by the French revolution and he paranoidly suspected individuality, whether of a linguistic, religious, or ethnic nature, to be the womb of nationalism and a direct challenge to the cohesiveness of his dictatorship. The Decembrist Revolt in 1825 and the Polish Revolution of 1830-1831 reinforced Nicholas' propensities and spurred him on to root out all differences and cudgel a uniform Orthodox state. In regard to the Catholic Church in Russia, his first and, as it turned out, his principal preoccupation was to incorporate the Uniate Church into the Russian Orthodox Church. Stalin, some one hundred years later, manifested Nicholas' paranoia of ethnic distinctions and, like Nicholas, utilized the Orthodox religion as a vehicle for fashioning a uniform citizenry, especially in his relations with the Uniates of Galicia and Transcarpathia. However, there were distinctions between the two Russian rulers which should be briefly noted. Stalin was not as much an ideologue as Nicholas and he revealed an extraordinary degree of flexibility. Secondly, Stalin was a Marxist-Leninist and, even though he used Orthodoxy to enhance his power (an example of his flexibility), he looked to Marxism-Leninism as the main, quasi-religious vehicle to create a uniform and leveled citizenry. Both believed, however, as Nicholas Berdyaev eloquently put it, that "the profession of some orthodox faith" was "always the criterion by which membership of the Russian people is judged.''[43]

Before the Polish Revolt of 1830-1831, Nicholas had already taken steps to undermine the truncated Uniate Church. On February 9, 1826, he issued a *ukaz* forbidding the sale of Uniate literature in places where Uniate churches did not exist.[44] On October 9, 1827, he prohibited the Basilian order, which was the backbone of the Uniate religious, to accept candidates of the Latin rite in their monasteries.[45] Since the Basilians relied upon Latin Catholics to help staff their order, the law was a significant blow to the Uniates.[46] By 1827 Nicholas located a Uniate priest, Joseph Semashko, who was willing to serve as a trojan horse to deliver the Uniate Church "legally" into the grasping hand of the Russian Orthodox Church.[47] It is interesting to note that Stalin pursued precisely the same tactic in handling the Ukrainian Uniate Church of Galicia. The Communists established a fifth column within the Ruthenian Uniate Church through a certain Father Gabriel Kostelnyk and, then, manipulated this Uniate priest to justify legally and canonically (which they did not do) the absorption of the Uniate Church into the Russian Orthodox Church in 1946.[48]

After the Polish revolt, in which some Basilian monks participated, Nicholas quickened the pace of his onslaught against the Uniates in Russia. Semashko was given broad authority over the Uniate Church and he worked diligently to prepare it for unification with Orthodoxy through an array of Russification techniques, such as permitting only the Russian language to be used in Uniate schools and in Uniate prayer books.[49] In 1837 the Church was officially subjugated to the authority of the Holy Synod.[50] On February 23, 1838, the one morally restraining block to effective annihilation of the Uniates, Metropolitan Josaphat Bulhak, died.[51] Again, this time by coincidence, there is a parallel to the Soviets' absorption of the Ruthenian Uniates. It was only after the leader of the Ruthenian Uniate Church, Metropolitan Andrei Sheptyts'kyi, died in November 1944 that the road was cleared for the forced annexation of the Uniates into the Russian Orthodox Church. At any rate, with Bulhak's death, Semashko was named Metropolitan of the Uniate Church by Nicholas and, on February 12, 1839, through the act of Polotsk, he announced the union of the Uniate Church with the Russian Orthodox Church.[52] Not surprisingly, the language of the synodal act affecting the union was very similar to the working of the Lviv *Sobor* which ended the life of the Ukrainian Uniate Church in 1946.[53] On June 23, 1839, Nicholas I, via a *ukaz*, officially sanctioned the union.[54] From that time on, the Uniate Church, except for the Cholm diocese in the Kingdom of Poland, ceased to legally exist within the Russian Empire. The only remaining centers of Uniate concentration were in Galicia and Transcarpathia, territories under the jurisdiction of the Austrian Empire.

Fortunately, the Latin Church, under Nicholas, did not face extermination. It did have many of its monasteries closed, diminishing from a high of 323 in 1803-1804 to 72 in 1846.[55] Latin convents were also occluded, decreasing from 40 at the beginning of the century to 34 in 1847.[56] However, Nicholas, while he concentrated on integrating the Uniates into Orthodoxy, deemed it unwise to engage the Catholic Church on all fronts and, thus, practicing a policy of bitters and sweets, agreed to work out a concordat with the Latin Church in 1847. The Soviet Government, between 1944 and 1948, pursued the exact same ploy: while it expunged the Uniates in Galicia and Transcarpathia, it refrained from attacking the Latin Church in Eastern Europe and actually offered to negotiate a concordat with the Vatican.[57]

According to the concordat of 1847, the Latin Church was permitted to re-structure its diocesan boundaries to conform to the civil administration of the empire. The archdiocese of Mogilev, which encompassed all of Russia, was divided into seven dioceses, which included Vilnius (patterned after the provinces of Vilnius and Grodno), Samogitia (contouring to the provinces of Kowno and Kurland), Minsk (encompassing the guberniia of Minsk), Lutsk-Zhitomir (embracing the provinces of Kiev and Volyn), Kamenets-Podol'ski (comprising the guberniia of Podolia), Kherson (containing the provinces of Astrakhan, Bessarabia, Kherson, Ekaterinoslav, Saratov Taurida, and the Caucasus), and, finally, Mogilev (embodying the provinces of Finland, Turkestan, and Siberia).[58] The concordat also stipulated that the new diocese of Kherson was to have an auxiliary bishop and a seminary located at Saratov. It further stated that the Catholics of the Armenian rite would be under the authority of the bishops of Kherson and Kamenets-Podol'ski until Armenian bishops could be assigned.[59] In 1848 the diocese of Kherson was replaced by the diocese of Tiraspol with the episcopal residence at Saratov and the jurisdiction of the bishop of Tiraspol was redefined to include the provinces of Saratov, Samara, Kherson, Ekaterinoslav, Taurida, and Bessarabia.[60] The Catholic settlements in the latter part of the empire date back to Catherine II's decree of July 22, 1763, when, desirous of populating these lands, she invited foreigners to settle them and promised, as an incentive, freedom of religion.[61] Despite the concordat, however, many problems still existed for the Latin Catholics and the Papacy, including the lack of free communication between bishops and the Holy See, the annihilation of the Uniates (which the Vatican vigorously protested), laws against proselytizing, etc.[62]

Under Alexander II (1855-1881) and Alexander III (1881-1894), the Latin Catholic Church continued to be badgered. After the Polish rebellion of 1863, Alexander II presumed it wise to attempt to suppress one of the major institutions of Polish nationalism, the Latin Catholic Church. In 1865 he abolished the diocese of Kamenets-Podol'ski and, in 1869, the diocese of Minsk. Throughout the 1860's hundreds of Catholic churches were shut down and, on November 22, 1866, Alexander unilaterally revoked the concordat of 1847 and broke relations with the Papacy.[63] The Catholic Church in Poland, like the Latin Church in Russia proper, was, as of 1867, subordinated to the Ecclesiastical College which, henceforth, served as an intermediary between tsarist-controlled Catholics and the Vatican.[64] Although Alexander, after strong papal protests, relented, in 1875, on this latter function for the Ecclesiastical College, he increasingly attempted to introduce Russian as the official language of Catholic services throughout his domain.[65] In 1875, he snuffed out the life of the last center of Uniatism by forcing the Uniates of the Cholm diocese in Poland to convert to Orthodoxy.[66] As a result of the latter event, there existed, as of 1875, no legal Uniate Church in either the Russian Empire or the Kingdom of Poland. Alexander III, following the policies of Russification which his father had initiated in Poland, continued to essay to pressure the Catholic Church to utilize the Russian language in its religious services. His leverage was outright force as well as a refusal to fill vacant episcopal seats unless Catholic officials first agreed to cooperate with the Government's policies of Russification.[67] Alexander III, like so many of Russia's rulers, feared individuality and he determined, like Stalin some sixty years later, that an orthodox, homogeneous populace was the best guarantee of the continuation of his rule.

With Nicholas II's accession, the Latin Church enjoyed some relief from ill-treatment. Nicholas, facing tremendous internal problems as Russia made the transition from a backward, agricultural anachronism into a modern, industrialized state, attempted to cool, however, slightly, the boiling cauldron on which he was sitting by agreeing to allow the archbishop of Mogilev, Boleslas Klopotowski, to fill, in 1897, several church offices (vacant because of the language dispute).[68] On April 17, 1905, with the state exploding into revolution, Nicholas further tried to defuse some tension and opposition to his rule by issuing an edict of religious toleration. The Catholic Church, naturally, after years of persecution, could not but interpret the edict as a boon. It promised not only freedom of worship for all religions but also permitted Orthodox Christians to convert to the Latin Church, although the process of conversion was tedious and drawn out. Nonetheless, within a few years, about 233,000 former Uniates took advantage of the edict and re-converted to the Catholic Church, although the Latin rite.[69] The decree, in addition, sanctioned the organization of a Russian Uniate Church.[70] The Papacy named, as the initial head of the new Church, the metropolitan of the Ukrainian Uniate Church, Andrei Sheptyts'kyi of Lviv, but the Vatican pursued a highly contradictory policy regarding Metropolitan Sheptyts'kyi's jurisdiction over the new Church.[71]

Despite these gains, however, the Government, after the revolution of 1905 subsided, began to hedge on complete religious toleration and continued its Russification policies among Catholic Poles.[72] For example, Edward de Ropp, the bishop of Vilnius, was exiled in 1907, for an array of "crimes," which included charges of "Polonizing" Lithuanians and Belorussians, demanding freedom of religion and conscience, and organizing a political party whose program basically demanded a termination of governmental interference in ecclesiastical affairs.[73] The Church continued to be discriminated against right up to the fall of Nicholas' regime in February, 1917.

The Provisional Government, which followed Nicholas, restarted what had been initiated with the edict of toleration in 1905 and a new era of freedom and toleration for the Catholic Church appeared to be on the horizon. In March the Government set up a commission to improve relations between itself and the Catholic Church in Russia, and surprisingly, many of its recommendations, beneficial to the Church, were accepted and made law. For example, on May 5, 1917, the imperial decrees which had suppressed the dioceses of Kamenets and Minsk were revoked.[74] On May 13, laws for conversion from Orthodoxy to Catholicism were liberalized and, on May 20, it was decided that Catholic authorities should have complete control over their ecclesiastical buildings.[75] On May 9, the Provisional Government allowed the exiled Bishop de Ropp to return to his office and diocese in Vilnius and, on May 20, requested the Vatican to name de Ropp archbishop of Mogilev and metropolitan of the Roman Catholic Church in Russia, a wish with which the Papacy complied on July 25, 1917.[76] The post at Mogilev, although officially vacant since 1914, had been administered by Bishop John Cieplak and he was now named bishop of Ochrid.[77]

In the summer of 1917 the Government continued to implement reforms advised by its religious commission. On July 14 it issued a decree which guaranteed freedom of conscience and, on July 26, it stipulated that the Vatican, in consultation with the Government, had charge of naming bishops and apostolic administrators in Russia and authority to appoint, without governmental approval, all other clerical positions.[78] Also on July 26 the Provisional Government gave the Vatican and Catholic authorities in Russia permission to reorganize, in accordance with their own wishes, Catholic dioceses and episcopal offices. The Church lost no time in taking advantage of this opportunity to strengthen its organization by the creation of deaneries in the vast parishes of Mogilev and Tiraspol and by filling the vacant episcopal sees of Minsk with Bishop Zygmunt Lozinski and of Kamenets with Bishop Peter Mankowski. The incipient Russian Uniate

Church, holding its first synod under Metropolitan Sheptyts'kyi, also restructed its hierarchical organization with the nomination of Father Leonid Feodorov as Exarch.[79]

The torrent of religious reforms continued in the late summer. The Church was eventually given permission to establish seminaries, to own a printing press, to repossess some confiscated monasteries, to open schools (in accordance with laws governing private educational institutions), and to form religious organizations and societies.[80]

In general, then, the Catholic Church under the Provisional Government experienced a renaissance and its ecclesiastical leaders looked forward to the future with a significant measure of optimism. Such buoyancy, however, was premature. The Catholic Church in Russia had been persecuted for centuries and the fact that a "Provisional" Government, whose very name symbolized impermanence, relaxed time-honored persecutory measures did not mean that the next government would abide by the decisions of the Provisional Government and would not, in fact, reinstitute many of the traditional, anti-Catholic practices and attitudes. And, as we now know, when the Bolsheviks toppled the Provisional Government in November 1917, they forthwith began again to abuse the Catholic Church, utilizing many of the tactics of the tsarist government. As a matter of fact, it would be tempting to find the source of Bolshevik anti-Catholic positions in the tsarist past, but such a unilateral solution would be not only misleading but mistaken. To be sure, the Bolsheviks would have recourse to populism, Third Romanism, nationalism, and the specific methods of measures of anti-Catholic persecution which the tsars developed and, in fact, Russian tradition was an essential ingredient in the Communists' relations with the Catholic Church, but Stalin's attack upon the Catholic Church sprung, in a much more fundamental way, from Marxism-Leninism. Stalin was a Marxist-Leninist and, although the influence of the past contributed to the fact the Catholic Church was brutalized, as *Bezbozhnik* claimed, more resolutely than other religions in Russia, he nonetheless harassed all religions, irrespective of their past history.[81]

CHAPTER II
MARXISM, LENINISM, AND RELIGION

Despite the existence of continuities in the religious policies of the Communists and the tsars, one should not conclude that the Soviet Government was simply attempting to realize, under new slogans, the goals of the past. The Communist Government's religious policy, in fact, was influenced more by the philosophy of Marxism and by Lenin's experience as a revolutionary in late 19th and early 20th century Russia than by the tsarist legacy.

Marxism's fundamental view on religion cannot be separated from Marx's materialistic interpretation of history or the role of economics in history.[1] All societies, according to Marx, are dialectically advancing from primitiveness to socialism. Religion's position in any given society is determined by the stage of that society's economic development, but religious alienation only develops, according to Marx, in antagonistic class societies. As Marx summarized, "the religious world is but the reflex of the real world."[2]

In early history, according to Marx, when the mode of production was quite crude, religion first appeared as the fruit of man's ignorance. Primitive man, uneducated and unable to divine the cause of such natural phenomenon as floods, drought, storms, pestilence, fire, etc., began, according to Marx, to worship what he did not understand.[3] Religion, as Engels neatly captulized, "is nothing but the fantastic reflection in men's mind of those external forces which control their daily lives, a reflection in which the terrestial forces assume the form of supernatural forces. In the beginning of history it was the forces of nature which were at first so reflected. . . ."[4]

In the course of time, the mode of production and men's relationships resulting therefrom became more complex. Men passed through the ages of slavery, feudalism, and, by the nineteenth century, had attained the highly sophisticated economic system of capitalism which, in turn, would be followed by socialism. Religion, notably Christianity, according to the Marxists, had played a progressive role in the transition of society from slavery to feudalism. According to Engels, "Christianity was originally a movement of oppressed people: it first appeared as the religion of slaves and emancipated slaves, or poor people deprived of all rights, of peoples subjugated or dispersed by Rome."[5] Religion, according to the Marxists, was the revolutionary clarion of the slave age. In the age of capitalism, however, Christianity and religion became "incapable for the future of serving any progressive class as the ideological garb of its aspiration. It became more and more the exclusive possession of the ruling classes, and these apply it as a mere means of government, to keep the lower classes within bound."[6]

With the era of capitalism, the mode of production became quite complex and the economic relationships between employer and employee quite exploitive and, in this context, religion became a tool of exploitation and repression in the hands of those who controlled the mode of production. The exploited and repressed, from the Marxist point of view, turned to religion for consolation and listened tearfully as the rabbis, ministers, and priests explained to them that all injustices on earth, their sufferings and heartaches would be rectified in the hereafter. Thus, as Marx says, "religion is the sign of the oppressed creature, the heart of the heartless world, just as it is the spirit of an unspiritual situation. It is the *opium* of the people."[7] Religion had its origin in man's ignorance of nature. Once natural nescience began to dissipate, religion was maintained by man's incomprehension of the changing economic process: the product of man's labor appeared to be an independent commodity as society adopted "elaborate schemes of division of labor, roundabout processes of production, and the confusion of competition."[8] Marx called this development the "fetishism of commodities."[9] Men, according to Marx, became confused and could not fathom the fact that their labor gave all products their value. For the working man, once a product became a commodity, "it . . . changed into something transcendent;" it took on a "mystic character," and became shrouded and indiscernible.[10] Man, once disconcerted by natural forces, was now, in the capitalistic period, according to Marx, mystified by social forces and, again, he turned to religion to find solace from his distress. Thus, as Marx summarized, "*religious* distress is at the same time the *expression* of real distress and the *protest* against real distress."[11]

Having made that general indictment of religion and having proclaimed religion's exploitative role as part of the capitalistic superstructure, Marx and Engels give very little in the way of political directives which socialists should assume in regard to religion. The omission is not haphazard, any more than is their lack of exhortations on foreign policy or economic planning for socialists. According to Marx and Engels, the socialist revolution which will supplant capitalism will eventuate only in highly developed industrial countries and as a result of an internal collapse of the political and economic system. When economic conditions are ripe in any given country, the socialist revolution will take place naturally and inexorably. It will not, according to Marx, be affected by international developments, such as imperialism, or by internal developments (other than economics), such as a violent pruning of exploitative religion. Engels specifically warned against a bloody crusade against organized religion on the basis that such a policy would do nothing but prolong the life of religion through the creation of a martyrology.[1] Persecution of religion, from the point of view of orthodox Marxism, will not hurry the forces of history but rather hinder them. Actually religion, according to the *Communist Manifesto,* is becoming less and less important in European society.[13] As the economy and civilization advance, religion, from Marxism's vantage point, has a decreasing effect on the destiny of people. Its exploitative nature is stripped naked as the clash of interests of the two hostile classes, capitalists and workers, accelerates and the working class is able to clearly depict and discard it as a tool of bourgeois manipulation. In a highly advanced industrial society, the working class will increasingly be capable of detecting all the methods of capitalistic exploitation, including the institutions of family, nationalism, and religion. Such factors, according to Marx, are means and not causes of exploitation. Naturally it would be futile for the working class and for socialists to expend their energies rooting out means. It is much more prudent as well as productive, according to Marxism, to take hold of the cause and let the methods—the superstructure of the capitalistic society—crumble of their own weight. Engels enveloped the lesson rather succinctly when, in 1878, he wrote that as soon as the working class takes control of the means of production, "the last extraneous force which is still reflected in religion (will) vanish; and with it will also vanish the religious reflection itself, for the simple reason that then there will be nothing left to reflect."[14] And Marx added that when the workers wield the economy the fetishism of commodities will disappear and with it, exploitation and poverty will go, once "the practical relations of everyday life offer to man none but perfectly intelligible and reasonable relations with regard to his fellowman and to nature."[15] With the disappearance of the fetishism of commodities, there will no longer be a need for an institution of consolation and solace. Thus, the basic support of religion in capitalistic society will evaporate. Accordingly, Marx does not waste time giving socialists tactical advice on how to deal with organized religion. Religion, from the Marxian perspective, will die a natural death and it is both foolhardy and wasteful to spend efforts attacking it directly.

As to the religious policy of a socialist state, again Marx and Engels say nothing. But again nothing is needed to be said for in a socialist state there will be no religion since the capitalistic juglar from which religion drew life would have been severed. Revolutions, of course, Marx admits, can happen in backward countries, but socialism will not develop unless and until the economic circumstances are mature and no amount of religious or political agitation will alter that fact.

Such in general is the main view of Marxist theory on the problem of religion in the future. But it is necessary immediately to inject an important qualification. Before it became apparent, with the Paris Commune and the developed organization of English and German social democracy, that socialists might be able to take power within the established systems of late 19th century western Europe, Marx and Engels had elaborated a more active stand for socialists against religion, which, while not contradicting their main point of view, still represented a different dimension of their thinking. In 1844, Marx, in a work entitled *Contribution to the Critique of Hegel's Philosophy of Right,* decried religion as the tool of the capitalistic oppressor but strongly suggested that a violent attack upon religion might advance the cause of the proletariat's struggle. He proclaimed: "The struggle against religion is, therefore, indirectly a struggle against *that world* whose spiritual aroma is religion. *Religious* suffering is at the same time an expression of real suffering and a *protest* against real suffering. Religion is the sign of the oppressed creature, the sentiment of a heartless world, and the soul of soulless conditions. It is the *opium* of the people. The abolition of religion as the *illusory* happiness of men is a demand for their *real* happiness."[16] Marx was forcibly intimating that religion was a brake on the progress of history and that its removal would speed up the revolutionary struggle. A few years later, in a column he was writing for a Cologne newspaper, Marx again denounced religion and implied action against the soporific of the working class:

> The social principles of Christianity justifed the slavery of Antiquity, glorified the serfdom of the Middle Ages and equally know, when necessary, how to defend the oppression of the proletariat, although they make a pitiful fact over it.
>
> The social principles of Christianity preach the necessity of a ruling and an oppressed class, and all they have for the latter is the pious wish the former will be charitable. . . .
>
> The social principles of Christianity declare all vile acts of the oppressors against the oppressed to be either the just punishment of original sin and other sins or trials that the Lord in his infinite wisdom imposes on those redeemed.
>
> The social principles of Christianity preach cowardice, self-contempt,

abasement, submission, dejection, in a word all the qualities of the *canaille;* and the proletariat, not wishing to be treated as *canaille,* needs its courage, its self feeling, its pride and its sense of independence more than its bread.

The social principles of Christianity are sneakish and the proletariat is revolutionary.

So much for the social principles of Christianity.[17]

Although Marx and Engels nowhere explicitly call for an open persecution of religion, certainly the seeds for developing such a theory and policy were contained in the canon of Marxist literature. And, as a matter of fact, much of the writing of pre-1870 Marx counsels socialists to pursue activist policies. Thus it was quite understandable why Herr Duhring, a confused obscure "convert" to socialism, picked up the antireligious, crusading strain in Marxism and, in the 1870's, began to call for the total abolition of religion through force. By that time, however, Marx and Engels had curbed many of their activist tangents, including the necessity of violent revolution, and reaffirmed with vigor their primary view on religion. A polemic against Herr Duhring, in 1878, became the chief vehicle for the reiteration of Marxism's nonpersecutory stand toward religion as well as for a classical exposition of dialectical materialism. Duhring, who some thirty years before would have been tolerated as a Marxist thinker, was now decried as a heretic. According to Engels, Duhring, having failed to detect basic social changes, was advocating the adoption of the methods of bourgeois persecutors, such as Bismarck who was then abusing the Catholic Church in Germany. Rather than attempting to exploit the discontentment of the persecuted, he "out-Bismarcks Bismarck."[18] And, even more seriously, wrote Engels, Duhring misinterpreted the laws of history and, accordingly, was calling for unnecessary and abortive action. Overlooking the axiomatic dictums of dialectical materialism which automatically doomed religion, Duhring will not and "cannot wait until religion dies this natural death."[19]

Such an approach, Engels declared, would not only reverberate to the disadvantage of socialism. He "incites his gendarmes of the future to attack religion and thereby helps it to martyrdom and a prolonged lease on life."[20] The message of post-1870 Marxism, in other words, was implicit and explicit passivity—"waiting for the priest to dig his own grave"—whereas earlier Marxism had implied religious persecution.[21] In the transition from activism to quietism, the religious enemy was revealed to be no longer all bad but a mixture of virtue and sin, contingent upon conditions. Early in its history, Christianity, according to Engels, preached a belief in the equality of all men that was both progressive and positive, although it did degrade that humanitarianism by depicting its origin in "original sin."[22] But the egalitarian tenet, ideally suited to the mentality "of the slaves and the oppressed," was suppressed when the Church gained legitimacy, organized its hierarchical structure, and initiated crusades against non-Christians. The advent of capitalism, however, brought a resurgence of the demand for equality by the newly disadvantaged class of workers, who, at first, based their claims "on primitive Christianity."[23]

Engels expounded even more profusely in praising early Christianity in his 1894-1895 essays "On the History of Early Christianity," which opened with a warm note of comparison:

The history of early Christianity has notable points of resemblance with the modern working-class movement. Like the latter, Christianity was originally a movement of oppressed people: it first appeared as the religion of slaves and emancipated slaves, of poor people deprived of all rights, of peoples subjugated or dispersed by Rome. Both Christianity and the workers' socialism preach forthcoming salvation from bondage and misery; Christianity places this salvation in a life beyond, after death, in heaven; socialism places it in this world, in a transformation of society. Both are persecuted and baited, their adherents are despised and made the objects of exclusive laws, the former as enemies of the human race, the latter as enemies of the state, enemies of religion, the family, social order. And in spite of all persecution, nay, even spurred on by it, they forge victoriously, irresistibly ahead.[24]

Furthermore, Marx and Engels actually could envisage the possibility of socialists allying with and supporting clerically-led and/or inspired revolutionary movements which tended to weaken capitalism and the status quo.[25] Thus, Polish nationalism was warmly endorsed by Marx, although at the time its source was mostly among Catholic clerics and the Polish upper and middle classes, because Polish religious nationalism and the thwarted Polish uprisings undermined, to a degree, the stability of the three states-Prussia, Austria, and Russia—which, from Marx's point of view, were not only reactionary but barred the development of social and economic conditions favorable to the evolution of socialism.

In general, then, the major thrust of Marxist religious policy was toleration. However, there was a possibility of violent persecution and, thus, in the last analysis, the inheritance of Marx on socialist religious policy must remain ambivalent. There is, in other words, a doctrinal justification in the Marxist canon for the antireligious inertia of the Social Democrats in Western Europe and for the persecutory onslaughts of the Communists in Russia.

To properly understand Leninism on religion, it is imperative to perceive the reason for the ambiguity in Marxism. In reality, it is a product of a dichotomous influence on Marx and Engels: materialism and positivism. Although Marx never carried historical materialism to its logical denouement, his early directives for violence against the capitalistic system demonstrated its existence. Materialism, for all practical purposes, dictates one moral priority and that is the accumulation of power, the control of men and things–materials–in a complete sense. In the middle of the 19th century, although Marx, under the influence of positivism and rationalism, framed his teachings in an axiomatic system, that is, although he argued that socialists must wait to take power in the historically proper circumstance, he nonetheless could not suppress the subcurrent of his position and, accordingly, exhorted socialists explicitly (by preaching the need for violent revolution) or implicitly (by suggesting attacks upon religion) to induce the birth of socialism. Marx, to put it another way, was buffeted by contravening winds: his materialism *sui generis* demanded that socialists clutch the crown but his education convinced him that the socialist imperium would only come in accordance with the iron laws of economics. Thus, the ambivalence of Marxism on practical policies.

After 1870, and increasingly as the large Social Democratic Party took shape in Germany and the English unions and working class began to organize and gain the vote, Marx and Engels, because they now realized that it was becoming possible for socialists to take power within the system, abandoned, in total, the incisive strain in their teaching and reaffirmed the progressive, rational approach of historical patience. Power, in other words, was at hand for the socialists in Western Europe and there was no need to resort to violence either against the system or against religion.

Circumstances, then, are the central difference between Lenin and his Bolsheviks and the Western European socialists. Lenin, of course, grasped the underlying message of Marxism, the basic heart of the doctrine—that power *per se* was the only value in life—but the backward conditions of 20th century Russia did not allow him to even contemplate taking control within that system. Thus, Lenin, motivated by the goal of power, was drawn irresistibly into the trenchant tactics of Marxism and simultaneously repulsed by its quiescent approach. Given the historical economic laws of Marxism, the next revolution in Russia was destined to be a bourgeois revolution in which Lenin, as a socialist, would have no role. But Lenin could not wait for economic requisites in Russia to become uberous for socialism and, accordingly, he began to modify Marxism to fit the historical *milieu* of Russia so that he would legitimately be able to participate in the coming Russian revolution. He started off in 1902 with a work entitled *What*

Is To Be Done which argued that conspiracy and elitist organization, characteristics forced upon his Bolshevik Party by a politically oppressive regime and by a Russian revolutionary legacy of violence, were 20th century essentials for all Marxist parties. Then, in 1916, in his *Imperialism,* he announced that propaganda and political and violent activism were the tools for socialist victory and that although socialism could not be achieved in a backward country such as Russia, socialists could take power in such a backwater area and act as the spark which would ignite socialist revolutions throughout the highly industrialized West. Lenin, in other words, emphasized revolutionary action rather than procrastinating until the economy dictated his admission to power. Implicit in his logic, of course, despite the fact that he did not theoretically admit it, was the additional deduction that once socialists were in power, even if the West did not take the cue and erupt in socialist revolutions, they would have to initiate, despite the inevitable laws of history, attempts to socialize the country in which they held authority in order to maintain their clutch on power. As Stalin forecasted in 1917: "It would be rank pedantry to demand that Russia should 'wait' with socialist changes until Europe 'begins.' That country 'begins' which has the greater opportunities. . . ." According to Stalin, "we must discard the antiquated idea that only Europe can show us the way. There is dogmatic Marxism and creative Marxism. I stand by the latter."[26] And, of course, once the Bolsheviks did assume control of the Russian state, they did immediately essay to socialize the vehicle of their power: in foreign policy, they introduced the Comintern; in economics, they inaugurated War Communism; and in religion, they began a persecution.

Thus, vis-à-vis religion, like in other aspects of world politics, Lenin was an activist. His writings and speeches on religion—few though they may be[27]—reflect Marx's influence, but they do modify Marxism's primary interpretation of religion. His activist stand, as already intimated, was affected considerably by the environment of late 19th and early 20th century Russia. In a very lucid study, Bohdan R. Bociurkiw has clearly pointed out that Lenin's critique of religion was prompted, in large part, by his perception of contemporary, Russian Orthodoxy's shortcomings and its position as a fundamental pillar of tsarist society.[28] Lenin, in fact, reflects the antireligious views of many of Russia's 19th century radical writers, including Belinksy, Herzen, Pisarev, Bakunin, and Chernyshevsky.[29] He considered an attack upon organized religion as a direct onslaught against an exploitive social system and, thus, in contrast to Marx, a practical means of advancing the revolution.

Such, in general, was Lenin's primary view on religion. He favored a direct attack, but, as with Marx's principal view, it is necessary to immediately inject an important and overriding qualification. Power, for the sake of establishing the socialist state, was the only meaningful value for Lenin and if religious abuse was a hindrance to the attainment of power, it would be foresworn. That is, no tactic was permitted to stand in the way of the socialists taking control of the state. In a tract which became of major importance in fashioning Communist, religious policy, Lenin wrote:

> A Marxist must be a materialist, i.e., an enemy of religion. But he must be a *dialectical* materialist, i.e., one who organizes the struggle against religion not on abstract, detached, purely theoretical grounds. . . . but concretely, on the basis of the *currently* proceeding class struggle, a struggle which is educating the masses more and better than anything else. A Marxist ought to be able to judge the concrete situation as a whole; he must always be able to determine the boundary between anarchism and opportunism (this boundary is relative, mobile and everchanging, but it exists); he must not fall either into the abstract, verbal, and, in fact, empty 'revolutionism' of the anarchist, or into the philistinism and opportunism of a petty-bourgeois or liberal *intelligent,* who is afraid of the struggle against religion, forgets about this task of his, reconciles himself with faith in god, and is guided not by the interests of the class struggle but by petty, meagre little calculations: not to insult, not alienate or frighten away, (in line with) a wise rule: 'live and let live,' etc.[30]

Once supremacy was won, of course, then the socialists could take steps to protect their position by attempting to erect a socialist society and that included maltreatment of religion.

Before 1917, that is, before the Bolsheviks toppled the Provisional Government, Lenin had to subordinate his antireligious principles to the policies of the *"dialectical* materialist." The reason was simply that the Bolsheviks, to wield the scepter, needed the support or acquiescence of movements or groups which either held religion sacred or believed it to be outside the purview of social democracy. In the latter category would be most non-Bolshevik socialists. These men held to Social Democracy's Gotha Programme (1876 version) which declared religion to be a private matter."[31] Lenin, to avoid completely alienating these socialists, carefully attempted, in his major article on religion, *Religion and Socialism* (1905), to draw a distinction between the role of the state and the party toward religion.

> We demand that religion be regarded as a private matter in relations to the state, but under no circumstances can we consider religion to be a private matter with regard to our party. The state must not concern itself with religion; religious societies must not be connected with the state power.

Everyone should be absolutely free to profess whatever religion he prefers or to recognise no religion. . . . There must be no discrimination whatever in the rights of citizens on religious grounds. . . . No subsidies must be paid to the state church, and no state grants must be made to ecclesiastical and religious societies, which must be absolutely free, voluntary associations of likeminded citizens independent of the state. . . . As for the party of the socialist proletariat, religion is not a private matter. Our party is a league of conscious, leading fighters for the liberation of the working class. Such a league cannot and must not be indifferent to lack of consciousness, ignorance or obscurantism in the shape of religious beliefs. We demand a complete separation of church from state in order to fight against ideological weapons—our press, our word. We created our league, the RSDWP, among other things, precisely for such a struggle against all kinds of religious deception of the workers.[32]

Lenin's position, however, remaind unacceptable to most socialists who continued to believe religion was of no concern for the party or the state. In the long run, Lenin's distinction was possible only as long as the party did not become the state, which, of course, it did become after the Communist coup.[33] But, in the short run, Lenin's stand, even if it did not win any converts, did tend to leave the impression among non-Bolshevik socialists that he had modified his anti-religious vehemence.

Among those who considered religion inviolate Lenin counted, as politically useful, the peasantry, the working class, and the minority nationalities of the Russian Empire. The Bolshevik leader knew that if he was to take power he needed the support of Russia's largest class, the peasantry, and, accordingly, to avoid alienating the deeply religious peasant Lenin downplayed the antireligious nature of Bolshevism. He found it much more politically prudent to talk, for example in his 1903 pamphlet, *To the Village Poor,* of everyone's "full right to profess any faith absolutely free," and to support such clerical figures who were popular with the peasantry such as the priest-duma deputy, Fr. Tikhvinski, whom he praised as a "fearless and resolute defender of the interests of the peasantry and the people."[34]

Like the peasantry, the working class in Russia, with one foot still in the rural village, was strongly religious and Lenin realized that an antireligious emphasis in his party would estrange what was the hope and flower of Russia's future socialist state. He did not even feel secure enough to include atheism as a principle in the party's platform. And, like the clercial heroes of the peasants, so Lenin found it convenient to take admiring note of such workers' heroes as Father George Gapon whom he identified with the growth "of a liberal reformist movement among some parts of the young

Russian clergy."[35] Although to the workers' ears Lenin's words sounded complimentary, one wonders what would have been their reaction had they known that he reserved some of his worst invectives for "liberal reformers."

Referring to the workers and peasants, Lenin neatly summarized the Bolsheviks' predicament: "unity in the revolutionary struggle of the oppressed class for the creation of paradise on earth is more important to us than unity of opinion among the proletarians about a paradise in heaven. That is why we do not and must not proclaim our atheism in the program; that is why we do not and must not forbid proletarians who still retain certain relics of the old superstitions to draw near to our party."[36]

Beyond the working class and peasantry, there was, of course, the force of nationalism which, in Russia, as elsewhere in the world, was as often as not, affiliated in either character or leadership with religion. Lenin, above all, realized that in the "Prisonhouse of nationalities," a term that still accurately describes Russia, the force of nationalism often transcended class identity and class interests. Naturally, wishing to exploit this force, as well as other sources of tension and turbulence in tsarist Russia, Lenin had to be careful not to offend such diverse groups as the Muslims, the Jews, and the Polish Catholics by coming down strongly against religion. It was much more fruitful, as turned out to be the case, to support the right of national self-determination and of all minorities to practice the religion of their choice. These tactics worked very well for the Bolsheviks during the revolution but, as with their other expediencies, they were really not intended as a permanent addition to the Russian scene but only as methods to push the Bolsheviks into power. Aside from the above described purposes, Lenin's advocacy of "Freedom of Conscience" served other goals: it tended to splinter the mutually supportive relationship—moral, political, and economic—between the church and the autocracy and it forged a temporary coalition with the liberal middle class against the tsarist government.[37]

Lenin, thus, was essentially tied to the activist-persecutory element in Marxism's catechism. He opted, however, to desist from his natural predilection for the sake of gaining power with which, once attained, he could do what he wanted. His legacy to the Communist state, then, was, like Marx's legacy to socialists, ambivalent—while propounding a virulent stand against religion as opposed to waiting for it to die a natural death, Lenin's directives could justify any policy, including religious toleration, which would buttress the maintenance and extension of power.

Stalin, who followed Lenin and ruled the Soviet Union till 1953, carried Leninism to one of its possible conclusions, although admittedly encrusting it with the crude tendencies of his own personality. Leninism, as noted above, was a political philosophy which worshiped power. But for Lenin, at least in his mind, it was not power for the sake of power but, rather, for the purpose of inculcating socialism. His desire was to usurp authority in Russia and, then, await the socialist revolution to sweep the industrialized West which, in turn, would help the Russians to socialize and, thus, secure their position. Once in power, however, Lenin did not hesitate "to prime" Russia for its socialist revolution in anticipation of Western Europe's socialist explosion. He initiated, for example, a series of economic policies called "War Communism" and, in the religious sector, he introduced antireligious legislation. By 1921, with the peasantry on the verge of rebelling against the economic polities and with it apparent that socialist revolutions would not be racing across Europe, Lenin made a tactical retreat, replacing War Communism with the New Economic Policy. From Lenin's point of view, this was purely and solely an expedient retreat and would be maintained only until his government was strong enough to forcibly industrialize and collectivize the land, to transform the peasantry into a proletariat and the economy into a socialist system. Only when Russia had been converted into a socialist state could Lenin's position, could the place the Bolshevik Party be guaranteed internally and only then could the classless society develop.

Although the Communists had been forced to make a tactical retreat on economic issues, they did not feel compelled to make any concessions to organize religion in Russia. There was no popular outcry against the Bolshevik's persecution of religion and this was the case, in part, because Orthodoxy, the major religion, had been compromised in the eyes of the peasantry through its support of the tsarist autocracy and through Bolshevik propaganda which falsely portrayed the Orthodox Church as unwilling to give up its property to help feed starving peasants in the 1921-1922 famine.[38] Thus, it was easy for the Communist Government to continue attacking organized religion. Again, however, Lenin would and could call a momentary halt to the religious attacks if there were some political advantages to be gained, but eventually religion had to be abolished.

It is debatable whether or not Lenin would have pursued the policies of Stalin in religion or any other realm, but it does seem to be beyond argument that Leninism at least made Stalinism possible.[39] Stalin, like Lenin, was moved by the quest for power, but the Georgian interloper changed, some would say vulgarized, the Leninist rationale for pursuing the political grail. Lenin, as already emphasized, sought power to establish socialism. Stalin tried to erect socialism to seek power. He, in other words, lusted after power for its own sake. Initially taking his cues from Lenin, Stalin, when he assumed authority, evidently decided that his position could be secured only through the creation of socialism in Russia. Accordingly, he began, with the five year plans, to systematically cudgel Russia into an industrial-ized and collectivized country. During the late 1920's and through the 1930's, he, in addition, bludgeoned organized religion until, on the eve of World War Two, it was languishing throughout the Soviet Union. His real purpose, however, did not actually seem to be to implement socialism but, rather, to guarantee his position. It just so happened that he was convinced that he could accomplish that ultimate goal through the establishment of a socialist state. His commitment to socialism seems to be primarily strategic dedication and not an ideological profession. If such were the case, the progeny of materialistic Marxism-Leninism had finally come home to roost. Stalin was, from all appearances, the living example of Machiavelism, a politician who would utilize any means, including Marxism-Leninism, to distend his power.

It should not be surprising, then, that it is Stalin who resurrects, in all its glory, Russian nationalism and who openly compares himself to such autocratic stalwarts as Ivan the Terrible and Peter the Great. It is also Stalin who reinstitutes one of the pillars of the tsarist order: alliance with the Orthodox Church. That policy would have made both Lenin and Marx turn in their graves, despite their flexibility, but it was the logical extension of their philosophy. Instead of attacking religion in general, Stalin, in the postwar period, struck out at "disloyal" or "anti-Soviet" churches and sects, clearly linking his religious policy to nationalism and not Marxism. However, the continued antireligious forays following World War Two were undoubtedly, in addition, designed to serve ideological purposes: to protect Stalin's position as leader of the Communist movement (interna-tional after the war) from the criticism that he was violating the atheistic norms of Marxism-Leninism and, very importantly, to instill atheism, admittedly at a much reduced rate, in Soviet society. The latter goal remained viable, at least as an ideal, because Stalin apparently continued to believe that, in the last analysis, his position could only be ultimately impregnable when Marxism-Leninism, with its essential atheism, had become the intellectual outlook of the Russian people. Stalin, in effect, could not allow Marxism-Leninism to be undermined through his adoption of apparently un-Marxist policies for Marxism-Leninism was the rationale for the status quo in the USSR. The same dilemma faces the Kremlin leaders today and for the same reason, as well as for others, they have continued to attack organized religion.[40]

Although the post Leninist Government in the Soviet Union was capable of any policy, it nonetheless preferred the atheism of Marxism-Leninism and, despite its eventual détente with Orthodoxy, it was naturally antago-nistic toward peddlers of heavenly bliss and citadels of reaction, especially the Catholic Church. In addition, it cherished the vestiges of Russia's cultural and political past. Moscow's use of Russian tradition as a policy against the Catholic Church was more than just a ploy. It was, in addition, a personal vendetta against a western culture which belittled xenophobic Russia, a reaffirmation of Moscow as the Third Rome, and a final turning back of the Polish-Catholic incursion of Brest in 1596. But again, despite this personal disposition, the Soviet Government would not pursue or tolerate any proclivity or bias if it tended to cramp or hinder its totalitarianism.

Thus, in regard to the Catholic Church, the Soviet Government's mental attitude, under Stalin, was political and its basic policy was attuned to its perception of the Church's utility. Beyond that intrinsic tenet, the Kremlin had a personal opinion of Catholicism which, molded by Marxist-Leninist atheism and Orthodox atavism, held the Church to be essentially repugnant.

The Bolshevik Revolution in November 1917 was greeted with mixed emotions by Catholics in Russia. The majority of the clerical leadership feared that the Communist take-over would issue in an era of persecution and cut in the bloom the tremendous strides the Church had made under the Provisional Government. A few, however, welcomed the socialists' victory, but, in a relatively short span of time, they had reason to regret their initial optimism.

In early 1918 the new Communist government issued a series of decrees separating church and state, nationalizing all church lands and property, and removing schools from religious control.[1] In the summer of 1918 the government published a new constitution which reaffirmed the earlier laws plus disenfranchised all clerics, denied them civil rights, and subjected them to the highest tax rate.[2] In late August, 1918, the Soviet regime passed the Instruction on Separation of Church and State which not only deprived all religious and ecclesiastical organizations of their legal personality and declared their property nationalized but ruled that church buildings and equipment could be used by groups which established a church council of twenty persons over eighteen.[3] In 1919 the government outlawed religious instruction (other than by parents) of children below eighteen.[4] In 1920 it began a massive liquidation of monasteries.[5]

The Catholic hierarchy protested the series of antireligious laws, but they themselves were divided as to what course to follow in response.[6] Monsignor Budkiewicz, the dean of the St. Petersburg clergy, demanded a tough, uncompromising stand, tantamount to refusing to comply with the legislation unless actually forced by the government.[7] Archbishop de Ropp, however, the archbishop of Mogilev and Metropolitan of the Catholic Church, deemed it best to obey the governmental dictates because he harbored the conviction that the Bolshevik government would soon be toppled anyway and, thus that the antireligious legislation was only temporary.[8] Archbishop de Ropp, though, was soon removed from the scene when in April, 1919, he was arrested. What prompted his incarceration was

Bolshevik pique over a 1919 expression of sympathy by the Pope for the Orthodox Church which the Communists were persecuting. In late November, 1919, the bishop was sent to Warsaw in exchange for Karl Radek.[9] With Ropp gone, Bishop John Cieplak took over leadership of the Latin Church and he, like Budkiewicz, was inclined to struggle against nationalization of ecclesiastical property, the establishment of church councils, and, by and large, the entire range of Communist antireligious statutes.[10] In late January, 1920, a Catholic clerical conference decided that Catholics could not belong to the Communist Party which was, although quite understandable, neither a pressing or prudent decision since it could do nothing but confirm, in the eyes of the Communists, the anti-revolutionary nature of the Catholic Church.[11] The Papacy's intervention for the safety of the Imperial family in 1918 and its vigorous objection to the religious persecution ongoing in Russia in 1919, of course, had already clearly pinpointed, in the mind of the young Communist government, the Catholic Church as a bulwark of reactionary and counterrevolutionary politics.[12] The anti-Soviet position of the Church was again clearly impressed upon the Communists when a number of the Catholic clergy supported Poland's invasion of the Soviet Republics in the spring of 1920.[13] Among the latter were the bishop of Minsk, Zygmunt Lozinski, the bishop of Kamenets, Peter Mankowski, and the bishop of Zhitomir, Ignatius Dubowski, all of whom were eventually forced to leave Soviet territory.[14]

By the time the Civil War and the Polish-Russian war had subsided, the Communists' attitude toward the Catholic Church had clearly crystallized into hostility, a disposition formed and reinforced by an atheistic ideology, Russian nationalism, and pre- and postrevolutionary experiences. Specifically, five interrelated motives seem to explain the Kremlin's persistently inimical feelings toward Rome. First, the Communists, as indicated earlier, considered Catholicism, as well as other religions, to be an illusion, a fraud, and a "false teaching," which could not be tolerated by the purveyors of socialist truth. Secondly, the Catholic Church was an independent institution which the Party could not control ideologically and which, furthermore, preached a reality which was irreconcilable with Communist political culture, thus, hindering the political socialization of part of the Soviet people. The Catholic Church was predominantly a religion of western national groups—Lithuanians, Latvians, Ukrainians, Germans, Belorussians, and Poles—and its principles seemed to impede these groups' assimilation into the Soviet system. Moreover the western orientation of the Church and the fact that many Catholics lived in the sensitive border territories of the Soviet Union made them potential threats to security. Thirdly, the commissars, again as indicated previously, could not completely stifle the traditions of the Russian past and they nutured a lingering suspicion and dislike of the Catholic Church. Fourthly, the young Soviet government believed, often without definitive proof, that the Catholic Church opposed its coup and policies, supported anti-Bolshevik forces during the 1917 Revolution, the Civil War, and the Polish-Russian war— beliefs which identified the Catholic Church as an instrument of the external and internal foes of the Communist system. Finally, the Catholic Church, from the Soviet vantage point, was a foreign, universal religion, controlled by an outside, supreme authority, the Vatican, which was not only superior to Communist internationalism but could stall and disrupt the Communist evangilization of the world and some goals of Soviet diplomacy.[15]

Despite the mordant mentality, however, the Soviet government, through 1921, did not accelerate its antireligious behavior or legislation against the Catholic Church. The reasons for the delay seemed to be linked to two factors. The regime was still consolidating its political position and preoccupied with the ramifications of the New Economic Policy which was sanctioned by the 10th Party Congress in March, 1921. Secondly, and most importantly, the Party, while united on the idea of creating an atheistic society, was divided in how to combat religion, over the means and pace of the antireligious battle, and the tactical utility of religion.[16] The Party *agitprop* and the Komsomol—"fundamentalists"—argued for a pervasive, uncompromising assault upon religion while the "practical" state workers and the police strove to utilize organized religion in the interests of the Soviet Government by granting temporary stays of execution in return for support.[17] Through 1921, the pragmatic approach to relations with the Catholic Church was adopted evidentally because the fledging Soviet state, in dire need of economic and political relations, perhaps hoped that the Catholic Church, with a large number of European adherents, might be able to serve as a bridge for establishing Soviet ties with the West. The Papacy's willingness to provide famine relief in the late summer of 1921 undoubtedly fed the Soviets' belief that the Vatican might be useful.

However, by the end of 1921, the Soviets probably came to the conclusion that the Vatican, while capable of providing some famine relief, could do nothing politically positive for their regime. Pushed by the "fundamentalists" the government apparently determined that all-out religious persecution would be more essential for its ultimate security than Catholicism's continued euphoria. At any rate, on December 26, 1921, censorship of sermons was inaugurated and in late February, 1922, the government began a systematic campaign of confiscating church valuables on the premise that they were needed for famine relief.[18] Catholic authorities, like Orthodox officials, refused to comply with this law as well as the multitude of heretofore mentioned antireligious legislation.[19] The regime reacted, first, by compromising the churches in the eyes of the starving peasants with the charge that the organized religions were hoarding wealth required for the purchase of food and, secondly, by forcibly sequestrating the precious chalices, crosses, etc., and closing down many of the churches in the process.[20]

The Vatican, still administering rations in Soviet-controlled territory, protested and offered to pay for the religious articles but its efforts were rebuffed.[21] The Polish government also complained to George Chicherin, the Foreign Minister, but evidently the Soviets were unconcerned with the disposition of the Polish government for its objections were also spurned.[22] The Rapallo Treaty with Germany in April, 1922, undoubtedly uplifted the spirits of the Communist government and convinced it that its antireligious salvos, against the Catholic Church and other religions, were not politically damaging in the eyes of foreign governments. The Soviets, of course, after WWI, like Germany, had been isolated economically and politically and, given their socialist ideology and their natural xenophobia, they no doubt felt, particularly after socialist revolutions failed to sweep across the industrialized world, that they were surrounded by capitalist nations who might very well find it within their interests to form a coalition and annihilate the world's one oasis of socialism. While they worked assiduously to preclude such a development, they simultaneously busied themselves with a number of policies geared to transform Russia into a socialist state, one of which was massive opposition to religion. In 1922, with diplomatic, economic, and military ties established with Germany, the Soviets not only removed the possibility of a capitalist alliance, since Germany would naturally be the leading and necessary integral in any such combination, but also had concrete proof that their policy of assaulting religion was not jeopardizing their relations with important countries and that the Papacy had very little international influence.

Accordingly, the Soviets' anti-Catholic thrust shifted into high gear in late 1922. In November of that year Bishop John Cieplak was notified that he and the clergy of Petrograd would be tried in early 1923 on the rather nebulous charge of counterrevolutionary and anti-Soviet activity.[23] Between March 21 and 25 the trial of the Catholic clergy was held and Bishop Cieplak, his assistant, Mgr. Constantine Budkiewicz, the Exarch of the incipient Russian Catholic Church, Leonid Feodorov, and twelve priests were found guilty of an array of crimes. The sentences were accordingly passed: Archbishop Cieplak and Monsignor Budkiewicz were to be executed for organizing anti-Soviets activities, leading a conspiracy of counterrevolutionaries, authorizing and inciting clerics and citizens to resist the government, and, finally, undermining the dictatorship of the working class.[24] Exarch Feodorov and Fathers Juniewicz, Chodniewicz, Chwiecko, and Ejsmont were sentenced to ten years' imprisonment, confiscation of their personal property, and loss of civil rights for joining a counterrevolutionary conspiracy.[25] Monsignor Malecki and Fathers Ivanov, Rutkowski, Toigo, Pronckietis, Wasilewski, Matulanis, and Janukowicz were to be interned for three years with loss of civil rights for cooperating with the so-called reactionary organization of Cieplak and Budkiewicz.[26]

The Papacy, naturally, objected to the trial and its conclusions,[27] but unconcerned about the Vatican, the Soviets went ahead and implemented all the sentences with the exception of the execution of Bishop Cieplak whose attainder they commuted to imprisonment for ten years.[28] The loss of so many clerical leaders was a staggering blow to the Catholic Church in the Soviet Union and, quite obviously, the Soviet action, especially the shooting of Monsignor Budkiewicz, was quite extreme. The explanation for such an escalation may perhaps be sought, as indicated earlier, in the temporary ascendancy of the left wing of the Party within the government. With strikes breaking out in the Ruhr in early 1923, the left fundamentalists, in control of the Comintern, evidentally concluded, once again, that the socialist deluge was about to engulf Europe and that the time was ripe not only to stimulate revolution in Germany but also, internally, to end NEP and emasculate religion with one swooping blow. Accordingly, the Catholic Church, as well as the Orthodox Church, whose Patriarch, Tikhon, was then in jail, experienced heightened hostility and even though, by the fall of 1923, it became obvious that the socialist utopia was not yet at hand, the attack against the Catholic Church persisted.

The Church, with the loss of its episcopal leadership, was reeling and the Soviet government pressed the issue. Catholic churches, chapels, and seminaries continued to be closed throughout the remainder of 1923 and into 1924. The Theological Academy in Petrograd was soon confiscated.[29] By the time of Lenin's death in 1924, there still were approximately 1,600,000 Catholics in the Soviet Union (same as at the time of the Treaty of Riga) but only a couple hundred priests (down from about 900 at the time of the Treaty of Riga).[30] The rest of the clergy had either fled, been exiled, or simply disappeared which meant the priests were either in prison, in hiding, in forced-labor camps, or in the earth, six feet under.[31] There was only one bishop, as of 1924, in all of the Soviet Union, Bishop Zerr of Tiraspol, and he was bordering on senility.[32] It was also in 1924 that the Soviets expelled the Papal mission for famine relief and, in 1925, organized, under the leadership of Emil'ian Iaroslavskii and a group called the League of Godless (Militant

Godless as of 1929-*Soiuz Voinstvuiushchikh Bezbozhnikov*), antireligious propaganda on a more systematic basis.[33] The Bolsheviks were great believers in the value of agitation and propaganda and well they might be for such were important keys to their victory in 1917.

1925 brought a respite to the sufferings of the Catholic Church in the Soviet Union. Stalin was, by then, directing the government and attempting to outmaneuver Trotsky and Zinoviev-Kamenev. The Dawes Plan and the Locarno Treaty, which respectively brought economic and political stability to Germany for the first time since the end of the war and reintegrated Wiemar Republic into the western community of nations, could not but reinstill with the Soviet leadership the fear of capitalist encirclement and, by extension, bring discredit to the policies of the left whose Comintern gambits in Germany had helped precipitate Dawes and Locarno. Under Stalin's leadership, the government, alarmed that the unique German-Russian relationship formulated at Rapallo was now in peril and that the USSR faced the grave danger of a capitalist coalition, attempted to open other avenues of contact with the western world. Fortunately for the Catholic Church, the Soviet government was desperate enough to make overtures to the Vatican, despite the fact that the year before they had shown complete disdain for Papal influence.

In early 1925 the Communists offered to the Vatican the chance to open negotiations on such diverse issues as finances, education of Catholics, the appointment of bishops, the publication of Papal Bulls, and the communication between the Papacy and Soviet Catholics.[34] The Vatican deemed this as not only an opportunity to discuss the various topics outlined by the Soviets but also as a crucial moment to reorganize its ecclesiastical structure. Thus, when Pius XI sent the French Jesuit Michel d'Herbigny to the USSR, he was commissioned not only to negotiate with the Communist leaders, but also to designate clandestinely, if need be, a new hierarchy.[35] D'Herbigny did precisely that and, although he was expelled in August, 1926, when discussions broke down, he did manage to consecrate eleven bishops and apostolic administrators.

Negotiations were ended in 1926 because Moscow was, by then, apparently convinced that there was no threat of a capitalist alliance forming against the USSR and because it was aroused by d'Herbigny's creation of a hierarchy. It must also be emphasized that other religions, especially Orthodoxy, were continuously tormented throughout the 1920s and that the temporary hiatus for Catholicism was not shared by other faiths, although Orthodoxy did obtain some relief after Metropolitan Sergei agreed to an unfavorable concordat in 1927.[39] One other point should be mentioned. Stalin, although he was individually persuaded that there was no threat of a capitalist coalition and, therefore, could drive ahead, full speed, with the warfare against religion as well, eventually, with the socialist-orientated but economically disruptive policies of collectivization and industrialization,[37] did not reveal his conviction to his fellow Communists but, on the contrary, emphasized, to the point of creating a war scare in the Soviet Union, that the USSR was in mortal danger of being victimized by a capitalistic concert. The reason for the pretense was simply to continue to anathematize the left wing of the Party[38] and, in that endeavor, Stalin was significantly buttressed by the British breakage of diplomatic relations in 1927. Had Zinoviev and Trotsky and, for that matter, the right wing of the Party been attuned to the Stalinist government's changing attitudes toward the Papacy, they might have been able to divine the political trap which was being set for them.

The attrition of the new Catholic hierarchy began with d'Herbigny's expulsion. In 1926 Mgr. Theophil Skalski, dean of the St. Alexander Church in Kiev and the new Apostolic Administrator of the Zhitomir diocese, and Mgr. Vincent Ilyin, the Apostolic Administrator of Kharkov, were arrested.[39] Mgr. Skalski was charged with espionage and counterrevolutionary activities, found guilty eighteen months later of only the latter charge, and sentenced to ten years imprisonment.[40] The desire to remove Skalski was more than simply anger over the creation of a new Catholic hierarchy. Skalski was, in addition to being Apostolic Administrator, a powerful and influential figure among the Polish minority in the Soviet Ukraine (comprising some 476,000 people) and he stood like a barricade against the "sovietization" of the Poles. More so than any other Catholic minority the Poles (there was almost 100,000 more in Belorussia) were synonymous in the interwar period with the Kremlin's "Catholic problem." This was evidenced by the surfeit of antireligious materials, including a bi-monthly periodical directed solely against the Catholic Church, published in the Polish language.[41] It is noteworthy, furthermore, as Walter Kolarz has pointed out, that the 12th Party Congress in April, 1923, openly admitted, in its resolution, "the growth of nationalist-clerical influence among the Polish minority in the USSR" and condemned the Catholic clergy's growing hold over schoolchildren.[42] What magnified Soviet concern with the Catholic Poles was that they were clustered in the strategically exposed borderlands and the Soviet inability to absorb them was a constant embarrassment to the state which claimed the right to lead the world (including the Poles) to the socialist nirvana.[53] Skalski's arrest, in fact, did nothing to alleviate the problem, but as one Soviet source allowed, enflamed it since he was eulogized as a martyr.[44]

Anti-Catholic propaganda, which had been published since the Communist coup, also increased in the mid-1920s.[45] This was probably a by-product of the improved organization of the antireligious forces under Iaroslavskii.[46] One major development in the mid-twenties was the godless organization's success in helping to fashion an international adjunct to its struggle against religion and, especially, against Catholicism. On June 1, 1925, the International of Proletarian Freethinkers was borne, a rather curious amalgam of West European Social-Democrats (fighting mainly against clerical-Catholic influences in politics) and the fundamentalist Communists who viscerally wanted to wipe out religion and the very concept of God. The Russian godless especially hoped to infiltrate the Catholic affiliates of the International and to push upon them a militant program for combating the Catholic Church. In this pursuit, however, the Kremlin, although exercising considerable influence over the International, found itself and its policies increasingly frustrated by the controlling Social-Democrats. By the end of the 1920s, the Russians, with growing attacks upon the social-democratic Freethinkers, verged on organizing a more pliable tool to fight international Catholic and Christian unity.[47]

In late 1927 Mgr. Boleslas Sloskans, the new Apostolic Administrator for Mogilev-Minsk, was incarcerated. Although he was a Latvian, he spoke and sermonized in fluent Belorussian and showed a high degree of respect for the Belorussian nationality. The Belorussian and Latvian Catholics in Belorussia were, like the Catholic Poles, stanchly faithful to their beliefs and, accordingly, somewhat impervious to "sovietization." Like with Skalski, however, the removal of Sloskans did not demoralize or weaken the faith of the people.[48]

In April 1929, the Apostolic Administrator for Kazan, Mgr. Michael Joudokas, was arrested and executed.[49] That extreme development was undoubtedly, in part, a consequence of the terror which Stalin had unleashed to hack the Soviet Union into collectivization, industrialization, and, above all, complete subservience to his will. Under Stalin, there were to be no independent institutions. The Catholic Church in the Soviet Union, from the beginning of the Five Year Plans, was victimized, cajoled, and beaten for the remainder of the 1930s. It was not alone, of course, and, in fact, because it was already so fragmented and small, its suffering paled in comparison to such institutions as the Ukrainian Autocephalous Orthodox Church, the Russian Orthodox Church, the trade unions, and, even, the Communist Party.[50] Stalin, using the police as a cutting edge, savagely chopped the Soviet *corpus* to fit into his perception of a socialist society. He, without a doubt, felt that the time was ripe for his policies: internally, he had the force necessary to create the workers' state which would guarantee the Party's (and his) continuation in power; internationally, capitalism, as evidenced by the depression, was on its last leg and, thus, circumstances demanded that he quickly transform the USSR into a totally socialist state so that it could be prepared to lead the international socialist revolution. There was no reason, either foreign or internal, to restrain the "fundamentalist" antireligious campaign. Apparently the only factor, at least during the First Five Year Plan, restricting persecution was priorities. In 1929, a constitutional amendment removed from churches and sects the right of religious propaganda and was interpreted as demanding believers to practice religion only among themselves. The new Law on Religious Associations of April 8, 1929, updating and codifying all previous religious legislation, proscribed the organization of church groups and societies and strengthened central control over the churches. In effect, believers and churches were at the mercy of the regime.[51]

The Vatican, which was naturally upset over the sequence of events since d'Herbigny's forced exit, condemned the Soviet government's policies.[52] In addition, it signed, in 1929, the Lateran Treaty with Mussolini partly in the hope that the solving of the Church-State problem would make Italy more stable and less vulnerable to Communism. It had earlier signed, for partly similar reasons, concordats with Livonia (1922), Poland (1925), Lithuania (1927), Romania (1927), and a *modus vivendi* with Czechoslovakia (1928).[53] On February 8, 1930, the Vatican's counteroffensive reached a climax when Pope Pius XI protested the "horrible and sacrilegious outrages" being perpetrated in the Soviet Union and proclaimed that he was going to celebrate a Mass, on March 19, "for the salvation of so many souls put to such dire trials and for the release of our dear Russian people and that these great tribulations may cease." The Pope denounced the Communist persecution of all religions and hoped that Christians from throughout the world would lend their voices to his Mass of expiation in a world-wide Day of Prayer.[54]

The Papal action provoked a response from both other church leaders and the Kremlin. The Anglican and the Lutheran Church of Germany, in particular, joined the Catholic Church in praying for the persecuted believers of Russia. The Communists, who could only see a political threat in the Vatican-proclaimed Day of Prayer, amazingly feared that the Papal initiative might become the fillip for a capitalist crusade against the Soviet Union.[55] They responded by denying that the Soviet government persecuted religion, by strengthening their defenses, and by temporarily halting, with the publication of a decree on March 15, the antireligious campaign in the countryside.[56] *Izvestiia,* commenting on the Pope's supplication, paid reluctant respect to the Catholic Church's political power: "The idiots and simpletons who underrate the political significance of the most reactionary

force of present-day capitalist society have received an object lesson. . . .
The Catholic Church is a powerful motor capable of inducing journalists to
write, politicians to deliver speeches and organizers to go into action."[57]

Within a month of the Vatican's Day of Prayer, the Soviet government,
apparently deciding that the depression was for real and that a capitalist
crusade a remote possibility, again revived its onslaught against religion
and, particularly, against the Catholic Church. Before the year was out, the
Apostolic Administrators for Kamenets, Mgr. Swiderski, for the Volga
region, Mgr. Augustin Baumtorg, for the Caucasus, Mgr. John Roth, for
Leningrad, Mgr. Anthony Malecki, and for the Aremenian rite Catholics,
Mgrs. Carapet Dirlughian and James Bagaratian, were arrested.[58] On June
30, 1930, Pope Pius XI, responding to the continued persecution, ruled that
prayers after Low Mass throughout the Catholic world would henceforth
have as their principal aim the expurgation of the evils afflicting the Russian
people.[59]

In November, 1930, the Russian *Bezbozhniki* finally broke with the
International of Proletarian Freethinkers because of the latter's refusal to
accept the Russian's extremism and set up a rival international which, using
the same name, declared itself to be its successor. The new Communist
Freethinkers' International initially had seven affiliates (Belgium, France,
Poland, Czechoslovakia, Germany, Switzerland, and the USSR) and, using
this as a base, the Kremlin launched violent attacks against religion and the
Catholic Church.[60] In 1931 the International, to its great satisfaction, added
a Mexican affiliate and, then, in 1932, a Spanish body, the "*Liga Atea.*" The
addition of these countries was of particular importance in the international
fight against the Catholic Church because of their predominantly Catholic
make-up.[61]

The Stalinist revolution continued, on all levels of Russian society, into
the 1930s. Internally, opposition to the trend of events from the people and
Soviet institutions was being met or would be met with brute force. The
purges of the 1930s which cut deeply into the ranks of the party and the
military were only the smoke of a raging fire. Externally, the only
frightening event in the early thirties was the Japanese invasion of Manchu-
ria and Moscow moved quickly to stymie that threat diplomatically.
Initially the Soviet Union's major hopes for arresting the Japanese peril
rested upon the United States and apparently it expected, once it had
established diplomatic relations with the Americans, a Japanese-American
imbroglio. The United States, of course, still in the throes of the depression,
did not immediately satiate the Russian hope (eventually in 1941 it did), but
quite interestingly the American recognition of the USSR in 1933 was a
significant development for Catholic-Soviet relations. Roosevelt, as part of

the provisions of recognition, stipulated that the United States had the right to appoint clergymen to serve the personnel of the U.S. Embassy in Moscow.[62] The Vatican, upon learning of the provision, requested that an American Assumptionist, Father Leopold Braun, as it turned out, be assigned to the American Embassy in Moscow. The American government agreed and, thus, began the American Assumptionist presence in Moscow which has persisted to this day. Braun took up his post in 1934 and did not reliquish it until 1946. The Kremlin must have been impressed with the far-reaching influence of the Vatican, but, if such was the case, it did not lead to any relaxation in the internal campaign against the Catholic Church. (The Japanese threat ebbed when Japan and China went to war in 1937). In fact, during the First Five Year Plan, when collectivization of agriculture reached its nadir, the regime concluded that the village Catholic priest was extremely dangerous, not because he opposed the collective farms, but rather because he attempted to infuse them with a religious spirit, with mercy, and with love.[63] Accordingly, in the early 1930s hundreds of village priests were separated from their flocks, not only in the Ukraine and Belorussia, but also in the Crimea and Volga regions where more than 350,000 German Catholics resided. Anti-Catholic propaganda flooded into the Ukrainian Soviet Republic, the Belorussian Soviet Republic, the Crimean Autonomous Republic, and the Volga German Autonomous Republic.[64]

In 1933, with the emergence of Hitler, the international scene became much more ominous and led to the beginning of Moscow's collective security policy. These events, in turn, forced the Communist to re-evaluate their attitude toward the Catholic Church not on the internal level, where collectivization and its accompanying struggle against religion were being pushed harder than ever, but in the international realm. The Kremlin reluctantly and slowly recognized that the Catholic Church, despite the fact that it signed a concordat with Nazi Germany in 1933, was opposed to Nazism and was itself attacked by the Nazis.[65] The recognition made not only the international fight against the Catholic Church wasteful and imprudent, since fascism was obviously the main opponent of Communism, but it aborted the possibility of a united front between the Catholic opponents and victims of Nazism and Communism. Accordingly, in the summer of 1934, the International of Proletarian Freethinkers dropped its intransigent struggle to abolish religion in favor of a campaign to draw religious-minded members of the working class, especially Catholics, into a joint attack against political oppression and economic injustice. The sections of the International were, simultaneously urged to infiltrate Catholic and fascist organizations for political purposes, not to spread atheism. The

International even cautioned its backers against militant antireligious activities. In 1935 Moscow forced the International Freethinkers' organization to work for the inclusion of Liberals and Social-Democrats—groups whom it had earlier denounced. In the spring of 1936 the Proletarian Freethinkers' International fused with the Brussels Free--thinkers' International and pledged itself to struggle against anticlericalism and fascism. From this point on, the Freethinkers' International disappeared as a significant force for Moscow. The Soviet leadership had obviously lost all interest in an international anti-Catholic campaign.[66]

From the middle of the 1930s it was the Communist leaders themselves and not the Russian *Bezbozhniki* or the Freethinkers who directed policy vis-à-vis the Catholic Church. Under Moscow's tutelage, Maurice Thorez, the leader of the French Communist Party, then the largest in Europe, offered on April 17, 1936, "la politique de la main tendue," or the policy of the "extended hand" to the Catholic Church.[67] Thorez's overture to peacefully co-exist with the Church was soon followed by similar offers from the German and Belgian Communist parties and by an official blessing from Moscow.[68] In fact, the Kremlin proclaimed the policy a success when, in 1939, *Antireligioznik* said that "millions of believing Catholics in Germany, Italy, Austria, France, Spain and all countries of the world" had joined the "Communist struggle against Fascism and war, for bread, peace, and freedom."[69] The policy of the "extended hand" was more than simply an expedient in response to the dangers inherent in Mussolini's invasion of Abyssinia, Hitler's remilitarization of the Rhineland, the Spanish Civil War, and the Anti-Comintern Pact; it was also a confession that the Catholic Church was being maltreated in Germany and that earlier Communist propaganda had been wrong in claiming that the Church was a lackey of Hitler and Mussolini.[70]

The Communist "popular front" policy, despite Moscow's assertions of its success, was doomed because of the Soviet Government's continuing campaign against religion in the USSR. In 1936, Bishop Eugene Neveu, the Apostolic Administrator for Moscow and the pastor of the only Catholic Church in Moscow, St. Louis-des-Français, (consecrated by d'Herbigny) who was protected from Soviet attacks because of his French citizenship, was denied permission to return to Moscow after he had left to seek medical care in Paris.[71] Leopold Braun, the American Assumptionist, assumed Neveu's responsibilities and, although he was also insulated from physical violence because of his nationality, he was soon victimized by a series of staged "incidents," interrogations, and constant surveillance.[72] These torments continued right up to the Nazi invasion of the USSR. In 1937 the last bishop ordained by d'Herbigny, Mgr. Alexander Frison, Apostolic Administrator for Odessa, was arrested and executed.[73] The only bishop left in the USSR was Mgr. Maurice Jean-Baptiste Amourdru (he succeeded Mgr. Malecki), a French Dominican, who served as Apostolic Administrator for Leningrad until his expulsion in 1941. It was also in 1937 that the authorities made large-scale arrests of the remaining Catholic priests apparently in an effort to break down the resistance of the Catholic minorities to collectivization. Most of the priests were charged with espionage for Poland and Japan and economic sabotage.[74]

In 1937 the Vatican reacted to the persistent persecution in the USSR and to the Communists' offer for a popular front against international fascism. On March 19, Pius XI published the encyclical *Divini Redemptoris* which not only excoriated the Communist *Weltanschauung* but also the Popular Front policy.[75] The Church's response came on the heels of a similar diatribe against Fascism, the encyclical *Mit Brennender Sorge* of March 14,[76] and, thus, left the Communists with a rejected "extended hand," but also without a base to propagandize the Church as an ally of fascism. The Soviets groped for an answer to the Papacy's novel position of anti-Fascism and anti-Communism. They felt constrained to conditionally sanction the Pope's condemnation of fascism's racial theories.[77] At the same time, however, they accused the Church of wanting a peaceful resolution of the fascist problem, of supporting Japanese militarism (a new charge), and absurdly of forming a united front with Trotskyites instead of the true Communists.[78]

The Kremlin's anti-Vatican propaganda, on the even of the war, was actually quite equivocal. On the one hand, particularly as the Soviet Union's potential involvement in war seemed to grow, the Communists thought it of paramount import to emphasize the Catholic Church's opposition to fascism. Soviet media praised the Czech Catholic Party and the Archbishop of Prague, Mgr. Kašpar for their stand against fascism. They also publicized the resistance and subsequent arrest of Catholic priests throughout Austria by the Germans. The Communists even lauded the anti-fascist attitude of Basque Catholics in Spain.[79] On the other hand, the Kremlin thought it necessary because the Church refused to work with the Communists and because the regime was beginning to revivify the Russian national-Orthodox tradition with its strong anti-Catholicism, to attack the Church. Thus, *Antireligioznik* denounced what it claimed was the pro-Nazi outlook of Slovak clergymen. Viennese Cardinal Innitzer's support of the Nazi *Anschluss,* and the Catholic Church's historical hatred of the Russian people.[80] In conjunction with the last charge, Orthodoxy was commended as a positive force in the development of the Russian state, a clear sign that the Stalinist government, aroused by the external threats, was hoping to embrace nationalism as an ally.[81]

By the latter half of 1938, Moscow seemed to have finally perceived that its public purges and its economically chaotic policies gave an impression of weakness and, thus, were damaging to its international position and attempts to eschew war. Accordingly, after the last great show trial in March, 1938, that of the Anti-Soviet Bloc of Rights and Trotskyites, public purges stopped and Soviet news media began to emphasize how strong and powerful the USSR was.[82] By the end of 1938, of course, the international situation was quite forbidding. In March, Germany had assimilated Austria and in September, at Munich, the West again appeased the insatiable German appetite by sacrificing Czechoslovakia. For the Soviet Union, the situation was desperate and pregnant with danger. Stalin had weakened his country's economy, its basic institutions, and its *esprit de corps*. His government was, to say the least, in no position to fight a war and, yet, war seemed, in 1938-1939, to be at every turn. In the Far East, where Japan was involved against China, the Soviet Union could have easily been drawn into the conflict. In Europe, England and France showed little inclination to stand up to Hitler who, as a vehement anti-Communist and racist who considered the Slavs an inferior people, was quite dangerous as he moved the Third Reich's border in an easterly direction. The Kremlin, however, shrewdly perceived that the West, after Munich, would tolerate no further extension of the German *Lebensraum* and, in that perception, saw the seeds of an intra-capitalist war which could potentially leave the USSR neutral. Through brilliant diplomacy which involved conveying to the world a propagandized picture of Soviet strength and, thus, usefulness as an ally, Moscow, by early 1939, had both the English-French and Germans inquiring about the possibility of an alliance.

1. West Ukraine, West White Russia, Leopold Braun: 1939-June 1940

Pursuing the goal of an atheistic society, the Soviet government, by 1939, had undermined the institutionalized structure of the Catholic Church in the Soviet Union. With the Church hierarchy decimated, churches closed, the clergy scattered and fragmented, there remained for Moscow only one chief avenue, aside from the continuation of propagandistic attacks, to lacerate Catholicism in the USSR: the pillory of Leopold Braun.

In the months preceding the outbreak of World War Two, Braun's life in Moscow simulated a pressure-cooker. There were no physical assaults on his person, but the NKVD unleased a vicious program to give him ulcers. On an almost daily basis, Braun was subjected to a guantlet of prostitutes and black marketeers who attempted to ensnarl him in some compromising situation. Added to these plagues, the police intensified surveillance of Braun and St. Louis Church such that he could not feel comfortable discharging either his natural or supernatural functions. This situation actually continued up to the Nazi attack upon the USSR in June 1941.[1]

The Vatican, of course, could and did take some rather languid comfort from the fact that the Soviet government could no longer storm against the Catholic Church in the Soviet Union, even if it still had Braun to torment, but, by March 1939, when Pius XII was elected Pope, the Papacy's rather hollow quietism was quickly being transformed into gnawing inquietude. By then, war was in the air, but what was even more disturbing, from Rome's point of view, was that the main antagonists, the French and English on the one hand, and the Germans on the other, were, by May, both seeking out the USSR as an ally.[2] The consequences of the culmination of either of those diplomatic moves certainly made the Vatican officials shudder, particularly the new Pope who as Papal Nuncio to Germany in 1919 had faced death at the hands of the Communist Spartacists. If the USSR should join France and Britain against Germany, Germany might be defeated and all of Catholic eastern and central Europe would then be exposed to the rage of Communism. If Germany should be victorious, the Soviet menace would disappear but three great Christian nations (including Poland), and no doubt more, would become the victims of Nazism, which the Church viewed, because of its racism and antireligious bent, as only a stripe above the Communist abomination.[3] If the USSR should join Germany, the Soviet Union would either become a direct ally of the Germans and go to war against France, England, and Poland or it would remain neutral. In either case, the Communists would gain. In the first event, Germany would no longer be a bulwark against the Soviet Union but its military ally, aiding and abetting the expansion of Communism throughout eastern and southeastern Europe. Could the French and English, despite their reputed prowess and Russia's believed weakness, stand up to such a combination? In the second case, the Soviets could sit on the sidelines while the Germans, French, and English (and possibly the Italians) weakened themselves in battle. The memory of World War One, with its attritious warfare, was fresh in the minds of the Catholic leaders and, after all, Communism did obtain its first chances for success during the tumultuous times of the first world war. Would not a war-torn, weakened Europe be easy prey to the Soviet Union which, unscathed by the ravages of the conflict, could sweep into Europe and dictate its will?

To prevent such vexatious possibilities, Pius XII launched a series of policies, beginning in May, geared first to avert war from breaking out in Europe and, thus, the need for a Soviet ally by either side and, secondly, if war was inevitable, to turn it into a Nazi-Soviet clash. Pius' initial and major effort at achieving his goals came in early May when he called upon the French, British, Germans, Poles, and Italians to come together in conference and discuss the outstanding problems dividing them.[4] The implicit assumption of such a proposal was that Hitler had a legitimate grievance against Poland and that, of course, was why the conference failed to materialize for neither the French, Poles, or English were willing to endorse that underlying premise. The Papacy did not, at this time, make explicit what was implicit in its proposal, namely that Poland give into German demands on Danzig and the Corridor, but, nevertheless, as the British and French stated in their refusals to participate, the element of appeasement was certainly latent.[5] How would further appeasement of Hitler achieve the Papacy's objectives? Placation on Poland, naturally, would remove the immediate cause of war between the Western Allies and Germany and, simultaneously, create a *casus belli* between Germany and the USSR. The Vatican knew that Germany's desire for an accord with the USSR was geared solely to avoid the old German nemesis of a two-front war and, thus, if the Western Allies yielded on the Polish problem, that the basis for a Russo-German detente would be removed.[6] Contemporaneously the Papacy, aware of Hitler's anti-

Communism and his appetite for war as well as the USSR's reputed military weakness, could legitimately conclude that the Nazi leader, if he was not preoccupied with war against France and England, would strike, if and when he was so proned, the USSR after Poland.

Unfortunately, however, from the Vatican's point of view, the May peace initiative failed. Through June and July the Papacy pursued a number of other avenues in the hope of finding the road to guarantee peace. It first encouraged Hitler, through the medium of Mussolini, who, it was almost universally believed, had a special hold over the Nazi dictator, to seek his objectives through peaceful means. On three different occasions, June 6, June 30, and August 29, Pius XII essayed to utilize Mussolini as a buffer on Hitler to prevent the outbreak of war over the Polish issue.[7] It is also logical to assume, although there is no evidence as of yet to support the contention, that the Vatican looked to Mussolini as a stoker who could keep the fires of Hitler's anti-Communism burning. Mussolini himself was a vehement anti-Communist and, as is known, did encourage Hitler, after WWII began, to break the Molotov-Ribbentrop Pact.[8] Another tactic which the Vatican improvised to keep the war clouds from bursting over Europe was to impress forcibly upon Hitler the fact that Britain and France would wage war with Germany if the Nazis struck Poland, a contingency which the Vatican knew Hitler did not seriously countenance.[9] Up to the eve of the war and even after the war started, Hitler continued to believe that the British would not hoist the battle flag against Germany.[10] To dispell that delusion, Cardinal Maglione, the Papal Secretary of State, relayed to the Italian Ambassador, on two different occasions in early July, a British and French confirmation that war would follow any German aggression against Poland. The Nuncio in Berlin also approached Ribbentrop and impressed upon him the danger of war with the West.[11] Such a course of action was shrewd for, as is known today, the possibility of war with Britain was a restraint on Hitler, as indicated by the fact that he postponed the invasion of Poland for a week after the British reiterated their commitment to Poland following the publication of the Molotov-Ribbentrop Agreement. The strategy of approaching Ribbentrop was particularly insightful since he apparently was the one who convinced Hitler that the West would not react to an invasion of Poland. But this Russophile was quite persuaded that in the event of a German-Polish war, the rapidity ("a few days") of the German victory would preclude Western intervention.[12]

One final approach the Vatican followed was to counsel the British, French, and Poles to be moderate in their actions and do nothing precipitately.[13] That advice, in conjunction with the peace conference initiative in May, could only mean to appease Germany. If the Polish issue could have been solved peaceably, obviously the French and English would not have needed the Soviets as allies and, thus, they could have become the audience while the Nazis and the Communists confronted one another in Eastern Europe.

The Kremlin was aware of at least the Vatican's May peace conference proposal and certainly cognizant of the repercussions of a peaceful settlement of the Polish issue. In fact the fear of a pacific solution for the Polish problem explains why Moscow was reluctant to sign a non-aggression pact with Germany in the summer of 1939. It knew that, if Hitler should manage to move his legions closer to the Soviet border at Poland's expense without military ramifications in the West, the Soviet Union would be, more than likely, Hitler's next victim. Accordingly, the Soviets did not want their hands sullied with a Nazi alliance if, a few weeks or months after Poland's capitulation, they would be forced to beckon the anti-Nazi West to aid them against Germany. By the same token, once Stalin could be warranted that England and France would unsheathe the sword of war against Germany over the Polish issue, he would have no reluctance to sign a non-aggression pact with the Nazis for this would keep the USSR out of the war and possibly allow it to become the broker of affairs in a war-weakened Europe if, as was the case during WWI, an attritious war evolved in Western Europe. Naturally, given such consequences, Moscow no doubt had a paroxysm when the Vatican attempted to find a peaceful resolution to the conflict over Poland. The degree of the Kremlin's fit can be measured by the fact that the Soviet news media did not comment on nor give any notice to the Vatican's May peace proposals until, five months after the war between Germany and the West started, *Izvestiia* bitterly criticized the Papacy for its appeasement efforts.[14] But, at the same time, the failure of the Vatican's efforts to stymie a bellicose climax to the Polish problem had to raise questions in Moscow's mind about the Church's influence with the major powers.

By August the Papacy's various exertions in favor of peace had met with failure, but still the Church was not prepared for the announcement, on August 23, of the Molotov-Ribbentrop Non-Aggression Pact. Stalin had brilliantly managed to play the English and French off against the Germans and vice versa and by this agreement had extracted the USSR from the inevitable conflict and, from appearances, placed it in the position of arbiter. With the publication of this treaty, the Papacy made one last, desperate effort to realize the fruits of its May proposal. In the crucial days at the end of August, Pius advised his Nuncio in Warsaw, Mgr. Cortesi, to advance to the Polish government the proposition that it return Danzig to the Reich, make concessions on the issue of the Corridor, and give guarantees concerning the safety of the German minorities. The British indicated to the Papacy that they, in turn, would compromise if Germany reduced its demands, but it was the Poles who refused to bend and who, thus, rendered the Vatican's final thrust vein. The Poles, lulled into a false sense of security from the Anglo-French pledge of protection, balked at the idea of making any concessions to the Germans[15]

On September 1, 1939, German troops marched into Poland and in a little over a week crushed Polish resistance. The Germans immediately began attacking the Polish Catholic Church because it was a principal source of leadership for the Polish people. The Nazi persecution was brutal and included the imprisonment and execution of clergy as well as the disruption of Catholic education.[16] The Vatican complained bitterly and Cardinal Hlond, the Polish Primate, issued in Rome a resounding condemnation of the Nazi practices.[17] But as trying as the Nazis' policies were, the Vatican was suffering under an even more disturbing anxiety: the fear of Soviet penetration of Catholic East Europe. On September 17-18 the Papacy's trepidation turned into a reality as the Red Army pushed toward the Vistula River. For the first time since the 1920s the Catholic Church faced the possibility of direct attack by the Communist government of Russia.

The first few weeks of the Soviet occupation of Western Ukraine and Western White Russia proved to be a capsule glimpse of the attitudes and policies Moscow adopted toward the Catholic Church until, in June 1941, its army was pushed out of Eastern Europe by the invading Germans. The nature of the Kremlin's relationship toward the Church, Latin and Uniate, was hostility. Such a disposition, as indicated earlier, stemmed from the historical memory, the ideological baggage, and the totalitarian aspirations of the Soviet government.

Although the Soviet disposition toward Catholicism in Eastern Europe was substantively inimical, the course of its specific policies was directed by the internal exigencies of "Sovietizing" the recent annexations and by the challenges to its position emanating from the swirl of foreign affairs. Compared to the violence of the 1920s and 1930s, Moscow's anti-Catholic deportment in Soviet-occupied Poland and, eventually, in the Baltic States, Bessarabia, and northern Bukovina was temperate. Virtually without exception the Communists restrained their antireligious inclinations in the new territories to non-violent administrative actions, such as taxing churches and removing crucifixes from classrooms. The Soviets did not organize or instigate a virulent or massive persecution throughout the period of the first occupation. The moderation was probably due to three motives. First, religious matters were, relatively speaking, of low priority.. The Communist occupiers were engrossed with integrating their East European territo-

ries into the Soviet structure as rapidly as possible. The scheme of incorporation was similar to that pursued in the Soviet Union where organized
religion was, during the first years of Bolshevik rule, left alone while the
Communists consolidated their position over political and economic affairs.
It is clear that the Soviet regime certainly intended to use violence
eventually against the Church in East Europe, but at first it was burdened
with the necessities of fashioning a political base. By mid-1941, of course,
antireligious malevolence was proscribed by the German attack against the
Soviet Union.

Secondly, Moscow was lenient toward the Catholic Church because it did
not wish to sacrifice, any more than it already had, Western public opinion
by precipitously assailing Catholicism. The Kremlin was certainly cognizant of the fact that all of the major powers had diplomatic ties with the
Papacy and that the Church had millions of adherents in Europe and the
Americas.

Finally and most importantly, during the first occupation, the Kremlin
treated the Catholic Church advertently because of its fear that sheer abuse
would produce benefits for Hitler in the newly absorbed but not yet digested
territories. The Soviets knew that Hitler controlled a powerful military
machine and that, in addition, he was an anti-Communist. As of the end of
September, 1939, and actually not until April of 1940, the Germans and the
Western states were not directly engaged in war and, then, once they did
fight, the Reich defeated France and pushed England off the continent by the
middle of June. At no time, except for a few months in the spring of 1940, did
the attritious European war, which Moscow had banked upon when it
signed the Nazi-Soviet Pact, burgeon or seem to be on the verge of
developing. Thus, it was imperative for the Soviets to forestall or remove
any complications in Russo-German relations for, without the requisite of a
Western-German front, there was a distinct possibility of Hitler ripping up
the Nazi-Soviet Pact and attacking the USSR. Moscow no doubt felt that an
unrelenting blitzkrieg against the Catholic Church in Eastern Europe would
place it at a disadvantage vis-a-vis Hitler. The Soviets surely appreciated
that there would be a popular reaction to blatant onsets against religion in
the newly occupied regions and that such opposition would confound and
possibly impair their control. The latter development, in turn, might induce
Hitler to exploit the Soviets' problems and invade but, even if it did not lead
to that extremity, it definitely would lower Hitler's opinion of Soviet
power and that deduction could move Berlin to neglect Soviet interests
and, eventually, persuade it that the Soviet Union had clay feet. To present
Hitler with such advantages was politically fatuous and the Kremlin was not
about to err so foolishly. An all-out persecution in Eastern Europe might, in

addition, excite Hitler's apparently latent anti-Communism. Antireligious savagery was a prominent Communist policy and, if the Soviets plunged into antireligious violence, Hitler might lose his illusion, which Ribbentrop had assiduously cultivated, of Stalin as a non-Communist, Russian national. Not only would Moscow appear to have clay feet, but *red* clay feet. Finally, the vast majority of the people in Soviet-occupied East Europe were Catholic— either Latins or Uniates—and the Kremlin had to know that Berlin had diplomatic relations with the Papacy. Such knowledge, despite the Nazis' impalement of the Church, had to be confusing: why would the most powerful country in Europe maintain formal ties with a man who had "no divisions?" The Soviets could not but realize that the Church was impor- tant, at least as a tool of expediency, for Hitler and that truculence against the Catholic Church might upset him because he had his own Catholic population of over thirty million in Germany to contemplate.

The basic policy, then, that the Soviet government adopted toward the Catholic dioceses which the Red Army occupied in eastern Poland in September, 1939, was, to be sure, a form of religious persecution but a moderate ill-treatment, mainly administrative malfeasance. All told, the Russian troops controlled, wholly or partly, six Latin dioceses, including Lviv, Peremyshl, Lomza, Pinsk, Lutsk, and Vilnius. On October 10 the Soviets permitted the Lithuanians, in a move calculated to appeal to their anti-Polonism, to annex the city of Vilnius and some surrounding land, but they kept control of the greater part of the diocese. Within the Communist pale there were approximately six and half million Latin Catholics. In addition to the Latin diocese, the occupied territories encompassed the greater part of three Uniate dioceses and a number of Uniate enclaves under Latin administration. The Uniate dioceses were Lviv, Stanislav, and Peremyshl and they had approximately three million, two hundred thousand believers.[18]

In general, in all Latin and Uniate dioceses and this would apply also to the regions the USSR annexed in 1940, the Soviets put in, at the onset of occupation, the following, broad policies: all churches and ecclesiastical properties were nationalized and assessed taxes; all schools were taken over by the state and religion was removed from the educational curriculum; all religious publications were prohibited; a number of Catholic clerics were arrested; monasteries and seminaries were, with few exceptions, comman- deered to quarter Red soldiers; the monks and religious were dispersed and forced to find new housing; antireligous propaganda was spread and supported by the new occupiers; communication with the Papacy was interrupted and rendered quite difficult; finally, Catholics were deported increasingly to Russia. One other general trait of the Soviet occupation was that the Russians dealt with the Uniates more harshly than the Latins.

As indicated earlier, the initial months of occupation set a tone and format of moderate persecution which the Soviets adopted for the length of their stay in Eastern Europe. And although there were official reports from only four occupied dioceses during 1939, the Vatican, by 1941, had received nuncio and bishops' descriptions on the religious climate from all Soviet-controlled dioceses and these corroborate the picture of antireligious leniency painted by the earlier sketches. In addition, unofficial reports, issued by both Soviet and Papal news media, the latter apparently based partly upon the official commentaries from the dioceses and partly upon other unidentified sources of information, supported the rather insipid representation of Soviet antireligious measures delineated in the 1939 accounts.[19]

One of the dioceses which succeeded in dispatching a description on religious conditions in 1939 was the Latin diocese of Peremyshl, one-third of which was under Soviet occupation (San River separated German and Russian forces in Peremyshl). On November 4, the Latin bishop, Mgr. Francis Barda, who was within the German held part of Peremyshl, reported to Pius XII that the Soviets controlled 250,000 Latin Catholics, one cathedral, one seminary, and one bishop (his auxiliary, Mgr. Francis Lisowski). But, according to Mgr. Barda, the Communists, as of his writing, had not interfered with either religious worship in the churches or with the duties of the clergy, most of whom were still at their posts. The only persecutory note the bishop sounded was that the Soviets, as soon as they moved into Peremyshl, forced the schools to drop religion and to add the "doctrine of Communism" to their course list.[20] There was one other antireligious measure the Soviets took, however, which the bishop did not mention but which Moscow Radio, on October 27, announced as general policy throughout the newly occupied territories and that was the nationalization of all ecclesiastical properties, including churches and schools.[21] In general, though, it appears from the sources available that the Communists were even more lenient in the Latin diocese of Peremyshl than in other Latin or Uniate dioceses for they did not, as was usual, shut down the Latin seminary.[22] The explanation for the unusual treatment must have been related to the fact that two-thirds of the Latin diocese of Peremyshl was under German control and the Soviets, even though the Nazis were stifling the Catholic Church, wished to keep this vulnerable, showcase borderland calm.

The second diocese on which Rome obtained an early summary was Pinsk. On November 22, 1939, the chargé d'affaires at Kaunas, Mgr. Joseph Burzio, informed Secretary of State Maglione that, thus far, religious life in

Pinsk was normal, except for the nationalization of ecclesiastical properties and antireligious propaganda, and that no clerics has been incarcerated.[23] His statement was laconic: the Russians had not organized any Neronian onslaught against the Catholic Church.

The diocese of Vilnius was also described in Burzio's November 22 report to Cardinal Maglione. The religious fortunes of Vilnius were quite similar to those of Pinsk and Peremyshl, although complicated by the fact that the Lithuanians, who, as mentioned, received the city of Vilnius at the beginning of October, had very little sympathy or use for the Polish Archbishop of the diocese, Mgr. Romuald Jałbrzykowski, or his Polish auxiliary, both of whom resided in the city of Vilnius.[24] Be that as it may, Mgr. Burzio informed Maglione that the Soviets ruled 294 of Vilnius' 365 parishes and that, to date, they had neither closed down any churches nor inhibited the clergy from performing its religious functions. According to the chargé, four priests were killed during the initial, confusing moments of the Communist occupation but they were victims of some local extremists' hatred. The Soviets, the chargé wrote, had not arrested nor executed any priests and, thus far, had simply demanded that clerics refrain from involving themselves in political affairs.[25] Of course, as in all dioceses, Soviet atheistic law became applicable in Vilnius once eastern Poland was assimilated into the Soviet Union and that happened shortly after occupation. Nonetheless it was clear in Vilnius as elsewhere in the Soviet-held regions that the Communists did not wish to arouse any popular resentment over religion. They also hoped no doubt, at least in the case of Vilnius, to impress the Lithuanians and other Baltic peoples that life under Soviet auspices was not all that bad.

On December 18, 1939, the Latin Archbishop of Vilnius, Mgr. Jałbrzykowski, sent chargé d'affaires Burzio a current assessment on Vilnius. He declared that a few priests had been interned by the Communists, including most recently Rev. Antonius Manturzyk, a catechismal scholar and the reactor of a church in Podrodzie. Other clerics, according to the archbishop, had to find new housing because Soviet troops had been quartered in their residences. Religious instruction in school had been replaced by atheistic teachings and antireligious propaganda was profuse. Additionally, the Soviets had prevented some priests from visiting the sick, the deceased, and one another. But, in general, the episcopal leader insisted, religious life was continuing unobstructed: churches were open, the faithful regularly attended mass and sacraments, and priests recited their divine office.[26]

The final reports that the Vatican received during 1939 all issued from and described the conditions of the Uniate diocese of Lviv. Here, the stronghold of Uniatism, the Russians faced an irreconcilable dilemma which they did not encounter in Latin dioceses. On the one hand, the Soviets wanted to represent themselves to the Ukrainians (and this would certainly be true of the Uniate dioceses of Peremyshl and Stanislav as well) as liberators from Polish cultural suffocation and to exploit the historical differences between the Poles and Ukrainians.[27] In pursuit of those objectives, they established a "Ukrainian University" in Lviv, "ukrainized" a number of Polish schools in the same city, and, of course, extensively heralded their redemptive role.[28] At the same time, however, the Soviets planned to crush the Ukrainian Uniate Church. They no doubt realized that it would be impossible to persuade the Uniate Ukrainians that they were emancipators if they persecuted the Uniate Church. But the Russians were committed to both policies, contradictory though they be. As logic would have it, they only convinced the Uniates, as Archbishop Sheptyts'kyi commented, that rather than bringing liberation they brought "enslavement."[29]

As previously mentioned, the Uniate Catholics were treated more severely than the Latins, although neither group suffered crippling blows. Possibly, however, the Ruthenian Catholics might have been victimized even more stringently than they were if it had not been for the rather far-reaching popularity of their leader, Metropolitan Andrei Sheptyts'kyi, Archbishop of Lviv. He was respected and liked by Ukrainians in and out of Galicia, irrespective of their religious affiliation.[30] As far as the specific events in the Uniate diocese of Lviv in the early months of occupation were concerned, a fairly detailed summary emerged from the reports of the Papacy's Berlin Nuncio, Mgr. Cesare Orsenigo, and of Archbishop Sheptyts'kyi.

On November 25, 1939, Nuncio Orsenigo wrote Cardinal Maglione that Metropolitan Sheptyts'kyi was still at his post but that the authorities had recently taxed him the outrageous sum of 600,000 *zloty* and refused to give him credit for paying 35,000 *zloty* in taxes. The Nuncio also reported that the Redemptorist and Basilian monasteries in Lviv had been disbanded, the priests dispersed, and the property confiscated. The Convent of the Sisters of the Sacred Heart, according to the Berlin representative, had also been partly confiscated. The Nuncio ended by intimating that the Soviets were attempting to exploit the cultural cleavage between the Poles and Ukrainians in Lviv.[31] Two days later, the Vatican gave Metropolitan Sheptyts'kyi permission to name Mgr. Joseph Slipyi coadjutor with right of succession to the Lviv diocese and, in a secret ceremony on December 22, Monsignor Slipyi was consecrated.[32] Evidently both the Vatican and Metropolitan Sheptyts'kyi wished to firm up the Uniate Church's ecclesiastical organization in the face of what portended to be a harrowing experience.[33]

On December 26, Metropolitan Sheptyts'kyi himself filed a summary on the religious situation in Lviv with Cardinal Domenico Tardini, the Secretary of the Congregation of Extraordinary Ecclesiastical Affairs. According to the Metropolitan, the Communists had no charity or benevolence for the poor. Additionally, their system of government was based upon fear and threats and complicated by jurisdictional and functional disputes between Soviet bureaucrats and administrators. The most prominent institution of the new Communist order, according to Mgr. Sheptyts'kyi, was the secret police. It dictated antireligious policy from the advent of Soviet control. Metropolitan Sheptyts'kyi claimed that all schools had been taken over and religion had been banned from the curriculum. Some priests, though, dressed in secular garb, continued to teach in the schools. Various church institutions, such as orphanages and religious societies, according to the archbishop, had either been appropriated or suppressed by the state. Atheistic propaganda had also been spread "fanatically" and every means— dances, music, games, etc.—had been utilized to undermine religion and promote atheism. The Soviets, furthermore, reported the metropolitan, had closed down the theological academy in Lviv and dispersed its faculty and, simultaneously, shut down all monasteries, including those of the Basilians, Redemptorists, Studites, and Hieronoines, dispersed the monks, and confiscated the monastic buildings. The archbishop also informed the Vatican that arrests had been ongoing among the population, but that it was impossible to tabulate the number of imprisoned. The bishop, in addition, wrote that the Soviets had taken away his printing press and that its removal had caused some communication difficulties with the pastors, priests, bishops, and faithful of Lviv. But, notwithstanding the described encumbrances, the metropolitan asserted that religious life in Lviv continued to flourish. Members of the Ukrainian Uniate clergy, according to the archbishop, had not been arrested and, although some fled their parishes with the Bolshevik arrival, the vast majority were still administering Lviv's 1,267 parishes. The metropolitan also stated that the faithful, who regularly attended church, protected the priests' personal property and the churches from sequestration. The Ukrainian archibishop concluded his resume by offering an explanation for the Communists' crusade against religion and their general antireligious behavior: "The system *en masse* was diabolically possessed."[34]

In addition to the specific episcopal and ambassadorial information that was given to the Vatican in 1939, there were other descriptions, written after the Soviet retreat, which summarized religious conditions in Lviv and Stanislav during the entire Soviet occupation. These reports and summaries will be elaborated upon in their proper, chronological sequence, but all of them, plus chronicles from the rest of the dioceses in 1940 and in the first half of 1941, emphasized, like the 1939 reviews, that the Soviets had not been frenzied in their antireligious measures. This conclusion was, furthermore, supported in general statements on religious conditions issued by Vatican Radio and L'Osservatore Romano.[35] And, finally, it was confirmed by the fact that Leopold Braun, who was still victimized by NKVD solicitude, experienced no intensification of pressure in 1939, except for a minor robbery of St. Louis Church on December 6. In other words, by the end of 1939, the religious position of the Catholic Church under Soviet control was, relatively speaking (particularly when compared to the Nazi persecution or to Stalin's policy in the 1920s and 1930s), tolerably good.

As previously emphasized, three reasons can be adduced for why the Church's status can be described as "quite good": the Church's posteriority in the process of Sovietization, Moscow's fear of compromising Western opinion, and, finally, the Soviets' concern over Germany. By the end of 1939, it seemed that the latter two reasons, touching on foreign affairs, loomed temporarily as dominant in Moscow's relations with the Catholic Church. By then, the Soviets, who were still desperately attempting to avoid becoming involved in war, must have been on the brink of epitasis. The Reich was still not engaged on the western front: the so-called "phony war" was in session. But the Russians, on November 30, had invaded Finland and, instead of the easy victory they had anticipated, the Finns proved themselves to be stubborn defenders, thus leaving the Soviets in the unenviable position of increasing their commitment to a minor conflict at a time when Germany's army was unoccupied. The Soviets could easily deduce that their difficulties with Finland presented Germany with an opportunity to extract concessions from the Kremlin and, if the war continued to engross the USSR, it might draw the dangerous conclusion that the Soviet Union was weak and easy prey itself. Furthermore the Soviets had already irritated the Germans by waging war on the Finns for they knew Hitler considered the Finns to be racially superior to the Communist Slavs and they were also aware that Germany received valuable raw materials from Finland. Added to these problems, the western states were enflamed over the Soviet invasion of Finland and verged on going to Finland's aid. Obviously, when the Kremlin initiated the war with Finland, it took a large gamble, even though it had expected a facile triumph. The reason, of course, that the Soviet Union was willing to involve itself in such risks was that, on balance, it considered it more important for the USSR to obtain strategic advantages vis-a-vis Germany in the eastern Baltic than not to annoy Hitler. And, as regards the West, the Soviets had no reason to anticipate the ground swell of sympathy for Finland in western countries and, at any rate, they foresaw, as mentioned, a quick victory.

Actually the Russo-Finnish war throws a great deal of light on Moscow's decision-making processes and, to a point, its religious policy. As the USSR moved its troops into the Western Ukraine and Western White Russia, it dreaded Germany and its consternation would continue to grow, amidst temporary lapses, until the end of the Battle of Stalingrad in 1943. Naturally Moscow wanted to avoid war with the Reich (as well as with the West) and, accordingly, it would eschew any policy which would exacerbate Hitler unless the lack of such a program was deemed in and of itself to weaken the USSR. Obviously the Soviets determined that they needed to push the Finnish border back from Leningrad and that, even though this would enrage the Germans, it was necessary for the defense of the Soviet Union. Likewise in late June 1940, after the French defeat, the Kremlin demanded and annexed, even though it incensed the Reich, Bessarabia and northern Bukovina from Romania because these lands were strategically located and populated with pockets of Ukrainians whom the Germans could manipulate, as centers of irredentism, against the Soviet Ukraine. Similarly, when it can to religion, the Soviet government determined that religious persecution might antagonize Hitler (as well as world opinion), but, yet, that it was useful to the evolution of socialism.[36] The latter premise, as previously cited, was based on the Leninist tenet that religion's demise could be a means of advancing the socialist revolution. However, in converse to the Finnish and Bessarabian-Bukovinian decisions, the Kremlin concluded that its war against religion would be more harmful to its security than no war and that deduction led and was leading Moscow, from September 1939 onward, to a reorientation of its religious policy. Since the First Five Year Plan the "fundamentalists" had been directing the Soviet antireligious campaign. But, by the end of the 1930s certainly, the "fundamentalists" were being pushed aside (but not abandoned) and superceded by the "pragmatists," those who wanted to use religion to serve the interests of the USSR and who based their stand on the other Leninist axiom of expediency. The orthodox, atheistic position remained strong and would rear its head during and after the war, but, from the fall of 1939, the heights belonged to those functionaries who favored toleration of religion for immediate advantages. So entrenched, in fact, did the "pragmatists" become during the war that religious persecution for the sake of creating an atheistic society did not revive in the USSR until the last five years of Khrushchev's reign.[37]

The Vatican's reaction to the 1939 persecution was multifarious. To begin with, the Papacy condemned the anti-Christian philosophy of Communism and its antireligious machinations.[38] Logically this policy had two goals: to vent the Church's anger and frustration over the Communist assaults and, secondly, to depict the Bolsheviks as the anti-Christs and the inalienable enemy of western civilization. The latter objective, in turn, could produce, from the Vatican's point of view, two happy consequences. It could serve as an implied rebuke to Germany for allying with the Communists and it could also keep the Soviet menace before the eyes of the world.

A second major tactic the Vatican espoused in reply to the Communist incursions in Poland was an explicit disapprobation of Germany for siding with the USSR in the Molotov-Ribbentrop Pact and for, consequently, aiding and expediting "the Communist triumph."[39] On Christmas eve, 1939, Pius XII warned the Germans to come to their senses and halt the war because a Europe, impoverished by war, was the easy prey of Communism which laid waiting "to give the final blow to Christian Europe."[40] The unveiled end of this tactic was to break the Nazi-Soviet agreement. The Vatican, before the Molotov-Ribbentrop Pact, had not been forced to make a choice between Nazism and Commuisn—it condemned them both. Now, however, for the sake of splitting the combination, the Papacy felt compelled to rein in its public denunciations of Nazism and to continue its opposition, at the public level, to Communist totalitarianism. The Vatican's decision was based not only on the fact that *public* anti-Nazism would go hard on the tens of millions of Roman Catholics under German control but, more importantly, the moral determination that Nazism, bad as it was, was not as abomitable as Communism *under Stalin*. Many East Europeans, including eastern Slavs, reached the same conclusion.[41]

A third strategy the Vatican effected was a proscription of the USSR's act of aggression against Finland. The Vatican was mute over the German-Soviet thrust into Poland, no doubt because Germany, which the Vatican supported as its hope against Communism was involved. But when the Soviets warred upon Finland, Pius XII, no longer restrained by the German presence, denounced as a violation of international law the Soviet Union's "calculated act of aggression against a small, industrious and peaceful nation, on the pretext of a threat which was neither real nor intended, nor even possible."[42] This policy, while reflecting the Vatican's genuine sentiments, was also geared, quite naturally, to water Hitler's apparently latent anti-Communism by reminding him that Nordic Finland was, as Adam Ulam summarized, "being sacrificed to the Moloch of Bolshevism."[43] Again the Vatican was attempting to drive a wedge between the Soviet and Nazi allies.

Another measure, albeit indirect, of retaliation was the Vatican's continuing efforts to limit the war, primarily by keeping Italy neutral.[44] Part of the motivation for this ploy, aside from the Papacy's ever-present wish to avoid more blood shed, was that the Vatican knew Italy's involvement would be directed against France and the Church leaders wanted, as long as possible, to keep the becalmed western front from boiling over into a hot theater of war. And certainly the Papacy did not want Italy joining Germany at a time when the Reich was tied to the USSR.[45]

A fifth approach which the Vatican might have pursued, but for which, as indicated earlier, records are not presently available, was to manipulate Mussolini to enflame Hitler's apparently de-emphasized anti-Communism. Mussolini did, in fact, particuarly after the Russo-Finnish war seemed to reflect Soviet weakness, urge Hitler to strike the USSR.[46] But *Duce* was a vehement anti-Communist in his own right and he needed little encouragement, if indeed any was provided, from the Vatican to commend an anti-Soviet policy to Hitler.

The Papacy's final reaction came, on December 24, in the form of Pius XII's five-point plan for peace.[47] This proposal, aside from representing the Vatican's genuine desire to tranquility, was, in addition, a sophisticated move against the Soviet Union. Obviously, if peace was forthcoming, the USSR would be stranded in a perilous position, morally compromised in the eyes of the English and French for signing the Molotov-Ribbentrop Pact, and concomitantly contraposed to the awful power of the Nazi military machine. And whether or not a war broke out between the USSR and Germany, the Soviet Union certainly could not, in the foreseeable future, advance its boundary further westward at the expense of western Christendom. However, the warring parties were unwilling, at that juncture, to halt the warfare and, thus, the Vatican's initiative for peace fell on deaf ears, no doubt to the great relief of Moscow.

As of the end of 1939, the Soviet government paid no noticeable heed to the Papacy's sundry policies. In fact, Soviet antireligious organs lashed the Church, especially the Uniate rite, as a tool not of fascism but of Polish reaction.[48] The Kremlin, however, must have increasingly become unsettled by the moves of the Papacy for any event or circumstance which essayed or tended to worsen Russo-German relations had to be disturbing. And, of course, Moscow was aware that Germany, as well as Italy, Japan, France, Great Britain, and the United States, the latter as of December, 1939,[49] maintained formal relations with the Papacy. The fact that the world's powers had diplomatic personnel at the headquarters of the "troopless" Pope must have affected the Soviets' evaluation of the Catholic Church as well as of religion in general.

In 1940 the situation of the Catholic Church did not significantly change from that of 1939 with the conspicuous exceptions of the diocese of Pinsk and Leopold Braun. Their especial positions will be touched upon later, but, aside from them, the Soviets continued to espouse a diminutive antireligious position, in fact, one that overall, if juxtaposed to the 1939 performance, abated. Official diocesan reports for 1940 emanated from Lutsk, Lomza,

Pinsk, Lviv, and from the newly occupied Baltic States and all of them, again with the exception of Pinsk, reflected a relatively mild degree of Soviet persecution. In addition, unofficial Vatican sources, throughout 1940, presented a Lilliputian picture of antireligious activity in the Western Ukraine, Western White Russia, and, eventually, in the Baltic States and Bessarabia-Bukovina.

The first official expositions on the status of the Church in Eastern Europe came from the Latin diocese of Lutsk. On January 13, 1940, Nuncio Orsenigo informed Secretary Maglione that the bishop of Lutsk, Mgr. Adolfo Szelazek, was at his post and performing his functions. The Nuncio also added that religious life in Lutsk, aside from the Soviets' standard antireligious measures, was normal.[50] Six days later, Orsenigo relayed another account on the religious situation in Lutsk which was sent to him by Mgr. Petro Verhun, the Apostolic Visitor for Ukrainians in Germany. According to Verhun, the churches in Lutsk were open and the faithful were not in the least obstructed from attending religious services. The Soviets, the Apostolic Visitor wrote, had, thus, far, accorded the clergy-Latin, Ruthenian, and Orthodox-full liberty to perform its religious duties on the condition it did not preach against the Soviet regime. The monasteries and religious houses, according to the monsignor, had been confiscated and were being used to quarter Soviet troops. The residents of the sequestrated buildings, the cleric stated, had been forced to find new housing.[51]

From the time of Verhun's report until May, the Vatican received no official reports, which it has published, from Soviet-occupied East Europe. However, Vatican Radio and *L'Osservatore Romano* as well as Soviet and world news media provided a fragmented commentary on what was generally happening. From the end of January through March, the Papal outlets, in a series of stories, announced that the Communists in Soviet Poland had forged a policy of oblique religious persecution. According to the narrations, the Russians did not directly attack the Church, but, rather, attempted to slowly erode its position through the assessment of high taxes, the closure of monasteries and seminaries, the abolition of religion from schools, the proliferation of atheistic propaganda, the impropriation of church-controlled cemeteries, and, finally, the jamming of Radio Vatican.[52] On January 22, Radio Moscow confirmed that the Soviets had dispossessed landowners (large) and monasteries throughout Soviet Poland.[53] On April 28, the *New York Times* reported that an atheistic organization in Lviv had usurped Metropolitan Sheptyts'kyi's library.[54] Although the latter episode, since it did take place in April,[55] was inconsistent with the waning persecutory stand of Moscow, it was more than balanced by the fact that the Soviets, also in April, did not interfere with Metropolitan Sheptyts'kyi's holding of the first Uniate Synod in Lviv since 1918.[56] On May 4, the Radio Vatican again broadcasted a general summary of conditions in Soviet Poland. According to the newscast, the Communists still had not openly assaulted the Church, but were plying circuitous methods of persecution.[57]

On May 5, the Latin archbishop of Vilnius, Romuald Jałbrzykowski, sent an up-to-date summary on the diocese of Pinsk to Nuncio Centoz at Kaunas. His recapitulation, in contrast to all other official reports received by the Vatican in 1940, revealed an increased antireligious campaign. The archbishop began by informing the Nuncio that Pinsk was without a bishop since Mgr. Casimir Bukraba, the ordinary, was ill in a clinic in Lviv and since Mgr. Charles Niemira, the auxiliary, was in Warsaw. The diocesan administration, according to the archbishop, was in the hands of the vicar general, Rev. Vitold Iwicki, and, although he was very capable, the Soviets had recently started to interfere with his work. Churches remained open, according to the archbishop, but lately the authorities had increased the tax rate on each church to about 100,000 rubles and had threatened to convert the churches into cinemas or other diversions unless the impossible taxes were paid in full. The archbishop also asserted that the Soviets had recently obstructed Latin priests in their duties and "suddenly suppressed" the Oriental Rite of the Catholic Church in Pinsk (probably a remnant of Exarch Leonid Feodorov's Church). The bishop ended by claiming that the Russians had also increased the deportation of the population from the Pinsk diocese.[58]

Archbishop Jałbrzykowski's exposition, as stated earlier, went against the swing of the pendulum, i.e., inconsistent with the denouement in the Kremlin's antireligious policies. But, although the report on Pinsk was the only official indication from the dioceses of Soviet Poland that there was an about-face in Moscow's non-persecutory inclination, it was not an isolated bolt from the blue. In fact, the Pinsk document was paralleled by three other developments which indicated, at least, obliquity from the Soviets' declining antireligious policies. First, as already pointed out, Metropolitan Sheptyts'kyi had property taken in April. Secondly, through the spring, Soviet sources called for a resuscitation of the waning atheistic struggle.[59] Finally, the Soviets, also in the spring, quickened the pressure on Braun by pillaging St. Louis and demanding that he pay an exorbitant income tax. Braun futilely protested the former and refused to pay the latter, but the Russians pressed the tax matter, eventually informing the new American ambassador, Laurence Steinhardt, that they would consider exempting Braun if he discontinued his "relations with Russians." Braun, however, neither paid the tax nor stopped his increasing contact with Soviet citizens and soon the Soviets, when it appeared as if the affair might disturb

American-Russian relations, allowed the income tax issue to dissipate.[60]

Why did Moscow, at this particular time, permit a resurgence of his anti-Catholic policy in the USSR, why did the scale rather suddenly tip, in the spring of 1940, in favor of knouting the Catholic Church? There seems to be three reasons for the twist in the Kremlin's position. One, as the Soviet government turned toward an acceptance of religion as a potential support, it riveted first on Orthodoxy. That posture, of course, had its own characteristics and propensities, a chief one of which was animosity for Catholicism and, foremost, for the Uniate and Eastern Rites of the Catholic Church and, logically, for any Catholic cleric, such as Braun, who administered to Russian citizens. Thus, as Moscow drew closer to Orthodoxy, it naturally adopted the traditional Orthodox bent for what might be described as "Catholiphobia." The Orthodox religion, in fact, was beginning to experience a revival, even though the antireligious movement in the USSR was simultaneously growing.[61] One case in point and a case that demonstrates the regime's awareness of Orthodoxy's utility was that in early 1940 it allowed the Moscow Patriarchate to appoint a Russian archbishop, Nikolai Iarushevich, metropolitan of Lutsk and Volynia and exarch for the newly annexed western *oblasts* bf the Ukraine and Belorussia. His function was to extend the authority of the Russian Orthodox Church over the large Orthodox diocese of Volynia, encompassing at that time three bishops and some 800 parishes, and potentially to serve as a jumping off point to reintegrate the Uniates into the Orthodox Church.[62] At the same time, the NKVD applied growing pressure upon the well-known Lviv priests, Dr. Havryil Kostel'nyk, a controversial personality known for his public criticism of the Papacy's Uniate policies, to start a schism within the Uniate Church to separate it from Rome.[63]

Secondly, the foreign pressure, Western opinion and especially fear of Germany, which was a root-cause of Moscow's antireligious slump, was rather significantly diminished in March, April, and May. In March, the Soviets finally terminated the Finnish war and toward the end of the month they must have had some hint, possibly from espionage sources, that the Germans were preparing a major offensive against the West. On April 10, of course, Moscow was informed by the German government of the Reich's invasion of Denmark and Norway and, without a doubt, that news was a great relief to the Kremlin: the "phony war" in the west had at last boiled over into a hot war and there was little chance now that Germany could tear up the Molotov-Ribbentrop pact and strike the USSR. By May, Germany was engaging the French and the English and the Soviet government certainly had visions of settling back for the next few years and watching the capitalistic states fight a war of attrition. Accordingly, as wave after wave of relief crested over Moscow, the less it felt a need, the less it was under foreign duress (either from the Allied or Axis camps) to modify its policies, including the antireligious measures. The time was opportune, in other words, to push on with creating a socialist society. Possibly the "fundamentalists" gained transient control of the antireligious machinery and launched an attack against the Catholic Church—Orthodoxy was off limits—under the banner of Orthodox nationalism. This policy had the added advantage of providing concrete evidence to Communists throughout the world that Stalin's government was not abandoning, through its diminution of the atheistic drive, the theoretical basis of Marxism-Leninism. Stalin knew, despite his purges, that there were still many, potential Trotskys in the world Communist movement and that they might jump at the opportunity to turn a non-persecutory stand into a wedge to use against him.

Finally, and most importantly, the Soviet government no doubt wished, while the West and Germany were preoccupied, to accelerate the absorption of its new Eastern European lands into the Soviet system. Such a goal, perforce, demanded increased deportation of recalcitrants and control, achievable only through force, of such independent institutions as the Catholic Church.

At any rate, violence did expand in Pinsk in the spring of 1940 (as well as in Moscow against Braun), but, at the same time, it did not appreciate in the other dioceses, with the minor exception of Sheptyts'kyi's experience in Lviv. Evidently the reasons for this situation were that Pinsk was the most eastern of the Church's dioceses, that is, closest to the pre-1939 borders of the USSR, and, thus, geographically a logical place for an inchoate policy plus there was no bishop in Pinsk and, ergo, it would be vulnerable because of the lack of recognized, ecclesiastical leadership. By the end of May, of course, the British were retreating, France was on the ropes, and the German pressure reappeared. The USSR was suddenly confronted with the frightening reality of being the only power standing in the way of a complete, Fascist conquest of the European continent. The return of the Nazi adversity, more redoubtable than ever, in turn, snuffed out Moscow's anti-Catholic rekindling, thereby, precluding its dispersion from Pinsk to other dioceses and returned the Soviets to their pre-March position: an evolving belief that a nonpersecutory stand against and, potentially, an alliance with organized religion (all religions) were actions which could meaningfully enhance the interests of the USSR. The "pragmatists," in other words, were in firm control of the religious wheelworks.

For the remainder of May, the only information on events in Soviet Poland came from two Radio Vatican broadcasts. On May 13 and 14 the radio announced that the tax rate for clerical domiciles and for churches under Soviet control was 4.5 rubles per square meter and 8 rubles per square meter respectively.[64]

On June 6 an official report on the Uniates in Lviv was sent by Mgr. Petro Verhun to Nuncio Orsenigo. According to the Ukrainian Apostolic Visitor, religious life in Lviv was thriving. The monsignor claimed that the churches were crowded and that the clergy operated and performed its functions without too many impediments. In the spring of 1940, according to Verhun, the Soviet authorities did not impede the convocation by Metropolitan Sheptyts'kyi of two archdiocesan *Synods* and did not hinder the archbishop from offering theological courses for some thirty seminary students.[65] Quite obviously, at a time when the Soviets were increasing the pressure against the Catholics in Pinsk, the situation in the diocese of Lviv, despite the fact that Archbishop Sheptyts'kyi's library was confiscated, was evidence of the changing nature of Moscow's antireligious policy. Aside from the overall trend from an antireligious to an areligious posture, what also undoubtedly motivated Moscow was its unwillingness to cross swords with the Metropolitan, who, if he had been prevented from staging his *Synods,* undoubtedly would have attempted to hold them anyway and, secondly, its desire to convince the Ukrainian Uniates that indeed the Russians were liberating them from the cultural fetter of Poland.

2. Baltic States, Bessarabia-Bukovina, West Ukraine, West White Russia, Leopold Braun: June 1940-June 1941.

In the middle and latter part of June, with France under the guillotine, Moscow moved to gather, as quickly as possible, the remaining territory allotted to it, as well as some not apportioned, by the revised Molotov-Ribbentrop Pact. On June 14-15 Soviet troops occupied the Baltic States, which were allocated to the USSR according to the Nazi-Soviet agreement, but they also, on June 26, marched into Bessarabia, which the Germans had only recognized as an area in which the Soviets had an "interest," and northern Bukovina, which was not even mentioned in the accord with Germany. The Soviet Union wanted the Baltic States to improve its defenses in the west and it desired Bessarabia and Bukovina not only to protect the USSR's underbelly but also to assimilate Ukrainian *terra irredenta.* As of the end of June, the only major, Ukrainian-populated region that was outside the boundaries of the Soviet Union was Trans-Carpathia and the Kremlin had to wait until Germany was defeated before it could unite that gnat with the elaphantine Soviet Ukraine.[66]

Once the Russians occupied these new regions, the antireligious measures

which had been instituted the previous year in Soviet Poland were introduced. The Catholic Church in the Baltic States, particularly in Lithuania,
was a substantial organization. In Lithuania the Church represented eighty
percent of a population totaling three million inhabitants. When the war
began there were three archbishops, eight bishops, six dioceses, and one
prelature served by more than 2,000 priests and religious. Since the
concordat in 1927, religious instruction was required in all primary and
secondary schools and Canon Law was respected by the State.[67] In Latvia the
Church had approximately a half million adherents which represented
about twenty-five percent of the population. Nonetheless the Church, by
virtue of an agreement in 1922, owned 7,500 acres of land and received an
annual donation from the government for the Church's upkeep. The Latvian
clergy was numerous and there was a sizable number of Catholic organizations and publications.[68] In Estonia the Catholic Church was insignificant.
Only two percent of the population or 2,000 people were Catholic in 1938.
Since 1926 a German Jesuit, Mgr. Edward Profittlich, residing in Tallinn,
had served as the Apostolic Administrator for all of Estonia. He was aided
by eleven secular priests and some twenty nuns and religious priests who
were principally German missionaries.[69] In the Romanian territories of
Bessarabia and northern Bukovina, the Catholic Church, like in Estonia, was
inconsiderable. The major Christian religion was Romanian Orthodoxy,
but there were numbered among the population a few Uniate and Latin
Catholics.[70] The Baltic States were formally annexed into the Soviet Union
in early August and the Romanian-speaking portions of Bessarabia were
soon thereafter added to the former Autonomous Moldavian S.S.R. to form
the new Moldavian S.S.R. while the Ukrainian-speaking sections of
Bessarabia and northern Bukovina were grafted onto the Ukrainian S.S.R.
(The incorporated portion of Bukovina lies mainly between the Suceava and
Cheremosh Rivers, extending north to the upper Dniester).

   The first official report from the Baltic States was a letter, dated June 17,
from Nuncio Centoz in Kaunas. He wrote simply to inform the Vatican that
the Soviets had removed the government of President Anatas Smetona and
erected in its place a puppet regime headed by J. Paleckis, President, and
V. Kreve-Michevicius, Vice-President of the Council of Ministry of
Foreign Affairs.[71] Although the Nuncio made no mention of religious
persecution, the Vatican, preparing for the worst, extended, on June 25,
extraordinary faculties to the bishops of the Baltic States.[72] On July 3,
Nuncio Centoz informed Cardinal Maglione that the new Lithuanian
Government had denounced the concordat with the Church but the prelate
emphasized that the government, in doing so, took pains to make sure its
action would not be construed as an attack upon the Catholic Church but,

rather, as a move to up-date Lithuania by introducing the modern principle of separation of church and state.[73] On that same day, in another letter to Maglione, Nuncio Centoz reported that recently the bishops of Lithuania had gathered in Kaunas under the leadership of Archbishop Juozapas Skvireckas to review the religious conditions in Lithuania.[74] Although the Nuncio did not summarize the conclusions of this body, the fact that it occurred was evidence of the moderate policy which the Soviets were practicing toward the Church. On July 5 Moscow Radio indirectly confirmed that the Lithuanian-Catholic concordat had been voided by reporting that the new Lithuanian government had halted "the vast sums" which Anatas Smetona's regime had given to the clergy and the churches.[75] Radio Moscow also announced, in a series of broadcasts in early July, that monastic lands in Bessarabia and northern Bukovina had been confiscated and, in patent parallel to Soviet policy in Galicia and to the populist policies of the tsars, that the Russians had come to free the Ukrainians from their Romanian exploiters.[76]

On July 5 and 9, in a move to strengthen its episcopal structure in Pinsk, Lomza, and Lithuania, the Vatican informed Nuncio Centoz that Mecislovas Reinys had been appointed auxiliary bishop of Vilnius and Vencentas Padolskis had been named auxiliary of Vilkaviskis and, finally, that he should name apostolic administrators for Lomza and Pinsk.[77] On July 16 Nuncio Centoz asked Nuncio Orsenigo to inform the Vatican that the Communists had arrested and expelled a few priests from Lithuania.[78] It was impossible to identify the clerics of whom Nuncio Centoz was speaking or the reason for the arrests and exiles, but, more than likely, in view of the Soviets' assuasive antireligious policy, the priests were either Poles, whom the Soviets would logically expel to impress the Lithuanians with the cultural liberator role they were donning, or they were Lithuanians energetically blocking Soviet annexation.[79]

On July 21 Archbishop Jałbrzykowski of Vilnius relayed a few details to the Vatican on the situation in the dioceses of Pinsk and Lomza. In Pinsk, according to the archbishop, the episcopal administration was still in the hands of Father Vitold Iwicki. In Lomza, the archbishop declared, Mgr. Stanislaw Lukomski was still performing his duties and that he had moved his residence to Kulesze which was near the city of Lomza. The auxiliary bishop of Lomza, Mgr. Thaddaeus Zakrzewski, according to Jałbrzykowski, was also still functioning and was located at Ostrwo Mazow, in the western part of the diocese.[80]

On July 29 Vatican Radio announced that the usual Soviet antireligious practices had been implemented in the Baltic States: church land and property had been nationalized, theological and philosophical faculties at the universities had been suppressed, and "exorbitant taxes" had been placed on the clergy.[81] On August 4 Radio Moscow broadcasted that the University of Chernovtsy in Bukovina would soon be offering a socialist curriculum.[82] Apparently that meant that theology and philosophy were on the verge of becoming extinct.

On August 6 Nuncio Centoz sent a current picture of the Church's position in Lithuania. According to the Nuncio, the Soviets had sequestrated the seminaries of Vilkaviskis, Vilnius, and Telsiai for quartering Russian troops. And, claimed Centoz, the Communists were planning to confiscate, for the same purpose, the Curia's premises in Kaunas as well as the dwelling of Mgr. Karasas, the head of the Curia.[83] On August 13 Radio Vatican reported that, throughout the Baltic States, antireligious propaganda was widespread, religious schools had been taken over by the state, religious instruction in the schools had been forbidden, and that the only religious meetings permitted by the authorities were church services. Some church property, according to the report, (evidently referring to monastic lands) had been confiscated and the Soviets closed the theological department at the University of Riga.[84]

On August 14 Nuncio Centoz, again in a letter to Cardinal Maglione, reported that, in Lithuania, the Russians had restricted clerics to nine square meters of dwelling space per person and had confiscated the remaining portion of dwelling space for billeting soldiers. The only seminary that was still open, according to the Nuncio, was the one at Kaunas.[85] On August 13 Nuncios Arata at Riga and Centoz at Kaunas informed Cardinal Maglione that their respective embassies had been closed by the Communists and that they had been requested to leave.[89] On August 14 Maglione requested the Nuncios to stay at their posts as long as possible.[87] But on August 19 and 24 the Latvian and Lithuania Nuncios respectively were forced to abandon the countries to which they have been charged.[88]

On August 21 Radio Vatican announced that church lands and properties in Bessarabia and northern Bukovina had been nationalized.[89] Ten days later Bishop Brizgys of Kaunas wrote to Nuncio Centoz, now in Rome, that the Seminary of Kaunas was scheduled to commence, on September 16, a new academic year with himself as rector, Mgr. V. Padolskis (auxiliary of Vilkaviskis) as dean of the Theology Department, and some professors from the closed seminaries of Vilkaviskis and Telsiai on the faculty. The bishop also reported that the archbishop's quarters had still not been occupied and that the bishops of Lithuania held another pastoral conference in Kaunas on the problems of administering the Kaunas Seminary and on general pastoral conditions. He concluded his letter by asserting that thus far the Communists had been restrained in their conduct toward the Church.[90]

On September 17 Vatican Radio gave a short summary on religious circumstances in the Baltic States. According to the broadcast, the Soviets, although they had appropriated religious colleges, had not as of yet closed churches nor excessively interfered with clerical duties.[91] On October 2 Nuncio Orsenigo reconfirmed for the Vatican that the seminaries in the diocese of Vilnius had been sequestrated.[92] Also in early October Bishop Brizgys managed to send an up-to-date report to Nuncio Orsenigo on ecclesiastical life in Lithuania. According to the bishop, the Kaunas Seminary was functioning with 180 students under his rectorship and the vice-rectorship of Mgr. Francis Ramasauskas. The Soviets had confiscated, according to the report, the mansion of the Seminary but that was the only building. The bishop also declared that all church property had been nationalized, that the possessions of the religious orders had been taken over, that all schools had been transformed into state institutions, that religious instruction, prayers, crucifixes, religious mementoes, etc., were outlawed in schools, and, finally, that atheistic propaganda was widespread. The bishop also mentioned that teachers had been obligated to attend atheistic training sessions and that civil matrimony had been made compulsory for everyone. The bishop concluded by informing Orsenigo that the Soviets had hindered communication between the church leaders and the faithful and had restrained missionary work, arresting, in September, Fr. Bruzikas, S.J. of Sasnava for his missionary zeal.[91]

On October 2 Nuncio Orsenigo wrote Cardinal Maglione that the Soviets had closed the Uniate seminary in Lviv.[94] That was an escalation on the part of Moscow, but it was directed solely against the Uniates for the Latin seminary continued to operate, although on a reduced scale, and it was tempered by the fact that Metropolitan Sheptyts'kyi was able to hold theological courses for a dozen students in his home.[95] Nonetheless it was evidence of the Kremlin's anti-Uniate orientation and its willingness to give vent to the traditional passions that were welling up as the government moved closer to embracing Orthodoxy. It could have also been a by-product of a growing need: More room to house more soldiers in view of the Nazi menace.

At approximately the same time that Orsenigo penned the above letter to Maglione, the Vatican learned that between September 17, 1939, and September 17, 1940, Archbishop Sheptyts'kyi had secretly named four exarchs for the Soviet Union and territories occupied by the Russians to govern the affairs of Uniate Catholics. He named Mgr. Mykola Charnets-'kyi the exarch of Volynia and occupied Poland, Rev. Klement Sheptyts'kyi exarch of Great Russia and Siberia, Mgr. Josyf Slipyi exarch of the Great Ukraine, and Rev. Anthony Niemancewycz, S.J., exarch of White Russia.

The Metropolitan did this by virtue of the powers granted to him by Pius X in 1907. On May 30, 1940, however, Piux XII had limited the Metropolitan's powers to name exarchs to Galicia alone but Sheptyts'kyi did not learn of the Papal qualification until four months later by which time the exarchs had already taken up their posts. To say the least the situation was "canonically embarrassing," and Pius decided, as an expedient measure, to change the exarch's designations to apostolic administrators with only temporary powers. His rationale for doing so was simply that he felt the Poles would claim the Concordat of 1925 had been violated if the appointments were permanent since some of the territory the Metropolitan assigned already fell under the jurisdiction of Latin Polish bishops.[96] But, despite the canonical "embarrassment," the affair revealed that Metropolitan Sheptyts'kyi wanted to strengthen his Church in the face of growing Soviet anti-Uniatism.

It was also on October 2 that Nuncio Orsenigo sent the Vatican a report on the situation in the dioceses of Lutsk, Lomza, and Pinsk. In a rather general summary of conditions which had been in effect from the time of the Bolsheviks' arrival, the Nuncio told Maglione that in all three dioceses the seminaries and monasteries had been closed and sequestrated for the use of soldiers, that all church property had been nationalized, and that atheistic teachings and propaganda were diffuse.[97]

On October 9 Radio Vatican announced that atheistic teachings were still being vigorously propagated throughout the Soviet portion of Eastern Europe.[98] On October 25 it broadcasted that the Russians had increased the pressure on the small Uniate enclave in Bendey, Bessarabia.[99] On that same day, for the first time since the Soviet occupation of the Baltic States, an official report was forwarded to the Vatican from Estonia by the Apostolic Administrator, Mgr. Edward Profittlich. The prelate wrote that the Soviets were on the verge of requiring all foreigners to leave the country, which meant himself as well as the bulk of the Catholic clergy, and he wanted to ascertain if the Papacy would object if he changed from a German national to a Russian national.[100] The Vatican quickly answered that he should feel free to choose the citizenship which was best for him.[101] On October 31, the Estonian delegate reported to the Vatican that all Germans had been asked to prepare to return to Germany and those who refused had to apply for Soviet citizenship and would probably be sent to Siberia.[102]

Radio Vatican, on December 12, broadcasted fresh data on the situs of the Church in Lativa. According to the Radio, mass arrests or executions of priests had not taken place, although church property had been nationalized and some priests' houses had been confiscated for the use of the occupying troops. The report claimed that all clerics had been barred from old age relief, that religious teaching had been outlawed in all schools, and that confessional schools had been shut down. Also religious festivals and holidays, according to the newscast, had been abolished and Protestant and Catholic theological faculties at Riga University had been suppressed and the teaching staffs dismissed without compensation. Teachers, claimed the broadcast, had to attend antireligious meetings and have been prohibited from having their children baptized. Additionally the religious press had been silenced and superseded by atheistic literature. The word "God," asserted the summary, had been banned and could not even be used in obituary notices. The Radio did admit, however, that religious worship in Latvia, despite the Soviet measures, was flourishing and signed off by adding that Communist antireligious tactics had changed from the violence and brutality of the 1920s to sophistication and subtlety, but that their aim remained the same: "The extermination of Christianity and every religion."[103]

The Vatican's reactions to the persecution in Soviet-occupied Eastern Europe during 1940, by and large, paralleled its policies in 1939. It continued to denounce the antireligious nature of Communism and the threat which that atheistic philosophy held for mankind and Western civilization.[104] Bishop Vincent Brizgys of Kaunas and Reverend Carl Fulst, the head of the Jesuits in Lithuania, specifically requested Radio Vatican to tone down its Lithuanian transmissions.[105] The Papacy, in addition, persisted in reproving Germany, publicly and privately, for its alliance with the Soviet Union.[106] The Church's most forceful disapprobation came on March 11, 1940, when Foreign Minister Ribbentrop was asked, during an audience, by Pius "If Germany had nothing to fear from its union with Communism."[107] Ribbentrop attempted to blunt the edge of Pius' reproach by emphasizing to the Pope as well as to Secretary of State Maglione that National Socialism and Hitler were the world's salvation from the Communist menace, but Pius was not quick to agree and, quite understandably, in view of the Nazi-Soviet détente.[108] The Vatican also worked steadfastly with the United States to keep Italy out of the war and, simultaneously, pressured the United States to obtain data on the Soviet anti-Catholic activities in Eastern Europe. The first tactic helped safeguard France and stymied a stimulus to the German-Russian alliance while the second, apart from mirrowing Rome's natural desire for information, reminded the Americans that the Soviets were Communists and ravishers of God's temples and, thus, hopefully cooled any real or potential American penchant for the USSR.[109] The Vatican, furthermore, sustained its condemnations of Soviet aggression. At the beginning of the year, with the Soviets bogged down in Finland, Radio Vatican anathemized the Soviet onslaught against Finland and, simultaneously, pointed out the supineness of the USSR as proven by its inability to defeat the Finns.[110] The Papacy explained Soviet weakness on the grounds of the "inborn wickedness of Bolshevik Communism," and while that approach stressed its policy of denigration, its emphasis upon the USSR's palsied condition was perhaps a red herring, dangled to persuade Hitler that the Red Army was, in Mao Tse-tung's words, a "paper tiger."[111] By June of 1940, when the Soviet Union incorporated the Baltic States, Bessarabia, and northern Bukovina, the Vatican again caustically censured what it called Communist aggression and, by way of reproof to Hitler, added that "whoever likes Stalin has not the right to call himself a paradigm of civilization."[112] By then, the Vatican's denunciations of Communism and Russian incursions acted not only to upbraid Germany but also to proscribe what, after the defeat of France and the advent of deterioration in German-Soviet relations, was becoming a clear possibility, namely, a move by the British to ally with the Communists.

The Papacy also continued its efforts to secure peace. The Vatican's principal activity along these lines came after France's capitulation, when Cardinal Maglione telegramed the Italians, English, and Germans, inviting them to negotiate a settlement.[113] The Nazis favored peace and, in fact, made a peace overture themselves to the English, but, as could be anticipated, London answered that "they are determined not to allow Europe and Britain themselves to fall under Nazi domination, and they are ready to fight against this to the end."[114] Despite the English disposition, the Vatican sought peace through the remainder of 1940.[115] If tranquility had been obtained in the West, the Soviet Union obviously would have been in extreme danger for she could not have dependend on England if the Germans, after gaining peace in the west, launched an invasion against her.

From the middle of 1940 onward, the Vatican increasingly became aware of the strain in German-Russian relations and no doubt that perception brought not only relief but also a faint ray of hope for the future. As a series of notes written by Cardinal Tardini reveal, the Papacy was cognizant of the rupture in the totalitarian states' alliance as early as June 29 and, for the rest of the year, it received strong hints of the impending Axis' invasion of the Soviet Union.[116] On August 8 its Apostolic Delegate in Sofia reported that German-Russian relations had significantly soured.[117] In early October, after the Brenner Pass meeting between Hitler and Mussolini, the Italian Ambassador to the Papacy cogently intimated to church leaders that the Axis were preparing an offensive against the USSR.[118] Possibly to reinforce the new direction of events, it was announced, also in early October, that the Vatican was preparing a major encyclical warning Catholics throughout the world of the dangers of Bolshevik philosophy and "communistic influences."[119] That report, however, while no doubt buoying up the anti-

Soviet tendency of the Nazis, set in motion a remonstrance by the British government which had to shroud the ray of hope which the Vatican was glimpsing. The Papal Nuncio in London, Cardinal Godfrey, informed Maglione on January 17, 1941, that the Church would lose influence in Great Britain if it took a strong stand against "Bolshevism and atheistic Communism" and did not simultaneously condemn "the anti-Christian theory and menace of Nazism."[120] That letter contained a dismal prospect which the Vatican had been fearing ever since the defeat of France: that Great Britain was moving closer to the USSR and wished to form an alliance.[121] From the Church's point of view, an Anglo-Russian agreement in place of the German-Soviet accord was hardly an improvement and the potentiality of such a combination, now that Russo-German relations were strained, plagued the Vatican for the remainder of 1940. Apparently the torment was enough to defer the issuance of the anti-Communist encyclical for none was forthcoming.

By the close of 1940 the Papacy's démarches got a rise out of the Kremlin.[122] By then, the Russians' apprehension over Germany had evolved into abject fear. The French, one of the great powers of Europe, had collapsed and the English were desperately attempting to defend their island. Hitler had become insulting and impudent toward his Communist ally. In November, Moscow had requested that the Germans allow the Soviets to take territories in Bulgaria, but Berlin never even so much as told the Russians no. Such temerity by the Nazis and indeed the Soviet desire to bolster its defensive position at Bulgarian expense were both pellucid signs of the low state of German-Russian relations. In light of the burgeoning defiance of the Germans, Moscow certainly had to interpret Rome's anti-Communist forays with fear and trepidation, for whether or not the Kremlin held them to have added to the loosening of Nazi-Soviet bonds, it undoubtedly understood that they were tending to better its relations with Berlin.

By the beginning of 1941, the Kremlin apparently determined to try to ameliorate its relations with the Papacy in the hope of, at least, watering down Rome's vituperative anti-Communism. The ultimate purpose was to erase a possible issue in the declension of Nazi-Soviet ties but, simultaneously, Moscow's policies revealed that it had virtually made a *volteface* in its evaluation of religion as a political weapon. The Kremlin's initiatives for impressing the Papacy were oblique and confused by four factors. One, as religion *per se* seemed politically significant, Orthodoxy, perforce, loomed as Moscow's most essential ally and that reality *ipso facto* strained ties with Rome because of Orthodoxy's anti-Catholic (particularly anti-Uniate) tendencies. Practically this implied that the Soviet regime, by embracing

Orthodoxy, was *a fortiori* shunning Catholicism. Specifically it led to heightened attacks upon Uniate Catholicism as well as on the Papacy's Apostolic Administrator, Leopold Braun, since he was ministering to Muscovites. Secondly, Moscow perhaps felt obliged to hide the antinomy of a Marxist government climbing into bed with organized religion to preclude being cited by the Trotskys of the world with emasculating the atheistic principles of Marxism. It needed, in other words, to show an active antireligious image, if not against Orthodoxy, at least against some religion and since the Communists were already tending, due to their growing ties with Orthodoxy, toward an anti-Catholic stance, it would be convenient to keep the Catholic Church as a target of invective. Thirdly, the Kremlin logically wanted to shore up its ramparts in the West and that meant an increase in troops and an accelerated deportation of persons deemed anti-Soviet. Specifically this tact induced Moscow to billet more troops in the houses which had not yet been taken from the Catholic Church and, additionally, to deport sizable numbers of Catholics since they were considered more untrustworthy, for atavistic reasons, than Orthodox, borderland peoples.[123] Finally, as indicated earlier, the Soviet government, planning for Sovietization, wanted to yoke the Church and fracture East European nationalism (of any type). The Church, as a foundation of national identity for many of the East Europeans and an apologist for a world view irreconcilable with Soviet ideology, stood in the way of Eastern Europe's rapid, successful assimilation and, thus its vigorous members and leaders were marked all the more for deportation, abuse, and discrimination.

Thus, the Soviet government, in its wish to curry favor with the Papacy, was in a dilemma. Nonetheless for the sake of palliating, even slightly, the German *Juggernaut,* it essayed to square the circle by, first, having Catholic clerics in Lithuania report to the Papacy that the religious conditions in the Russian-controlled portions of East Europe were satisfactory and that the Vatican should halt its fallacious announcements on Soviet persecution.[124] Secondly, Moscow contacted the Papacy directly by sending, on January 11, 1941, its new ambassador to the Reich, Vladimir G. Dekanosov, to Nuncio Orsenigo to impress upon the Papal emissary that the Soviets were not attacking the Catholic Church in Russia or the Baltic States and that the Church's position in those countries was the same as it was before the war.[125] Finally, it did not significantly increase, until the fateful month of June, its persecutory attitude toward the Catholic Church in Eastern Europe. The latter claim is supported by episcopal descriptions of the religious situation in Eastern Europe during the first half of 1941. These materials, summarized below, arrived at the Vatican as late as 1943. In addition to the bishops' reports, Radio Vatican and a summary report, dated September, 1941, on

Soviet religious policy and evidentally written by Myron C. Taylor, corroborate the claim.[126]

As far as the official, episcopal reports on the religious situation in eastern Poland were concerned, the initial one came, on August 5, 1941, from the Uniate auxiliary of Lviv, Bishop Slipyi. He simply wrote Pius XII that, during the Soviet occupation, the clergy and the faithful fulfilled their religious duties and obligations.[127] On August 6, 1941, the Uniate Bishop of Stanislav, Hyrhorii Khomyshyn, reported to Nuncio Rotta at Budapest that the Russians, while they held his diocese, did not substantially interfere with his duties, those of his auxiliary bishop, Ivan Liatyshevs'kyi, or his priests who numbered over five hundred. The Soviets, however, did tax the clergy and churches, according to the bishop, as well as confiscate the diocese's seminary for the use of soldiers. Some of the clergy, who resided in the sequestrated seminary, were eventually conscripted into the Red Army, according to the bishop. In the last days of the Soviet occupation, the bishop asserted, deportation of Uniates was increased and the Russian soldiers became quite violent toward the Uniate clergy, killing at least three priests. It was also at that time, according to the bishop, that the Communists tried to poison him and his auxiliary. Eight priests were arrested and deported and, the bishop added, a similar fate would have befallen more priests except that they took refuge in the woods and private homes. Before then, however, according to the Uniate leader, aside from the atheistic propaganda and the ban on religious instruction in schools, religious worship was tolerated.[128] A Vatican report, mentioned above, placed the number of deported priests at over seventy and revealed that some of the deportees were "barbarously murdered."[129]

On August 30, 1941, Archbishop Sheptyts'kyi sent to Nuncio Rotta a rather detailed sketch on the Soviet occupation in Lviv. The metropolitan maintained that the Bolsheviks were dedicated assassins of all religions, but that they proceeded slowly so as not to excite public or international reaction to their murderous policies. The archbishop asserted that the Soviets did not obstruct the operation of divine services in church and did permit a modicum of religious freeom. According to the Uniate archbishop, the bulk of the Communists' antireligious campaign was directed at attempting to make atheists out of the children and youth. The young people, claimed the metropolitan, were not allowed to learn religion in school, but, instead, were forced to devote a considerable number of hours to the "science of communism and atheism." Many of the young, the archbishop wrote, were enlisted into the Pioneers or *Komsomols* where the Communists essayed to systematically demoralize them. Deportations and arrests, according to the Uniate leader, continued throughout the period of occupation although not until the end were sizable numbers of Uniate clerics and faithful incarcerated, deported, and, in some cases, executed. The archbishop affirmed that "in the last days of the Bolshevik occupation . . . . the lives of thousands of faithful were taken (nearly 6,000 at Lviv alone)." In addition, according to the metropolitan, the Communists, before they fled Galicia, arrested nearly fifty of his priests and it was feared they had killed eleven of these clerics, although he had certain proof of only six executions. The Uniate seminary in Lviv, the archbishop declared, was eventually closed, but he was able to organize "with great pain" a course of theology at his residence with a dozen students. The Uniate leader also noted that he was treated differently than the other clerics in his diocese: his cathedral and domicile were not, for example, at first confiscated when other clerics were being forced out of their dwellings and when the religious orders and monks were being dispersed and having their monasteries expropriated. The archbishop thought the reason for the distinction in treatment was a Soviet ploy to compromise him in the eyes of his flock. Be that as it may, it was certainly an oblique recognition by the Soviets of Metropolitan Sheptyts'kyi's widespread popularity and influence. The archbishop also detected that the Latins of Lviv were treated with more leniency than the Uniates. He noted specifically that all the Latin monasteries, in contrast to the Uniate monasteries, were not confiscated by the authorities and that the Latin seminary in Lviv managed to operate throughout the entire period of occupation, again at variance with the Uniate situation where the seminary was suppressed. The metropolitan speculated that the motive for the differences in conduct was due to the fact that the Soviets knew the Germans were going to attack them and, thus, wanted to remain on good terms with the Polish people and their English supporters. That was a possibility, but since all available evidence indicates that the Soviets did not believe, at least before 1941, that the Germans were preparing an invasion of the USSR, it is more probable that the Soviet discrimination was attributable to the traditional, Russian animosity for Uniatism as well as to a Soviet belief that the Uniates would be more easily absorbed into the Russian system than the Latins. As far as the overall religious life in Lviv was concerned, the metropolitan concluded that the clergy performed its duties and the faithful regularly attended religious services.[130]

On November 7, 1941, Metropolitan Sheptyts'kyi had an opportunity to reevaluate the religious situation in his diocese following the Bolshevik retreat. He estimated that for his diocese alone there was a loss, primarily through deportation, of 200,000 persons and for the entire western Ukraine about 400,000. He also added that, in his diocese, eleven or twelve priests were assassinated and thirty-three deported and that from the Uniate diocese of Peremyshl twenty priests were killed.[131]

On March 7, 1943, the Latin archbishop of Lviv, Boleslaw Twardowski, informed Pius XII on the conditions of religious life in his diocese under the Soviets. The archbishop declared that the Church was not openly or violently attacked by the Communists. Their official stand, according to the bishop, was that religion was free and a private affair. However, the archbishop charged, the Communists were not as tolerant as their official position indicated. In fact, according to the archbishop, their official stand was contradicted by an array of indirect maneuvers against religion. The religious orders and monasteries, the archbishop asserted, suffered the worst fate at the hands of the Soviets. Most of the religious and monks, according to the Latin leader, were forced out of their houses and monasteries which the authorities then confiscated and used as barracks for Russian troops. All church property, the archbishop claimed, including churches, ecclesiastical equipment, schools, hospitals, orphanages, and monasteries were nationalized and the latter four institutions were appropriated. Churches, according to the archbishop, were taxed at an exorbitant rate. Religion, wrote the archbishop, was removed from schools, including secondary and primary schools and the University of Lviv, and replaced, at least in the case of the former, by courses on atheism and Communism. The archbishop charged that two youth groups, the Pioneers and *Komsomol,* attempted to inculcate atheistic ideas in the minds of the young. Civil marriages and divorces, according to the bishop, were made obligatory and permissible respectively. All parish records and archives as well as the Curia's diocesan archives, the bishop reported, were confiscated by the authorities. Bishop Twardowski also claimed that he and his auxiliary, Mgr. Eugene Baziak, were forced from their residences and that all their furnishings were despoiled. The students and teachers at the diocesan seminary, according to the archbishop, were forced to find new living quarters. The major efforts of the occupying officials, wrote the archbishop, went into atheistic propaganda, which they spread fanatically and by every conceivable means: books, magazines, journals, public meetings, shows, cinemas, plays, and special atheistic information sessions which they held in factories, hospitals, private homes, etc. Anyone who opposed the Soviet practices or criticized the terroristic methods by which they kept the population in tow, according to the archbishop, was subject to imprisonment and possible execution. The archbishop asserted that, aside from the murder of ten priests and six religious brothers during the Soviet retreat and the loss of eighteen priests who fled to Hungary when the Soviets first marched into Poland, all priests, approximately 753, were at their posts and performing their tasks in the diocese's 412 parishes. In conclusion, the archbishop reported that the Soviets did permit the church officials to hold regular clerical meetings, recite divine office, teach catechism to the young in church, and administer to the spiritual needs of the faithful.[132]

As far as the official, episcopal reports from the Baltic States during 1941 were concerned, the initial one came, on March 21, from the auxiliary of Kaunas, Bishop Vincent Brizgys. He wrote Cardinal Maglione that the Soviets impeded the broadcasts of Radio Vatican, closed the seminary at Kaunas, and continued to arrest sisters and priests (the number of priests detained, he reported, had reached thirty). But, the bishop also emphasized that the profession of faith and the practice of religion had not ebbed and that even Soviet military personnel visited churches and practiced religion, although they did so under the pain of prison.[133]

On May 15, Father Leopold (Gumppenberg) von Ebersberg, O.F.M. Capp., the head of the Capuchins in Estonia and Latvia, who had been forced to leave the Baltic States in March, 1941, and then took up residence in Rome, summarized for Pope Pius XII the religious conditions in Latvia. According to the priest, the Communists harassed the clergy, confiscated church buildings, and interfered in religious instruction. But, the priest claimed, the hierarchy remained faithful to the Church and the clergy were full of zeal.[134]

The Baltic States, of course, by the end of June, were firmly in the hands of the Germans, but correspondence with the Vatican continued to summarize the religious conditions during the Soviet occupation. On September 18, Cardinal Maglione received bad news from Nuncio Orsenigo in Berlin. The Nuncio reported to the Secretary of State that the Soviets, on June 28, 1941, deported Edward Profittlich, the Apostolic Administrator in Estonia, across the Urals.[135]

On September 20, 1941, Bishop Springovics of Riga wrote to Piux XII to inform him of the religious condition in Latvia during the Russian occupation. According to the bishop, all bishops in his province were alive and well. Ten priests were lost during the Soviet occupation, according to the bishop, and seven of them had been cruelly murdered and the remaining three deported to Russia. The number of faithful lost to the Russians in his province, claimed the bishop, was around 10,000 (he said a total of 100,000 citizens had actually been deported). When the Soviets initially occupied Latvia, the bishop went on, they implemented all of the standard antireligious laws of their own country. By August of 1940, according to the bishop, the Communists had spoiled many of the Church's immovable goods which were a principal source of sustenance for the clergy and ecclesiastical servants. The only churches left intact, offered the bishop, were those with attached cemeteries. Most priests and bishops, claimed the bishop, were expelled from their residences and had to find housing among their parishioners, although in the large cities the priests and bishops were allowed to continue living in truncated ecclesiastical residences, but these domiciles were heavily taxed. In March, 1941, according to the bishop, all churches and church goods were nationalized. When the Germans attacked, claimed the bishop, the Soviets, before evacuating, burned two churches. The Communists, claimed the bishop, eliminated religion from the schools and promulgated atheism. The Communists also, according to the bishop, forced the faithful to work on Sunday and suppressed the seminary in Riga and the Catholic Theological Faculty at the University of Riga. But, in conclusion, the bishop wrote that Christian life had not diminished under the Bolsheviks, that religious education, although with great difficulty, continued in homes and churches, and that, finally, in April, 1941, four men were ordained presbyters.[136] The Vatican also reported, in September, that thirty Latvian priests had been taken and probably killed by the retreating Russians.[137]

On October 10, 1941, Joseph Skvireckas, Archbishop and Metropolitan of Kaunas, communicated to Pius XII the situation in Lithuania under the Bolshevik yoke. The bishop reiterated that the Soviets, upon occupation of Lithuania, terminated the Church-State concordat and exiled the Nuncio. They also, cited the archbishop, replaced religious instruction with atheism in the schools, suppressed and confiscated the goods of all Catholic associations, prohibited the printing of religious journals and tracts, despoiled much of the movable and immovable property of the seminaries, monasteries, and bishoprics, left only the barest minimum necessary for worship in churches, quartered troops in ecclesiastical residences and buildings, refused to excuse Catholics from work on religious feast days, imprisoned 30 priests and many Catholic laymen, who held important posts, especially in Catholic Action, as well as about a thousand other citizens, and, finally, attempted to weaken the faith of the clergy through incessant interrogations. By the middle of June, 1941, with the German attack on the horizon, the bishop claimed that the Soviets began a massive deportation of educated and professional Lithuanians, about 40,000 in all. (According to the Vatican, large scale deportations began on June 14 in all three Baltic States and during the period from June 14 to June 17, it estimated that about 34,260 were deported to Russia.) When the Germans actually invaded, according to the bishop, the Bolsheviks, in their flight, killed a great number of laymen and eighteen priests and deported forty priests whose fate is unknown. On the positive side, according to the archbishop, the Catholic clergy showed prudence in handling money and fortitude in their faith; the faithful frequented the churches and the sacraments; many parishioners, who before had been indifferent or retarded in their faith, according to the bishop, recuperated during the occupation; and, finally, many young scholars, asserted the religious leader, revealed a strong faith.[138]

On February 14, 1942, Archibishop Jalbrzykowski, in a letter to Cardinal Maglione, briefly summarized the experience of the diocese of Vilnius under the Soviets. In general, according to the archbishop, church life in Vilnius remained strong. The Communists did arrest and detain six priests in the territory of Vilnensi, did deport fifteen priests, and did abrogate the seminary of Vilnius. When they retreated, the Russians, claimed the bishop, deported more than 100,000 people from the diocese of Vilnius and barbarously murdered six priests.[139] On March 19, 1942, Bishop Skvireckas of Kaunas, in a laconic note to Cardinal Maglione, stated that the Bolsheviks held up Papal correspondence.[140]

On August 8, 1942, Bishop Springovics of Riga capsulized, for Cardinal Maglione, the position of the Catholic Church in Estonia. According to the bishop, there were approximately 2,340 Catholics in Estonia in 1942 which was close to the prewar total. But the priests, who numbered fourteen before the war, according to the bishop, had been reduced, mainly through expulsion, to four. The bishop also confirmed the fact that Edward Profittlich, the Apostic Administrator, had been deported, on June 27, 1941, to the USSR.[141]

A final letter, dealing with the Bolshevik occupation, was received at the Vatican in October, 1942, from the Lithuanian bishops as a whole. The signatories included Joseph Skvireckas, Archbishop of Kaunas, Anton Karosas, Bishop of Vilkavishensis, Justin Staugaitis, Bishop of Telsensis, Casimir Paltarokas, Bishop of Panevezensis, Joseph Matulaitis-Labukas, Vicar of Kaisedoresis, Vincent Brizgys, Auxiliary of Kaunas, Vincent Borisevicius, Auxiliary of Telsensis, Vincent Padolski, Auxiliary of Vilkaviskensis, and Mecislas Reinys, Apostolic Administrator the archdiocese of Vilnius. The bishops informed the Pope that during the Soviet occupation, the bishops became the peoples' leaders and the staunch defenders of religion. According to the letter, the bishops were not permitted by the Communists to meet in assembly or to write pastoral letters to the faithful, publish religious journals, or give religious instruction. Twenty-two priests from Lithuania, reported the bishops, were killed and many others were arrested, tortured, and deported. The Bolsheviks also, claimed the bishops, deported thousands of citizens.[142]

As these reports reveal, the Soviets, although certainly continuing to persecute the Church, did not increase their incubus against the Catholic Church in Eastern Europe during 1941. In fact, joined to their policies, cited earlier, to persuade the Vatican that they were not pillorying Catholicism, they indicate, admittedly nebulously, a proclivity on Moscow's part to placate the Vatican. Certainly the Kremlin's propensity to assuage its bad reputation in Rome was propelled by a series of events in early 1941. First, the Japanese Foreign Minister, Yosuke Matsuoka, with whom the Soviets were anxiously trying to arrange a non-aggression pact, visited Pius XII in March. [143] That event must have impressed Moscow with the fact that the Pope, even if he did not have any divisions, had some influential friends. Secondly, Germany was becoming more menacious than ever before. In March, the Nazis started overflights into the Soviet Union and, in April, with incredible ease, conquered Yugoslavia and Greece.

Unfortunately, no doubt, from the Soviet point of view, their attempts to impress the Papacy were contradicted by the complicating measures outlined above: their growing anti-Uniate position (or pro-Orthodox propensity), their desire to demonstrate an atheistic frontispiece (not a major concern), their need to bolster defenses, and, lastly, their authoritarian proclivities. These components, singularly or in combination, led Moscow, first, to name, in March, 1941 an Orthodox bishop, Panteleimon Rudyk, for the Uniate diocese of Lviv, whose obvious purpose was to prepare the Uniates for "reunion" with the Russian Orthodox Church and to increase pressure on Kostel'nyk to organize a split from Rome within the Uniate Church.[144] Secondly, they induced it, in January, to confiscate Kaunas Seminary which, until then, was the only seminary open in Lithuania.[145] Thirdly, they moved the Soviets to instigate a terroristic campaign (under the NKVD) of arrests, torture, executions, and deportations which grew in proportion to the proximity of the German invasion.[146] Finally, they compelled the Kremlin to exacerbate Leopold Braun's tribulations. Beginning on December 25, 1940, and stretching to February 14, 1941, the Soviets, on three occasions, robbed and vandalized St. Louis Church. Braun angrily reported each of the thefts to the proper authorities, but they always responded, upon investigating his complaints, that there were no clues. After the last theft, however, the Russians went one step too far by presenting Braun with a bill of "several thousand" rubles on the grounds that, according to law, all church property and, thus, the stolen goods, belonged to the state. Braun, naturally, exploded over the government's impudence and decided to take his case to the American Embassy as well as to Henry Cassidy, the head of the Associated Press Bureau in Moscow. The news shortly led to an official United States' protest as well as remonstrances from other embassies. These developments soon moved the police to produce the robbers and most of the stolen property. From that time until the Nazi attack, Braun, except for the usual annoyance of surveillance, was not nettled.[147] The Kremlin, at a time when the German Gorgon was looming, evidently wanted to keep relations with the United States smooth and, possibly, wished to remove this thorn from the side of the Catholic Church just in case it might improve its standing with the Vatican and lead to a decrease in Catholicism's anti-Soviet broadside.

The Vatican did not requite the Soviets' overtures for even without the contravening factors that accompanied their policies, it still thought of Communism as the dire threat of Catholicism, Western civilization, and humanity. During the spring of 1941, the Vatican pursued the policies it had followed against Communism in 1939 and 1940.[148] Accordingly the Papacy was certainly animated by the increasing number of Nuncios' transcriptions that adumbrated a Nazi-Soviet war. On February 7, Nuncio Angelo Roncalli, the future Pope John XXIII, then the legate to Turkey, reported to Cardinal Maglione that the Nazis were building up their troops in Romania.[149] A little over a month later, Nuncio Filippo Bernadini in Bern, Switzerland, wrote that rumors of a clash between German and the USSR were volitant.[150] On June 13, Nuncio Andrea Cassulo in Bucharest informed Maglione that a break in the Nazi-Soviet alliance was very near.[151] Finally, on June 19, Nuncio Bernadini wrote the Papacy that hearsay had it that war was imminent between the Communists and Fascists.[152] Moscow, which was also aware of such rumors and information, was certainly, in contrast to the Papacy, depressed and unnerved.

CHAPTER V
HIATUS: JUNE 1941-1944

The invasion of Soviet Russia by the Axis powers on June 22, 1941, precipitated diverse reactions in Vatican City and Moscow. In the former, there was relief and a twinge of hope. The relief stemmed from the fact that the Nazi military machine was ending Communist persecution in Eastern Europe and the hope from the fact that the Nazis were giving a respite to the Allied forces. The only somber conditions which prevented the Vatican from actually celebrating the irruption were, one, that the Nazis, if they should smash the Communists, might return to besiege the West and, secondly, that the Allies might form an alliance with the USSR to preclude the Fascists from annihilating the Soviets. Ideally, no doubt, the Papacy would have preferred a Nazi Pyrrhic victory in the East, one in which the Communists, to be sure, would have been obliterated but also one in which, at the same time, the Germans would have been so weakened as to allow the Western Allies to defeat or force a conditional peace upon the Axis.[1]

In Moscow the Nazi plunge was met with speechless anxiety. The Kremlin, which had jeopardized itself internally through forced collectivization and externally through the Molotov-Ribbentrop Pact, seemingly lay exposed to the *Wehrmacht*. Allies, however, some from surprising quarters, were close at hand and soon rallied around the beleaguered government of Stalin. The West, led by England, extended without delay the hand of alliance to the Soviet Union which the Soviets, probably with an element of incredulity, quickly if unceremoniously accepted.[2] Internally the people, partly in response to the exhortations of the Moscow metropolitan, reacted to the German incursion as patriots and girded themselves for battle.[3] Undoubtedly, for the Kremlin, the most shocking event during the first week of the assault was the willingness of the people, the army, the Church, and the other ravaged institutions of Soviet Russia to fight for the regime. The Church's response, in particular, must have been surprising for even through Metropolitan Sergei had pledged Orthodoxy's support to the government in 1927, the Communists never trusted the Church and persisted in rebuffing and persecuting it. Now, with the Church proving its loyalty by condemning the Nazis and envoking the Russian people to expectorate the "Nazi phlegm," the regime allowed itself to be convinced that Orthodoxy had, at last, accepted the verdict of the 1917 revolution.[4] In fact, from this point on, Stalin's government adopted, with near exclusivity, the "pragmatists' " principle for determining religious policy: toleration in proportion to a church's loyalty and/or utility to the regime. The state bureaucracy, with the Party apparatus obviously at perigee, strove to embrace the Church, an envelopment to which the ecclesiastical leaders, now conditioned via decades of maltreatment to political docility, warmed and reciprocated.[5]

Eight interrelated reasons suggest themselves for what N. S. Timasheff calls Moscow's "religious N.E.P." First, toleration of Orthodoxy could bring social cohesion under the banner of "Soviet patriotism" whereas continued persecution might divide the Soviet population. Secondly, a concord with Orthodoxy could provide moral legitimacy for the government's war effort and boost popular morale. Thirdly, the Church, as an ally, could channel Soviet influence both upon the believers in the lands lost to the Nazis and on foreign public opinion. Fourthly, religious toleration could make the West more comfortable allies of an avowed atheistic government. Fifthly, it might also rob the Germans of a propagandistic weapon, particularly in the lost regions where religion was experiencing an amazing revival, against the Soviet Union. Sixthly, it would undercut both foreign churches' (especially the Vatican) and the Russian emigres' charges of the Communists as Neros and, possibly, might even draw the Vatican over to the Communist side. Seventh, Orthodoxy could be used as a sophisticated and less obvious tool of "sovietizing" and/or "re-sovietizing" the Russian and non-Russian peoples and institutions, particularly the Ukrainian Uniates, once the Soviet army recaptured lost land and extended its writ into neighboring countries. Finally, the Church oculd make a significant contribution in support of Soviet foreign policy.[6]

The "religious N.E.P.," evolving over the course of the war, was the government's *quid pro quo* to the Church. Officially, the government's concessions to the Church did not mean, with possibly one exception which will be touched on in Chapter VI, a repeal of the 1929 Law on Religious Associations, but comprised a different interpretation of the law such that the Church was permitted to have seminaries and monasteries, to lease buildings for worship, to organize religious meetings, and to publish religious journals (the chief one was the *Zhurnal Moskovskoi Patriarkhii* begun in September, 1943). The regime, in addition, opted to facilitate the collection of church revenues from believers, to allow the Church to elect a Patriarch, Sergei in 1943, and to disregard some of the more capricious prohibitions against religious activities, such as pilgrimages, private religious instruction of children, etc.[7] The government also curtailed its antireligious propaganda, dissolving the League of Militant Atheists (never officially) and such publications as *Bezbozhnik* and *Antireligioznik*.[8]

Obviously some of the same reasons which led to the Kremlin's reversal with Orthodoxy could have induced *rapprochement* with the Catholic Church. A friendly Catholic Church could bring international moral support for the Soviet war effort and, conversely, deny it to the Axis powers. The Kremlin was certainly aware of the fact that Catholicism was a major moral force in Italy, France, Germany, Belgium, Luxemburg, Ireland, Spain, Portugal, Austria, Hungary, Czechoslovakia, North America, and Latin America. At the same time Moscow was probably cognizant, from British sources if from no where else, that the Axis powers were pressuring the Vatican to publicly support their invasion of the USSR.[9] The Communists could easily deduce that if Papal approval was important for the Axis, the lack of such a sanction or, even more, a Catholic endorsement of the Soviet war effort could have a demoralizing effect on Russia's enemies and deliver a psychological boost to the image of the Soviet Union, somewhat still tarnished by the memory of the Molotov-Ribbentrop Pact. The 1941 denunciations of fascism by Cardinal Hlond, the Polish Primate in exile at Lourdes, provided exemplary evidence of such a weapon in use.[10]

A benevolent Vatican could also help to diffuse the anti-Sovietism of Catholics, Poles, Balts, Belorussians, and Ukrainians, and, simultaneously, unite these German-controlled peoples, their partisan movements, and the governments-in-exile with Soviet battle plans. Lithuania and Poland both maintained ambassadors at the Vatican and the Polish-government-in-exile at London, under General Sikorski, made it perfectly clear to Ivan Maisky, the Soviet envoy to Britain, before and after the signing of the Russo-Polish Alliance in July, that the Polish government desired Polish refugees in the USSR to be administered by Catholic priests.[11] The Soviets certainly realized that an amiable Catholic Church would improve their standing with the Poles especially and, in 1941, that was crucial for the Communists were stained by their collaboration with the Germans in partitioning Poland and their internment of thousands of Polish refugees. (They also, by this time, although it was not discovered until April, 1943, had murdered thousands of Polish military officers).[12] A friengly Poland, in turn, would erase the moral stigma of the Molotov-Ribbentrop Pact, would strengthen the Soviets' alliance with Britain and the United States since both of these powers backed, at that time, the Sikorski government, and most importantly, place the Poles in, at least, a disarmed frame of mind for Soviet endeavors to keep the earlier annexed lands of the West Ukraine and West White

Russia. A well-disposed Catholic Church, in fact, might even serve as a pressure on the Sikorski government to recognize Soviet territorial claims.

An amicable Vatican could, in addition, greatly improve the Soviet Union's image in the West, particularly in the United States and Britain, the two chief allies of the Kremlin. Moscow was undoubtedly conscious of the fact that the British were drawing close to the Vatican, immediately after the German invasion of the USSR, to prevent the Church from supporting the Nazi onslaught and, secondly, to keep the goodwill of the Vatican.[13] It was public knowledge also that the British, to accomplish the latter goal, impressed upon the Vatican the fact that its support of the Soviet Union did not mean that England backed Communism.[14] It would not have been too difficult for the Soviets to realize that an ameliorated relationship with Pius XII would have pleased the English and, no doubt, added to their alliance. At the same time, it was crystal clear that the American government, in 1941, wanted Vatican backing for its policies, including aid to the USSR, and hoped that the Church would adopt a friendly or, at least, neutral posture toward the Soviet Union. These realities were impressed upon Moscow by a veritable deluge of Rooseveltian ploys that erupted in August and September. First, at the end of August, Roosevelt's good friend, Bishop Patrick Hurley, publicly came out in favor of aid to Communist Russia.[15] Then, in early September, Supreme Court Justice Frank Murphy repeated the bishop's message to a Knights of Columbus assembly in Washington, D.C.[16] On September 9, Myron C. Taylor, acting as Roosevelt's personal envoy, made a well publicized, two week trip to the Vatican.[17] On September 11, in a conversation with the Soviet ambassador, Konstantin A. Umansky, President Roosevelt obliquely connected American aid with the relgious issue in the USSR by suggesting that "some publicity" regarding the freedom of religion in the USSR "might have a very find educational effect before the next lend-lease bill comes up in Congress."[18] At the end of September, Roosevelt, furthermore, in a press conference, declared that the Soviets allowed "freedom of religion" in accordance with article 124 of their constitution.[19] Finally, also at the end of September, W. Averell Harriman, who was in Moscow with Lord Beaverbrook to work out the details of Lend-Lease for the USSR, informed Molotov and Umansky (as did U.S. Ambassador Laurence Steinhardt) that the American Government wanted a declaration on freedom of religion from the Soviet Government.[20]

Finally, a détente with the Catholic Church could deny an important ear and base to anti-Communist émigrés and, eventually, give the Communists a diplomatic base in the heart of Italy. The Soviet government certainly was aware that émigré groups were in constant contact with the Vatican and, at the same time, it undoubtedly appreciated the fact that diplomatic representation at the Vatican, aside from the moral significance, had important political overtones. All of the major states and many of the minor countries had envoys there and, thus, representation could be useful as an international sounding-board, an information exchange, and a limited espionage service.

As far-fetched as some of these possibilities seem, they were, nonetheless, real, although the Soviet government did not make a strenuous effort to crystallize them. What blocked a "Catholic N.E.P.", during the first stages of the Nazi invasion, was that the burgeoning nexus with Orthodoxy dictated an anti-Uniate mentality, that the Catholic Church was insignificant as an internal institution and, thus, could be of no immediate assistance in the overwhelming preoccupation of rallying the *Soviet* people and stopping the Germans, that too many concessions, some striking at the heart of the totalitarian controls, would have to be given to appease the Vatican, that the quantum leap of aligning with the Catholic Church, the arch-foe of the "fundamentalist ," might have been too much of a strain for the Party atheists, and, finally, that the Papacy reaimed adamantly hostile and, although it did not approve,[21] did not condemn the Nazi invasion. The result of subtracting the prophylatics from the fruits was that the Kremlin was interested but unenthusiastic about closer ties with the Catholic Church. It decided, while the Nazi threat was imminent, to devote its efforts to strengthening the home front and not wooing the Catholic Church. But the regime did make minor concessions or overtures to the Papacy and tried to use its détente with Orthodoxy to convince Rome and its friends that atheism had been dropped in the USSR.

The first policy Moscow delineated in its modified courting of the Catholic Church was the issuance of praise, beginning in late July, for Papal and Catholic clerical efforts to halt and limit Nazi atrocities against human beings.[22] Secondly, in September, the Soviets freed some Catholic priests from prison and permitted Catholic chaplains to be assigned to the combat units of displaced Poles which were organized in the Soviet Union following the Russo-Polish agreement of July. The chaplains were also allowed, although not without difficulty, to visit and administer Polish civilian enclaves near their military posts.[23] Thirdly, the Kremlin impressed upon the Allied governments, which were so concerned about concessions to the Vatican, that there was religious freedom in the USSR. Ivan Maisky, on September 23, announced, at a press conference in London, that "religion in my country is not persecuted and every citizen has the right to believe or not to believe, according to his or her conscience." The "believers," claimed Maisky, "practice their religions freely."[24] Litvinov, who became Soviet ambassador to the United States in December, informed Harriman, while the latter was in Moscow with the Beaverbrook mission, that there was religious freedom in the Soviet Union.[25] On October 4, in Moscow, Assistant Commissar for Foreign Affairs, Solomon A. Lozovsky, read a prepared statement in which he emphasized that all religions, including Catholicism, were free in the USSR.[26] Fourthly, Stalin's government significantly improved its treatment of Leopold Braun. This was, no doubt, attributable not only to the desire of the Soviets to exhibit a friendly posture toward the Catholic Church but also, especially in view of the fact that Harriman interviewed Braun while he was in Moscow, to poultice any real or potential inflammation in Soviet-American relations. At any rate, life did take a dramatic turn for Braun in the late summer and early fall of 1941. According to Braun, as the Nazis pushed in toward Moscow, police surveillance of him and St. Louis Church halted. He also claimed he was allowed to administer Muscovites, including Red soldiers, without harassment. For the first time since he had come to the USSR, Braun discovered, in the fall of 1941, that he was able to obtain building supplies and materials for the repair of St. Louis Church. The new Soviet attitude so impressed Braun that, in late September, before Harriman left Moscow, he informed Harriman that he should carry back to the Vatican and the United States his firm conviction that religious conditions had so improved in the USSR that the time was ripe for "negotiating a *modus vivendi* between the Church and this Government."[27] The final policy Moscow pursued belonged in the category of omission rather than commission. In September and October, rumors of a Soviet-Vatican accord, touched off by the close proximity of Taylor's visit to Rome and Harriman's sojourn to Moscow, circulated throughout Europe. The Allies reacted with joy and the Fascist powers with disconcertion to the rumors.[28] The Vatican immediately branded the reports as false, but, significantly, the Soviet government neither repudiated the rumors nor denied that the possibility existed for a Soviet-Vatican *rapprochement*. Although it is doubtful that the Soviet had anything to do with stimulating these initial *on dit,* they certainly sensed, from the reaction of the other powers, their utility once they were in motion. Accordingly, it is not too difficult to believe that the Soviets perpetrated the rumor of a Soviet-Vatican détente that rocked Europe in 1942.[29]

The responses of the Catholic Church to Moscow's policies and, in general, to the consequences of the Nazi invasion were manifold. The Papacy, of course, was quite perturbed about the major deportation of Catholics from Eastern Europe during the initial stage of the German attack and its anger was not, in the least, soothed by the Kremlin's about face toward religion in the USSR and, more specifically, toward the Catholic Church in the late summer of 1941. The Church leaders clearly knew that Moscow had changed its tactics, but they were not at all convinced that the halt in the antireligious policies was permanent. The Church, however, did not issue any anti-Soviet or anti-Communist propaganda. This reaction was a reversal of pre-invasion policy, but the Church chose evidentally to follow it, despite the deportation of Catholics by the Communists, because of the alliance existing between the Western democracies and the USSR. The Church did not want to appear publicly pro-Axis by patently castigating the Russians and it wished to avoid confusing Catholics, especially Americans, who were in the process of bearing arms with atheistic Russia.[30] Another policy which the Church implemented and continued through 1941 and 1942 was also a revision of pre-invasion effort. No longer did the Papacy *constantly,* as before June, 1941, call publicly for peace. Between June and December 23, the Vatican made no declarations in favor of peace, despite the fact that Myron Taylor specifically requested one during his September visit.[31] The sudden dearth of peace pleas can be attributed to one of two causes or, more likely, a combination of both. One, the Papacy, as it claimed, had already outlined its peace proposals and it was futile to reiterate them.[32] Two, the Vatican did not want peace at this precise moment for the Nazis and Communists were finally locked in a death struggle and there was a genuine hope that both movements, especially the Communist, might be totally destroyed. It seems, in view of the fact that the Papacy did again agitate fastidiously for peace after the Battle of Stalingrad, and eventually for a conditional peace between the Allies and Germany, that the second point was the more weighty motive for the curtailment of the Vatican's peace efforts following the Nazi invasion of the USSR.[33] A fourth measure which the Vatican elaborated was one geared simply to take advantage of the Western alliance with the Soviet Union. It attempted, primarily through the agency of the United States, to care for, in a spiritual sense, Catholic prisoners of war in the hands of the Communists.[34] The Papacy, however, was frustrated in this desire because the United States was reluctant to intercede for it with the Soviets.

The Papacy's final and most significant response to the events of 1941 was a two-sided policy geared to neutralize Soviet Russia as a threat to the Catholic Church in the event that the Soviets and the Western Allies were victorious over the Axis. The first side of this policy represented a negative thrust. It amounted to an attempt to convince the Western Allies, notably Britain and the United States, that the Soviet Union was a Trojan horse, which, although appearing to be innoculous as an ally, was in fact a dire threat to western civilization. Cardinals Maglione and Tardini again and again emphasized, in talks with British and American representatives, that the Soviets, if Germany should be defeated, would sweep into Europe and take control, that the Russians would do precisely what the Allies were attempting to prevent Germany from accomplishing: establish hegemony in Europe.[35] The Church leaders, in addition, attempted to persuade the Westerners that the Soviet Union was a menace not only to Europe, but also to western civilization, to Christianity, and to humanity in general.[36] To prove their assertions, the Cardinals cited numerous examples of persistent religious persecution in the USSR, including the recent deportations, and also pointed out the aggressive 1939-1940 Soviet attacks upon Poland, the Baltic States, Finland, and Romania.[37]

Why were the Church leaders so condemnatory of the Soviet Union? The answer is multifaceted. The Church, first, was hostile because it continued to view the Soviet government as fundamentally atheistic and intolerant of religion. Secondly, the Church feared the expansion of non-Catholic Russia into Catholic East Europe. Even if the Communists had not been atheistic, the Church would have objected to their control of Eastern Europe because their tradition was Orthodox and anti-Catholic. For that reason, the Vatican could sympathize more with Germany and Italy than the USSR and acquiesce—but not condone—in Axis control of Eastern Europe. By the same token, it is conceivable that the Church could have or can subscribe to Soviet control of Eastern Europe if Moscow would have or would guarantee, at the minimum, tolerance of the Catholic Church. Thirdly, the Catholic Church remained antagonistic because of its persecutory experience in the Soviet Union and in Eastern Europe during the first Soviet occupation. Finally, the Church was inimical because the new Pope, Pius XII, since his days as Papal envoy to post-WWI Germany, was an implacable foe of Communism.

The Church, accordingly, tried to arouse the western states against the Soviet Union, at least to the point where they would prevent the USSR from expanding any further west than it had in 1939. The Church, however, as the present status quo in Europe reveals, was quite unsuccessful in awakening the western states to what the Church considered was the danger of Soviet expansion. The reason the West did not listen to the Papal Cassandra was that it perceived that the Vatican's opposition to the USSR was based upon ideology and personal experience and not upon abstract justice or the rights of people to chose their own government. The western observers sensed that the Church, although not supporting the Axis openly, certainly acquiesced in their control of Eastern Europe and that by taking an anti-Communist stand, although it was private, implicitly backed the Nazis.[38] Logically the westerners concluded that if the Church could endure the Axis it could also sustain the USSR and that the Church really, although it constantly warned against Soviet expansion into Eastern Europe, was not concerned about expansion *per se* but about the antireligious or, better yet, anti-Catholic ideology of the USSR. Thus, the westerners, especially the United States, in order to obtain Vatican approval for their policies, felt compelled to prove to the Vatican that the Soviet Union was not antireligious. Instead of obtaining from the Soviets guarantees for the freedom and independence of Poland and the Baltic States to appease the Papacy, the West sought cursory concessions on religious freedom. Myron C. Taylor, for example, after his two week visit to the Vatican in September, 1941, was not in the least disturbed about the danger of Communism or of Soviet expansion into Europe despite the fact that the Church leaders daily subjected him to anti-Communist and anti-Soviet propaganda.[39] He, rather, was much more intent upon persuading the Vatican that it was wrong about the USSR. Accordingly, after leaving the Vatican, he immediately wired Harriman, who was in Moscow discussing lend-lease provisions, to request a declaration of religious freedom from the Soviet government and also, apparently, to consult with Leopold Braun about religious conditions in the Soviet Union.[40] His message, of course, led to the Soviet declaration of October 4 on religious freedom in the USSR and also to Braun's late September declaration claiming that conditions had so drastically changed in the USSR that the time was ripe for a *modus vivendi* between the Church and the Soviet government. It was a year, however, before Taylor had the opportunity to present the fruit of his Moscow telegram to the Vatican, although in the United States, the administration used Braun's note, Harriman's discussions with Litvinov, and the Soviet government's October 4 announcement to attempt to convince Cardinal Cicognani that religious worship was open and free in the Soviet Union.[41]

The second side of the Church's policy to neutralize Soviet Russia, in contrast to the first, represented a positive approach. The Vatican decided that a sure way of ending the anti-Catholic posture of Stalin's government was to convert the Russian people to the Catholic faith. This was a two dimensional policy involving, first, the strengthening and consolidation of the weakened Church in Eastern Europe, especially the Uniate Church, so it could be used as an institutional springboard for eastward expansion and, secondly, the export of missionaries into the lands evacuated by the Communists.

In the case of the former, the Baltic Church attempted to reclaim much of what it had lost under the Bolsheviks, but to its dismay, it soon discovered that the Germans were almost as intolerant of Catholicism as the Communists.[41] However,, because the Church was so strongly anti-Communist, the Germans put up with it[43] and directed most of their persecutory measures against the Polish clergy in the Baltic States, arresting on March 3, 1942, the Polish archbishop of Vilnius, Mgr. Romuald Jalbrzykowski, and most of the

Polish clergy in his archdiocese.[44] Lithuanian auxiliary bishop Reinys was permitted to succeed to the administration of the archdiocese as an Apostolic Administrator with the full faculties of a resident bishop. In Estonia, the Germans maintained the position the Church was in at the time of the Bolshevik retreat, although they did permit Reverend Henry Werling, S. J., to assume the duties of Rev. Edward Profittlich, the Apostolic Administrator of Estonia whom the Bolsheviks deported when they retreated.[46] In Latvia also the Bolshevik status quo was continued by the Nazis, although, according to Archbishop Springovics of Riga, personal life was more secure.[47] The Latin Church in the West Ukraine and West Belorussia, which had been under Soviet auspices, was, in contrast to the Baltic Church, violently persecuted, particularly in the late stages of the war. The archdiocese of Lviv, though, did manage to hold the line on its pre-Nazi position.[48] As far as the Uniate Church was concerned, the Germans, like with the Latins, were initially tolerant for the political advantages to be gained. Under the more liberal German umbrella, the head of the Uniate Church in Galicia wished to strengthen the Uniate position in Eastern Europe by extending his authority over the Axis-occupied Ukraine and, then, use his church as the vehicle for uniting all Ukrainians in a single national church.[49] The Ukrainian Orthodox, themselves split with schism, and the Germans, however, were unwilling to see Sheptyts'kyi's dream come to life.[50] By August, 1942, Metropolitan Sheptyts'kyi, frustrated in his designs and increasingly aghast at the German atrocities, especially against the Jews, wrote Pius XII that the German regime, although a stripe above the Bolsheviks, was "bad, almost diabolical."[51] In general, then, needless to say, the Vatican's hopes of using a re-invigorated Church in Eastern Europe-Latin or Uniate—as a means of reaching the Russian people were dashed by the Germans. The Church was fortunate, in most cases, to maintain its stature at the time of the Communist retreat.

The second dimension of the Church's positive policy vis-à-vis the Soviet Union crystallized shortly after the Nazi attack. In late June and early July Cardinals Tardini and Maglione contacted the superior general of the Jesuits, Rev. Vladimir Ledochowski, S. J., the head of the Capuchins, Rev. Donato da Welle, OFM, Cap., and the leader of the Basilians, Rev. Denis Tkachuk to formalize a plan to send missionaries into the Russian lands occupied by Italians, Romanians, and Hungarians.[42] The Church leaders also wished to dispatch priests into the German-controlled territories, but the Nazis would allow, according to Nuncio Orsenigo and Archbishop Jalbrzy-kowski, only "schismatic priests" to go into their occupied zones. Although numerous priests from Poland, Galicia, and Lithuania attempted to penetrate the German zones and some made it as far east as Smolensk,

Orsenigo and Jalbrzykowski claimed that they were mostly expelled.[53] The explanation for the Germans' intransigence in not allowing Catholic priests into the USSR, according to Nuncio Orsenigo, was simply that they were angered that the Vatican had not approved their attack and had not preached, as expected, an anti-Communist crusade.[54] Despite the German attitude, a few priests did manage to enter the Soviet Union through the zones under Hungarian, Italian, and Romanian control. The exact number of missionaries in Russia during the invasion has not been released, but it is known that, by March of 1942, 42 Jesuits, "who had been officially authorized to go into Soviet territory," had been captured and imprisoned by the Red Army, that Mgr. Marc Glaser, who had been the rector of the Jassy seminary in Romania, had become bishop of the territory between the Dnieper and the Bug Rivers (including Odessa), and that there were at least two priests, the Italian Jesuit Pietro Leoni and the French Assumptionist Jean Nicholas, in Odessa.[55] In one sense, the Vatican's "crusade" represented a legitimate need and right to rebuild its decimated church in the Soviet Union and, in another sense, it reflected the Vatican's age-old desire to reunify the eastern and western branches of Christianity. The Vatican's proselytizing effort, however, fell short of achieving either goal, as indeed the Vatican must have suspected for the Church rested its main hope of paralyzing the Communist threat upon arousing the western allies to be vigilant against Soviet expansionist aims. However, the Papacy must have also realized that this negative policy, as it has been described, was also aborting for Cardinal Tardini constantly summarized the Allied opinion of the Soviet Union, especially that of America, as dangerous and superficial.[56]

As 1942 dawned, the Soviet government carried on its limited and one-sided détente with the Catholic Church. The policy of benefaction was reinforced by a number of demonstrations of the Church's far-ranging influence in the Allied and Axis camps, but, at the same time, it was circumscribed by the internal needs of the regime. The foreign events which perhaps corroborated the Kremlin's concession-orientated behavior included the following developments. In late January Japan requested and soon received full diplomatic ties with the Papacy.[57] Germany also continued to attempt to induce the Vatican to buttress publicly its anti-Bolshevik "crusade" and, as the publication, in 1942, of the Moscow Patriarchate's amazing book, *The Truth About Religion in Russia,* implied, the Kremlin realized that the Church was not fulfilling this German request.[58] The British and the Americans, for their part, also persisted in indicating to Moscow their desire to have Papal support for the Allied cause and, thus, obliquely their wish that the USSR would appease the Vatican. By the end of the summer of 1942, it might have been clear to the Soviets that their two principal allies had become disenchanted with the Papacy, primarily because of the Church's willingness to establish full diplomatic relations with the Japanese, but, at least through the first half of 1942, they could not but conclude that dispensations to the Church would score points with the western democracies. Moscow had to be impressed with such developments as the American hierarchy's declaration of support, in January, for Roosevelt's policies, including alliance with the USSR,[59] and Myron Taylor's two-week return visit, in September, to the Vatican.[60] In addition, the Kremlin was probably affected, in early 1942, by British representations in favor of Catholics in northern Persia, which since the Anglo-Russian accord on Persia in August, 1941, was under Soviet occupation.[61] The Free French mission, under Roger Garreau, also, when it arrived in Moscow in March, revealed to the Soviets a great concern about religious liberty in the USSR and about the Russian government's attitude toward the Catholic Church.[62] Besides all of these indications of Papal influence, Moscow must have also been aware that, in 1942, an array of nations, some intimately touching the interests of the USSR, either established or strengthened their ties with the Vatican. These included China, Turkey, Finland, Lithuania, Poland, and a bevy of Latin American countries.[63] Finally, the Soviet authorities were no doubt cognizant, given the priorities of the Soviet secret police, that a Russian émigré group, headed by a Mr. Wolkonsky, was in contact with the Papacy in 1942.[64]

As a result, Moscow persisted in not propagandizing, throughout 1942, against the Catholic Church. In fact, the Patriarchate's book, *The Truth About Religion In Russia,* found room to praise Catholicism's valiant fight against Nazism.[65] The government also continued to placate Leopold Braun.[66] The Kremlin's treatment of Catholics in northern Persia was also exemplary and a vivid contrast to its pre-mid 1941 attitude toward Catholics in Eastern Europe.[67] On April 19, furthermore, the Soviets made, for them, a magnanimous gesture to the Catholic Church by permitting Mgr. Joseph Gawlina, a Polish bishop, to cross into Russian territory and organize the work of the Polish Catholic chaplains working among the Polish armed forces. The action was tempered, however, by the fact that the Communists, with Gawlina's arrival, refused to permit the military chaplains to visit civilian centers and, shortly thereafter, with the removal of the Polish army to Iran, demured from allowing Polish priests, including Gawlina, to remain in the USSR to cater to civilian refugees.[68] Nonetheless the Vatican was quite thrilled about Gawlina's work and, in fact, named him Ordinary of Catholic Poles in Russia with full powers of a resident bishop.[69]

In the summer of 1942 the placating measures persisted. In July the Free French Mission, apparently at the behest of the Soviet government for

Garreau certainly would not have acted on his own, informed the Apostolic Delegate in Syria, Mgr. Lepretre, that the Soviet Union now permitted religious freedom and wanted *rapprochement* with the Catholic Church.[70] The Vatican responded, through Lepretre, that the Soviet government was still committed to the atheistic doctrine of Communism and had not completely made an about face from its pre-war anti-Catholicsm and, thus, no accord was possible.[71] The Church leaders also realized perhaps that there would be little benefit and much heartache, mainly in the Church's relations with the Axis powers, if the Vatican concluded a *modus vivendi* with the USSR. More than likely Moscow anticipated the Papacy's response but its offer to bury the hatchet, as the Soviets certainly calculated, demonstrated to the western allies its open attitude toward the Catholic Church. If the Vatican would have accepted, Moscow would have undoubtedly signed a concordat, but, for reasons which have been and will be touched on again, its concessions to the Catholic Church would not have appreciably increased.

One final event in Soviet-Vatican relations in 1942, although it cannot be classified as an essayed concession on Moscow's part, demonstrated, if, in fact, it can be held accountable for it, the Kremlin's willingness to exploit the Church for its own advantage. In March, a Romanian paper published a report that Stalin had sent a handwritten letter to the Pope informing Pius XII that the Soviet government had nothing but good intentions toward the Catholic Church and religion in general. The report was spurious, but it has been generally assumed by all, including the Vatican, that the Nazis were the authors of this rumor.[72] Although there is no evidence, of a definitive nature, to prove or disprove authorship, logic dictates that the Soviets, not the Nazis, planted the rumor. The Nazis had nothing to gain by demonstrating that there was a growing bond of friendship between the Vatican and the USSR. They were desperately attempting to obtain Vatican support for their policies and they were actually purporting that the Church backed their invasion.[73] The Germans knew they could not procure benefits from such a ploy for the similar rumors of late 1941, which redounded to the advantage of the Allies, including the Soviets, served as an object lesson. Conversely, of course, the same lesson would serve as a fillip for Moscow to perpetrate such rumors and, in fact, the Soviets did reap the fruits of the rumor. The Americans and English were quite literally overjoyed at the news of Stalin's letter for they were looking for just such a propaganda lever to rally Catholic public opinion, in their respective countries, behind the Russians.[74] The Catholic hierarchy in Eastern Europe, particularly the Uniates, were totally confused.[75] Did this report mean that the Church was redefining its attitude and relationship with the Soviet government? And that an accord was in the air? The Soviets, of course, directly benefited from the use to which the Allies put the rumor and from the consternation among the Uniate hierarchy for this group, like many religious who had lived under the persecutory hand of the Soviets, welcomed and backed, at least until it realized that the Nazis were no more tolerant than the Communists, the German invasion and occupation as a crusade to unshackle religion.[76] The rumor also held out the possibility of encouraging Nazi-controlled Poles and Lithuanians to join the anti-Nazi partisan movements. Finally, the Soviet government did not object, as did the Nazis, to the substance of the rumor.[77] Moscow made no attempt to impugn the veracity of the report printed in the Romanian paper.

In sum total, the Soviet government's 1942 efforts to propitiate the Church were controlled and restrained. The Vatican did not trust the Communists to begin with and their half-way measures did nothing to diminish that opinion. By and large, through 1942, the Papacy pursued the same policies vis-à-vis the USSR that it had followed in 1941. The Vatican continued to attempt to convince the Allies to use their influence with the Russians to obtain permission for the Church to administer Catholic prisoners of war in Soviet prisons.[78] The Church also wanted the Western Powers to ask the Soviets to release Bishop Profittlich who was deported from Estonia in June. [79] As before, the western states were reluctant to make such requests of the Soviets on the grounds that such intercessions represented interference in the Soviet Union's internal affairs. In 1942, the Papacy maintained, as in 1941, its low profile on peace proposals. Pius XII, for the entire year, made only one international plea for peace and that was on May 13, his episcopal jubilee.[80] The Vatican again, as in 1941, denied all reports that there was an accord or the possibility of an agreement between the Holy See and the Soviet Union.[81] Finally, the Vatican persisted in pursuing its two-sided policy of neutralizing the Soviet Union as a threat to Catholicism. On the positive side, the Church continued to try to penetrate the Nazi-held territory of the USSR with missionaries and, in September, gave Metropolitan Sheptyts'kyi permission to organize ecclesiastical life in Russia.[82] On the negative side, and this encompassed the main activity of the Church for 1942, the Papacy sought to keep the West, especially the United States, apprehensive about the dangers of Communism and Soviet expansion. The Papacy was firmly convinced that the western democracies were naive in their assessment of Soviet intentions and, thus, the Vatican felt an enormous obligation to jar the Allies out of their stupor. Naturally, the Church's ability to disquiet the West was directly dependent upon the Vatican's influence and leverage with the English and Americans. In fact, the *sine qua non* for the Church, in terms of achieving its over-all goal of keeping the West weary of Communism, was close and smooth relations with the British and American governments. As will be seen, the Church failed to accomplish this requisite and, thus, its ultimate objective.

In January, the Vatican, pursuing its policy of pressuring the Western States, requested and received assurances from the British that Anthony Eden had not promised any territory to Stalin during the former's December 1941 visit to Moscow.[83] These assurances, however, were counterbalanced by reports by Turkish Nuncio Roncalli that Stalin had informed Eden that the Soviets wanted and were planning to annex the Dardanelles and that to obtain the Straits the Soviets would go so far as to conclude a separate peace treaty with the Germans.[84] As preposterous as that report seems, the Vatican no doubt took it to heart for the Papacy harbored a suspicion of the Communists as great, if not greater than, the Communists' mistrust of the capitalists. The British assurances were further dissipated when, in late January and early February, Cardinal Godfrey reported to the Vatican that British public opinion was quickly turning pro-Soviet and, ominously, anti-Vatican.[85] And, then, on February 9, the British assurances were all but shattered when the British ambassador, d'Arcy Osborne, informed the Vatican that the British government did not anticipate that the USSR would try to "bolshevize" Europe but, rather, would respect the rights of all nations. Osborne explained that significant changes had occurred in the Soviet social and political system, particularly, in regard to religion, and that the Russians had "demonstrated no interest in encouraging Communism in Germany and *western* Europe."[86] The fact that Osborne did not mention *eastern* Europe must have gravely perturbed the Vatican and increased its fears that the British had, in fact, given up eastern Europe as Stalin's legitimate sphere of influence.

The Papacy's policy of pressuring the British against granting concessions to the Soviet Union was geared to produce confidence that the English had not, in fact, committed themselves to territorial adjustments favorable to the USSR. Instead of generating sanguine expectations, however, the British response to the Church's nettling yielded dismay and desperation. The Vatican pursued the same policy with the Americans, querying Harold Tittmann, who became American charge d'affaires in December 1941, about American policy toward the Baltic States. Although Tittmann, on February 5, assured the Papacy that the United States' position on the independence of the Baltic States had not been modified, the Church, on February 6, received word from the Lithuanian Legation at Vatican City that Soviet war aims included the incorporation of the Baltic States, Bessarabia, and Bukovina.[87] Albeit the Lithuanian chargé did not impinge Tittmann's promise; it still had to fill the ecclesiastical leaders with a sense of groping and uneasiness about the possibility of secret agreements existing between the powers ranged against the Axis.

All told, the Vatican's tactic of keeping the danger of Bolshevism before the eyes of the West was not paying handsome dividends. But, at least, the Vatican and its charges were taken seriously enough to merit an answer and verbal reassurance. In other words, the Papacy had the respect of the Western Powers and, all things considered, had good relations with the British and American governments. By the end of the first week in February, however, the Papacy announced a policy that undercut its influence with the West and, by and large, corroded its cordial relations with the Western States. On February 5, the Church informed both Tittmann and Osborne that it had agreed to establish full diplomatic relations with Japan.[88] The explanation provided by the Vatican to the Western representatives was that Japan and the Catholic Church had ties stretching back to 1919 and that it was afraid for the spiritual safety of Japanese Catholics if it did not accommodate the government of Herohito.[89] The British were amazed and officially objected to the Vatican's announced intentions on February 19 and again on February 23.[90] Without a doubt the Papacy's decision to establish ties with Japan increased the feeling in Britain that the Vatican was pro-Fascist and it also undoubtedly helped precipitate England's newly announced directive demanding that Italian clerics be removed from the Middle East and East Africa.[91] Although the British were amazed, the Americans were shocked and flabbergasted. Tittmann officially protested on March 2 and 5 and, again, on March 11, when the representation, finally sinking in, was laced with such words as "deplorable, incredible, unspeakable," etc.[92] The American press (and the British press) immediately became hostile to the Church.[93] The American hierarchy was thrown into disarray and confusion by the Papal action.[94] Finally, Roosevelt himself informed Pius on March 14 that he simply did not believe that the Pope had actually agreed to establish full ties with Japan.[95] Needless to say, the Vatican's action revealed an incredible obtuseness and ignorance of American psychology and the American *raison d'etre* for fighting the world war. The Papacy attempted to redress its blunder by extending diplomatic ties to China, but it was an insufficient gesture.[96] The Americans wanted, and held up as a test of the Vatican's neutrality, the Church to establish relations with the USSR. The American suggestion left the Papal officials aphonous but soon Cardinal Montini responded that "Roman Catholic interests in Japan and Japanese-occupied territories were more important than in Russia at the present time. Furthermore, the Church had been attacked in Russia, while in Japan it had been tolerated so far."[97] To emphasize the Church's abject fear and, at the same time, its refusal of the American *quid pro quo,* Cardinal Maglione told Tittmann, on March 2 and again on March 5, that the Vatican would receive the USSR "only if and when the Holy See were satisfied that Soviet doctrine and methods in religious matters had been revised."[98]

The Papacy's general behavior went far to compromise the Church in the eyes of the Americans and British and led to a waning of what influence the Vatican had with the Allied Governments. The ramifications of the Papacy's loss of leverage are hard to calculate, but certainly for Lithuania and Poland, which were relying upon Vatican influence with the Allies, they were tragic. Needless to say, it might have been beneficial for Roosevelt and Churchill, as they approached the Teheran Conference, to have an advisor sound the anti-Communist theme, even if the counsel was based upon a fear of atheism. And undoubtedly, the Vatican's fall from grace lessened the coaction on Moscow to grant amenities to the Catholic Church. Additionally, it is worth mentioning that the Papacy's loss of influence would compromise all Papal efforts to mediate a less-than-unconditional surrender for the Axis.

Before 1942 ran out, the Papacy's lowered stature with the Allies was clearly revealed. In July the English imprisoned 450 Italisn clerics in Egypt and Palestine on the grounds that they were pro-Fascist and, simultaneously, refused to admit into Britain Mgr. Alfredo Pacini, a newly named Papal envoy to the Polish Government-in-exile.[99] If they respected and wished to keep the favor of the Vatican, the English would have never taken such drastic actions. In September, Myron Taylor arrived at the Vatican for another two week visit and his style was indicative of a changed relationship. After presenting letters from President Roosevelt to the Pope which made it clear that the West was going to obliterate Nazism and refuse a conditional peace with Germany, Taylor outlined three arguments to persuade the Papacy to jettison its anti-Communism and come out in full support of the Soviet Union. First, he pointed out to the Vatican Hitler's criminal policies, especially his persecution of the Jews, and urged the Pope, on moral grounds, to condemn such abominations.[100] Cardinal Maglione responded to this maneuver by impressing upon Taylor the fact that the Pope was well aware of Hitler's atrocities and that His Holiness had, on numerous occasions, denounced all governments which mistreated peoples and individuals (which meant, among others, the Communists as well as the Nazis), but that the Pope could not descend to particulars for this course of action "would immediately draw His Holiness into the field of political disputes, requires documentary proof, etc." The Cardinal added, by way of a rebuke, that "people have short memories in matters of this kind and that many would have the Pope speak out daily in denunciation of these evils."[101] Church officials also reported that the Church was discreetly helping the

Jews and cited examples of its work in both France and Italy.[102]

Taylor's second approach was more direct. He simply tried to convince the Vatican that it should adopt a pro-Soviet posture because the USSR was needed in the battle against the Nazis, that the Soviet Union's close association with Christian states offered firm hope for postwar peace and stability, and that, at any rate, the Russians were, perforce, going to play a major role in Eastern Europe after the war.[103] Taylor argued that "it would seem logical, both from a moral as well as a practical standpoint, that the effort should be earnestly made to bring Russia more and more completely into a world family of nations, with identical aims and obligations." He asked: "Who shall say that, as an ally in a Cause so just, even the Russian Government itself may not yield to the influence of an association with Christian allies and the great moral force of their Cause and become a responsible and beneficient member of the family of peace-loving nations dedicated to the future prevention of war."[104] Taylor added, no doubt to disarm the Vatican, although the effect was certainly the opposite, that the Soviet Union was willing to take on the burden of guaranteeing the independence and autonomy of the countries of Central Europe and of preventing Germany from rearming and precipitating another war."[105] Finally, Taylor concluded, throwing in what he no doubt felt was the *coup de grace,* that the Soviet Union was no longer interested in Communism but Capitalism.[106] Taylor's second argument, of course, could do nothing but alarm the Vatican. It was clear-cut evidence that the United States was moving into blissful blindness vis-à-vis the Communist regime of Stalin and that the Americans had gone far down the path of conceding Eastern Europe (including Germany) to the USSR. Quite obviously Taylor's remarks presaged the Teheran concessions to Stalin and lucidly revealed that the Western Allies, who, in 1941, claimed they had not conceded anything to Moscow, were disposed to consider Poland, the Baltic States, part of the Balkans, and, possibly, Germany, within the Communist sphere of influence for only under such a development could the USSR "guarantee" Central Europe's "independence and autonomy." Both Cardinals Tardini and Maglione remonstrated with Taylor and rather brutally pointed out that they felt the United States was minimizing the Communist danger and Tardini forecasted that the United States' stand would lead to Communist domination of Eastern Europe.[107]

Taylor's final contention was purely that the USSR was no longer attacking religion and, thus, there was no reason why a *modus vivendi* could not be worked out between the Church and the Kremlin. Taylor also produced the letter of Braun, from September 1941, which attested that conditions had so improved in the USSR that an accord between the Soviet government and the Vatican was possible.[108] Cardinal Tardini countered Taylor by emphasizing that Stalin's tolerant attitude toward religion "may be explained easily in the light of the circumstances of the present state of war, without supposing a change in the general program of Communism with regard to religion."[109] He also ridiculed Braun's claim by stating that "it is always damaging when missionaries involve themselves in political questions!"[110]

Roosevelt's determination to smash Nazi Germany and Taylor's general arguments, with all of their terrible implications, were extremely unsettling for the Church leaders for they felt the Americans, and the British for that matter, were closing their eyes to reality.[111] But just as agitating, if not more so, to the Papacy was the fact that Myron Taylor did not even both, as he had in 1941, to allay the Church's diffidence over Communism. The Papacy, like in 1941, subjected Taylor to a barrage of anti-Communist sentiment and evidence that the Soviets were still hamstringing religion, but Taylor did not even make an attempt to rebut the Cardinals or quell their apprehensions.[112] It appeared as if he could care less about the Church's positions or attitudes on Soviet Russia and it was obvious that his style was indicative of a changed opinion in Washington on how to deal with the Catholic Church. In 1941, the Americans made deliberate efforts to accommodate the Vatican, to answer its objections, etc. By September, 1942, there was only an attempt to force the American point of view on the Papacy without even giving so much as cursory consideration to the Vatican's convictions about the danger of Communism. The Vatican, with Taylor's visit added to the earlier British actions, had to be aware, by the end of 1942, that its counsels and fears were no longer being seriously contemplated by the Western Allies. The Church was not even able to obtain a binding agreement from the Allies to forego bombing Rome. (Rome was only bombed twice by the Allies, in July and August of 1943. The Vatican was bombed once in November, 1943, by an unidentified plane). In these circumstances it was obvious that substantive concessions and, for that matter, serious auditions were no longer possible.[113] The Vatican would continue to voice its fear of Communism, either directly or indirectly through the American hierarchy, but its premonitions were disregarded for the remainder of the war. At the same time, with it fairly clear by December, 1942, that the Axis were going to be defeated, the Church wanted to take a more public anti-Nazi stand. The Pope's dilemma was well portrayed in his Christmas address in 1942. On the one hand, he attacked ideologies which put the State above the family and persecute people because of race or nationality (an obvious reference to Nazism). On the other hand, he decried all totalitarian systems and pointedly declared that the working class was worse off under Statist regimes than Capitalist governments (a clear reference to Communist Russia). For his effort the Pope was roundly criticized by the Western Allies for not condemning Nazi Germany more stringently. And the British ridiculed the "bogey of the Bolshevik peril" as Nazi propaganda.[114]

Admittedly the Vatican was extreme in its anti-Communism and its polarization cost the Church sway with the West. The Church, however, did not think it was unreasonable in refusing to warm up to Moscow. It continued to hold that the Soviet government was antireligious and that only wartime conditions coerced it to give up its atheistic measures. However, although this was the Church's official position, it was amenable to actions which proved the contrary. Cardinal Tardini suggested to Myron Taylor, during his 1942 visit, a number of specific actions which the Soviet government might implement, including opening up closed Catholic churches and releasing the Catholic clerics who were still in Soviet prisons.[115] Archbishop Gawlina, in a letter to Cardinal Stritch of Chicago, added a few more desirable developments, including the release of confiscated religious objects and freedom of movement in the USSR for the Polish military chaplains.[116] The Church also wanted a public statement by the Soviet Government guaranteeing religious freedom. Archbishop Mooney, who was chairman of the administrative board of the National Catholic Welfare Conference as well as bishop of Detroit, drafted, in 1941, the following proposition which the Vatican wanted the Soviet government to publicize as official policy:

> In view of the loyal participation of all our people in the defense of the Fatherland under the direction of constituted authority in the State, the Soviet Government, interpreting and applying Article 124 of the U.S.S.R. Constitution, publicly proclaims complete religious freedom, including freedom of worship and freedom of religious teaching, in all the territories of the Soviet Union.[117]

The Church's demands, however, from the Kremlin's point of view, were unrealistic. Moscow was strengthening its alliance with Orthodoxy and steadily reviving the nationalist-historic leimotifs of the Russian Orthodox Church. In 1942 the publication of *The Truth About Religion In Russia* by the Orthodox Patriarchate confirmed the growing bond between Stalin's government and the Orthodox Church. Also in 1942, Moscow, becoming quite perturbed about the growth of religion in the territories occupied by the Germans, used the Church to attempt to cause a schism and to encourage anti-German guerrilla activities among Nazi-controlled believers.[118] In 1943 the government centralized, at the federal level, its control over the Church by placing it under the Council for the Affairs of the Russian Orthodox Church, headed by G. G. Karpov.[119] (A year later, a similar council was created for non-Orthodox religions under I. Polyansky). Also in 1943, with the naming of an Orthodox Patriarch and the publication, once again, of the *Zhurnal Moskovskoi Patriarkhii,* Orthodoxy became a full-fledged partner in the alliance against the western invaders. What this cooperation meant, in religious terms, was that antagonism for Catholicism, especially the Uniates, dramatically increased in Russia. The government was not about to dampen the Orthodox link, particularly when the German pressure was at its zenith and, concomitantly, a tremendous revival of religion was taking place in the German-occupied regions of the USSR. And, of course, the Vatican's policies of "union," as its sending of priests into Axis-controlled parts of the Soviet Union and Metropolitan Sheptyts'kyi's efforts in 1941-1942 could be interpreted, simply reinforced traditionally inspired anti-Catholicism.[120] Secondly, a continued, if diluted, anti-Catholic position provided some evidence for the die-hard atheistic supporters that Marxism's antireligious principles were still being upheld. Thirdly, the Catholic Church did not seem, from Moscow's point of view, to respond positively to the already proffered concessions, so there was no incentive for the Kremlin to concede more. Fourthly, relations between the Allies and the Vaticans were, by the end of the year, strained and, thus, the Soviets were not as pressed, as they had been in 1941-1942, to cater to the Vatican for the sake of appeasing the Anglo-Americans. Fifthly, a full-blown détente with the Catholic Church offered no substantive, internal proceeds since the Catholid Church was inconsequential in Russia. Sixthly, the demands of the Vatican for religious freedom and for the unfettered movement of foreign priests violated the authoritarian and xenophobic instincts of the Stalinist government. Finally, any public announcement about a new governmental policy of religious freedom would have been tacit acknowledgement that such freedom had not existed previously.

1943 was the decisive year in World War Two. It was obvious, during the course of that year, that the Allied forces were going to be victorious and that the Axis faced ignoble defeat and destruction. The year witnessed the removal of Mussolini, the Allied invasion of Italy, and, most momentous, the defeat of the Germans in the east at Stalingrad and Kursk. The Russian victory, in fact, was the turning point in the war and, by late summer, the Soviet Army, in a series of coordinated and massive drives, pushed into the west. On August 26, 1943, Kharkov was captured; on September 14, Smolensk, gateway to Moscow, was taken; Kiev was occupied by the Soviets on November 6; the twenty-nine months' siege of Leningrad was broken on January 26, 1944; Odessa was freed from the Axis on April 11. In mid-January, 1944, the Russians crossed the pre-1939 Polish border and, in March, bridged the Dniester into Bessarabia and Bukovina. By the end of July, 1944, the Red Army had swept to the Vistula River and through the Baltic States, capturing in the process most of the territory it held at the beginning of the Nazi invasion. In August the Russians opened an offensive in the Balkans, quickly overran Romania, Bulgaria, and Trans-Carpathia (in October), and joined forces with Tito in Yugoslavia. By November, Budapest was being besieged. In January, 1945, the Russians pushed out from the Vistula line. Since June, 1944, of course, the Western Allies had been driving toward Germany from beachheads along the Atlantic. In April, with Germany on its last leg, the Russians took most of Czechoslovakia and pushed to the Oder River while the West reached the Elbe River. In May, the war in Europe ended, leaving the Soviet army in sole occupation of the Baltic States, Poland, Hungary, Czechoslovakia, east Germany (including East Prussia), Romania, and Bulgaria.

Once the Soviet army pushed westward, the relationship between the Catholic Church and the Kremlin changed drastically. The Uniate Church, with its enthusiasm for Ukrainian separtism and its traditional controversy with Russian Orthodoxy, had a foreboding future and rightly feared, as Metropolitan Sheptyts'kyi wrote on May 8, 1943, to Cardinal Tisserant, the reimposition of the Bolshevik yoke.[121] The Baltic Church, the backbone of Lithuanian nationalism, also confronted a dismal tomorrow and correctly dreaded, as Bishop Vincent Brizgys and Lithuanian lay leaders communicated, on March 12, 1943, to Pius XII, persecution and re-incorporation into the Soviet Union.[122] For the Vatican, of course, the prospect of Soviet domination of Catholic East Europe now had to be faced and the Church could not but feel anguish. For the Soviet government, the Catholic Church, with its numerical predominance in Eastern Europe and its Latin and Uniate rites, was now a major problem which had to be reconciled with the interests, internal and foreign, of the Soviet Union. The multiple nationalities and the dual rites of the Catholic Church elicited, from the Soviet government, by 1944, three distinct policies. The first two fall under the category of what Cardinal Tardini called the "Extended Hand"[123]: 1) toleration of Latin Catholics in those regions of Eastern Europe which had not been or would not be directly annexed into the USSR 2) initial toleration but eventual persecution, but not institutional annihilation, of Latin Catholics in territories assimilated by the Soviet Union at the end of the war (West Ukraine, West White Russia, Baltic States). The final policy might best fall under the genre of "Extended Sword": persecution and institutional absorption of the Uniate Church throughout Soviet-controlled or annexed East Europe:

West Ukraine, West White Russia, Romania, Carpatho-Ukraine, Czechoslovakia, and Poland.

CHAPTER VI
THE UNIATE CHURCH: 1944-1949

By 1944-45 with the Red Army in control of most of the regions of Eastern Europe where the Uniate Church was a force, the Soviet government initiated, in 1944, a campaign to harness the Uniates. The Soviet policy toward the Uniates was in marked contrast to its relative tolerance of Latin Catholics in those parts of Eastern Europe not annexed into the Soviet Union. The difference, quite obviously, was both strategic and political. Strategically, Moscow was simply following a *divide et impera* tendency— there was no need to arouse *all* Catholics at one time. The Kremlin also probably hoped that its quiescent approach would neutralize the Vatican to the point where it would, at least, adopt a wait-and-see position regarding Soviet control of Latin-dominated Eastern Europe. Politically, the Uniates represented much more of a threat to "sovietization" and political cohesion and, thus, had to be corraled as soon as possible.

The Uniate Churches under Soviet control included the Ukrainian Greek Catholic Church, the West Belorussian Uniate Church (30,000 believers), the Romanian Uniate Church (4 dioceses with 1.4 million adherents), and the Hungarian Uniate Church (1 diocese with about 142,000 faithful). The Ukrainian Greek Catholic Church, by far the largest, was centered in Galicia and the Carpatho-Ukraine (both annexed into the Ukrainian S.S.R. by 1945) with significant congregations in Poland and the Presov diocese in northeastern Slovakia. In the West Ukraine, the Ukrainian Uniate Church at the time of its forced demise embraced four dioceses with a metropolitan-archbishop, seven bishops, some 2,400 priests, over 1,000 nuns and 600 monks, and close to four million believers. In the Mukachiv diocese in the Carpartho-Ukraine, there were, before the war, one bishop, 354 priests, 35 monks and 50 nuns in 3 convents and 5 monasteries, 459 churches in 281 parishes, and 461,555 faithful.[1] This chapter will devote itself to a study of the fate of the major Uniate congregations in the Soviet Union; later chapters will take up the history of the other various Uniate Churches throughout East Europe.

A number of factors can be suggested for the Soviet thrust against the

Ukrainian Uniate Church. There were, of course, the constants of Soviet anti-Catholicism including Marxism-Leninism, suspicion of the Church's foreign domination and influence, abhorence and frustration over Catholicism's relative imperviousness to "sovietization," the atavistic rivalry with Orthodoxy, the irreconciliability of word views, and, finally, the identity of the Church, dating from the first years of Communist rule, with the regime's foreign and domestic enemies. To these perennials the war years seemingly added a new source for invective: the Soviets identified, either because the Vatican did not line up behind the USSR or because of the Church's neutrality, the Catholic Church with the Axis forces.[2] It is difficult to determine with certainty if the Kremlin made these charges out of conviction or for propagandistic advantages, but, given the Soviet penchant of treating those who were not supporting the USSR as opponents, the former would seem to be the case. In regard to the Ukrainiane Uniate Church, the Soviets had another, exclusive motive for animosity. The Uniate Church proved itself during the Nazi sojourn in the USSR to be a pillar of Ukrainian separtism and its clergy to be both religious and political leaders. In the 19th century the tsars ended the institutional existence of the Uniate Church in the Russian Empire because the Uniates, at that time, represented the avant-garde of Orthodoxy's chief rival, the Catholic Church, were a symbol of earlier Polish and western advances in the east, and, finally, but most importantly, blocked or interfered with the "russification" of the Ukrainian and Belorussian people.[3] In the 1940s the remaining Ukrainian Uniate strongholds (Galicia and Carpatho-Ukraine were under Austrian jurisdiction in the 19th century and, thus, avoided the fate of the Uniates in the Russian Empire) emerged, shorn of Polish influences, as a new reservoir of Ukrainian nationalism and, accordingly, loomed in the eyes of the Soviet government not only as a counterforce to the "sovietization" of the western Ukraine but of the total Ukraine. The Soviet government, having lost control of the Ukraine for three years, was desperately preoccupied with re-integrating its people and rooting out all seeds of nationalism and anti-Sovietism. The Ukrainian Uniate Church, like the Ukrainian Autocephalous Orthodox Church, was thus marked for formal extinction.

The return of the Soviet authorities to the West Ukraine in 1944 caught the Ukrainian Uniate Church in a much more pregnable position than during the first Soviet occupation. Almost 300 Uniate priests as well as an untold number of Ukrainian intellectuals fled before the Soviet offensive, leaving the Uniate Church's lay and clerical leadership seriously damaged.[4] On November 1, 1944, the respected leader of the Uniate Church, Metropolitan Andrei Sheptyts'kyi, died, cutting the Church adrift at a time of unparalleled danger.[5] No longer did the Soviets share an uneasy border running through the West Ukraine with the Germans. The Church also was susceptible because of its support of the Ukrainian nationalist movement to accusations of collaborating with the enemies of the Soviet Union.[6] Furthermore, the Uniate Church had to confront a revitalized Russian Orthodox Church which had the backing of the Soviet government. This was evidenced not only by the 1943 "concordant" between the government and Orthodoxy, but by the fact that in 1945, by the Decree of the *Sovnarkom,* the Russian Orthodox Church (and other pro-Soviet churches) were assigned the rights of a juridical person, including the right to own property (excluding ecclesiastical and monastic buildings) and to manufacture liturgical goods. This development represented a major modification of the 1929 Law on Religion Associations (and implicitly the 1918 Decree) and a high point of Stalin's "religious N.E.P."[7]

The method, in fact, by which the Ukrainian Uniate Church was to be liquidated was "reunion" with the Russian Orthodox Church, a policy borrowed directly from the tsars. The Communists elected this method of handling the Uniate problem, rather than such precedents as hatching a "schism," purging the recalcitrant leaders, or whittling the Church into docility by *Yezhovshchina* techniques, because of a number of pressing advantages. The political boons were such, moreover, that they evidently outbalanced the contradiction of an officially atheistic state working hand-in-glove with a "state" church. The self-immolation tactic or, more drastically, the naked suppression of the Uniate Church would have unquestionably precipitated a strong local and foreign polarity, precisely at a moment when the Soviet government's "democratic" facade was, in the wake of the Warsaw Uprising, under re-examination. Brute force, in addition, might unduly alienate the Vatican, the East European Latin Catholics soon to be under Soviet occupation, and, possibly, disturb other religious groups, including the Orthodox, in the Soviet Union. The simple annihilation of a church structure, moreover, did not eliminate religious practices or beliefs but, if anything, created a catacombs which complicated control and surveillance. A staged "reunion" with Orthodoxy, conversely, gave the regime a tool to parade, more convincingly, the "conversion" as voluntary, to control, with greater success, extra-legal ecclesiastical activities, and to manipulate, possibly, issues dividing the Unite clergy. In addition, Russian nationalism, which had centuries earlier sanctioned the alter and throne alliance as a weapon of defense and expansion, undoubtedly suggested to the Soviet leadership the utility of the Russian Orthodox Church in liquidating a wellspring of Ukrainian nationalism.[8]

The attack upon the Uniate Church by the Soviet government was prefaced by a series of preparatory anti-Catholic declarations and actions. Following the Battle of Stalingrad, the first concrete indication that the Uniate Church would be persecuted emanated from the Uniate Archbishop of Lviv, Metropolitan Andrei Sheptyts'kyi.[9] On May 8, 1943, after the tide of battle had turned in favor of the Soviets, he wrote the Vatican that he feared "we will fall under the yoke of the Bolsheviks."[10]

The metropolitan's anxiety was corroborated by an anti-Catholic, verbal onslaught that began in early 1944. Both the Soviet government and the recently revived Orthodox Patriarchate criticized the Catholic Church on levels ranging from politics to religious doctrine.[11] At the turn of the year the new Russian Patriarch revealed the direction of the anti-Catholic campaign by inviting the Uniate Church to voluntarily rejoin the Russian Orthodox Church.[12] This announcement was made at the local *Sobor* in late January, 1945, which evidently made the preparations for the "legal" destruction of the Uniate Church.[13]

Bishop Josyf Slipyi, who succeeded Metropolitan Sheptyts'kyi, essayed a tactful policy in dealing with the ominous situation. In the hope of stabilizing relations with the Soviet government and the Moscow Patriarchate, Metropolitan Slipyi, in early 1945, sent a special delegation, including Father Havryil Kostel'nyk, to Moscow to apparently donate 100,000 rubles for the Soviet Red Cross and to pay tribute to the new Patriarch of Moscow, Alexei, on the occasion of his coronation in January, 1945.[14] His tact, if indeed the commission's purpose was to improve relations with the Soviets, went unrewarded, since the Soviets demanded, as the price for a *modus vivendi,* that the Church give a helping hand in the suppression of the Ukrainian anti-Soviet partisan movement.[15] The metropolitan nebulously complied by exhorting the Ukrainians to obey and respect their lawful superiors.[16] The Russian authorities, in turn, reacted by increasing their anti-Catholic attack. Soon all normal lines of communication between the Uniate hierarchy and the diocesan clergy were impaired and the priests were obligated to attend anti-Uniate propaganda meetings.[17]

On April 6, 1945, an article by Iaroslav Halan in *Vil'na Ukraina,* attacking the patriotism of the Greek Catholic clergy, presaged open persecution.[18] It was soon followed by a barrage of slanders and accusations, imputing to the Greek Catholic Church everything from espionage to "parasiting on the wounds of mankind."[19] On April 11, 1945, the hierarchy of the Uniate Church in the Soviet Union was arrested and this included Metropolitan Slipyi, Mgr. Nykyta Budka, his auxiliary bishop, Mgr. Mykola Charnets-'kyi, Apostolic Visitor for Volyn, Mgr. Hryhorii Khomyshyn, Bishop of Stanislav, and Mgr. Ivan Liatyshevs'kyi, his auxiliary.[20] Bishop Josaphat Kotsylov'kyi of Peremyshl, and his auxiliary, Bishop Hryhorii Lakota were extradicted by the Poles to the Soviet authorities in June, 1946. The hierarchy's arrest was evidently soon followed by the arrest of the leading members of the monastic and secular clergy.[21] With the hierarchy and the leading priests removed, the Church was ill prepared to contest the Russian plan of incorporation that was soon to unfold. At the end of April, 1945, Patriarch Alexei again requested the Uniates to dissolve their ties with Rome and unite with the Russian Orthodox Church.[22] At the same time, the Soviet authorities prevented the vacant sees from being filled or administered and demanded that all churches in the Western Ukraine comply with the 1929 Soviet church law.[23]

After nearly a year in prison, the Uniate bishops were sentenced for their "criminal complicity" with the "German Fascist occupier," especially the Gestapo and the German intelligence service, and for sending Ukrainians to forced labor in Germany.[24] Mgr. Hryhorii Khomyshyn was sentenced to ten years of forced labor but died in prison in January, 1947. Mgr. Josyf Slipyi, Mgr. Nykyta Budka, and Mgr. Ivan Liatyshevs'kyi were interned for eight years of forced labor and Mgr. Mykola Charnets'kyi for five years.[25] Metropolitan Slipyi, on the expiration of his sentence, was re-sentenced to another five years and, then, in 1959, to an additional seven years. In 1963, John XXIII arranged for his release and Bishop Slipyi has since resided at the Vatican.[26]

Together with the internment of the Uniate hierarchy in early 1945, an "Action Group for the Reunion of the Greek-Catholic Church of Galicia with the Russian Orthodox Church" suddenly materialized. It was headed by Father Havryil Kostel'nyk who, for various reasons, including constant threats to his family by the Soviets and a deep and growing personal aversion for the chauvinism of the Polish Catholic clergy, was apparently working, with enthusiasm, for the assimilation of the Uniate Church by the Russian Orthodox Church.[27] Two other Uniate priests, Antonii Pel'vets'kyi of the diocese of Stanislav and Mykhail Mel'nyk of the diocese of Peremyshl, patently assisted Kostel'nyk.[28] The Moscow Patriarchate also directly intervened by naming a Kievan priest, Makarii Oksiiuk, the new Orthodox bishop for the Western Ukraine. His function was to help the "Action Group" in the program of reunification.[29]

Kostel'nyk, Pel'vets'kyi, and Mel'nyk, at first, occupied themselves with anti-Vatican propaganda.[30] On May 28, however, they invited the entire Uniate clergy to take part in the movement for reunion with Orthodoxy.[31] A contingent of Uniate priests immediately protested to the Soviet government the actions of Kostel'nyk's group and simultaneously asked that the arrested episcopate be freed.[32]

The protestations of the Uniate clergy were answered on June 28 by the

recognition of the Soviet government of Kostel'nyk's group as the administrative organ of the Uniate Church.[33] It was authorized to prepare the
Uniate Church for reunion with the Orthodox Church and to report any
recalcitrant clergy who refused to cooperate.[34] By 1946 there were some 800
"recalcitrant" clergy in prison.[35] The stage was now prepared for the direct
incorporation of the Ukrainian Uniate Church into the Russian Orthodox
Church.

The method chosen for the annihilation of the Uniate Church was the
same as that which Nicholas I used to extinguish Uniatism in the Russian
Empire in 1939: a Church council or *Sobor*. In preparation for this event,
Kostel'nyk, Pel'vets'kyi, Mel'nyk, and a small group of their supporters
went to Kiev in February, 1946, to visit the Orthodox Exarch of the
Ukraine, Metropolitan Ioann.[36] At this meeting, Pel'vets'kyi and Mel'nyk
were "secretly" ordained as Orthodox bishops and Kostel'nyk and a few
others were received into the Orthodox Church. In celebration Kostel'nyk
declared: "The yoke imposed on the Galician people by the Roman Popes is
now being removed."[37] The apparent reason for the ordination of Pel'vets-
'kyi and Mel'nyk to the episcopacy was to validate the convocation of a
Uniate Church council. Only a bishop could call a council into session and
since the entire Uniate hierarchy refused to cooperate, the Soviets skirted
the issue by ordaining two of the Uniate renegade clerics. However, as
Bohdan Bociurkiw has pointed out, the Soviets' maneuvering rendered the
Sobor illegal and uncanonical: "Paradoxically, the *Sobor* of the Greek
Catholic Church was to be convoked and directed by clerics who had
already ceased to belong to that Church."[38]

Nonetheless, on March 8-10, 1946, Kostel'nyk summoned a *Sobor* at Lviv.
Circumventing procedural rules, the "Action Group" named itself the
leader of the council and also outlined the program. Kostel'nyk, the head of
the Action Group, quickly took charge and announced that the *Sobor* had
been called to deal with the question of reunion with the Russian Orthodox
Church. The 216 clerics and 19 lay "delegates" in attendance, all of whom
had been pre-selected for participation in the *Sobor* by the Action Group,
voiced no objection, although one cleric moved that the question of reunion
be postponed.[39] This one dissenting voice was rapidly suppressed and
Kostel'nyk moved the proceedings forward with a trenchant attack upon
the Vatican. He declared that the Uniates had "wrongly retained bad seeds
of faith received from the Roman Popes who worked always with violence,
cunning, deceit, trampling on the sacred truth in the name of their love of
power and their satanic pride."[40] Kostel'nyk then proposed a break with
Rome and a reunion with the Russian Orthodox Church.[41] His proposal read
in part that

... the Church Union was imposed upon our people in the sixteenth century by the aggressive Roman Catholic Poland as a bridge towards Polonization and Latinizaion. Under present circumstances, when, thanks to the heroic feats and the glorious victory of the Soviet Union, all the Ukrainian lands were gathered together, and the Ukrainian people became the master of its entire territory, it would be unreasonable to support further Uniate tendencies and it would be an unforgivable sin to continue the hatred and fratricidal war within our people, of which the Union was the cause in history and must always remain so.[42]

The *Sobor* accepted Kostel'nyk's proposal and resolved "to annul the Union with Rome, to break off the ties with the Vatican, and to return to the Orthodox faith and to the Russian Orthodox Church."[43] The *Sobor* further added that

The Vatican was completely on the side of bloody Fascism and came out against the Soviet Union, which saved our Ukrainian people from slavery and destruction and united all our lands . . . thus liberating us from national and religious oppression.[44]

At this stage in the proceedings, the two newly ordained bishops were introduced apparently "to resolve the problem of the canonical validity of this gathering and to allay fears that henceforth the clergy would be ruled by the ethnically alien hierarchs."[45]

The remainder of the *Sobor* was dedicated to the circumstantial details of "reunion" and to politics. The *Sobor* shortly sent a message to Patriarch Alexei asking him "to receive us into the bosom of the All-Russian Orthodox Catholic Church,"[46] and also a notice to the Ukrainian Supreme Soviet "that it may note and recognize this historical change and take under [its] protection our, henceforth Orthodox again, Church."[47] Kostel'nyk, Mel'nyk, and Pel'vets'kyi also sent a telegram to Stalin expressing "the most profound gratitude for your great deed—the gathering into one of the Ukrainian lands without which it would have been impossible even to dream of liquidating our religious separation."[48] Another letter was sent to "the clergy and faithful of the Greek Catholic Church" to advise them of the reunion and also to warn "recalcitrants" to adhere to the new reality.[49]

In April, 1946, Kostel'nyk, in an interview with *Tass*, declared to the world that the reunion was accomplished without duress.[50] On September 20, 1948, this man, whom the *Journal of the Moscow Patriarchate* eulogized as one who "skillfully refuted the lying proofs of the Latin hyprocrites," was murdered in Lviv. The Soviet authorities blamed the assassination on an "agent of the Vatican", while Ukrainian Catholics in Rome stated it to be the work of Ukrainian partisans who apparently did not believe that the reunion had been completed without coercion.[51]

In Transcarpathia, the Union preserved a little longer than in Galicia but not much longer. The same Lviv *Sobor* of 1946 which proclaimed the "reunion" of the Ukrainian Uniate Church in the Western Ukraine was declared, by the Soviet authorities, to extend to all Soviet lands. Even though the clergy of the Makachiv-Uzhhorod diocese in the Carpatho-Ukraine were unrepresented at the Lviv *Sobor,* they were suppose to conform to its decisions. However, until early 1949, the Patrarchate and the Kremlin, despite the existence of a large Orthodox minority in the Carpatho-Ukraine, were able to produce only one "joiner" among the Uniate clergy, Reverend Irenei Kondratovych of Uzhhorod. Accordingly, he was nominated as the official "spokesman" and given the honor of proclaiming the "Act of Reunion" on August 28, 1949. Bishop Theodore Romzha of Muchachiv-Uzhhorod successfully blocked Soviet efforts to force him to convert to the Orthodox Church until his still unresolved and mysterious death on November 1, 1947.[52] Bishop Aleksander Khira, Romzha's successor, was arrested by the NKGB and sentenced to forced labor for ten years. It was only in February, 1949, when Orthodox Bishop Makarii from the Ukraine arrived in the Carpatho-Ukraine that an organized campaign to liquidate the Uniate Church got under way.[53] Mass arrests and deportations followed his demands that the clergy submit to the "reunion". No figures on how many eventually did "reunite" with the Orthodox Church have been announced. By the end of 1949 not a single Uniate Church in the Carpatho-Ukraine (and Galcia for that matter) remained; all had been absorbed by the Russian Orthodox Church.[54]

The Uniate congregation in Belorussia, some 30,000 strong at the time of the German occupation, was also subject to the decree of the Lviv *Sobor.* The Uniate Church there, however, was already quite weak because of German persecution[55] and, thus, easily assimilated into the Russian Orthodox Church.[56]

In addition to the direct assault upon the Uniates, Moscow also, because of the necessity of attacking the leader of the Uniate Church, the Papacy, launched a vicious propaganda barrage against the Vatican beginning in 1944. This tactic, obviously, when one considers that the Kremlin was simultaneously attempting to neutralize the Vatican, was self-defeating, yet the Soviets apparently thought they could sooth the Papacy by concomitantly taking a benevolent attitude toward the Latin Catholics in Eastern Europe. At any rate, the soul and substance of the Communist verbal onslaught was an attempt to discredit the Vatican on the grounds that it supported fascism dusring WWII. *Izvestiia, Pravda,* and Radio Moscow carried the burden of the anti-Vatican campaign, but the *Zhurnal Moskovskoi Patriarkhii* joined in, increasingly, to slam the Papacy on both the political and doctrinal levels.[57] At the Local *Sobor* which elected Alexei the new Patriarch of Orthodoxy and which also apparently outlined the plans to destroy the Uniate Church,[58] the Orthodox leaders charged that the Vatican was seeking "to shield Hitlerite Germany from responsibility for all the crimes committed by it" and was aiming to perpetuate the anti-Christian Fascist doctrines after the war.[59] M. M. Sheinman, the expert on Vatican affairs, and Iaroslav Halan as well as other antireligious writers came out with a series of publications criticizing the Vatican.[60] Their works ranged over the entire postwar period and asserted that the Papacy was everything from a murderer of Orthodox Christians to the "citadel of world obscurantism."[61]

The Vatican's response to the anti-Uniate campaign and the anti-Vatican propaganda assault was multifarious. It, of course, from the inception of the anti-Vatican attacks, denied the various charges and allegations of the Soviet press.[62] As a matter of fact, the Papacy responded to the Soviet propaganda by launching a series of diatribes against the Soviet government. Its attacks ranged from criticism of the Soviet Union's lack of freedom to a pointed reminder that although "the signatures of Von Ribbentrop and Molotov" both appear "on the pact of Russian-German friendship . . . Von Ribbentrop is accused at Nuremburg and Molotov is shining in the sun in Moscow."[63]

In addition to refuting Soviet propaganda, the Vatican also increased its efforts to turn the Western Allies, especially the United States, against the Soviet Union and, at least, to be on guard against Soviet machinations.[64] Pius XII impressed upon both Churchill and Myron Taylor that Stalin could not be trusted and that Communism was a dire threat to western civilization.[65] In 1944 the Papacy pleaded for a negotiated peace with Germany.[66] It still was convinced, despite the growing public information on the Nazi crimes against humanity, that Germany was preferable to the Soviet Union and that Germany was really the only feasible barrier against the spread of Communism and of the USSR's borders.[67] The Papacy thought it ridiculous to destroy any bastion, however corrupt, which could help hold off the atheistic menace.[68] Pius XII made it quite clear that he did not believe that the German people should be punished for the mistakes of their leaders.[69] Once it became obvious that a negotiated peace was unacceptable to the Allies, Pius XII and other Catholic leaders requested, with increasing anxiety, that American and English troops remain in occupation in Italy and throughout Europe to avert the diffusion of Communism.[70] The Pope, particularly, wished to have safeguards against Soviet encroachments in Poland, the Baltic States, and the rest of Eastern Europe.[71]

The Vatican's principal reaction to the mounting suppression of the Uniate Church came in early 1946 when the Holy See issued the encyclical *Orientales Omnes Ecclesias*. Basically the Papal decree was a condemnation of Moscow's revival of Orthodox animosity toward Catholicism and of the ongoing incorporation of the Uniate Church into the Russian Orthodox Church.[72]

CHAPTER VII
"EXTENDED HAND": POLAND, HUNGARY, CZECHOSLOVAKIA, 1944-1948

In 1944, while Moscow was stalking the Latin Catholics in the USSR and laying the foundation for the forced assimilation of the Ukrainian Uniate Catholic Church into the Russian Orthodox Church, it contemporaneously was inchoating a scheme to conciliate or, at least, neutralize the Latin Catholic Church in those countries of Eastern Europe where the Catholic Church was the predominant religion and which were not destined for incorporation into the Soviet Union: Poland, Hungary, and Czechoslovakia. The plan, stretching to 1948, also was geared evidentally to include overtures of friendship to the Vatican. However, the entire policy was obfuscated and negated by the superficiality of the Kremlin's gestures to the Vatican, by the brutal and heavy-handed suppression of the Uniates, by the Soviets' attack upon Latin Catholics in the USSR, especially in Lithuania, and, finally, the shrill anti-Vatican propaganda which accompanied not only the public and disingenuous onset against the Uniates and the Latin Catholics in the USSR but also Moscow's eventual although more subtle, campaign to control those Latin Catholics in the non-annexed satellites.

A number of motives can be postulated to explain the Soviets' "Extended Hand" policy. In 1944-45, the Catholic Church was the strongest institution in Poland, Hungary, and, possibly, Czechoslovakia. The hierarchy and clergy in these countries were, by and large, intact. Many of the Church's leaders, with a few notable exceptions, were identified with the anti-Nazi struggle and revered as war heroes. The church, furthermore, was firmly grounded and, in the case of Poland, equated with nationalism. Obviously it would be imprudent of the Communists to unduely arouse such a powerful opponent without first consolidating their own position. The position of the Catholic Church in Poland and Hungary (and to a point, in Czechoslovakia) was vastly different than that of Orthodoxy at the time of the Communist take-over in Russia. The Catholic Church could not be easily compromised in the eyes of the people for supporting an exploitative *ancien regime* or an enemy. The process of controlling, if not annihilating, the Catholic Church would thus of necessity be slow, evolving, and, to a point, proportional to the government's consolidation of political power.

In addition, the Communists, operating on the theory that one catches more bees with honey than vinegar, certainly entertained the hope that toleration would induce the Church to cooperate with the government's policies in and out of the Bloc. The Catholic Church's position in Poland and Hungary was similar to that of Orthodoxy in Russia. As such, it could, if it so chose, buttress social cohesion, endow the Communist governments with moral legitimacy, strengthen the Communists' hold on power, rob the governments-in-exile (especially the Polish government in London) of moral support, and, finally, uphold foreign policy goals.

Furthermore, in 1944-45, Germany was still not defeated and that remained the main preoccupation of the Communists. An anti-Church campaign would have divided the anti-Nazi forces and, possibly, created more enemies, not only internally among the partisans and governments-in-exile opposed to the Germans but also externally among the Allies.

The situation in Eastern Europe in 1944-45 was, moreover, still fluid. After the Teheran Conference, the Soviets believed that they had the West's commitment to place Poland (and, thus, the more easterly Baltic States) within their sphere of influence. But the question of Soviet control of Poland was still undefined; the West had not agreed explicitly to a Communist government in Poland, only to the USSR's right to annex the Polish lands of West Ukraine and West Belorussia. And beyond Poland nothing had been decided about the rest of Eastern Europe except that it was generally understood (at least by the Soviets and East Europeans) that the fate of Poland would adumbrate the future of all of Eastern Europe for it was the largest and most strategic of the countries. This reality was evidenced by the fact that the leader of the Czechoslovakian-government-in-exile, Eduard Beneš, immediately after Teheran, moved quickly, in December, 1943, to sign a treaty of alliance and friendship with the Soviet Union. It was obvious to Beneš that Soviet control of Poland, implicit in the Teheran agreement, meant the Soviets would hold the balance of power in Eastern Europe after the war. As part of the agreement with Beneš, the Soviets demanded and received "rectifications", which eventually consisted of Soviet annexation of the Carpatho-Ukraine in northeastern Czechoslovakia. It was also quite apparent, at least to Beneš and the Soviets, that the position of the respective armies (Red or American-British) would be deterministic in a fluid situation and that the Soviety Army, in 1944-45, was rapidly filling the East European vacuum. But, needless to say, it would be foolish of the Communists to take on the Catholic Church in Eastern Europe when the political question was still muddled.

Finally, once the Soviet did occupy Eastern Europe, they were not the sole political forces.[1] In some countries, they deliberately contrived multiple political parties and personages to take in western public opinion, but, in others, they faced genuine, although futile, political challenges. In Poland, the Soviets upon occupation set up a Communist-controlled Provisional government but it included, as of July, 1945, a popular non-Communist representative, Stanislaus Mikolajczyk, the leader of the People's Peasant Party. Mikolajczyk, it is true, became a virtual prisoner of the Communist government, but, nonetheless, he was popular and had a base of support among the Polish people. And, furthermore, there were other political parties, besides Mikolajczyk's group, existing along with the Communist Polish Workers' Party. Of course, it would be naïve to maintain that these non-Communist political parties and personalities were anything more than windowdressing but, nonetheless, their existence gave the strongest institution in Poland,[2] the Church, a political medium to oppose Communist totalitarianism.

In Hungary, following the end of the war, an Allied Control Commission, on which the United States, Great Britain, and the Soviet Union were represented, oversaw political affairs. In a gross miscalculation of Communist support, the Soviets allowed free elections to be held in October, 1945. The elections led to the establishment of a republic and a coalition government under the leadership of the Small Farmers' Party headed by Zoltan Tildy and Ferenc Nagy. The Communists, to their dismay and embarrassment, received only seven percent of the vote.

In Czechoslovakia, a coalition government, in which the Communist Party was the most powerful, was set up in March, 1945, under the leadership of a non-Communist president, Eduard Beneš. Beneš and the Czech people had a pronounced propensity for the Soviets due to the Western sell-out at Munich and to the much needed land reform which the Communists carried out in Czechoslovakia. This disposition culminated in a freely elected, Communist-controlled government (38 percent of the vote) in May, 1946.[3] But the new Czech government was still under the nominal leadership of Beneš and there were non-Communist ministers, including Jan Masaryk, son of the founder of the republic, in the government.

In total, the existence of these political centers, independent, even though, in some cases, only nominally, of the Kremlin, tended to inhibit the Communists' campaign to yoke the Catholic Church in Eastern Europe. This varied, however, according to the nature and strength of the oppositional center and its position in the Soviet orbit.

The policy of "toleration" to the Latin Church in parts of Eastern Europe and to the Vatican formally got off the ground with the unfolding of a rather curious development known as the Orlemanski Affair. In April, 1944, Stalin invited an unsophisticated and naive American-Polish priest, Reverend Stanislaus Orlemanski, to the Kremlin. Orlemanski, who was held by the United States government to be pro-Soviet and unrepresentative of most Polish-Americans, had written to the Russian Consulate in New York for permission to go into the Russian military zone in Eastern Europe and study for himself the religious "question" in Poland.[4] Stalin replied by inviting him to Moscow to discuss not simply the persecution of the Catholic Church in Poland, but to examine the persecution of the Church throughout the world.[5]

Orlemanski accepted the invitation and during two interviews, Stalin managed to convince him that he held no animosity toward the Catholic Church and that he was willing to negotiate an understanding.[6] After having his picture taken with Stalin and Molotov and broadcasting pro-Soviet statements "to the people of Poland," Orlemanski immediately flew back to the United States and dutifully held a news conference in Chicago on May 12 to tell the world of Stalin's warm feelings toward the Catholic Church.[7] He reported that he had had two conferences with Stalin that lasted approximately two hours and fifteen minutes apiece. He stated that he found Stalin "very democratic, very open." And he added that "as an American citizen I stood up as a man to man and talked to Stalin."[8]

The purpose of Father Orlemanski's trip was expressed succinctly: "I told Stalin that the most important problem to solve is the religious problem."[9] Orlemanski disclosed that Stalin rejoined his statement with a question: "How would you go about this? What would you do?" The unapprized priest announced that he then retorted with two questions: "Do you think that cooperation with the Holy Father, Pope Pius XII, in the matter of struggle against coercion and persecution of the Catholic Church is possible"[11] Stalin reportedly answered: "I think it is possible."[12] Then Orlemanski asked: "Do you think it admissible for the Soviet Government to pursue a policy of persecution and coercion with regard to the Catholic Church?"[13] Stalin answered: "as an advocate of freedom of conscience and that of worship I consider such a policy to be inadmissible and precluded."[14] The remainder of the two interviews apparently was taken up with Stalin's policy toward Poland which Orlemanski summarized thus: "Stalin gave me a promise that he will do all in his power to cooperate with the Church so that there will be no persecution."[15]

Moscow promptly backed up Orlemanski's announcement with a double-barreled offensive. *Pravda* under the heading of "Statements by Father Orlemanski" stated that there certainly was a possibility of closer relations with the Vatican in combating persecution of the Catholic Church.[16] This was supplemented by action: some Polish children in the Soviet Union were permitted to have Roman Catholic religious education by priests. In addition, Bibles and prayer books were printed at the government's expense and a few Latin rite churches were re-opened in the Western Ukraine.[17]

The Vatican, however, did not respond positively to the Soviet government's overture. Orlemanski was suspended from his priestly functions and packed off to a monastery, an action which was generally viewed "as a Vatican rebuff to Stalin's peace offer."[18] The Church, of course, found the Kremlin's proposals and means of delivery outrageous and incredible, particularly in view of the burgeoning onslaughts against the Ukrainian Uniate Church.

The Vatican's attitude elicited a response of shocked innocence from the Soviets. On May 22, Radio Moscow broadcasted a lengthy report which expressed bewilderment that Orlemanski had been punished for his discussions with the Soviet government. The broadcast cited instances, such as the Yugoslav partisan movement and the French Committee of National Liberation, in which Catholics have collaborated and continued to work with Communists. The report paraphrased a *Christian Science Monitor* article as follows: "If a *rapprochement* on a wider basis between Moscow and the Vatican is possible, it is evident that Stalin is willing to undertake this *rapprochement* and difficult to believe that the Vatican—traditionally well versed in solving questions in new circumstances—would refuse to recognize the new international position of the Soviet Union. Should a *rapprochement* become impossible because of the old ideological conflict, this would seriously hamper the development of inter-Allied collaboration." The broadcast went on to quote from other newspapers, including the *Chicago Sun* of May 15 which was paraphrased to underline the major theme of the entire broadcast: "that apart from what the Church leaders think of the propriety of Orlemanski's visit, new efforts . . . [should] now be made to achieve . . . a *rapprochement*."[19]

The Vatican's response, however, did not deter the Soviet authorities from continuing to tolerate Catholicism in the Eastern European satellites. As the countries of Eastern Europe quickly slipped under Soviet hegemony in 1944-45, the Communist authorities unveiled an overall, non-persecutory policy toward the Church in those parts of Eastern Europe not annexed into the Soviet Union. The attitude was general throughout the Soviet-controlled countries of Eastern Europe, but particularly noticeable in the states where the majority of the population was Catholic: Poland, Hungary, and Czechoslovakia. For the sake of spatial limitations and in the belief that not much is missed, Catholic-Communist relations are dealt with in detail below and in the following chapters only in the above-cited countries and the USSR.

At the end of the war, the Catholic Church in Poland, as already indicated, was a formidable political, social, and religious institution. Not only was it the principal pillar of Polish nationalism, it was also, despite the loss of three bishops and 1,847 priests to the Nazis,[20] a superbly functioning organization with an intact hierarchical and clerical administration. Numerous schools, charities, publications, and lands and buildings belonged to the Church and, even though the Nazis had confiscated much of this property, the Church, once Poland was freed from the Nazi grip, not only claimed but began operating and managing its prewar holdings. The Church leaders, furthermore, were revered as embodiments of Polish nationalism and war heroes.[21] In addition, the Church, after the postwar territorial adjustments, was able to claim adherence of 95% of the population. Poland lost the mixed Orthodox-Catholic regions of West Belorussia and West Ukraine, but it gained, in 1946-47, from these territories over 500,000 Latin Catholics whom the Soviets resettled in Poland mostly on the former German lands.[22] In addition, the Soviets ceded to Poland, in 1945, the region of Belostok which included 478,000 Latin Catholics.[23] The so-called "recovered territories" (up to the Oder-Neisse Rivers) from Germany with its forced removal of thousands of Germans (many non-Catholic) also increased Catholicism's percentage of the population. Finally and most tragically, the Nazi decimation of the Jews further enhanced it.

Of necessity, then, the Communist government, supported only by Soviet political and military forces and not by the people, decided to temporize and forestall any showdown with the Polish Church. Ultimately, it hoped to control this awesome institution and use it as a buttress for its internal and foreign programs, but until such a time as the government felt it could directly challenge the Church it opted for toleration. Undoubtedly the government's decision to appease the Church was reinforced by the hope that the policy might spawn some other rewards, such as, swaying the Church to back the government, disarming the Church for the inevitable conflict, providing a favorable image among religious believers in the West, especially those some five million Polish voters in the United States, and, finally, keeping the home waters calm while the Communists manipulated for position.

From the very beginning of Soviet control of Poland, the authorities revealed a tolerant attitude. In January, 1945, the *New York Times* reported that the Polish Provisional government was "meticulously and scrupulously correct" in dealing with the Catholic Church.[24] Polish Church leaders, in early 1945, furthermore, declared that there was "complete liberty of religious education, religious services and Church administration."[25] The government also announced, in early 1945, that it had decided not to include Church land in the general postwar division of large estates.[26] In April, 1945, the British Legation in Moscow reported in a communique to the Vatican that:

> All reports agree that the Catholic Church is being very carefully handled in Poland. There is no interference with public worship and priests are not molested. The provisional authorities have also been at great pains to conciliate the Catholic hierarchy. For example, at a recent meeting at Cracow in honour of General Zymierski, Archbishop Sapieha was treated with great honour and held up as a model Pole who had shown outstanding qualities in resisting the German invaders. . . . Church lands have hitherto been spared the treatment suffered by private estates.[27]

The government's end-of-the-war attitude of appeasement was taken full advantage of by the Church. In March, 1945, the Cracow Curia started publishing a weekly, *Tygodnik Powszechny,* which soon became a respected and thoughtful chronicle of current happenings.[28] By the fall six more Catholic journals started publishing and before the year was out the Catholic University at Lublin and numerous Catholic schools and seminaries re-opened. Catholic charities and groups picked up where they had left off when the Nazis arrived.[29] Church land, about 450,000, remained exempt from the agrarian reform announced in January, 1946. Numerous churches were rebuilt with state assistance and the Church could count upon the army to assist in religious holiday processions. Religious worship was not restricted and, in fact, Boleslaw Beirut, the Polish Workers' Party leader, and other high Communist officials openly attended religious ceremonies.[30] In September, 1945, the Ministry of Education confirmed the provisions of the 1921 Constitution making religious instruction in public schools mandatory.[31]

There were, to be sure, some restrictions. A few Catholics associations were denied governmental approval; as of January, 1946, civil marriage was the only type recognized by the state; the Catholic press was liable to the censorship laws. Of a more serious nature, the Church's legal status was undermined. The government, although affirming the 1921 Constitutional provisions requiring mandatory religious education, never obliged itself to support those regulations in the repudiated Constitution which guaranteed the Church's primacy among the religions of Poland and the Church's right to be ruled by Canon Law.[33] In addition, on September 12, 1945, the government unilaterally repudiated the 1925 Concordat. The explanation provided was that the Vatican had violated the Concordat by authorizing, in 1940, German bishops to administer Polish territory annexed by the Reich.[34] The real reasons, though, seem to have been that the Papacy refused to name permanent Polish bishops for the "recovered territories," did not curb the jurisdiction of the Polish bishops in the regions attached to the Soviet Union, refused to grant diplomatic recognition to the Provisional Government (Papacy still recognized the Polish government in London), and, finally, corroborated, in the regime's eyes, the unreceptive and even hostile attitude of the Polish hierarchy to the government's policy of toleration.[35]

The government also tried, increasingly, to splinter the Polish Church. This effort was multileveled and began with an attempt to separate the Polish Church from the Vatican. The quashing of the Concordat represented part of this two dimensional campaign; its other aspect was a propaganda foray, beginning in 1945 and never really abating during Stalin's tenure, to associate the Papacy in the minds of the Polish people and, if possible, church leaders, with pro-Germanism and anti-Polonism.[36] In Poland, the government also applied its divide and conquer philosophy and initiated, in the fall of 1945, an organization called Social Catholics, led by Boleslaw Piasecki, the erstwhile head of the prewar fascist group, "Falanga." Its objective, as reflected in its weekly organ, Dzis i Jutro (complemented by a daily newspaper, Slowo Powszechne, in March, 1947) was to educate the Poles to accept socialism and to bridge the differences between Marxism and Catholicism.[37]

In general, though, the government was uninterested in coming to blows with the Church. It made a series of offers to improve relations and to establish channels of cooperation and communication. For example, in June, 1946, at a meeting of the Workers' and Socialist Parties, Cyrankiewicz called for a modus vivendi with the Church. The hierarchy replied, through Tygodnik Powszechny, that the Church was ready to work with the government, but only if the regime accepted Catholic principles and programs. The journal, in addition, admonished the Communists that a democratic system, which they claimed as their goal, necessitated the tolerance, in power, of different political parties and programs.[38]

The hierarchy was keenly aware of the fact that the government was a puppet of the Kremlin's and, by its very nature, inclined towards totalitarianism. It could not, therefore, compromise with the system without risking being swallowed into the vortex of the ever looming storm of Stalinism. The episcopate had to keep its guard up and be quick to criticize, as it did through its press and pastoral letters, every governmental trend towards statism, towards collectivization, towards arbitrary and whimsical administration of justice, and, above all, towards efforts to splinter and compromise the

Church. The Social Catholics' philosophy of attempting to reconcile Marxism and Catholicism was denounced as false teaching. At the same time, the bishops wanted Catholic participation in the new parliament (to be elected in January, 1947) to guarantee Catholic input in the formulation of, at least, the school legislation, marriage laws, and the cultural and arts programs. The bishops, in addition, called unsuccessfully for the organization of a truly Catholic political party.

The Communists, although rebuffed again and again, still did not want to alienate Catholic opinion through coercion. Naturally they were uninterested in having Catholic representation in the government, but, in an obvious attempt to satiate the basic demands of the Church, the Communist-dominated bloc stipulated, as part of its platform, that the new constitution (to be framed after the 1947 election) would guarantee freedom of religion and recognize the special rights of the Catholic Church.[39]

The Church, however, was unimpressed with what it interpreted as another Communist ploy to disarm it. In September, 1946, as the time for the first postwar election neared, Cardinal Hlond issued a pastoral letter which declared that "Catholics may not belong to organizations or parties, the principles of which contradict Christian teaching, or the deeds and activities of which aim in reality, at the undermining of Christian ethics." Moreover, the Cardinal ordered that "Catholics may vote only for such persons, lists of candidates, and electoral programs, as are not opposed to Catholic teaching and morality, and that Catholics may neither vote, nor put themselves forward as candidates for electoral lists, the programs or principles of which are repugnant to common-sense, the well being of the nation and the state, to Christian morality, and to the Catholic outlook."[40] The Communists censored the letter.[41]

When the January, 1947, election took place, the Church patently supported Mikolajczyk's opposition party.[42] To its dismay, however, the Communists rigged the election and won an "overwhelming victory." Henceforth, with the Communists no longer simply the leaders of a provisional government, the Church decided to halt it adamant struggle against the government and to pursue a course of gaining the regime's recognition of the Church's rights and obligations.

On March 17, 1947, the episcopate presented its "bill of rights" to Premier Cyrankiewicz in the form of a document called the Catholic Constitutional Postulates. Basically, the bishops wanted included in the new Constitution safeguards for traditional liberties, private property, the Church's autonomy and its rights to organize and run schools, charities, and publishing enterprises.[41] In the months following its presentation, the Church attempted to demonstrate to the government, in the partial hope of

having the Postulates accepted, its utility as a moral force. Not only did the
Church come out strongly against hooliganism, alcoholism, abortion, and
postwar demoralization, especially among the young, but it also urged the
people, while rejecting materialism, to cease resistance to governmental
programs seeking to create "a better tomorrow for the working classes."[44]

The Communist government rejected the Postulates and did not respond
to the Church's efforts to improve relations. Instead it began preparations
for a struggle. In 1947, it tried to outflank the Church by essaying to offer the
Vatican, through the Social Catholics, a Concordat. The Papacy, however,
passed up the opportunity claiming that the Polish government had to first
work out an accommodation with the Polish Church. With that failure, the
government exacerbated its anti-Vatican pelts and, increasingly, in 1947 and
1948, included obloquies against the Polish hierarchy and clergy. The Polish
Catholic leaders were charged with "non-cooperation, and this was
represented as bordering on treason."[45] In March, 1948, the Pope presented
the regime with an explosive weapon when he publicly sympathized with
the plight of expellées in West Germany. The government quickly interpreted the letter as proof of the Vatican's pro-German propensities and that
as the explanation for why the Papacy refused to sanction a permanent
ecclesiastical administration for the "recovered lands." The regime's
propaganda evidently scored some success at undermining the Church's
position in Poland for even the Polish Catholic leadership felt compelled to
complain to Rome.[46]

1948 was a critical year in Church-State relations in Poland. It saw the
government's generally tolerant attitude change to outright hostility. This
development was not unique to Poland, however, but, rather, quite
characteristic of developments in the other major Catholic countries of
Eastern Europe, Hungary and Czechoslovakia.

In Hungary, like in Poland, the Communist authorities from the beginning exercised restraint and laxity toward the Catholic Church. In the
Church, the regime faced a vigorous, functioning institution which com-
manded, at least nominally, the adherence of 68% of the population and
which was identified with the deepest roots of Hungarian nationalism.[47] In
the prewar period its strength was reflected in the fact that its bishops were
ex officio members of the Upper House and its name was affiliated with a
plethora of journals and newspapers, political parties, publishing houses,
trade unions, and social movements and associations. Above all, its influence
was demonstrated by the fact that it controlled nearly half of all the
educational institutions in Hungary (the other Christian churches administered most of the rest).[48] It also owned a huge *latifundia*, comprising one-
eighteenth of all arable land and a great variety of other tangible assets.[49]

While the Church traditionally was a supporter of the established order and pre-industrial values, it was not opposed to change and, in fact, in the 1930s, organized the mamouth Catholic Agrarian Youth League (KALOT) which called for far-reaching reforms, including land reform.[50] It was, in other words, a preminent social, political, and economic institution.

The war did not significantly affect the Church's influence but, if anything, enhanced it as a guardian of traditional values against the dehumanizing philosophies of both Nazism and Communism. It opposed, during the war, the Hungarian government's rightist tendencies and when the Germans installed the Arrow Cross government in October, 1944, the Church assumed a position of noncooperation and actively incited opposition. The Prince Primate, Jusztinian Cardinal Seredi, in fact, approved the largescale underground Catholic resistance against Sźalasi's government. The Church, despite the fact that the WWII Hungarian government fought with Germany, could not be compromised as pro-Nazi by the Communists and was, in fact, identified as one of the main institutions offering both moral and political contravention to Nazism.

With the end of the war, accordingly, the Communists, preoccupied with garnering political power, did not impinge measurably on the Church's position.[51] Catholics were permitted, in 1945, to organize their own political party, the Christian Democratic People's Party led by Count Joszef Palffy.[52] Two small weekly Catholic newspapers also appeared simultaneously. The authorities did not interfere with religious worship, the duties of the clergy, or the issuance of pastoral letters.[53] With the death of Cardinal Seredi in March, 1945, there was no effort to block the election of Joszef Mindszenty as his successor or to curb the new Primate's far-reaching influence.[54]

The relationship, however, was not without its strains. In March, 1945, the Apostolic Nuncio was ordered out of the country, but that action was modified by the fact that all other foreign delegations were also expelled.[55] In addition, in 1945, the Communist authorities undertook major land reforms and decided to include the property of the Catholic Church in the new arrangements. The Church vigorously but unsuccessfully objected to the government's action because the maintenance of the Church's schools and buildings was derived, in part, from the income produced by its landed properties.[56] In 1946, as a by-product of the Communist effort to weaken the Nagy regime and the Small Farmers' Party (of which the Catholic Church was a major backer), the Communists were able to force the dissolution of the Catholic youth organization.[57] In 1947, after forcing the Small Farmers' Party out of power, the Communists took over control of the Church's large, charitable organization, Kartasz.[58] With the Communists firmly entrenched by the end of 1947, a foreboding future awaited the Church.

In Czechoslovakia also the Communist authorities confronted a strong institution, although the Church, like the state, broke down along lines of Czech and Slovak nationalism. Anti-clericalism, a residue from the days when the Church wielded enormous power in the Hapsburg Empire, and resentment, at least by the Czechs, of Monsignor Tiso's pro-Nazi government in Slovakia placed the Church in a much more vulnerable position in Czechoslovakia than in Poland or Hungary.[59] Despite these fissures, however, the Church, at the end of the war, still counted over seventy-eight percent of the population in its fold and owned some 797,930 acres of lands and 248 buildings.[60] The hierarchy and clergy were still functioning. Many of the priests and bishops, most notably Archbishop Joseph Beran of Prague, were war heroes and not only balanced Tiso but tended to identify the Church, at least in the Czech lands, as a main opponent of the Nazis.

Like elsewhere in Eastern Europe, the Soviets treated the Church in Czechoslovakia with kid gloves. The Church leaders and clerics were not hampered in the performance of their duties and, in general, the Church operated without restraints. There were a number of laws passed by the coalition government to weaken the strong Catholic Party in Slovakia,[61] but this was advertised as measures to punish Nazi-collaborators and not as an effort to antagonize or attack the Catholic Church.[62] It was also primarily on the grounds of Nazi affiliation that the Czechoslovakian government nationalized Roman Catholic schools and dissolved Roman Catholic associations in Slovakia during the immediate postwar period.[63] Despite these actions, however, the Catholic Church remained generally untouched and the Church leaders did not strenuously object to the regime's decisions in Slovakia. On May 13, 1946, the government exchanged representatives with the Holy See. Mgr. Xavier Ritter became Internuncio to Prague while Dr. Arthur Maixner took up residence as the Czech envoy in Rome.[64] This relationship was to change drastically during 1948, but as late as March, 1948, after the February coup put the Communists in exclusive power, the Communist government assured Archbishop Beran that the Catholic Church had nothing to fear from the new regime.[65]

Baltic States, West White Russia, West Ukraine, Assumptionists, Anti-Vatican Propaganda, and Orthodox-Catholic Relations.

Initially, like in Eastern Europe, the Soviets showed modified deference to, at least, the Catholics of Lithuania-Latvia. The British legation in Moscow reported in April, 1945, to the Vatican that the Soviets had allowed a few priests to return to the Baltic States. In addition, according to the British report, the hierarchy and ecclesiastical organization had not been interfered with, worship restricted, nor the three seminaries (opened under the Nazis) closed. However, the British did assert that the Russians had cut off all contact between the Church in the Baltic States and the Vatican, prohibited religious instruction in schools (permitted by the Germans), and proscribed the publication of religious books and pamphlets.[1] The tempered approach, if such it could be described, did not last much beyond April, 1945, and, in fact, could not, with any measure of objectivity, be claimed, even before 1945, as general policy toward the Catholics in the Soviet Union.

Moscow's general approach, as it clearly crystallized with the end of the war, was to attack the Church. Its reasons for moving against the Church at home were probably tied to Moscow's desire to "re-educate" as quickly as possible the populations of the formerly German-controlled parts of the country and to "sovietize" without delay the previously annexed but temporarily lost regions of Galicia, West Belorussia, and the Baltic States. The Communists realized that they would not only have to overcome the anti-Sovietism produced by their first occupation, but they would also have to break the back of established and newly budding institutions of nationalism. In particular, the Kremlin knew it had to suppress the widespread anti-Soviet partisan movement which was especially strong in Lithuania and, secondly, control the Roman Catholic Church which fed the nationalism of the Belorussians, Lithuanians, and Latvians and blocked these peoples' political, cultural, and economic socialization into the Soviet system. Evidentally the Communists did not think that an onslaught against Catholicism in the USSR would significantly jeopardize their image in the

West. The Western Powers never mentioned at length the Baltic States at the various wartime conferences and this omission, from the Soviet point of view, was no doubt taken as an implicit recognition that these lands belonged to the Soviet Union. And the Western Ukraine and West Belorussia had already been explicitly confirmed as Soviet territory. Accordingly, the policies formulated in these lands were internal matters and, from the Soviet vantage, of no legitimate concern to foreigners. Hedging their bets, though, the Russians did not publicize their anti-Catholic drive, managed to effectively close off their country to western eyes, and, to explain those inevitable leaks about their persecution, promulgated the thesis that its deportations, arrests, executions, etc., were the product of wiping out centers of Nazi collaboration and Kulak nationalism.[2] The fact that the Communists were not hamstringing the Church in Eastern Europe in fact could lend credence to the Soviet charges. The Soviets might even have hoped that the Vatican, even though it was destined to become a target of invective, might remain passive either because of the "extended hand" in Eastern Europe or because of the fear that what was happening in the USSR could happen elsewhere in Eastern Europe if it denounced the Communists.

The campaign against the Catholic Church in the Soviet Union can be broken down into five subdivisions: West Ukraine—West Belorussia, Baltic States, Assumptionists (Apostolic Administrators in Moscow), Anti-Vatican propaganda, and Orthodox-Vatican relations.

The Soviet government's policy toward the national minority Catholics in Belorussia and the West Ukraine differed only in degree from its struggle to annihilate the Ukrainian Uniate Church. The authorities, to be sure, were inimical to the Latin Catholics, particularly those they suspected of collaborating or sympathizing with the regime's enemies—the Germans or the anti-Soviet partisans found in both the Ukraine and Belorussia. The government also was determined to make Orthodoxy, as much as possible, the dominant religion in Galicia and West Belorussia. However, the regime evidently decided immediately after the war, in contrast to the Uniates, that the Latins in the Ukraine and Belorussia could not be effectively absorbed into the Russian Orthodox Church and, thus, it opted for the alternative plan of mass deportation and/or cession of largely Catholic-populated territories to Poland and Lithuania with the intention of diluting Latin concentrations.[3] In 1945, Belostok (encompassing most of the episcopal see of Lomza) was detached and returned to Poland. This maneuver, presumably a blessing for the Catholics, reduced the Latin Catholics in the Belorussian SSR by 478,000.[4] The city of Vilnius and its adjacent lands (some 2,750 square miles), which had been ceded to Lithuania in 1940 and contained about 422,000 Catholics, was kept, upon the Soviet return, as part of Lithuania.[5] Finally, during 1946-1947, approximately 500,000 Belorussian Catholics were relocated in the Polish annexed Oder-Neisse territories.[6]

By such means, the Soviets reduced, by 1947, the number of Latin Catholics in Belorussia by at least a million and a half. When the Communists first occupied West Belorussia and the West Ukraine in 1939, six and a half million fell under their auspices. Even allowing for the significant losses due to the wartime attrition and the Communists' policies of deportation and cession (during and after the war), it seems, although no precise figures are available because of secrecy on the part of Poland and the Soviet Union, that a considerable number of Latin Catholics still inhabit the Belorussian SSR and the northwestern part of the Ukrainian SSR. The Orthodox Metropolitan of Minsk, Pitirim, claimed, in, 1958, that there were two and a half million in Belorussia which is a significant variation from the 800,000 estimate of one Catholic source.[7] Reliable figures on the number of Latin Catholics in the West Ukraine—the archdiocese of Lviv and the episcopal see of Peremyshl'—are just as difficult to come by. They, like their Belorussian co-religionists, were also subject to massive resettlement in various parts of the Soviet empire[8] No matter, though, how many Catholics were left by the end of the 1940s, they had no episcopal leadership and few priests.[9]

In addition to the drive against the Latin Church in Belorussia—West Ukraine, the Soviet authorities, in 1945, set about harnessing the Catholic Church in the Baltic States, all three of which reverted to SSR's. What lent earnestness to this dragooning effort was the well organized anti-Soviet partisan movement of the Lithuanians which raged on from 1944 to 1952. The Lithuanian resistance, which reached its zenith between 1944 and 1948 and then declined until its suppression in 1952, was fed by the memories of Soviet atrocities during the first occupation, by Moscow's immeidate attempts (beginning in 1944) to collectivize and sovietize Lithuania, by the Russians' campaign of purges and reprisals, by the Lithuanian leaders' hopes that the West would intervene, and, above all, by the Lithuanians' desire to establish their own independent, pro-Western government. The existence of an anti-Nazi underground, of course, provided the Lithuanians with the tool, experience, and momentum to oppose Soviet designs and hopefully realize their own hopes.[10] The Lithuanian resistance to incorporation, which was paralleled on a much reduced scale in the other Baltic States, keep Moscow from completely controlling the region for the better part of four years. Initially during 1944-1945 the Soviets bypassed the Church in Lithuania, but, by the end of 1945, they evidently decided that the Church was not only a backer of Lithuanian nationalism but of the anti-Soviet partisan movement.[11]

The Communists' first major move against the Church in Lithuania, aside from the fact that Soviet antireligious laws were introduced once again with the re-incorporation of the Baltic States into the USSR, was directed against the hierarchy. In 1946 the Lithuanian Commission for Internal Affairs requested that the bishops denounce the partisans and appeal for their surrender. When the bishops demured, the authorities, after issuing warnings, purged them. On February 3, 1946, Bishop Pranas Ramanauskas was interned and subsequently deported to Siberia. In the same year, Bishop Teofilius Matulionis of Kaisiadorys and Archbishop Mecys Reinys of Vilnius were arrested, tried, and sentenced to hard labor in Siberia. (On November 8, 1953 Archbishop Reinys died in jail near Moscow). By 1947, the only bishop in Lithuania was Mgr. K. Paltarokas of Panevezhys who was spared because of his advanced age.[12]

Simultaneously with the removal of the bishops, the priests were arrested, reaching 180 by 1949.[13] The number of priests free in Lithuania in 1954 totaled only 741 which was down from a 1945 aggregate of 1,470.[14] According to a Radio Vatican report of August 10, 1948, many of the arrested priests were deported to Siberia where they became a familiar figure.[15] The monastic clergy fared even worse than the secular priests. In 1947, monastic lands were confiscated, all monasteries and convents shut down, the monks and nuns dispersed and/or deported *en masse* to Siberia. Membership in religious communities was declared illegal.[6]

As the priests and bishops were atrophied, the Communist authorities quickly closed churches with the excuse that there were no priests to administer them. By 1948 the prewar total of 1,202 churches (including chapels) had been reduced to 711.[17] The three seminaries of Telsiai, Vilkaviskis, and Vilnius were occluded, leaving, by 1946, only the Kaunas Seminary whose enrollment and internal affairs were restricted.[18]

Catholic associations and charities were outlawed. The religious press, throughout all of the Baltic States, was effectively suppressed.[19] No longer was it possible, by 1948, to teach religion in school. In mid-November, 1948, the Vatican reported that the clergy still at large in Lithuania were rapidly being isolated and that secular education had been introduced into the schools.[20]

From the end of the war, the government also contrived to organize a National Catholic Church which could provide the base for a schismatic movement. Despite the methodical application of enticements and punishments to the clergy, the Communists were unable to persuade any clergymen to become the fulcrum for a *raskol*.[21]

The Church's economic and social base were significantly undermined by the loss of its monastic lands, religious associations, publications, and churches, and, especially, by the rigorous application of Soviet law which nationalized all church property. Possibly even more damaging to the Church was the Soviet policy of deporting intellectuals and lay leaders. In March, 1949, the Papacy declared that "400,000 Lithuanians, 200,000 Latvians, and an equal number of Estonians," that is, fourteen percent of the entire population of the Baltic States were in Soviet concentration camps.[22]

Even though the regime failed to fashion a splintering wedge in the Church, it did succeed, by 1949, in forcing some of the Lithuanian Church leaders to mouth propaganda in support of Soviet foreign policy goals. For example, in October, 1950, at the Second All-Union Peace Conference in Moscow, Canon Stankevicius urged

. . . all Christians to condemn those who are committing a crime against Christian morals and against humanity. . . . That is why we denounce the American and British invader who have kindled the fire of a new war in Korea. . . . Hypocritical are the assertions that America and Britain are now democratic countries. Any country that seeks to enslave others and encourage racial discrimination is not a democracy but a land of tyranny. We pray for peace every day and we call upon all believers to offset the danger of a new war through joint efforts.[23]

In Latvia, a similar experience visited the Catholic Church. When the Soviets retook this country, however, only the oldest bishop of the Catholic hierarchy remained, Archbishop Anthony Springovics (1875-1958). Since the Germans had forcibly removed the other three Latvian bishops, the Communists did not have to concern themselves with taking any action against them.[24] In June, 1947, however, Archbishop Springovics attempted to rebuild the hierarchy by consecrating two bishops, Mgrs. Peter Strods and Kasimir Dulbinskis. The Communists quickly arrested the latter and placed him in a hard labor camp in Siberia.[25] Bishop Strods was allowed to function and, eventually, with the death of Archbishop Springovics, assume the leadership of the Latvian Catholic Church.

The priests, like the bishops, were whittled down, although the losses were not as great as suffered by the Lithuanian clergy. Apparently fifty priests out of 187 at the end of the war were lost to Communist methods and others escaped the country after the German retreat. In 1959 the number of priests of Latvia stood at 126.[26] The Seminary at Riga was permitted to carry on, although, like Kaunas Seminary, its enrollment and activities were limited.[27] Churches were also closed and, in 1959, there were only about 250. The swath cut into the laity through deportations greatly weakened the

Church.[28] Although Archbishop Springovics gave only cursory approval to Soviet policies, the authorities found Bishop Strods much more accommodating. He, like many of the other young Catholic officials in the USSR, tautologized, as part of their payment for toleration, the regime's hackneyed phrases about Anglo-American imperialism. For example, in October, 1951, Bishop Strods, at one of Moscow's "World Peace" meetings, announced that

> the self-seeking capitalists of America and Britian, together with the revanchists of Western Germany and Japan, are trying to unleash war. They are preparing it first and foremost against our State—the Soviet Union. Most probably this war would already have begun if the fighters for peace, throughout the world, headed by the Soviet Union, had not given an energetic rebuff to the warmongers and if atomic energy and the atomic weapon had remained a monopoly of the aggressor.[29]

In Estonia, where Catholics were few and scattered, the regime easily suppressed the institutionalized Church.[30]

Not only did Moscow bear down against Catholicism in its annexed territories, but also in Moscow and through the media of propaganda and Russian Orthodoxy. In Moscow, the Communists decided, by 1944, that they had tolerated long enough Leopold Braun who, by then, had expanded his ministry to include a large number of Muscovites. Accordingly, through the year, Braun found himself once again the victim of rude searches and conspicuous and unnerving surveillance.[31] Undoubtedly Braun's travails would have been more severe if he had not been a citizen of the United States with whom the Soviets, in 1944-1945, still wanted good relations.

Braun reciprocated the Soviet hostility by bad mouthing the Russians, to their consternation, to every foreign diplomat and dignitary who would listen.[32] The Ameican Embassy even found Braun's unmitigated candor disquieting.[33]

In October, 1944, the Braun-Kremlin conflict reached a climax when Braun, paranoid because of the Soviet surveillance, throttled the caretaker-janitor of the French Embassy, one Knyazev, whom he believed to be a secret police agent.[34] The Soviets seized the opportunity to embarrass Braun undoubtedly in the hope of having him withdrawn or, at least, compromised in the eyes of the Americans. Braun was soon brought to trial on charges of assault. From his point of view, the entire scenario had been planned by the police.[35] As Braun expected, the court found him guilty, but within a few weeks it reversed itself and exonerated him completely.[36] In the interim the Soviets had evidently convinced the Americans that Braun was insufferable and a *persona non grata*. After the Yalta meeting, at which Stalin personally requested Braun's recall, Roosevelt sent Edward J. Flynn of New York, a close Catholic friend, to Moscow to survey the situation.[37] Flynn, after confering with the Soviets and Braun, decided that the priest was afflicted with fixed ideas.[38] He then flew on to Rome to presumably inform the Papacy of Braun's condition.[39] Reports also claimed that he was acting as an emissary to improve relations between the Kremlin and Rome, but, if that was the case, the Vatican, as with the Orlemanski Affair, rebuffed the opportunity to dialogue with the Soviet Union.[10] Flynn's mission, at any rate, set in motion the machinery that soon brought Father George Antonio Laberge, another American Assumptionist, to Moscow to replace Braun.[41] On December 29, 1945, Braun returned to the United States where he quickly became a harbinger of McCarthyism.[42]

Because Laberge was also fluent in Russian and soon, like Braun, was preaching to full churches of foreigners and Muscovites, the Soviets, particularly in view of the *Zhdanovshchina* and the revitalization of Orthodoxy, were no happier with him than with his predecessor.[43] In 1949, when Laberge requested an exist and re-entry visa to take a vacation in America, the authorities quickly granted him both, but canceled the latter after he left the country.[44] Father Jean Thomas, a French Assumptionist who had been at the French Embassy since 1947, assumed the administration of St. Louis-des-Français, but on May 13, 1949, the Council for the Affairs of Religious Cults, expelled him from the church on the grounds that he could not preach in Russian and was a foreign agent.[45] From then until now, the Assumptionists have been unable to reclaim jurisdiction as pastors of St. Louis. Thomas remained in Moscow until 1950, but from May, 1949, to the present, he and the Assumptionists who succeeded him have had to relegate their ministry to the foreign embassy community in a small chapel in the American Embassy. St. Louis Church was placed under the care of a Baltic priest and fell within the jurisdiction of the Archbishop of Riga.

While the Soviets effectively curbed the Vatican's sole line of communication with the Catholics of Moscow, they concomitantly enlarged their anti-Vatican propaganda. This was, in part, stimulated by the ongoing campaign against the Uniates and the Latin Catholics in the Soviet Union and, in part, by the Cold War. Throughout the immediate postwar years, Soviet propaganda held the Catholic Church to be its principal enemy on the international religious front and the volume of anti-Catholic books and pamphlets vastly outnumbered the tomes directed against other faiths.[46] Initially, the central themes of the anti-Vatican literature was that the Papacy was pro-German, a wartime collaborator of fascism, and an enemy of the Russian and Slavic peoples. M. M. Sheinman, the Kremlin's resident expert on the Vatican, led the propaganda campaign with a barrage of publications. In 1948, in a book entitled *Vatikan mezhdu dvumia mirovymi voinami,* he asserted that Pius XII was the protector of "Hitler's criminal band"[47] and that the Pope believed and spread "the fable of religious persecution in the USSR."[48] He also claimed that Benedict XV intervened in favor of the reactionary Russian clergy and the imperial family during the Russian revolution.[49] He went on to state that the Pope wished to rejoin Orthodoxy with Catholicism and to this end, the "Russicum" Seminary was founded in Rome.[50] But he concluded that the atheists of the Kremlin would never permit "the conversion of the people of the USSR to Catholicism."[51] In 1950 Sheinman published *Idiologiia i politika vatikana na sluzhbe imperializma* wherein he manipulated facts to prove that the Vatican was the enemy of the Slavic peoples and wished for war.[52] He quickly followed this volume with a pamphlet that elaborated upon his theme of the Pope's hatred of Slavic peoples. This was entitled *Vatikan, vrag mira i demokratii* and offered as proof of the Pope's inimical attitude to Slavs the allegation that "the Catholic Popes had massacred in Croatia one million Orthodox Serbs and had forced 300,000 Orthodox to become Catholics."[53]

Increasingly, as the Cold War became cooler, it was propounded that the Vatican was a supporter of American aggression and international reaction. All of the Papacy's decisions and actions, including changes in its internal organization, were interpreted as having the sole aim of pleasing reactionary circles in the United States.[54] In 1950 Sheinman wrote *Vatikan i katolitsizm na sluzhbe imperializma* "to prove" that the Vatican had been and was the ally of capitalistic-imperialistic groups.[55] He alledged that the Papacy "was sympathetically inclined towards fascist organizations everywhere, in France, Britain, Italy, the United States, and in countries of South America."[56] It was also charged that "close cooperation" had been established, via the Jesuits, between the Vatican and the "Fascist-Tito clique."[57]

In 1951 in *Vatikan vo vtorio mirovoi voine* Sheinman contended, among other things, that, in 1941, the fascists, supposedly under the orders of the Catholic bishop of Croatia, Aloysius Stepinac, openly massacred 350,000 Serbs.[58] In addition, Sheinman called attention to a tactic which Communists should utilize to curtail and terminate the influence of the Papacy. He called for the separation of the Catholic masses from the hierarchy and the hierarchy from the Pope.[59] This tactic of divide and conquer, of course, had long been a fundamental weapon in Moscow's arsenal.

In 1952, in his last major work before Stalin's death, Sheinman published *Sokrashchenie istorii papstva.* Herein he accused the Papacy of cherishing "world domination"[60] and of planning to unite the churches of the East with Catholicism.[61]

In 1950 the *Bol'shaia sovetskaia entsiklopediia* pinpointed the Vatican as "the rampart of the blackest reaction."[62] A compatriot of Sheinman, P. Pavelkin, followed up this accusation with a work entitled *Religiozne suerveriia i ikh vred.* Pavelkin ridiculed the Catholic Church, made sport of its rites, doctrines, and teachings, and claimed that it was not only reactionary but "the center of religious obscurantism."[63] In 1952 the work of one of the more famous of the antireligious writers was published, I. Halan's *Vatikan bez maski.* He pictured the Vatican as the "citadel of world obscurantism."[64] The Vatican's alleged reactionary role in world politics and civilization was a recurrent theme in all of the post-World War II antireligious literature. Halan also touched upon another continuing theme when he declared that the Papacy was a powerful force which was attempting to convert the Orthodox East through its priestly agents trained at the Collegium Russicum in Rome.[65]

The Vatican and the Catholic Church were also castigated in the Soviet news media. On June 26, 1948, Radio Moscow declared that the Catholic Church was the leader of obscurantism and that Pius XII was the "head of an enormous centralized and well-disciplined army of obscurantists."[66] Radio Moscow later broadcasted that Catholic Action was the chief agent of reaction in the French and Italian Trade Union Movement.[67] The Soviet journal, *New Times,* in an article entitled "The Vatican Apostles of Imperialism" criticized and berated the Vatican for supporting the western capitalistic nations and for interfering in the Italian national election of 1948.[68] Tass news agency summarily reported that the Vatican was on the side of exploiting forces, that its activities were directed against the masses of the people, that the Vatican was anti-Slav, that it was the promoter of war, and that it was the center of international fascism.[69]

On August 20, 1948, Radio Moscow declared that the Catholic Church stifled "free scientifice thought" and spread "obscurantism and mysticism."[70] Pursuing the attack four days later, the Russian radio claimed that the Vatican actively participated in espionage, sabotage, and the murder of well-known Communists. According to the broadcast, the Papacy's aspiration was "to recruit legionnaires to commit any crime for a small reward on behalf of Wall Street and the 'Holy' Catholic Church."[71]

In late September *Tass* circulated a report to the effect that Cardinal Spellman had sent a half-million dollars to the Vatican to combat Communism throughout the world.[72] Radio Moscow followed with a barrage of accusations. It claimed that the Vatican was the world's major reactionary force and, worst, a leading supporter "of the dictatorial pretensions" of General De Gaulle.[73] It further identified the Catholic clergy and the Christian Democratic Party as the mainsprings of Italian obscurantism and, finally, declared that the French Foreign Office was under Vatican influence.[74]

The invectives emanating from Moscow continued into 1949. At the turn of the year, the Papacy was harshly criticized for defending Hungarian Cardinal Mindszenty, whom the Soviet-controlled government had arrested, and, then, was berated as the main support of reaction and conservatism in the United States.[75]

On January 22 Radio Moscow analyzed some of the means the Vatican employed to maintain its influence. The broadcaster claimed that the Catholic Church had set up a powerful propaganda machine to support its worldwide policies of reaction.[76] The Catholic Church, according to the report, published thousands of daily and weekly newspapers and maintained its own news agency and correspondents. In addition, according to the broadcast, the Vatican exercised censorship over various American publications and had an influential hand in controlling the American trade union movement and educational system.[77] Finally, the report concluded, the Vatican had allied itself with the government of the United States to thwart the democratic forces of Communism.[78]

The Communist news media continued to blast the Vatican throughout 1949.[79] The theme of the reports was consistent and repetitive. The Vatican was displayed as an ally of Wall Street and the vanguard of world reaction headed by the United States.[80]

The Vatican, of course, was quite aware of its notoriety in Moscow's disseminations and it continuously issued denials to the Communists' various charges.[81] In April of 1949, however, the Papacy briefly went on the offensive and, in a perspicuous analysis of the Soviets' anti-Catholic tirades, Il Quotidiano argued that the anti-Catholic irruptions were intended to limit and, eventually, destroy the Vatican's influence in Eastern Europe.[82]

The Kremlin was not, however, wont to blast the Papacy simply with literary and proclamatory artillery. From July 8 to July 19, 1948, the Communists permitted the Moscow Patriarchate to summon an all-Orthodox Congress in Moscow to celebrate the 500th anniversary of the Russian Orthodox Church's autocephaly. The gathering counted among its number not only the leaders of the Russian Church, but also the Patriarch-Catholicos of the Georgian Orthodox Church, the Patriarchs of the Romanian and Serbian Orthodox Churches, and Metropolitan Stefan, head of the Bulgarian Orthodox Church. Representatives of the Patriarchs of Constantinople, Antioch, and Alexandria were also in attendance. The Greek, Albanian, and Russian Orthodox churchmen came from Czechoslovakia, Western Europe, the United States, Yugoslavia, Bulgaria, and China. The Catholicos-Patriarch of the Armenian Orthodox Church attended as a guest.[83]

One of the chief functions of the Orthodox Congress was to fulminate the Vatican on the religious level. This the Congress accomplished both in its conferences and its concluding resolutions. In the early discussions, the Vatican's College of Cardinals was criticized. It was claimed that the College was dominated by Italian and American Cardinals led by Cardinal Spellman of New York.[84] It was also pointed out that the Vatican was a political machine and not a religious-orientated institution.[85]

The early discussions emphasized the political role the Papacy played in Hungary, Czechoslovakia, Holland, Switzerland, Belgium, Germany, Austria, Italy, France, and other countries with a significant Catholic population, through its Catholic Action organization, its youth groups, its farm cooperatives, its political parties such as the Christian Socialists, the Christian Democrats, and the Popular Christians, and, finally, through L'Osservatore Romano and its some 2,782 different Catholic journals.[86] The Vatican, according to the congregated Churchmen, had been the prime instigator behind the Italian-German crusade against the Soviet Union.[87] And, according to the Orthodox conferees, the principle by which the Roman Catholic Church lived and operated was that "money has no odor."[88]

In later discussions the Congress elaborated upon this latter theme. It claimed that the Vatican made a profit from its clerical organization and that it executed "the directives of Italian imperialism . . . under the pretext of religious instruction" for the sake of self-gain and for the purpose of training young fascists.[89] According to the Conference spokesmen, it was a well known fact that the Vatican was a reactionary organization[90] and a close ally and confidant of the Anglo-American imperialists.[91] From time immemorial, it was asserted, the Papacy had despised the Slav people and this was evident from the efforts of the Vatican and the Catholic Church to "stifle" the life of the Polish people[92] and force Slavs in Romania and eastern Poland "to adhere to the Union."[93]

The Conference concluded with a resounding condemnation of the Catholic Church. It resolved that the Roman Catholic clergy was "under secular influence," and that the deposit of faith left by Christ had been misconstrued in the Catholic Church because of the Roman emphasis and belief in "filioque and Immaculate Conception, but, above all, because of papal authority and papal infallibility, a doctrine which is totally anti-Christian."[94] By "introducing this anti-Christian doctrine, the Roman Church has erected an enormous block to the unity of the universal Church of Christ and, in general, to the work of saving men on earth."[95] The Orthodox Churchmen condemned the Papacy and Catholicism because "these dogmas are purely human invention, not founded in Holy Scripture, not in Holy Traditions, nor in patristic literature, nor likewise in Church history."[96] It was further resolved that "the Living Church of God has been transformed by the Popes into a temporal and political organization."[94] Over the years and "up to our day the Papacy by bloody war and all sorts of violence has attempted to convert the Orthodox to Catholicism."[98] Today, the resolution continued, "the Vatican's activity is directed against the interests of the workers" because it "is the center of international intrigue against the interests of peoples, above all of the Slavs."[99] The Vatican is "a center of international fascism" and it "was one of the kindlers of two imperialist wars and at present takes an active part in kindling a new war and, in general, in the political struggle against world democracy."[100] The Orthodox Conference concluded its sessions by deeply regretting "to hear that the Vatican, the fortress of Catholicism, is promoting a new war and is praising the atomic bomb and similar devices for the destruction of human life."[101]

Catholic authorities, naturally, denied the allegations against the Vatican made at the 500th anniversary celebration of the Russian Orthodox Church.[102] But this did not deter a continuation of assaults by the Moscow Patriarchate. Following the Orthodox Congress, the *Zhurnal Moskovskoi Patriarkhii,* in an article entitled "Christianity's Mission For Contemporary Peace," identified the Russian Orthodox Church with the great moral drive for peace and accused the Catholic Church of promoting war and with meddling in non-spiritual affairs.[103] In late 1949, the Moscow Patriarchate again charged that the Papacy was always striving for world domination. For that purpose the Patriarchate alleged Pope Pius XII actively supported Mussolini and the Italian fascist war machine in their conquest of Abyssinia. In Germany, according to the Patriarchate, the Pope supported Hitler and the Nazis and blessed the conquests and attempted conquests of both Hitler and Mussolini. When these two fascist leaders fell from power, the charge continued, the Papacy came to depend on the United States as its major ally for world domination. Cardinal Spellman, the journal asserted, was the key figure and go-between in Vatican-Washington relations. Today, the article finally concluded, the Vatican and the United States were striving together to bring on a third world war in order to crush the new, progressive forces in Eastern Europe.[104]

In another article entitled "The Departure of the Vatican from the Foundation of Christianity," the Patriarchate charged that the Papacy had departed from the principles of Christianity through its opposition to socialism and its alleged support of the rich against the poor.[105] In 1950 *Zhurnal Moskovskoi Patriarkhii* castigated the Vatican for its opposition to progressive movements as evidenced by the Papacy's denunciation of liberalism and progress in the *Syllabus of Errors*.[106] The *Zhurnal* also accused the Papacy of siding with the oppressors of the landless peasants in southern Italy, backing the fascist groups in South Korea, Greece, and Spain, and supporting the colonial powers who continued to exploit the peoples of Indonesia, Indochina, and Malaya.[107]

The Patriarchal crusade against the Catholic Church was quite useful to the Soviet government since it appeared to be predicated upon religion and not politics.[108] But, of course, Orthodoxy's criticisms, as well as the antireligious literature and broadcasts and attacks upon the Vatican's representative in Moscow and Latin Catholics in the Soviet Union, were steeped in politics. By 1948 they were paralleled by a Soviet-sponsored persecution of the Catholic Church in Eastern Europe.

The Communists' synergetic efforts in the Catholic countries of East Europe came to an abrupt halt in 1948. They were superseded by a tightening pressure, in some cases violence, against the Church. The coaction had been foreshadowed and implicit in the Soviet regimes' attitude since 1945, but it was only in 1948 that a satellite-wide system was implemented to yoke the Catholic Church.

The motives for the Communist change-of-heart were certainly linked to the escalating nature of the Cold War. The Soviet position in Eastern Europe, from Moscow's perspective, was, by 1948, threatened and the Kremlin responded with a massive campaign to quickly consolidate its control. Communist relations with the West, mainly the United States, had been deteriorating since 1945 and pressure proportionate to the decline had been building to end the real and feigned independence of political parties and institutions in the East European satellites.

Since Yalta American-Soviet ties had degenerated over the status of Poland and eventually the other Soviet-occupied countries of East Europe. In 1945-46 the initial Soviet decision to remain in northern Iran further colored relations. The irritation precipitated by the break down of war reparations and American loans to the USSR added to the collapse of the wartime alliance. Soviet pressure, beginning in 1946, on Greece and Turkey reinforced the polarization.

Behind the growing repugnance between Russia and America and the Soviet thrusts into the Near East and the Mediterranean, there was of course the rivalry resulting from the inevitable jockeying for position and boon following the defeat of a common enemy. Added to that were the problems of American naivete and idealism, genuine semantical confusion over the already agreed upon provisions of Teheran, Yalta, and Potsdam, American monopoly of the atomic bomb, Russia's desire to assume, along with the United States, big-power status with the rights and privileges implied in that role, and Soviet willingness to resort to *realpolitik*. The major factor, however, which would have frayed American-Russian ties even if all other problems had been non-existent was Stalin's desire to reestablish his totalitarian system in the Soviet Union and eventually stretch it to Eastern Europe. His country was in economic ruin at the end of the war. But what was even more disturbing to the dictator was that millions of Soviet citizens had been under foreign control for three years or more and many had openly collaborated with and/or sympathized with the enemy. Many of these did so not because they were pro-Nazi but simply because they were anti-Stalin. A continuation of close ties with the United States might have brought economic aid to the USSR's beleagured economy but it would have also resulted in American awareness of Soviet weakness and frustrated completely the ability of Moscow to re-impose authoritarianism. Isolation from the West, on the other hand, with concomitantly measured hostility, held out the advantages of keeping the West ignorant of the USSR's political and economic impairments and the Soviet population in a mood to forego the wartime, promised "good life" and to accept the re-imposition of Stalinism. Soviet expansionist attempts, which led to hostile American reactions, not only provided proof to the Soviet people that the Anglo-Americans were threatening the Soviet Union and, thus, the need for the country to re-build and re-militarize as quickly as possible—most of the budget was therefore earmarked for heavy industry and military works, including the development of an atomic bomb—but indeed they might result in, if the Americans failed to respond, the enlargement of the Soviet empire.

In 1947 the United States made two moves which were viewed with considerable apprehension in Moscow. In March, 1947, the Americans, through the Truman Doctrine, provided military and economic aid to the Soviet-pressured governments of Turkey and Greece. This was significant for the Russians because it demonstrated that the Americans were beginning to take direct and formidable measures to block Soviet expansion. Two months later, Washington announced the Marshall Plan and, from the Soviet point of view, this was extremely dangerous and marked a major escalation of the Cold War. The Americans, from the Soviet vantage, were hatching an elaborate, multi-staged plan to "roll back" Soviet control of Eastern Europe.[1] The scenario, according to the Russians, had the United States first rebuilding the war-torn countries of Western Europe economically. This included a simultaneous effort to unify the western zones of occupied Germany. Secondly, the Americans planned to arm the West Europeans and then send them against Soviet East Europe. The Americans would, in turn, prevent Soviet intervention in the resulting wars by rattling and, if necessary, using their atomic weapons.

To the Kremlin, the American efforts brizzled with ominous implications. But, in 1947, the "roll back" scheme remained in the stage of an idea and not a reality. 1948, however, witnessed the unfolding of three events which moved "roll back" closer to reality and, in turn, demanded that Moscow consolidate its position in Eastern Europe as quickly as possible. The West began to seriously talk of unifying West Germany. That, from the Soviet perspective, was the essential first step if "roll back" was to materialize.[2] Secondly, in May, 1948, the Italian Communist Party lost an election it was supposed to win.[3] The Catholic Church and the United States worked closely together to defeat Togliatti's party.[4] This development had many dire implications. Not only might it encourage the Americans to take on Communism in Eastern Europe and elsewhere but the close collaboration between Rome and Washington revealed that the United States might have a powerful fifth column in Soviet-controlled East Europe, especially in Poland, Hungary, and Czechoslovakia.[5] The Church, from the Soviet point of view, had to be quickly corraled. Finally, the Tito-Stalin split in the spring of 1948 revealed for the entire world that the Soviet empire was not a unified monolith.[6] It might spur the Americans to develop and exploit further fissions and, above all, it was a bad example for other satellite rulers. The Soviets, accordingly, felt they had no choice but to rapidly "sovietize" and "Stalinize" East Europe.

While the Cold War, with its various implications, provides the background to the Communist incubus against the Church, there are other elements, some of which are dimensions of the complexities involved in the Cold War, but which for the sake of grasping the total picture of Church-Communist relations in the postwar years need to be highlighted. Stalin's personal antipathy to independent institutions and personalities certainly plays a role in the anti-Catholic onset in East Europe. The *Zhdanovshchina,* the purge of western influences in the Soviet Union and a factor in the Soviets' attack upon Catholicism within the USSR's borders, probably stretched to include forays against the Church in East Europe. Russian nationalism and Orthodox animosity for the Vatican undoubtedly corroborated the anti-Catholic campaign in the satellites. The Orthodox-Kremlin cooperation against the Uniates could have fired the expansionistic imagination of both Patriarchical and Soviet leaders. Finally, the Catholic Church in Eastern Europe and the Vatican were criticizing the Communists and showing no gratitude for the three years of relative toleration. The Communists could have concluded, in the best tradition of Pavlov, that the time was ripe to try the antipode of toleration in order to mold the Church in Eastern Europe into a manipulable institution.

In Poland, the ominousness apparent in the government's disposition toward the Church by early 1948 crystallized into a series of persecutory actions that stretched from the summer of 1948 to 1956. The campaign was multi-dimensional and encompassed increased attacks upon the Vatican and upon the loyalty of the Polish clergy, the arrest of clergy, attempts to secularize the schools and social norms, the confiscation of Church property, and, finally, efforts to split the clergy and the hierarchy.

In July 1948, the authorities organized the *Zwiajek Mlodziezy Polskiej* (Union of Polish Youth), modeled after the Soviet *Komsomol,* and obliged all young people to join.[7] Even though President Bierut attempted to allay Catholic fears with guarantees that the government did not intend to exclude influences other than its own on the youth, the Church leaders interpreted the state's aim as an effort to replace religion with Marxism in the schools and in Polish cultural life.[8] Simultaneously prayers in the schools were abolished and the time allotted for religious instruction was reduced in the lower grades and completely suppressed in some of the higher grades.[9] Priests and nuns, who held teaching positions in the public schools, were fired at an increasing rate beginning in the summer of 1948.[10] The excuses offered for such expulsions eventually included the alleged "demand" of parents and clerical refusal to participate in government sponsored programs, such as the Stockholm Peace Appeal.[11] In the late summer of 1948 a campaign was organized to remove crucifixes from classrooms and to suppress religious associations and to date Party demonstrations and work days to coincide with religious feast days.[12]

The summer of 1948 also witnessed the internment of priests, nuns, and monks. By the beginning of 1950, according to some sources, hundreds of clerics were in prison.[13] The excuses for the imprisonment ranged from such charges as collaboration with the Germans, cooperation with the underground, and sabotage to attempts to overthrow the government.[14]

The Vatican also was singled out for increased attacks during the summer of 1948. Repeatedly the Polish press and radio "recalled" that Cardinal Pacelli, as Papal Nuncio in Berlin, had always supported the "Germanization" of Poland and that, during the war, as Pope Pius XII, he backed the fascists.[15] The unwillingness of the Vatican to name permanent bishops for the Oder-Neisse territory was continuously offered as proof of the Church's pro-Germanism.[16] The Church denied these allegations and declared its hope that harmony might be achieved with the Polish government.[17] In late July the Vatican, reacting to the accelerated persecution, publicly accused the Polish government of initiating "a violent campaign against the Pope," intensifying "antireligious propaganda," and of attacking and threatening "the still remaining Catholic organizations."[18] By August the Vatican vehemently complained of the increased arrest of clergy and prominent Catholics.[19]

In September of 1948 the Roman Catholic bishops of Poland in the

"Manifesto of Wroclaw" protested the Polish government's actions and hostility toward the Catholic Church.[20] The government, wishing to assuage the worries of the hierarchy, quickly replied that compulsory religious instruction would continue in Polish schools.[21] But even while this public assurance was made, the government continued to remove priests from the classroom, to restrict religious instruction, and to take down crucifixes from school walls.[22] Before September was out, two prominent Catholic publications were suspended and the slander campaign against the Vatican magnified.[23] Throughout October arrests of priests continued.[24] On October 2, 1948, Cardinal Hlond, the Primate, died and was succeeded by Stefan Wyszynski. The government might have hoped that the transition, particularly in view of the fact that Cardinal Hlond was an implacable anti-Communist and Bishop Wyszynski was known to favor adopting the Church to modern life, would lead the Church to be more accommodating to its policies and aims,[25] or, on the other hand, would be more vulnerable to government pressure. At any rate, the Communists decided that the most suitable means to elicit a pro-government stand from the Church was intensification of its persecution.

In early November Premier Cyrankiewicz, the leader of the Communist government, endorsed a resolution of Communist educators which condemned the "liberal attitude" heretofore observed with regard to the Catholic Church.[26] The Vatican responded by denouncing the Polish government's arrests of priests and "attacks against Catholicism."[27] The Minister of Education answered the Vatican's complaints by implying that Poland would soon institute a new education program to inform the Catholic youth of Poland about the truth of Marxist philosophy.[28] In December, 1948, at the congress which united the Communist and Socialist parties into the United Workers' Party, the regime repudiated its earlier promise to include in the constitution the Church's rights and privileges and adopted the principle of separation of Church and State as its official position.[29] At the same meeting, the Vatican and the Catholic hierarchy were condemned for not supporting the government and its reforms.[30] The Papacy was particularly castigated for refusing to establish Polish episcopates in the "recovered territories."[31] The Catholic clergy was accused of backing criminal bands.[32]

The Church responded to the government's new educational platform by asserting that, while separation was not ideal in Poland, it could accept the principle if the government in fact did not interfere with the Church's schools, publications, properties, and welfare activities. The Church's reaction was a decided change from its immediate postwar attitude where it considered separation of Church and State totally unacceptable.[33] The

Vatican, meanwhile, rejected the various anti-Catholic charges made at the government's unifcation meeting in December and charged that the authorities were attempting to undermine religious education in Poland.[34]

In January, 1949, Premier Cyrankiewicz warned the Catholic clergy not to interfere in state affairs and cautioned them against exploiting the people's religious devotion for anti-government resistance.[35] The Vatican promptly announced that a hundred priests had been arrested since October of 1949 and imprisoned on the charge of "spreading an atmosphere of discontent."[36]

In early February Cardinal Sapieha, Bishop of Cracow, wrote President Bierut to urge that a joint Church-Government commission be established to settle apparent differences.[37] The secretary of the Roman Catholic Episcopal Council, Mgr. Sigismond Choromanski, put substance behind Cardinal Sapieha's request by shortly visiting Wladyslaw Wolski, the Minister of Public Administration, and informing him that the Church was willing to cooperate with the state, but that it would fight to preserve its status.[38] In the meantime, the Catholic bishop of Katowice, Mgr. Stanislas Adamski, publicly condemned the government's antireligious activities in a pastoral letter.[39] The government immediately responded to Adamski's accusation by denying that it was engaged in antireligious campaigns. The regime claimed it was simply prosecuting criminals and responding to the Vatican's anti-Polish attitude.[40] Ten days later two priests were charged with blessing a group of underground terrorists and three other priests, according to the Polish government, pleaded guilty to charges of cooperating with an illegal organization.[41] Another priest was charged with misusing the funds of a peasants' organization.[42] In late February the Vatican, taking the pulse beat of the religious situation in Poland, announced that the position of the Church was deteriorating "from week to week."[43]

On March 20, the Government formally answered Cardinal Sapieha and Mgr. Choromanski by presenting to the Monsignor an official eight-point statement of the government's position on Church-State relations. The tone of the declaration was foreboding for it was mostly preoccupied with assertions that the Vatican and the Polish hierarchy and clergy were treasonable and responsible for the state of unrest in Poland. The document emphasized that the government fully stood behind "freedom of religion" and denied that there was religious persecution in Poland. In brief, the state demanded complete loyalty from the Church and a permanent episcopal administration for the "recovered territories." In return, it pledged to maintain religious education in the schools and to allow the Church to run its internal affairs providing no civil laws were broken and religious freedom was not abused for political goals. The document, in addition, stipulated that a Church-State *modus vivendi* depended entirely on the good behavior of the Church.[44]

At about the same time the Warsaw authorities issued their eight-point declaration, they founded *Towarzystwo Przyiacial Dzieci* (Society of Children's Friends) which was commissioned to set up nurseries, kindergartens, primary and secondary schools, teachers' colleges, and recreation centers and camps for the young. Its purposes were to implement atheism and the tenets of proletarian society into the lowergrade curriculums as well as to promote loyalty to the regime.[45] Simultaneously the revision and redrafting of textbooks was begun and by May of 1949 fifty million revised textbooks, reflecting the philosophy of Marxism-Leninism, had been issued.[46] In late March the government refused Catholic newspapers the right to publish rebuttals of the clergy who were being tried in state courts.[47]

On March 21 the Vatican broadcasted a report that analyzed the regime's current relations with the Catholic Church. The broadcast saw as the basic reason for the increased persecution the Polish government's desire to control or remove the Catholic Church, the only important bulwark remaining against the advance of Communism. The methods being employed by the Communists to effect this end, according to the report, were to remove the clergy from the schools, to exclude religious teaching from the educational curriculum, and to close down completely parish schools.[48] Within a few days the Vatican again complained that priests were being arrested, schools closed, and children exposed to atheism.[49]

Shortly thereafter the government claimed that the Catholic Church in Poland "has full freedom in religious matters" and that the Vatican was Poland's historic enemy. The regime asserted that the annals of the Polish nation reveal that at the time of the people's greatest need, "when the fate of the Nation was at stake, when all that was noble in our Nation joined in the battle for freedom and a better future, the Vatican was not on our side."[50]

On April 10, 1949, the Catholic hierarchy replied to the statement the government had presented to Mgr. Choromanski on March 20. The Catholic bishops implied that the government had not spoken the truth in its official statement and admonished the government that it should "be convinced that it is certainly not by being traitors to God that you will build a better Poland."[51] The episcopate, however, went on to propose the nomination of a mixed commission to examine the serious problem of internal Church-State relations in Poland. As for the Oder-Neisse question, the hierarchy claimed that was beyond its jurisdiction and had to be taken up directly with the Vatican.[52]

The government did not initially respond to this proposal. It was still seething over the remarks Archbishop Wyszynski, the Catholic Primate of

Poland, made in an April sermon in Warsaw. He claimed that "once again we have concentration camps and the jails are packed to overflowing. The bricks and stones of war-damaged churches are being used to build penitentiaries. Many priests are in prison."[53]

The authorities reacted swiftly to the Catholic Primate's accusation by charging that the policy of the leaders of the Catholic clergy was incompatible with the good of the country, religion, and the best interests of the Polish Church.[54] The Polish Army daily, *Polska Zbrojna,* charged that the Catholic hierarchy, though its opposition to the state, was attempting to create an artificial division between believers and non-believers, but that in reality its continued opposition would result in the hierarchy's "complete isolation from the progressive part of the nation."[55]

The Polish episcopate supported Archbishop Wyszynski's remarks and charged that the government had closed many Catholic schools, discriminated against and arrested many priests, coerced the youth to join organizations hostile to the Church, removed crucifixes from the classroom, and stringently censored Catholic publications.[56]

In mid-April the Vatican again closely examined the religious situation in Poland and concluded that the increasing number of imprisoned priests and the unusual harshness of court sentences indicated that the Warsaw regime intended "to deprive the country of the clergy."[57] In a discerning diagnosis a few days later, the Vatican declared that Moscow was behind the "campaign of hate against the Vatican and the Polish clergy."[58] Cardinal Joseph Slipyi, the Uniate Metropolitan imprisoned by the Soviets, supported that contention and opined that the Kremlin was behind the anti-Catholic campaign throughout East Europe.[59] The Polish government, in turn, denounced the Vatican's slanderous remarks and criticism and claimed that the Catholic Church alone was preventing a Church-State accord.[60]

In early June the Communists, after having announced once again that there was complete freedom of religion in Poland, seized and nationalized all Catholic printing works.[61] Simultaneously they arrested one of the principal leaders of the Polish episcopacy, Mgr. S. Kaczynski, on the grounds that he was a "member of an anti-government organization" and took part "in activities harmful to the state."[62]

In July the Vatican summed up the situation in Poland: the teaching of religion in Polish schools had been prohibited, the activities of religious organizations had been hampered, the Catholic religion was attacked and persecuted, the Catholic press was censored, the sick and imprisoned were deprived of religious solace, correspondence between the Holy See and the Polish hierarchy and faithful had been made impossible, and, finally, all religious practices were increasingly difficult to perform.[63] In a radio address to a Catholic congress in Berlin Pius XII openly declared that there was no longer religious freedom in Poland.[64]

It was also in July that the government and the Church finally agreed to begin negotiations to establish a *modus vivendi,* but the atmosphere in which the discussions proceeded did not augur well for a mutually happy resolution of the Church-State problems. The authorities attempted to break the independence and unity of the Church and weaken the Church's hold on the people. The clergy was accused, with acclerated vehemence, of supporting in the past and present imperialists, reactionaries, and fascists and indulging in immorality, bribery, sabotage, and espionage.[65] At the same time, the regime was able to organize a small group of priests, called "priests-patriots," who, without breaking with the bishops, openly disagreed with the hierarchy and demanded that an agreement be concluded on the government's terms.[66] Initially the "priests-patriots" group was comprised of priests who had been chaplains in Polish units of the Red Army or prisoners in Nazi concentration camps.[67] It was later enlarged by the addition of many priests who reputedly had been suspended by the hierarchy because of unpriestly conduct.[67] In September the "priests-patriots" promised their complete backing to the government and the authorities responded by bestowing favors upon the these priests not only in the hope of creating a separatist, loyal church but also to entice other clerics. The group was given financial assistance, allowed to have its own journal, *Glos Kaplana* (The Voice of the Chaplain, later replaced by *Ksiadz Obywatel* (Citizen Priest)), and, eventually, its members were placed in teaching and administrative positions in Catholic seminaries, Catholic University at Lublin, and in the diocese of the Oder-Neisse region.[58] The hierarchy deplored the "priests-patriots" movement from the beginning.[69]

In addition to these blows, the government legislated, during the ten months of negotiations, a number of disabling decrees. On August 4, 1949, the decree on Freedom of Conscience and Religion, supposedly protecting the right of religious and antireligious activity, was declared. It meded out heavy punishments to anyone who infringed on the "rights" of the irreligious individual and, furthermore, who would deny "another access to a rite or religious ceremony because of his activities or his political, social, or scientific views."[70] On September 21, 1949, Catholic hospitals were nationalized under the Ministry of Health.[71] Schools operated by the religious orders were also nationalized.[72] On January 23, 1950, the Church's social and charitable organization, *Caritas,* was placed under a government controlled trusteeship council on the incredible grounds of fraud and mismanagement and, on March 20, Churchlands exceeding two hundred and fifty acres were confiscated. The Church lost about 375,000 acres.[73]

Despite the regime's pulverization, the Church in Poland did not noticeably bend. The hierarchy attempted to meet the government's thrusts at every turn. A stream of pastoral letters encouraged the faithful to remain steadfast in their faith and behind their leaders, to give the young a strong religious foundation, and to eschew the government's atheistic programs. The bishops also complained directly to the government. On Feburary 16, 1950, the episcopate, in a letter to President Bierut, charged that there was no religious freedom in Poland, that a "war against God" was being waged, and that the authorities were essaying to coerce the Church into an agreement. Particular objection was made to Minister Wolski's efforts to convince the lower clergy to sign a separate concordat with the government.[74]

In this charged environment, on April 14, 1950, a nineteen point Agreement was finalized. The government agreed to protect religious worship, to keep religious instruction in the schools, to allow a Catholic press and schools, to permit religious orders and associations and welfare organizations, to grant religious care in the hospitals, prisons, and army, and to recognize the Vatican's spiritual authority. The Church, for its part, pledged to instruct the faithful to respect the government, to support Poland's foreign policy, to request the Papacy for permanent bishops in the "Recovered Territories," to buttress reconstruction, to stop opposing collectivization, and to resist "the exploitation of religious feelings for anti-state activities."[75]

The new agreement did not in the least diminish the Church-State conflict. Each side put its own interpretation on the various provisions and soon the Church, which though it had gained both administrative and spiritual autonomy, found itself confronting increased violence that did not subside until 1956.

The government, however, despite its police powers, was unable to fashion the Polish Catholic Church into an institutional lackey. The Church was much too powerful and, if anything, the Communist efforts consolidated the people behind the Church and increasing set the government off as both anti-Polish and a servant of the Soviets. By 1949 this was already apparent and the Vatican which was closely following the Polish anti-Church onset, as well as the Communist attacks elsewhere in Eastern Europe, published in July, 1949, a major Papal decree which was not only a retaliation but undoubtedly an attempt to drive a wedge between Catholic nationalists and the Eastern European Communists.

The small Uniate enclave in Poland, alluded to earlier, also faced persecution. The oldest Ukrainian diocese, that of Peremyshl' was liquidated by the Polish government, acting apparently at the behest of the Soviets, when it arrested Bishops Iosafat Kotsylov'kyi and Hryhorii Lakota. In June 1946, they together with their senior priests were extradited to the Soviet Union. In the autumn of 1947 Bishop Kotsylov'kyi expired in prison and in June, 1951, Bishop Lokata died in a Vorkuta concentration camp.[76] A number of Uniate priests resettled in Poland and they with the small Ukrainian Uniate minority have managed, with the support of some of the Polish clergy and, since 1956, the liberalization of the government's minority policy, to maintain forty-one parishes and a monastery in Warsaw.[77]

In Hungary, Stalin's requital against the Vatican revolved mainly about
one man, the Catholic Primate, Cardinal Joszef Mindszenty. The Catholic
Primate traditionally was one of the most important individuals in the life of
the Hungary people. Hungary was sixty-seven percent Catholic but because
of the honorary position and privileges bestowed upon the Catholic Primate
by the Hungarian State until the Communist take-over, the influence of the
Primate, in this case, Cardinal Mindszenty, touched not only the Catholic
but most Hungarians.[1] Mindszenty was an influential man and he became the
reality and the symbol of not only the Catholic Church's resistance but of
the Hungarian people's opposition and repugnance to Stalinism.[2]

Before April, 1948, there had existed between the Communist Government of Hungary and the Catholic Church a mutual distrust and hostility
that was interrupted periodically by denunciations. There was not, however, a unified campaign by the Government to curtail the influence of the
church of the Catholic Primate over Hungary's 9,316,000 citizens.

In late April, however, there was a noticeable shift in the Government's
policy. It began to accuse the Catholic Church of persecuting teachers in
Catholic schools and of displaying an anti-State attitude.[3] These accusations
were the beginning trickles of a deluge that soon would pound against the
institutionalized structure of the Church and shake that body to its very
foundation. In April the Government announced that it felt nationalization
of Catholic schools would be a correct and worthwhile action. The regime
began to work out a plan for that end and a few so-called "Peace Priests,"
who argued for accommodation with the authorities, supported the action.[4]
Cardinal Mindszenty promptly threatened to excommunicate any Catholics
who backed the scheme to nationalize Church schools and prohibited
Catholic teachers from participating in conferences on the subject organized by the Government.[5] The Vatican directly supported him and declared
that "education is the task of the Church. . . . Only force can prevent the
Church from fulfilling its educational mission."[6] The Vatican somewhat
bitterly added that the slogan "Free Church, Free State" is a catch-word to

conceal the "confiscation of the rights and property of the Church. When everything has been taken from the Church, they say 'Now, you are free.'"[7]

Mindszenty pursued his threat by issuing a pastoral letter in which he condemned the Government's nationalization proposal on the grounds that it interfered with parents' rights to educate their children.[8] He said the Church would not abide by "tyrannical laws."[9] Once again Pope Pius XII supported him and called upon the Catholics of Hungary to thwart "the Government's anti-Church policy."[10] The Vatican announced that the Hungarian Church was experiencing much persecution.[11]

The Government, in turn, accused Mindszenty of trying to cause a "flare-up," but added that the Cardinal's pastoral letter was an exercise in futility since the vast majority of Catholic teachers and clergy supported school nationalization.[12] The Government then asked the clergy to make a formal declaration of loyalty to the Government and appointed a formal commission to study the problem of school nationalization.[13] Mindszenty was also approached by the Government on the possibility of entering into negotiations for a *modus vivendi*. Mindszenty replied on May 19 that before any negotiations could begin the Government had to abandon its proposed nationalization.[14] This answer aroused the Communist leaders. Vice Premier Rakosi countered by declaring that the time had come "to purge the educational system of reactionary elements," to stop the intolerable situation where the core of the enemies of the Hungarian people hides behind the church, and first and foremost the Catholic Church."[15]

Cardinal Mindszenty turned to the Catholics of Hungary to support the Church and oppose nationalization.[16] In a pastoral letter on May 29 he denied a number of Government assertions, namely that the Catholic bishops had failed to agree among themselves on nationalization, that local priests had opposed the bishops and refused to read pastoral letters, and that where pastoral letters were read they were interrupted by shouts of protest from the congregations. It was not true, he declared, that teachers had desired the nationalization of schools, that the only step blocking national prosperity was the nationalization of schools, and that the Church and the Government had begun negotiations for a concordat.[17] On that same day Mindszenty addressed a letter to the Minister of Education, Gyula Ortutay. Herein he claimed that Government-sponsored violence against the Church and schools had reached an all-time high. He added that teachers and students at ecclesiastical institutions were continually threatened and discriminated against and that the press had consistently ridiculed and insulted the Church and its ecclesiastical dignitaries. Mindszenty concluded that these were "Kulturkampf tactics" directed towards "moral compulsion and permanent deprivation of religious liberty."[18] One day later Pope

Pius exhorted the Hungarian people to triumph "in spite of violence and intimidation."[19] The Vatican reported that 200 priests were in prison.[20]

In early June Cardinal Mindszenty followed up his letter to Ortutay with a denunciation of the Hungarian Government. He called the Government the worst in history and forbade Catholics to read Government publications or to listen to Government broadcasts.[21] The Government responded by nationalizing the Catholic printing works in Budapest, St. Stephen Publishing House, and thus forced Mindszenty to rely on typists to reproduce his pastoral letters. On June 3 the Government arrested 200 Catholics in the eastern village of Pocspetri for demonstrating against school nationalization.[22] The Hungarian Minister of Education blamed Mindszenty's excommunication threats for the disturbance and in an open letter to the Catholic Primate he wrote:

> It is now clear that agitation against Hungarian democracy and the Hungarian Republic is going on in Church circles in connection with the democratic school reform. By means of reactionary fascist catchwords the clergy are trying to rouse their flock against Hungarian democracy. The events in this village are the first serious warning to the Catholic Church.[23]

On the same day that Ortutay penned his letter to Mindszenty, a Government weekly, *Uj Magyarorszag*, denied that the Hungarian State was persecuting the Catholic Church.[24]

On June 12 Mindszenty reiterated his previous warning that anyone contributing to laws which would infringe on the rights of the Church would be excommunicated.[25] It was obvious to the Government by this time that Mindszenty was the backbone of the Church's resistance in Hungary, and so, it was determined to meet him head-on and drive him into submission.[26] On June 12 the Cabinet received the bill for the nationalization of schools.[27] This was done amidst protests by some Catholics, but on June 13 Vice-Premier Rakosi revealed to Catholics and Mindszenty that henceforth a hard-line was to be taken against the Catholic Church.[28] The Vice-Premier warned that "anyone who opposes the country will be smashed by the fist of democracy."[29]

Cardinal Mindszenty responded to the Government's hard-line by ordering special masses held and Church bells tolled on June 18 in protest against the Government's planned nationalization of schools.[30] On June 16 the Hungarian Parliament ratified the bill nationalizing confessional and private schools and hostels and kindergartens related to them.[64] According to the provisions of the bill all teachers would be state employees as of July 1, 1948. The state would be responsible for supervision of the schools and for the preparation of new textbooks; seminaries were not to be included, and religious instruction was to continue and remain in the hands of the clergy.[65] On July 1 the Government defended its action by comparing the new Church-State relationship in Hungary to the Church-State relationship in the United States.[66]

The Government now offered to work out an agreement with Mindszenty but he demanded that before an agreement could be reached the law nationalizing schools would have to be voided.[64] Then the Cardinal excommunicated all the Catholic Deputies in the Parliament who had supported the nationalization program.[35] Following a Government warning to refrain from his campaign Mindszenty next excommunicated all Roman Catholics who supported the nationalization program.[36] He pursued this tact by instructing Catholics to stop teaching in Government schools, and advising clerical instructors to leave Hungary unless their presence was absolutely necessary.[37] He exhorted Catholic parents to give religious instruction at home.[38] The Government struck back by arresting a number of Catholic priests, including Rev. Edmund Lenard, the Secretary of Catholic Action. The Priests were accused of complicity in an alleged Vatican-United States plot against the Government.[39] The Secretary of the Hungarian Women of Catholic Action, Mercedes Sprenger, was also arrested without a reason being given.[40] The Communist press now accused the Catholic Church of using its clergy as agents to distribute funds to support anti-Government activities and to incite peasants against the Government.[41]

As charges followed countercharges, the Government responded by increasing its campaign.[42] In early June three more priests were arrested, including the director of Catholic Action, Zsigmond Mihalovitch, for "agitating against Hungarian democracy."[43] The Government also jammed the Vatican Radio, prohibited all contact between the Hungarian hierarchy and the Papacy, and ended all Hungarian religious broadcasts.[44] Amidst an increase in clerical arrests, the Hungarian episcopate formally announced its rejection of the Government's nationalization program.[45]

On August 1 Cardinal Mindszenty requested that Catholic families receive into their homes and occupations the 4,500 Catholic teachers whom he expected to give up teaching.[46] The Government had already ousted 600 teachers for their opposition to nationalization.[47] Throughout August and September the Government passed laws forbidding all processions and pilgrimages and banned loudspeakers for Church use.[48] In late September the Vatican declared that the government of Hungary continued "to obstruct all Church activity," but, the Vatican announced triumphantly that "out of over 3,000 priests and religious of both sexes, only five have agreed to continue teaching in nationalized schools."[49]

In early October the government identified Mindszenty as the leader of the forces of reaction and claimed that religious manifestations had become the occasion of political demonstrations.[50] The Vatican defended the Primate, by asserting that "if a high Church dignitary defends the Catholic religion and education, that cannot be considered political activity."[51] Later the Vatican sarcastically added that Cardinal Mindszenty's defense of the Catholic Church and of Catholic education was certainly "an anti-democratic act."[52]

The Communist leaders of Hungary, however, showed no appreciation for the Vatican's derisive remarks. Once again the Government accused Mindszenty of being the leader of Hungarian reaction and of meddling in political affairs.[53] An organized campaign now began to remove Mindszenty from office. The Communist press and Government clamored and demanded in the name of liberty that the "reactionary" Primate be removed.[54] A new word was coined, "Mindszentyism," which was defined as "black reaction and ecclesiastical intrigue allied with capitalism against the State."[55] Priests and nuns who supported Mindszenty were arrested in mass. According to the Vatican more than 600 of them were imprisoned by the beginning of November.[56]

Mindszenty and the bishops of Hungary reacted sharply to the Government's intensified onslaught. The episcopate denounced the attacks upon the Cardinal and expressed its complete support for the Catholic leader.[57] Mindszenty, for his part, penned a scathing denunciation of the Government in what proved to be his last pastoral letter. On November 18 he wrote that in recent weeks he had been accused of counter-revolution and of reactionary activities. He claimed that these accusations were untrue and that the Government manufactured them. The reason, according to the Cardinal, was that the Government could not tolerate any opinion that differed from its own. Dejectedly he wrote: "The country is condemned to silence and public opinion has been made a mere frivolous jest. If a man dares to raise his voice in contradiction," he is imprisoned "because of his criticism of democracy."[58]

The Vice-Premier, Matyas Rakosi, ominously responded to the Cardinal's pastoral letter on November 27:

Now there can no longer be any political tolerance. This tolerant policy, which used kid gloves for dealing with spies, traitors, smugglers, adherents of the royal Hapsburgs and other reactionaries moving about in the gowns of priests or those of a cardinal, is over and done with forever. The law must be applied, not only to small clerical criminals. We cannot allow such organized shock troops of Fascism as clerical reaction to disturb any longer our reconstruction and stabilization.[59]

On November 16 the libraries, art treasurers, and furnishings belonging to the Chruch were nationalized.[60] On November 19 the Cardinal's secretary, Father Andrew Zakar, was arrested and on November 23, Fathers Imre Boka and Janos Fabian, members of Mindszenty's staff, were also seized.[61] Budapest Radio announced that the Government would soon abandon its restraint against reactionary clergy. Cardinal Mindszenty, the Radio claimed was the "focal point" and it added that the Government could not allow raging "Mindszentyite" enemies "to mislead, to incite the Hungarian peasants to hoodwink them against their own interests."[62] Throughout December the Government publicly attacked and ridiculed Mindszenty.[63] In mid-December the new Prime Minister, Mr. Dobi, hinted at what was in store for Mindszenty. He declared that there was no possibility of accord with the Catholic Church while Mindszenty remained.[64]

On December 20 the Cardinal, in a letter to the clergy asked for perseverance in the face of persecution.[65] One week later he made a statement that he was later forced to recant:

> Since I have not taken part in any plot I shall never resign. I shall not speak. If after this you hear that I have confessed this or that, or that I have resigned my office (even though this should be authenticated by my signature), you should realize that such a declaration is but the consequence of human frailty. . . . Likewise I declare null and void any confession which may be attributed to me from this day forth. . . .[66]

On that same day he was arrested on charges of high treason, espionage, illegal dealings in foreign exchange, and crimes aimed at the overthrow of the Republic.[67] The Government reported that it possessed evidence of Mindszenty's guilt and proceeded to arrest other Roman Catholic leaders.[62]

The Vatican's first reaction was to protest Mindszenty's arrest and excommunicate any Catholic who was involved with the arrest.[69] Pius XII then issued an opostolic letter to the episcopate of Hungary in which he deeply lamented the great injustices against the Church in Hungary and deplored the arrest of Cardinal Mindszenty.[70] The Vatican next issued its own explanation for the arrest that went to the heart of the Church-State confrontation in Hungary. It claimed that Moscow was behind Mindszenty's arrest and that the Soviets were conducting all-out persecution of the Catholic Church in Eastern Europe.[71] Finally the Vatican held that the charges against the Cardinal were fraudulent and it challenged the Hungarian Government to publish its so-called "evidence."[72] Within a few days the Papacy asked the world to take a firm stand against Hungary because what was at stake was not only Hungary but all of Eastern Europe.[73]

The Government, in turn, castigated the Vatican and the world press supporting Mindszenty for their interference in Hungarian affairs.[84] The Communist authorities declared that they had evidence connecting Mindszenty to a royalist plot to overthrow the Government.[75]

The Vatican, responding to the turn of events in Hungary and to the contemporaneous onset against its position in the rest of Eastern Europe, broadcast in mid-January a thorough diagnosis of exactly what was happening in Stalinist-controlled Eastern Europe. The Vatican declared that Stalin had designated Moscow as "the home of the national Catholic Church which the Communists would like to organize in the countries behind the Iron Curtain." Stalin, according to the Vatican, wanted to cut off Eastern Europe from Rome and thus open "the way for the national Church under the auspices of Moscow."[76]

The Hungarian Government, possibly in defensive response to the hail of criticism emanating from the Vatican and the western press, asserted that there was "complete religious freedom," in Hungary and that the Vatican was responsible for the rupture of Church-State relations.[77] On January 19 the Communist leaders published a *Yellow Book* which contained the "evidence" against Mindszenty and his alleged confession.[78] The Papacy promptly ridiculed the *Yellow Book* claiming that never in the history of democracies had a government published a "yellow book, or blue, or green to explain to the world what applies to itself. But this is done in police regimes, suffering from bad conscience, to justify its violence. . . ."[79] The Government thereupon accused the Pope of wanting to overthrow the Hungarian regime.[80]

On February 3 Mindszenty's trial began.[81] After publicly retracting his pre-trial letter discrediting any future confession he might make, Mindszenty was found guilty of treason, illicit trading in currency, espionage, and leading an organization aimed at overthrowing the Government.[82] The Cardinal was sentenced to life imprisonment.[83] The Vatican, of course, denounced the trial as a sham and the punishment as a miscarriage of justice.[84] It directed the Hungarian people to remain steadfast in the face of such adversity.[85]

With the removal of Cardinal Mindszenty, the resistance of the Church in Hungary was substantially weakened. Religious instruction in schools became optional on September 3, 1949, and complicated regulations and extensive pressure on parents reduced the number of children receiving religious teaching in school to only 11% by 1952. The Government also moved quickly to close down Catholic schools and seminaries and to "re-educate" teachers. An accord was forced on the Hungarian bishops on

August 29, 1950, by which they agreed to the new political and educational changes. Eight gymnasiums were returned to the Church, and, since then, the administration of these schools is the only legal function of the Catholic orders in Hugnary.[86] In May, 1951, a State Office for Church Affairs was established to oversee ecclesiastical affairs and to supervise and coordinate the actions of the Hungarian bishops.[87] In June, 1951, Archbishop Jozsef Grosz, Mindszenty's replacement, was arrested.[88]

Although the Catholic religion in Hungary remained, as it did in Poland, Lithuania, and Czechoslovakia, an inscrutable and unmalleable problem, Stalin, nonetheless, by 1949, had deeply grooved its institutionalized framework. In January, 1949, Jean Thomas, in Moscow, noted and lamented that reality.[89] In early July, when the Hungarian Supreme Court upheld Mindszenty's conviction, the Vatican was ready to retort and it warned, following the failure of Mindszenty's final appeal, that "the last word has not yet been said."[90]

CHAPTER XI
CHURCH-STATE IN CZECHOSLOVAKIA, 1948-1949

In Czechoslovakia, as in Hungary, the Government, after April of 1948, initiated a campaign to weaken the influence and independence of the Catholic Church. There were 10,000,000 Catholics in the country out of a total population of 12,000,000 but, still, the Stalinist Government logically did not anticipate an extremely difficult reaction in weakening the Church because of the prevalent anti-clerical and anti-western feeling of the Czechoslovakians.

In early May the Government expelled some forty Catholic nuns on the grounds that they were "provocative elements."[1] Simultaneously three Catholic weeklies, the *Nedele (Sunday)*, the *Bozsevan (The Sower)*, and the *Katolik (Catholic)*, each with a circulation of about 150,000, were banned.[2] On May 23 Radio Prague, in a rather ominous broadcast, declared that "the leaders of the Czechoslovakian People's Party believe that it is the duty of every Christian or Catholic to do all in his power to preserve peace."[3]

On June 3 the Vatican reported that Mgr. Beran, the Archbishop of Prague and recognized leader of the Catholic Church in Czechoslovakia, was forbidden to print letters or circulars without prior authorization and that his duplicating machine was sequestered.[4] On June 11 the Government announced that all primary and secondary schools were to be nationalized.[5] Premier Gottwald, the leader of the Communist Government, told Beran, however, that the Catholic schools were to be excluded from nationalization providing the Archbishop honored the new Communist regime with a *Te Deum* in the St. Vitus Cathedral in Prague.[6] The Archbishop assented, but on September 30 all schools, including the Catholic institutions, were placed under State administration.[7] It was obvious Gottwald had simply used Beran and that he had not intended the least concession.

In July the Czech Government issued instructions to local Communist groups ordering them to undermine the dignity of the Vatican and the people's confidence in it, to create divisions between the bishops and the clergy and between the clergy and the people, to allow the General Secretariat alone to negotiate with the Catholic hierarchy, to create rival

Church groups to perform actions which the Church opposed, to support the National Czechoslovak Church as the rival and alternative to the Roman Catholic Church, and to stress collaboration between Czech Church groups and the Russian Orthodox Church. The Party was to discredit the Catholic Church by the following arguments: the unreasonableness of celibacy, the economic power and wealth of the Church, the connection between the Catholic Church and capitalism, the immortality of priests, homosexual trials, etc.[8] On July 8, Premier Zapotocky[9] announced that the Roman Catholic Church must not allow Church services to be "the occasion for abusing our democratic People's Republic and for appeals to refuse the carrying out of civic duties."[10]

In mid-July the Vatican discerned that in Czechoslovakia there were "quiet, steady efforts to eliminate the influence of the Church, to restrict its field of activities. . . ."[11] On July 29 the Vatican became more specific and accused the Government of closing Catholic schools.[12]

In August Archbishop Beran and his fellow bishops responded to the growing anti-Church campaign in a pastoral letter. The bishops claimed that the Government was antagonistic toward the Church, that it was breaking promises to reach an agreement on religious questions, and that it was restricting religious publications, religious meetings, charitable works and institutions.[13] The Vatican denied Government accusations that the Catholic Church "had never condemned fascists as war instigators, [that] the Pope was defending the 12 million evicted Germans," and that the Vatican had adopted "a hostile attitude toward the Soviet Union and the people's democratic countries, including Czechoslovakia."[14] It supported the allegations of Beran and his fellow bishops.[15]

On September 13 Archbishop Beran was expelled from the Union of Anti-Nazi Resistance Fighters for suspending Father Plojhar from the priesthood.[16] Father Plojhar was the Minister of Public Health and the personal secretary of President Gottwald.[17] In late September the Czech Defense Minister warned that "if the members of the clergy impede the work of the Government . . . the defense of the Republic will not halt before their altar."[18] In early October the Government made civil marriage compulsory and prohibited the "reading from the pulpit of Papal encyclicals and pastoral letters if these contained anything concerning the 'People's Democracy.' "[19]

The Government increased its prohibitions against the Catholic press and finally in November nearly all Catholic publications were suppressed by a decree from the Ministry for Information.[20] The Pope promptly condemned the Government's action.[21] The Communist press reacted by claiming that the Vatican, its cardinals and archbishops, had now become the spokesmen of fascism in Central Europe.[22] Prague Radio again accused the Vatican of a hostile attitude toward the Czech people and state. It claimed that the Catholic clergy were hostile toward the Government and that they were the "leaders of reaction."[23] Throughout November and December laws were passed which had the cumulative effect of outlawing all organizations formed on a religious basis.[24] This accomplished the suppression of all Catholic Action associations.[25] Simultaneously various Catholic charitable organizations, notably *Caritas,* and Catholic hospitals were transformed into Government institutions.[26] On top of this, all ecclesiastical real estate was nationalized during the final months of 1948.[27] This left the Church impoverished and economically dependent upon the State.[28] The Vatican maintained that the Communist attacks against the Catholic Church had become more intense.[29] The Government simply retorted that the Vatican was meddling in East European affairs.[30]

In late December Dr. Nejedly, Minister of Education, stated that the origin of anti-state actions could be traced invariably to a monastery, church, or priest. These acts, he added, were most likely coordinated by the Czech hierarchy and the Vatican. Soon, he concluded, Catholics would be forced to choose whether they wished to be good citizens or whether they wished to condone treacherous acts against the Republic.[31]

As the new year came in, the communist campaign against the Catholic Church moved into high gear. Another set of directives was given to local Communist groups. Now they were to confiscate the lands of parochial benefices, to prohibit all pilgrimages and religious functions outside the Church, to forbid the printing of ecclesiastical publications, to dissolve all remaining religious associations, to search the houses of persons suspected of helping priests with food and clothing, and to help priests willing to collaborate.[32] The objectives of these directives were fourfold:

1. To separate the bishops and the priests by the suppression of the *Acta Curiae;* to weaken the religious spirit of the priests by the prohibition of all meetings, retreats, clerical congresses, etc.
2. To separate the priests from the laity who might help them.
3. To limit religious activity to the inside of the Church buildings and to control it even there.
4. To liquidate whatever remained of Church property and thus to deprive the clergy of all economic independence.[33]

Almost concomitantly with the issuance of new directives, plans for establishing an independent Czechoslovakian Catholic Church were rumored.[34] The Roman Catholic hierarchy quickly warned against any such attempt.[35] Archbishop Beran and the Council of Catholic Bishops followed this warning with a number of accusations toward the end of January. The bishops charged that the Government had interfered in the duties of Church officials, that clerics who refused to join in political demonstrations had been branded as suspect, that the Government had restricted without adequate cause Catholic schools, institutions, organizations, press, and meetings, that Church property had been confiscated without compensation, that the Vatican had been attacked, and that the Government had been attempting to split the Catholic hierarchy from the people.[36] The Vatican itself claimed that the Czech Government was vilifying it and the Czech episcopate as being anti-Czech and pro-Nazi.[37]

In early February the Communist press reported that the people were demanding that the Government take remedial action against priests accused of anti-Government activities.[38] Radio Prague claimed that only the Catholic Church had refused to support the Government.[39] In mid-March the Government press announced that the leaders of the Roman Catholic Church had slandered the national hero and Protestant reformer, John Hus.[40]

In April Archbishop Beran reported that all the Catholic schools in Moravia and Slovakia already had been closed and that the liquidation of those in Bohemia was almost complete.[41] On April 29 the Catholic bishops, well aware of the Government's direction, circulated a letter among the Czech clergy. They declared that "today we have a further and undeniable proof that the Government has launched an all-out campaign against the Church, using all the means at its disposal. . . ."[42] The letter went on to outline the actions of the Government against the Church in the past months.[43]

On May 11 the Government began issuing its own "Catholic" newspaper called *The Bulletin of the Catholic Clergy*.[44] Archbishop Beran promptly forbade Catholics to read *The Bulletin* and the Government, in turn, claimed that the directives of the Catholic episcopate and all other ecclesiastical instructions were not valid or binding upon the clergy and the faithful unless and until they were printed in *The Bulletin*.[45] The official diocesan bulletin, *Acta Curiae*, which usually carried these various episcopal instructions, was banned in April.[46] In late May and early June the Government also began publishing a number of "Catholic" newspapers to replace the restricted Catholic press.[47]

In late May Archbishop Beran, knowing that the Government was working to set up a "Catholic Action Committee" of apostate priests to act as an organizational group for a schismatic Catholic Church, publicly condemned the Government for its attempts to form a separate National

Catholic Church.[48] Beran threatened excommunication for any Catholic aiding the Government in such an endeavor.[49] *Il Quotidiano,* commenting on developments in Czechoslovakia, declared that the Czech Government left the Catholic Church "only a single freedom, the freedom to choose the manner of its death."[50]

In early June Beran protested that Government action was making Christian educational work impossible and illegal.[51] He accused the Government of forcing lectures in political science on theological students, making it impossible for the clergy to maintain contact with the people outside Church buildings, and sequestering the theological seminaries.[42] The Government reacted by assigning special instructors to Roman Catholic seminaries to give lessons on history and politics.[53] *Rude Pravo,* the Communist Party organ, followed with a number of accusations on exactly why there was tension in Church-State relations. It claimed that it was the Roman Catholic Church's "political envy, hatred against all that is progressive, against the Soviet Union and against this country that operated against an understanding."[54]

On June 10, despite the warning of Archbishop Beran, a number of priests and laymen met in Prague to form the "Catholic Action Committee."[55] They established guidelines for a new "Catholic Action" movement whose main purpose was to ameliorate Church-State relations.[56] The new "Committee" concluded their first meeting on a note of warning to the Czech hierarchy and the Vatican:

> We hope that our bishops will regard our action with understanding. However we exhort those who might dare to penalize in any way our priests or the Catholic people because of their attitude to the State to note well that we have with us the overwhelming majority of the faithful. . . . We cannot accept any order of a political nature from outside the country.[57]

The Czechoslovakian Government immediately recognized this pseudo-Catholic Action movement as the official representative of the Catholic Church.[58] It provided subsidization and placed *The Bulletin of the Catholic Clergy* under the new group's auspices.[59] Simultaneously the Government arrested the Secretary of the authentic Catholic Action, Dr. Antonin Mandl.[60]

The Catholic bishops replied with a pastoral letter in which they summarized the status of Church-State relations. They declared that the Catholic Church would accept no subsidization which enslaved and deprived it of its liberty and that a betterment of Church-State relations presupposed that the Christian concept of society would be respected and permitted in the Czech society. The bishops demanded that the Government acknowledge the supremacy of the Pope and the bishops in Roman Catholic ecclesiastical affairs, that all limitations on religious freedom for Roman Catholics be removed, that *The Bulletin of the Catholic Clergy* and the pseudo-Catholic Action movement be terminated, and that all interference in Church life be ended.[61] Vatican Radio also condemned the Government's "Catholic Action" group.[62]

On June 15 Czech police raided Archbishop Beran's consistory and removed his official seal. The Government directly began sending out pastoral letters to the clergy bearing the official seal of the Archbishop.[61] Three days later the Government vehemently denounced the Vatican for interfering in Czech affairs.[64]

On June 19 Beran was shouted down by Government supporters during a sermon in which he criticized the Communists.[65] On that same day he was placed under house arrest and the Czechoslovakian episcopate denounced what they termed "a systematic persecution of the Catholic Church in Czechoslovakia, well prepared and methodically executed."[66] One day later the Vatican officially condemned the government's "Catholic Action" movement.[67] In late June the government again decried what it termed Vatican interference in Czech affairs and it described Archbishop Beran as a pawn in the Vatican's game of politics in Eastern Europe.[68]

At the John Hus Memorial Day services in early July, various government spokesmen assailed the historic "reactionary" role of the Papacy in Czechoslovakian affairs. Deputy Premier Fierlinger stated in Husince that "Hus fought not only against the immorality of the Catholic Church but also against the increasing German influence in Bohemia which was backed by the corrupt Catholic hierarchy and the Pope. Now the battle between Czechoslovakia and Rome is renewed."[69] At Devin, Premier Zapotocky declared that the "Catholic clergy are traitors and are in the pay of foreign capitalists."[70] And at Sazala, Education Minister Nejedly claimed that "the Catholic Church is an enemy of socialism and of the Slav people. The State will deal with those bishops who are in the service of a foreign power as traitors. The clergy should not follow their bishops."[71]

In early July a Communist Party circular attacked the Catholic Church as the principal enemy of the Czechoslovakian people and stressed that it was necessary to cut the thread linking the Vatican to the Catholic hierarchy.[42] The circular also pointed out the need, if the Vatican's authority was to be undermined, to build a great dam against the bishops and archbishops, to set honestly thinking Catholics against Beran, and to agitate for the government's "Catholic Action." According to the circular, the regime-backed "Catholic Action" had to be particularly well grounded in rural areas since the peasants had not yet understood that its purpose was not to destroy the Church but to prevent it from fighting the Republic.[73]

On July 13 the Czech government ousted the Vatican's acting charge d'affaires, Mgr. Verolina. On that same day, Jean Thomas commented in Moscow that the Church in Czechoslovakia was being incessantly persecuted.[74] At the end of 1949 the clergy were required to swear allegiance to the republic and to cooperate in the building of socialism.[75] At the beginning of 1950 all Catholic monasteries were closed and confiscated by the government and many religious were deported.[76] One year later the Vatican estimated that some two thousand of its seven thousand clerics had either been imprisoned, deported, or subjected to forced labor.[77] In March of 1951 the government finally interned Archbishop Beran. By 1953, despite opposition, Communist officials had indirectly taken over, through the collaborationist clergy, the active direction of many dioceses.[78]

The Greek Catholics in the Ukrainian-speaking Presov area of Slovakia, as mentioned earlier, were also nettled and absorbed into the Orthodox Church. The main tool for "reunion" was the local Orthodox Church, and with the support of the Czechoslovak government, it organized an elaborate program featuring the creation of "committees" for "reunion," "re-education" courses by the police, and the imprisonment of "recalcitrant" clergy, including Bishop Pavlo Goidych. (Sentenced to life in prison in January, 1951, the Bishop passed away in the Leopoldovo prison on July 19, 1960). The campaign finally climaxed on April 28, 1950, with a lay-controlled "Conference" in Presov, which proclaimed itself a "Greek Catholic *Sobor*" and requested "unanimously" reunion with the Orthodox Church. Within a few weeks, the government ratified the action of the *"Sobor"* and declared that the Greek Catholic Church was no longer a legal institution in Czechoslovakia. The Auxiliary Bishop of Presov, Vasyl Hopko, who opposed the "reunion," was arrested in 1951 and stayed in jail until 1963.[79]

In Romania, the only other Eastern European country with a sizable Uniate concentration, "reunion" also went forward. In 1948, the Romanian Communist government, acting undoubtedly under orders from Moscow, forced the Romanian Uniate Church to self-immolate and merge with the Orthodox Church.[80] The sole surviving Ukrainian Uniate diocese in the Communist bloc—the Krizevci diocese in Yugoslavia—owes its existence to the Tito-Stalin break and Belgrade's subsequent relaxation of religious persecution.[81]

Although the Communists' attacks upon the Catholic Church had repressed its religious activities, Catholicism in Czechoslovakia, as elsewhere in Eastern Europe, remained indomitable. But, nonetheless, Moscow's policy of the "Extended Sword" in Eastern Europe had drawn blood and, by the middle of 1949, the Vatican was proned to react.

CHAPTER XII
CONCLUSIONS

The Church responded to the Communist persecution in Eastern Europe on July 13, 1949, when the Vatican issued the decree *Decretum: Responsa ad dubia de communismo* excommunicating any Catholic "who knowingly and freely defends or spreads the materialist and anti-Christian doctrine of Communism."[1] It was a sophisticated move against the Communist authorities because it clearly brought into focus that the Church-State conflict in the Communist world was both an ideological and a political struggle. The Catholic-Communist encounter went beyond differences of opinions on the organization of political-socio-economic institutions and policies to the ultimate control of men's minds, values, and philosophical outlook. At the same time, the decree underlined the fact that Moscow was trying to fashion a monolithic political system where all independent institutions, notably the Church, would be suppressed and where the people would only respond to the dictates of the Communist Party. The decree also threw the international spotlight on Moscow's religious persecution in the territories under its control and upon its totalitarian measures. As such the decree could not but damage the Kremlin's image—the country which was leading international peace campaign after peace campaign in the late 1940s and early 1950s was also unleashing a war against the people and institutions under its jurisdiction. Undoubtedly the decree reinforced the polarization of East and West at the end of the 1940s and set the stage for such anti-Communist movements as McCarthyism. It put all believing Catholics, and there were millions of them spread around the world, on guard against Communism as a force which had to be defeated at all costs. In the Communist world, the authorities had to be concerned that believing Catholics would never permanently accept the various Communist governments.

The decree, though, was a mixed blessing for it certainly forced Moscow to quicken its anti-Catholic step in Eastern Europe (clearly this was the case in Poland) and to add impetus to its campaign to control the Church in order to prevent the decree from having any effect.

The Church's attack was on two levels: the spiritual realm which the

Communists could not appreciate and the political level which they could divine and correctly assess as a dangerous thrust which aimed at ranging not only believers but nationalists (especially in Poland, Lithuania, and Hungary, and, to a point, in Czechoslovakia) against Communism. The Church was forcing Catholics to make a choice between itself and the Party and the Church was quite confident that most Catholics, in and out of the Soviet system, would choose, at least in their hearts, the Church. The Kremlin realized the seriousness of the Vatican's blow to the steel-trap society it was essaying to create in Eastern Europe and to the international prestige of Communism. Soviet propaganda agencies wasted little time in reacting to the Vatican's decree. On July 22 the *Soviet Monitor* declared that the "Vatican has taken its stand firmly on the side of the most extreme reaction. The Holy See has not the slightest intention of excommunicating those who publicly call for a new war, for dropping atom bombs."[2] The report went on to claim that now "all the enormous, ramified machinery of the Catholic Church is placed at the service of the cold war that the Anglo-American repressentatives are waging against the camp of peace."[3] The *Soviet Monitor* added that the "July 13th decree is actually one more Vatican contribution to this cold war."[4] What the Papacy wished, the report went on, was to "split the united front of people fighting for peace against the Anglo-American warmongers. . . ."[5] On July 29 *Izvestiia* published an account of what it termed the Vatican's "medieval decree." It claimed the decree threatened millions of Polish believers with "religious repression," and that Catholics the world over were rejecting the reactionary decree.[6] *Pravda* purported that the decree was dictated by international reaction and that it constituted an anathema against "one-third of mankind."[7] The Communist Party organ went on to state that historians of the Catholic Church "point out that the Holy Fathers have not belched such mass curses at least since the twelfth century. But, even then, the number of heretics to be burned did not reach such astronomical figures."[8] Patriarch Alexei, in turn, declared that the excommunication of all persons supporting Communism "fundamentally contradicts the main tenets of the Orthodox Christian faith."[9] He added that there was no conflict between Communism and Christianity.[10] For its part, the Communist news media in the occupied countries of Eastern Europe also denounced the Vatican's decree and castigated the Papacy.[11]

In addition to the propaganda, Moscow also reacted to the Vatican's decree by continuing, as demonstrated earlier, its intensive efforts to force the Catholic Church in Eastern Europe to kowtow. With complete political control and with the coercive institutions behind them, the Communists no doubt believed they could not only neutralize the Vatican's "declaration of war"[12] but also subjugate the Church.

The issuance of the Vatican's decree froze Catholic-Communist relations at the level of mutual hostility. It was the end of an era where the Church and the Communists, although harboring antagonism for one another, still made irregular attempts, for whatever reason, to seek a *modus vivendi* and the beginning of a new period where the Church and the Communist governments remained implacable foes and which only ended in the course of the 1960s. The Vatican had dropped its atomic bomb and, in the mind of the Communist leaders, it was identified, more than ever, as the opponent of Communism, Sovietization, and the ally of the United States. Compromise with the Catholic Church, from the Communist point of view, was no longer possible. What brought the Church to issue its decree? What pushed Communist-Catholic relations to that point?

The history of the events leading to the decree has already been reviewed. The Soviet government, from the beginning, possessed animosity for the Catholic Church. This was due, in part, to the atavistic antipathy between the Russian Orthodox East and the Catholic West which the Communists inherited from and shared with earlier Russian rulers. More fundamental, in causing the hatred, was the ideological baggage of the Bolsheviks: Marxism-Leninism. This philosophical outlook held religion to be an anchronism, an exploitive parasite to be expunged. In addition, Marxism-Leninism was a rival religion, a materialistic *Weltanschauung*. It strove to replace "spiritual" religion, to win men's minds and bodies, and to convince the masses that the Bolsheviks were the new high priests and their doctrine the only true doctrine. Religions which did not acknowledge the Communists as the highest authority had to be trammelled and superseded by Marxism-Leninism. The Catholic Church, not only because it was the largest Christian Church in the world but because it claimed to have an infallible authority, was a chief antagonist.

The already inbred hostility of the Communists toward the Church was sustained by their experiences with the Catholic Church once they assumed power. The Church was naturally fearful and suspicious of the Communists, given their ideology, but it was willing to give them a chance in 1917. The Bolsheviks immediate attacks upon Orthodoxy and their murder of the Romanovs aroused the sympathy of the Vatican and it publicly denounced these developments. In addition, some bishops in the western borderlands— human beings who could not pen up entirely their national predilections— openly sympathized with Poland when it invaded the Soviet Union. These events earmarked the Catholic Church as an incorrigible foe in the eyes of the young Communist government. The regime's suspicion and distrust of the Church was heightened by Catholicism's stronghold over the western national minorities: the Poles, Ukrainians, Belorussians, and Volga Germans. For the government's point of view, this reality was a strategic weakness, a block to the cohesion of the Soviet peoples and a prophylactic to eventual Sovietization and collectivization. Furthermore, the Vatican was a foreign center which had the allegiance of part of the Soviet citizenry.

Accordingly, the Communists launched a ruthless onset against the Catholic Church in the Soviet Union. The Church simply joined a long list of other institutions under assault in Soviet Russia. The Catholic Church in the Soviet Union was continuously, without restraint, ravaged to the point where, by the 1930s, it was institutionally decimated: the hierarchy was gone and there were only a few scattered churches and priests. Externally, however, the Soviet government's foray against Catholicism was uneven; it was, to be sure, always in the direction of pillorying the Church, but it was dotted with gaps and lapses. The Vatican was hit with fair consistency in Soviet propaganda, but there were ebbs. What dictated the ebb and flow was international conditions. The Communists varied their fulmination against the Vatican and international Catholicism in accordance with whether or not their position internally was threatened by shifting international developments. If placation to the Vatican was deemed useful, whether for an internal or external goal, the Soviets implemented it. It is most interesting to note that the Soviet leadership did not consider its conduct of internal policy to be the concern of a foreign power, that its internal policy should be a factor in its foreign relations. On a number of occasions in the 1920s and 1930s, when the USSR was or thought it was under foreign threat, it attempted to establish contact with the Vatican. In the mid-1930s, for example, the Kremlin offered to join forces with the Church in a popular front against fascism. But, at no time, did the Soviets' overtures to the Papacy stretch to the obvious rub in the Communist-Catholic relationship: the internal persecution of the Catholic Church. Assuming that the Soviets knew freedom for the Church in the USSR would be appreciated by the Vatican and that they were sincere in their desire to work with the Church, one can only conclude that they wanted foreign governments to overlook the domestic personality of the Soviet government and conduct foreign relations in a vacuum. Internal affairs, in the Soviet scheme of politics, were a private matter and completely and totally devoid from foreign affairs.

There is, of course, a direct connection between internal policy and foreign policy—they cannot be separated and compartmentalized and dealt with individually without relation to one another. Foreign policy, in fact, is often a reflection of or an effect of internal developments. A study of the history of Soviet foreign policy underlines this relationship again and again.[13] The Soviet leadership has tried, at the public level, to deny the connection and to conduct internal and external policies as if they were mutually exclusive. This attempt naturally involves dissimulation on a major scale and its goal is not to persuade the Soviets that there is no nexus but the outside world. The Vatican, an institution with centuries of political experience and savvy, refused to be taken in by such pretense. It could not bring itself to work out a *modus vivendi,* a popular front, or anything else at the international level while the Kremlin wasted the Catholic Church and other religions in the USSR and put the Soviet people through the excruciating torture of collectivization and industrialization with the consequent loss of millions of lives. The Papacy recognized the Soviet government for what it *was in the 1930s*: a totalitarian system which embodied the anti-humanist philosophy of materialism and aimed solely at the maintenance and expansion of its power and control. In March, 1937, in the encyclical *Divini Redemptoris,* the Vatican took it upon itself to denounce this philosophy and to reject the possibility of allying with this government. In the same month the Papacy condemned Marxism-Leninism, it also railed against another totalitarian movement, that of National Socialism. At that juncture, the Church did not have to make a choice between the two.

By 1939, the Vatican had to make a choice and it opted, by way of omission rather than commission, to reject National Socialism less than Communism. The Papacy did not support the philosophy of Nazism and its national churches, in the countries under Nazi control, worked to alleviate the sufferings of the persecuted Jews. The Church did not bless the Nazi invasion of the USSR and, in fact, Nazi-Vatican relations, for most of the war, were quite strained. But the Church did continue to condemn, through the war, in public and private, Communism while at the same time holding the line on its invectives against Nazism. The Church did not approve of Nazism and did not withdraw its earlier condemnation contained in *Mit Brennender Sorge.* The Church's official position was one of neutrality, but in fact it was pro-neutral toward Germany and anti-neutral toward the USSR. Was this position justified? Before that question can be answered, it must be determined if, in fact, the Church had to be neutral for either one, that is, if it had to abandon its earlier position of opposing both movements. Once the USSR and the Third Reich signed the Molotov-Ribbentrop Pact, they represented for the Church a combination that could control the world and threaten western civilization, Christian morality, and human dignity and worth. For the Vatican, it was difficult to conceive of any previous alliance or movement which held out a similar threat. If the Nazi-Soviet alliance should have blossomed and eventually been victorious, mankind, from the Church's point of view, was doomed. The only practical means of preventing that dismal prospect was to split the alliance. The alternative of encouraging the Anglo-French forces to extend their war against Germany to include the USSR was absurd. England-France and, to a point, the United States, decided upon the course of cleaving the Nazi-Soviet tandem. They, however, determined to support the USSR and, implicitly, Communism. They did not, although during the Finnish-Russo war they came periously close, declare war on the Soviet Union. The Western powers chose to woo the USSR, especially after the fall of France, because Germany was a more direct military threat to the West. This was quite understandable, but what was unjustified was the subsequent Western belief that the USSR had changed from a totalitarian, expansionist movement, worshipping power to a normal, democratic country content with its borders. Expediency dictated any attempt to break the Nazi-Soviet pact and to ally with the USSR, but only naïveté could explain the West's departure from reality.

The Vatican, on the other hand, concentrated its efforts on Germany, attempting to break the Nazi-Soviet pact by denouncing the USSR to the Germans and mutely siding with the Reich. The Vatican's choice was made on moral grounds: it chose the lesser of two evils and, on that basis, its position was justified. The Church had been tortured by the Soviet government in the 1920s and 1930s; it witnessed executions, arrests, deportations, and the unbridled use of administrative force and terror; it lived in the Soviet Union of the 1930s where human life and independent personalities and institutions were brutally crushed; between 1939 and 1941 the Church in Eastern Europe again tasted the bitterness of life under the Soviet regime. The Church, on the other hand, was also quite familiar with what the Nazis were doing in Germany and eventually throughout Europe. The Third Reich persecuted also the Catholic Church and massacred its own citizens and the Jews of Europe. It realized that both movements were dispicable. But which was worst: the movement of irrational emotion led by a mad man which attacked many but not all of the people or a movement of science and reason led by a cold, calculating dictator which violated everyone and everything. Stalinist Communism and Nazism were philosophies inherently tied to the personalities of Stalin and Hitler and both obviously could change with their death. But, in the third and fourth decades of the 20th century, the movements had to be viewed and weighed for what they were, not for what they might become.

The Vatican's decision to eschew Nazism less than Communism, naturally, had a political dimension to it. If faced with no other option, the Church would have tolerated Nazi control of Europe before Soviet hegemony. It is significant that millions of people who had direct experience with both movements, which the Vatican did and which England-France and the United States did not, elected, when faced with no other alternatives, the

Nazis: Lithuanians, Latvians, Estonians, Ukrainians, Belorussians, the so-called Vlasov men, and others.

Once the Nazis and the Soviets were at war, the Vatican consoled itself with the hope that both movements might extinguish one another. It was, thus, not at all pleased to see the Anglo-Americans extend an alliance to the USSR. Once the Communists turned the Nazi tide and began marching westward, the Papacy foresaw Soviet domination of Eastern Europe. It simultaneously found it astounding that the Western Allies did not realize that Nazi power would be replaced by Soviet power. For the Vatican, Soviet prefecture, direct or indirect, of Europe was the very worst outcome of the war. Repeatedly the Papacy warned the West of Soviet intentions, but it was a voice in the wilderness.

Since the Nazi invasion, the Soviets had made some efforts to allay the Vatican's anti-Communism, but they did nothing meaningful. The explanation for the lack of substantive concessions was due primarily to internal priorities but also to the lack of pressure from the Western Allies. The Anglo-Americans made no demands on the Soviet Union, as prerequisites for the alliance and for military aid, to change its internal structure, policies, or goals. It can be argued that the moment was not suitable for such demands since the important objective was to defeat the Axis powers. But the moment was right for something had to change: either the Soviets had to give up their designs of world conquest and revolutionary struggle by making appropriate internal changes, such as allowing basic freedoms, movements of peoples, etc. or the West had to believe, through self-delusion and Soviet pretense, that the Soviet Union had been transformed or, lastly, the West had to accept the idea of helping a future foe which would be just as redoubtable as the Nazis. The possibility which materialized was that the West decided *to believe* that the USSR had altered, that it was a different country and itself not as much of a threat as Germany. Since the West did not demand fundamental change, Stalin did not modify his system and, thus, did not offer any serious hope to the Vatican that Communism in the 1940s was going to be any different than Communism in the 1930s.[14]

However, the Soviet government did make tactical concessions and changes, in part, because it found it internally and externally useful to do so and, in part, to help the West along in its self-deception. The major tactical alteration came in the regime's religious policy. This was not the result of Western pressure but, rather, of a lesson Moscow learned under the pressure of the Nazi *Juggernaut*. Russian nationalism with its chief institution, Russian Orthodoxy, could be useful in the expansion and maintenance of the Soviet system. It was paradoxical that an atheistic movement would depend upon religion to spread itself, but the goal of distention, not the means, was paramount.

Once the Kremlin recognized the connection between nationalism and religion, it ascertained, as its forces advanced into Catholic East Europe, that the Catholic Church could be a powerful tool and ally for it was the dominant religion in Lithuania, Poland, Hungary, and Czechoslovakia. The joker in the deck, however, was the parallel Soviet-Orthodox intention of assimilating the Uniate Catholics of Eastern Europe into the Russian Orthodox Church.

As the Soviets moved forward and took control of East Europe, the Catholic Church rightly feared for its life. It saw that the change in Moscow's religious policy was a tactical change and not a fundamental transformation. The Church stood alone in East Europe, a force opposed to Communism, but an exposed and war-wearied force. The Church's hostility, however, was not immutable. National Catholic churches, in fact, attempted to work out concordats with the various Communist regimes. The Communists could have won the Church over if they would have allowed religious freedom. The Church might even have become a supporter of a status quo which included Soviet hegemony.

The Communists, however, did not allow religious freedom. Instead they pursued three policies vis-à-vis the Church. First, they annihilated the Catholic Uniate Church in East Europe. Between 1944 and 1949-50, all Uniate dioceses within the Soviet sphere of influence were absorbed into the Russian Orthodox Church. The Church condemned this campaign in 1946 in the encyclical *Orientales Omnes Ecclesias.* Secondly, the Soviets, after allowing a very brief period of toleration, commenced a massive persecution against Latin Catholics, especially Lithuanians and Belorussians, in the USSR. Both of the above policies were accompanied by strident propagandistic barrages against the Vatican. The final policy was a three year toleration of Latin Catholics in those parts of Soviet-controlled Eastern Europe not annexed into the USSR, followed by a violent incubus beginning in 1948. The latter campaign was intimately tied up with the shifting winds of the Cold War.

The Vatican responded to the Soviets' postwar struggles against the Catholic Church in 1949 with the decree *Decretum: responsa ad dubia de communismo.* The document said that the Soviets had not changed; that they were the same as before and that there was no chance for reconciliation between Catholicism and Soviet Communism at the present time.

1949 was a watershed year in Soviet-Catholic relations. In that year they became implacable enemies. But the year was significant in Communist-Catholic relations for other reasons also. The Soviets exploded an atomic bomb and to the Church that was an unsettling event for it meant that the Soviet Union was destined to remain strong and in control of Eastern

Europe. The year also saw the Chinese Communist victorious. No longer was the Soviet Union the sole Communist state or the only source of Communist exegesis. At the time, Mao's success was quite upsetting to the Vatican for it appeared as if Soviet Communism was advancing. But, in fact, it contained seeds which would eventually lead to changes in international Communism and concomitant alterations in the position of the Church toward Communism. Finally, the year saw the crystallization of NATO. For the Church, the emergence of NATO was a great consolation, albeit a belated one, for the West was finally creating the military alliance necessary to stymie further Communist expansion in Europe.

1. *The Russian Primary Chronicle,* trans. Samuel H. Cross, *Harvard Studies and Notes in Philology and Literature* (Cambridge, Mass.: Harvard University Press, 1930), Vol. xii, pp. 183-184.

2. Deno J. Geanakopolos, *Byzantine East and Latin West: Two Worlds of Christendom in Middle Ages and Renaissance* (New York and Evanston: Harper Torchbooks, Harper and Row, Publishers, 1966), pp. 85-86.

3. For excellent surveys of this episode and the entire course of Byzantine history, see: A. A. Vasiliev, *History of the Byzantine Empire 324-1453* (Madison: The University of Wisconsin Press, 1952) and George Ostrogorsky, *History of the Byzantine State* (New Brunswick, N.J.: Rutgers University Press, 1957); for the effect of the 4th Crusade on Kievan Rus, see: George Vernadsky, *A History of Russia* (New Haven and London: Yale University Press, 12th Printing, 1968), p. 42.

4. For background on the cultural history of Eastern Europe and Russia, see: Oscar Halecki, *Borderlands of Western Civilization* (New York: The Ronald Press, 1952); Wladimir Weidle, *Russia: Absent and Present,* trans. A. Gordon Smith (New York: Vintage Books, 1961); Francis Dvornik, *The Making of Central and Eastern Europe* (London: The Polish Research Centre, Ltd., 1949); Francis Dvornik, *The Slavs: Their Early History and Civilization* (Boston: Little, Brown, Inc., 1959); Vasily V. Zenkovsky, "The Spirit of Russian Orthodoxy," *Russian Review,* Vol. XXII, No. 1 (January, 1963), 38; Dmitri Obolensky, "Russia's Byzantine Heritage," *Oxford Slavonic Papers,* Vol. I (1950) (Oxford: Clarendon Press), 37-63; Eugenii E. Golubinsky, *Istoriya Russkoi Tserkvi,* 2 vols. (Moscow, 1901) (History of the Russian Church).

5. *Bezbozhnik,* Illustrated edition, No. 12, 1938.

6. J. V. Stalin, *Works* (Moscow: Foreign Language Publishing House, 1952-1955), IV, 240; Stalin reiterated the same message in an "election" campaign speech in 1946: *Pravda,* February 10, 1946.

7. Vernadsky, *History of Russia,* pp. 68 ff.

8. Adam B. Ulam, *Expansion and Coexistence: The History of Soviet Foreign*

Policy, 1917-1967 (New York-Washington: Frederick A. Praeger, Publishers, 1968), pp. 289, 299, 355.

9. In 1921, Stalin proclaimed that it was the duty of the Party to "crush the hydra of nationalism": Stalin, *Works,* V, p. 101. That position was, of course, at variance with the theme of national self-determination which Stalin (under Lenin's tutelage) propounded in 1913 in *Marxism and the National Question,* but, in 1913, Stalin was not in power.

10. The editor of Trotsky's biography of Stalin uses the term "Great Russian Russifyer," but the following authors all note Stalin's sense of Russian nationalism: Leon Trotsky, *Stalin: An Appraisal of the Man and His Influence,* ed. and trans. Charles Malamuth (New York-London: Harper and Brothers Publishers, 1941, printed 1946), pp. 359-360; Isaac Deutscher, *Stalin: A Political Biography* (New York: Oxford University Press, 1949), pp. 240-241; Milovan Djilas, *Conversations with Stalin* (New York: Harcourt, Brace, and World, Inc., 1962), p. 62; James H. Billington, *The Icon and the Axe: An Interpretive History of Russian Culture* (New York: Alfred A. Knopf, 1966), pp. 536-541; E. H. Carr, *Socialism in One Country 1924-1926,* I (New York: The Macmillan Company; London: Macmillan & Co., Ltd., 1958), 176-186; Adam Ulam, *Stalin* (New York: Harper, 1973); Robert Tucker, *Stalin As Revolutionary* (New York: Norton, 1973).

11. For studies of the theory of Moscow and Third Rome, see: Cyril Toumanoff, "Moscow the Third Rome: Genesis and Significance of a Politico-Religious Idea," *Catholic Historical Review,* XL (1955), 411-447; Dmitri Stremooukhoff, "Moscow the Third Rome: Sources of the Doctrine," *Speculum,* XXVIII, No. 1 (January, 1953), 84-101; Nicholas Berdyaev, *The Origin of Russian Communism* (Ann Arbor: The University of Michigan Press, 1966), p. 8; Gustave Alef, "Muscovy and the Council of Florence," *Slavic Review,* XX, No. 3, 389-401; Robert Lee Wolff, "The Three Romes: The Migration of an Ideology and the Making of an Autocrat," *Daedalus,* LXXXVIII (1959), 291-311; Michael Cherniavsky, "Holy Russia: A Study in the History of an Idea," *American Historical Review,* LXIII, No. 3 (April, 1958), 617-637; Gustave Alef, "The Adoption of the Muscovite Two-Headed Eagle: A Discordant View," *Speculum,* XLI (January, 1966), 1-21; E. Denisoff, "Aux Origines de l'eglise russe autocephale," *Revue des Etudes Slaves,* VII (1927), 224-240; Serge Zenkovsky, *Medieval Russia's Epics, Chronicles, and Tales* (New York: E. P. Dutton and Company, Inc., 1963), pp. 266 ff.

12. This is not to say that Russian Messianism and autocracy were solely the products of Third Romanism.

13. For an excellent study of Brest, see: Oscar Halecki, *From Florence to Brest (1439-1596)* (Philadelphia: The Westminster Press, 1950).

14. Dennis J. Dunn, "The Disappearance of the Ukrainian Uniate Church: How and Why?," *Ukrains'kyi Istoryk*, 1-2- (33-34), p. 57.

15. Deutscher, *Stalin*, p. 360; Robert Tucker, *The Soviet Political Mind: Studies in Stalinism and Post-Stalin Change* (New York: Frederick A. Praeger, Inc.; London and Dunmow: Pall Mall Press, 1963), pp. 37-45 ff.; Alexander Orlov, *The Secret History of Stalin's Crimes* (New York-London: Jarrolds, Publishers Ltd., 1953), p. 206; Roy A. Medvedev, *Let History Judge: The Origins and Consequence of Stalinism* (New York: Alfred A. Knopf, 1972), pp. 305, 323.

16. Stalin, *Works*, IV, p. 186.

17. For an excellent study of the Council of Florence, see: Joseph Gill, *The Council of Florence* (Cambridge: Cambridge University Press, 1959).

18. Vernadsky, *History of Russia*, p. 92.

19. Stremooukhoff, "Moscow the Third Rome," p. 91.

20. *Ibid.,* p. 94.

21. Halecki, *From Florence to Brest*, pp. 58-65, 352-55, 414-16. In 1646 at the Uzhhorod Union the diocese of Mukachevo (Carpathian Ukraine) was brought into union with Rome.

22. Vernadsky, *History of Russia*, p. 129. For an interesting study of the position of the Ukrainian Orthodox Church on the eve of Khmelnytsky's action, see Hugh F. Graham, "Peter Mogila-Metropolitan of Kiev," *The Russian Review*, Vol. XIV, No. 4, (October, 1955), 345-356.

23. James J. Zatko, *Descent Into Darkness* (Notre Dame: The University of Notre Dame Press, 1965), p. 8.

24. *Ibid.*

25. *Ibid.,* p. 9.

26. *Ibid.*; Wasyl Lencyk, *The Eastern Catholic Church and Czar Nicholas I* (Rome-New York: Ukrainian Catholic University Press, 1966), pp. 14-15.

27. Zatko, *ibid.,* p. 10; Lencyk, *ibid.*

28. Zatko, *ibid.,* p. 9.

29. *Ibid.*

30. Lencyk, *Eastern Catholic Church*, pp. 15, 19-20.

31. Zatko, *Descent Into Darkness*, pp. 1-11.

32. *Ibid.,* p. 11.

33. *Ibid.,*; Lencyk, *Eastern Catholic Church*, p. 15.

34. Lencyk, *ibid.*; Zatko, *ibid.,* pp. 10-11.

35. Lencyk, *ibid.,* p. 16.

36. Zatko, *Descent Into Darkness*, p. 14.

37. *Ibid.,* pp. 13-14.

38. Radio Vatican, *United States Foreign Broadcast Information Service, Daily Reports,* November 19, 1948, p. NN4 (hereinafter cited as *Daily Reports.*);

Albert Galter, *The Red Book of the Persecuted Church* (Westminster, Md.: The Newman Press, 1957), pp. 362-365; Ludwig Nemec, *Church and State in Czechoslovakia* (New York: Vantage Press, Inc., 1955), pp. 272-278.

39. Zatko, *Descent Into Darkness,* pp. 14-15; Lencyk, *Eastern Catholic Church,* pp. 17-18.

40. Lencyk, *ibid.*

41. *Ibid.,* p. 20.

42. For a good survey of the ideology of Nicholas' reign, see Nicholas V. Riasanovsky, *Nicholas I and Official Nationality in Russia, 1825-1855* (Berkeley: University of California Press, 1959).

43. Berdyaev, *Russian Communism,* pp. 9, 46.

44. Lencyk, *Eastern Catholic Church,* p. 26.

45. *Ibid.*

46. Zatko, *Descent Into Darkness,* p. 16.

47. Lencyk, *Eastern Catholic Church,* p. 31.

48. Bohdan Bociurkiw, "The Uniate Church in the Soviet Ukraine: A Case Study in Soviet Church Policy," *Canadian Slavonic Papers,* Vol. VII (1965), 89-113.

49. Lencyk, *Eastern Catholic Church,* pp. 32-88.

50. *Ibid.,* pp. 78-88.

51. *Ibid.,* p. 89.

52. *Ibid.,* p. 106.

53. Bociurkiw, "The Uniate Church in the Soviet Ukraine," pp. 104-106.

54. Zatko, *Descent Into Darkness,* p. 17.

55. *Ibid.,* pp. 17-18.

56. *Ibid.*

57. See Chapter VII, below.

58. Zatko, *Descent Into Darkness,* pp. 18-19.

59. *Ibid.*

60. *Ibid.,* p. 19.

61. *Ibid.*

62. *Ibid.,* p. 20.

63. *Ibid.,* p. 21.

64. *Ibid.,* pp. 21-22.

65. *Ibid.,* pp. 23-24.

66. Bociurkiw, "The Uniate Church in the Soviet Ukraine," p. 92.

67. Zatko, *Descent Into Darkness,* p. 24.

68. *Ibid.,* pp. 24-25.

69. *Ibid.,* p. 25.

70. *Ibid.,* p. 26.

71. *Ibid.*; See: Diakon Vasilii, OSBM, *Leonid Fedorov, Zhizn' i deiatel'nost'*

(Rome: "Studion" Publications, III-V, 1966).

72. Zatko, *ibid.*, p. 27.

73. *Ibid.*

74. *Ibid.*, p. 40.

75. *Ibid.*, p. 42. For the texts of these laws and other affecting religion, see *Sobranie Ukazonenii* (Collection of Laws), I, 1917, 2 Nos. 1014, 1099, 1134.

76. Zatko, *ibid.*, pp. 43-44.

77. *Ibid.*, p. 45.

78. *Ibid.*, p. 48.

79. *Ibid.*, pp. 58-59.

80. *Ibid.*, pp. 48-50.

81. *Bezbozhnik,* April 3, 1923.

NOTES TO CHAPTER II

1. For a compilation of Marx's view on religion, see Karl Marx and Frederick Engels, *On Religion* (New York: Schocken Books, 1964). For an excellent biography and interpretation of Marx's thought, see David McLlellan, *Karl Marx: His Life and Thought* (New York: Harper, 1973).

2. Karl Marx, *Das Kapital,* edited by Friedrich Engels and condensed by Serge L. Levitsky (Chicago: Henry Regnery Company, A Gateway Edition, 1961), p. 60.

3. M. M. Bober, *Karl Marx's Interpretation of History* (New York: W. W. Norton and Company, Inc., 1965), p. 147.

4. Frederick Engels, *Anti-Duhring* (New York: International Publishers, 1966), p. 344. Also see: Marx, *Das Kapital,* p. 60.

5. Lewis S. Feuer, editor, *Marx & Engels: Basic Writings on Politics and Philosophy* (Garden City, New York: Doubleday & Company, Inc., 1959), pp. 168-169.

6. *Ibid.*, p. 240.

7. *Ibid.*, p. 263.

8. Bober, *Karl Marx,* p. 148.

9. Marx, *Das Kapital,* p. 53.

10. *Ibid.*, pp. 50-52.

11. Feuer, *Basic Writings,* p. 263.

12. Engels, *Anti-Duhring,* p. 346.

13. Karl Marx and Friedrich Engels, *Harold J. Laski on the Communist Manifesto* (New York: Random House, Vintage Book, 1967), p. 147.

14. Engels, *Anti-Duhring,* pp. 345-346.

15. Marx, *Das Kapital,* p. 61.

16. Feuer, *Basic Writings, p. 263.*

17. *Ibid.,* pp. 268-69.

18. Engels, *Anti-Duhring,* p. 346.

19. *Ibid.*

20. *Ibid.*

21. Harvey Fireside, *Icon & Swastika: The Russian Orthodox Church under Nazi and Soviet Control* (Cambridge: Harvard University Press, 1971), p. 14.

22. Engels, *Anti-Duhring,* p. 114.

23. *Ibid.,* p. 117.

24. Feuer, *Basic Writings,* pp. 168-69.

25. Marx and Engels, *Communist Manifesto,* pp. 177-78.

26. Stalin, *Works,* III, pp. 186, 200.

27. For the most complete collection of Lenin's writings on religion, see *V. I. Lenin ob ateizme, religii i tserkvi* (Moscow: Misl, 1969). For a good, although somewhat dogmatic and occasionally distorted, treatment of Lenin's views on religion, see M. I. Shakhnovich, *Lenin i problemy ateizma* (Leningrad: Izd-vo Akademii Nauk SSSR, 1961). Also see the recent collection *Deiateli Oktiabria o religii i tserkvi* (Moscow: Misl, 1968). In late 1976, a book which many students of Soviet religious affairs thought had to exist finally surfaced in the West: V. A. Kuroedov (present chairman of the Council of Religious Affairs) and A. S. Pankratov (Deputy Procurator General of the USSR), eds., *Zakonodal'stvo o religioznych kultakh* (Moscow: 1971). This work, stamped "for official use only," is the Soviet regime's reference work on legislation affecting religious cults.

28. Bohdan R. Bociurkiw, "Lenin and Religion," in Leonard Schapiro and Peter Reddaway, eds., *Lenin: The Man, The Theorist, The Leader: A Reappraisal* (New York and London: Praeger, 1967), pp. 107-34.

29. *Ibid.,* pp. 110-11; Shakhnovich, *op. cit.,* p. 13; Erwin Adler, "Lenin's Views on Religion," *Studies on the Soviet Union,* Vol. X, No. 1 (1970), 11.

30. *V. I. Lenin ob ateizme. . . .,* pp. 72-73.

31. See F. Megruzhan and Iu. Kogan, "Programmnii dokument proletarskogo ateizma," *Antireligioznik,* No. 1, 1936, 8-23.

32. *V. I. Lenin ob ateizme. . . .,* pp. 44-46.

33. The pretense that the party and state are separate continues in the Soviet Union, and, not surprisingly, Lenin's distinction between the party and the state vis-a-vis religion has also continued. For official commentaries on Soviet religious policy, see G. T. Utkin, "Religion and the Church," in *Bolshaia Sovetskaia Entsiklopediia* (Moscow: Gosudarstvennoe Isd-vo Sovetskikh Entsiklopedii), Vol. 50, 1957, pp. 642-43; Vladimir A. Kuroedov, *Religiia*

i zakon (Moscow: Znanie, 1970).

34. *V. I. Lenin ob ateizme. . . .*, pp. 33-34; V. I. Lenin, *Sochineniia,* 4th Edition, 35 Volumes (Moscow: Institut Marksa-Engel'sa Lenina, 1941-1950), XII, p. 261.

35. Lenin, *Sochineniia,* VIII, p. 86. It should be noted that Lenin condemned attempts by various socialists to either unite with organized religion against the regime *(bogoiskatel'stvo)* or to interpret Marxism as a religion *(bogostroitel'stvo).* See Shakhnovich, *op. cit.,* pp. 28-32, 48-50, 490-511; *Kommunisticheskaia partiia Sovetskogo Soiuza v rezoliutsiiakh i resheniiakh s' 'ezdov, konferentsii i plenumov Tsk* (Moscow: 1953), Vol. I, p. 222.

36. Lenin, *Sochineniia,* X, pp. 68-69.

37. Bociurkiw, "Lenin and Religion," p. 113.

38. See Alexander Solzhenitsyn's *Gulag Archipeligo* (New York: Harper and Row, 1973-74), pp. 343-47.

39. Stalin seems to have adopted Lenin's religious views and policies wholeheartedly. He had few thoughts himself on religion, if his writings are any guide. See Bociurkiw, "Lenin and Religion," pp. 128-29.

40. For an excellent analysis of Soviet motivation in persecuting religion, see Bohdan R. Bociurkiw, "Soviet Religious Policy," *Problems of Communism* (May-June, 1973), pp. 37-51.

NOTES TO CHAPTER III

1. For details, see Kuroedov and Pankratov, *Zakonodal'stvo,* pp. 53-66; for early party and state directives on religion, see pp. 20-31 *passim.* Also see: Shakhnovich, op. cit., pp. 566-72; Boleslaw Szczesniak, *The Russian Revolution and Religion* (Notre Dame: University of Notre Dame Press, 1959), pp. 34-35; John S. Curtiss, *The Russian Church and the Soviet State, 1917-1950* (Boston: Little, Brown and Co., 1953) p. 46.

2. Zatko, *Descent Into Darkness,* p. 71.

3. Kuroedov and Pankratov, *op. cit.,* pp. 63-66; Szczesniak, *op. cit.,* pp. 40-48.

4. See "Resolution of the Commissariat of Education," April 3, 1919; "Resolution of the All-Russian Central Executive Committee," June 13, 1921; and Article 121 of the 1922 Criminal Code of the RSFSR.

5. *Revoliutsiia i tserkov,* No. 9-12, 1920, 83.

6. Francis McCullagh, *The Bolshevik Persecution of Christianity* (New York: E. P. Dutton and Co., 1924), pp. 160-61, 174.

7. *Ibid.,* pp. 160-61.

8. *Ibid.,* pp. 159, 210, 233.

9. *L'Osservatore Romano,* December 28, 1919; March 22, 23, 1920; Nedesh-da Teodorovich, "The Roman Catholics," *Religion in the USSR* (Munich: Institute for the Study of the USSR, 1960), p. 84; Paul Mailleux, S. J., "Catholics in the Soviet Union," in Richard H. Marshall, Jr., ed., *Aspects of Religion in the Soviet Union 1917-1967* (Chicago: University of Chicago Press, 1971), p. 361; S. Tyshkevich, *Sovetskoe bezbozhie i papstvo* (Soviet atheism and the papacy) (Rome: 1950), p. 1.

10. McCullagh, *op. cit.,* pp. 161-62, 202-3; N. V. Krylenko, *Sudebnye rechi, 1922-1930* (Court Speeches) (Moscow: 1931), p. 18.

11. McCullagh, *ibid.,* pp. 157, 205.

12. *L'Osservatore Romano,* June 28, April 2, 1919; M. M. Sheinman, "Vatikan i rossiia v period mezhdu fevralem i oktiabrem 1917 g.," (The Vatican and russia in the period between february and october 1917), *Voprosy istorii religii i ateisma,* V (Moscow, 1958), pp. 87-89.

13. Zatko, *Descent Into Darkness,* pp. 96-97.

14. *Ibid.*

15. For excellent analyses of Soviet antireligious motives see Bociurkiw, "Soviet Religious Policy," pp. 38-39 and Walter Kolarz, *Religion in the Soviet Union* (New York: St. Martin's Press, 1961), pp. 176-77.

16. Bohdan Bociurkiw, "Church-State Relations in the USSR," Max Haywood and William C. Fletcher, eds., *Religion and the Soviet State: A Dilemma of Power* (New York: Praeger, 1969), p. 81.

17. The agencies in charge of religious policy included from the very beginning the Commissariats of Justice with its department for the Implementation of the Separation of the Church from the State, otherwise known as the Eighth and, later Fifth Department of the Commissariat of Justice (existed from 1918-1924 under Krasikov); the Commissariat of Internal Affairs or the NKVD with its Section of Cults; and the Cheka-GPU with its subdivision for ecclesiastical affairs (headed during the 1920s by E. Tuchkov). In 1924 a higher level agency was organized to supervise governmental controls over religion. It was called the Secretariat for the Affairs of Cults attached to the All-Russian Central Executive Committee (Vse-Rossiiskaia Tsentralnaia Ispolnitelnaia Kommissiia (VTsIK)), (renamed in 1929 the Permanent Commission of the VTsIK for the Affairs of Cults). These various agencies worked under other bodies organized at the highest levels of the Government and the Party, the chief one of which was the Commission on the Implementation of the Decree on the Separation of the Church from the State, which was set up under E. Iaroslavskii (he replaced Trotsky as the central figure in charge of antireligious work) in 1922. For more

detail, see Bociurkiw, "Church-State Relations," pp. 77, 81-82; and Joan Delaney, "Origins of Soviet Antireligious Organizations," *Aspects of Religion,* pp. 105-109.

18. Zatko, *Descent Into Darkness,* p. 116; McCullagh, *op. cit.,* p. 110; *Izvestiia,* February 24, 26, 1922.

19. Zatko, *ibid.,* pp. 104-105, 120-121; McCullagh, *ibid.,* pp. 8, 14-15; Curtiss, *Russian Church,* p. 116 ff.

20. Zatko, *ibid.,* pp. 121-27; McCullagh, *ibid.,* pp. 154-71; Alexander Solzhenitsyn, *Gulag Archipelago* (New York: Harper and Row, 1973-74), pp. 343-47.

21. Edmund A. Walsh, *The Last Stand: An Interpretation of the Soviet Five-Year Plan* (Boston: Little, Brown and Co., 1931), pp. 182-83.

22. Zatko, *Descent Into Darkness,* p. 125.

23. McCullagh, *op. cit.,* pp. 112-13.

24. *Ibid.,* pp. 142-276, 364-65; Szczesniak, *op. cit.,* pp. 113-26; Krylenko, *op. cit.,* pp. 3-34.

25. McCullagh, *ibid.,* pp. 142-287; Szczesniak, *ibid.;* Krylenko, *ibid.*

26. McCullagh, *ibid.;* Szczesniak, *ibid.;* Krylenko, *ibid.*

27. Zatko, *Descent Into Darkness,* pp. 157-58. Few other foreign governments, however, with the exception of Poland, supported the Vatican's vigorous objections. See Szczesniak, *op. cit.,* pp. 130-31, 139-44.

28. McCullagh, *op. cit.,* pp. 365-66; Galter, *op. cit.,* p. 44; Maxime Mourin, *Le Vatican et l'URSS* (Paris: Payot, 1965), p. 53.

29. Zatko, *Descent Into Darkness,* p. 173.

30. *Ibid.,* pp. 171, 183; Szczesniak, *op. cit.,* pp. 226-33; Walsh, *op. cit.,* pp. 184-87; Galter, *op. cit.,* pp. 39-40.

31. Leopold Braun, *Memoirs* (my title) (Unpublished manuscript located at the Assumptionist Provincial House, New York City, 1961), pp. 148-49; Serge Bolshakoff, *Russian Nonconformity* (Philadelphia: The Westminster Press, 1950), pp. 149-50; D. E. Mikhnevich, *Ocherki iz istorii katolicheskoi reaktsii* (Outlines of the history of catholic reaction) (Moscow: Izd-vo Akademii Nauk SSSR, 1953), p. 241; Galter, *ibid.*

32. Zatko, *Descent Into Darkness,* p. 183.

33. *Ibid.,* pp. 118-19; Curtiss, *Russian Church,* p. 206; Conquest, Religion in the USSR, p. 82. Mikhnevich claimed the Vatican's efforts were tinged with politics, *op. cit.,* pp. 240-41. On the rise of Iaroslavskii, see Delaney, "Origins of Antireligious Organizations," pp. 103-29.

34. Sir John Maynard, *The Russian Peasant and Other Studies* (London: Victor Gallancz, Ltd., 1943), p. 363; Mourin, *op. cit.,* pp. 52-56.

35. Sacra Congregazione Per La Chiesa Orientale, "Communicato," *Acta Apostolicae Sedis,* XVIII (1926), 62 (hereinafter cited as A.A.S.); PP. Pius

XI, "Provisio Ecclesiarum," *A.A.S.,* XIV (1927), 242ff; Father d'Herbigny was the director of the Vatican's Pontifical Institute of Oriental Studies. For his exploits and viewpoints see Michel d'Herbigny, *Eveques russes en exil* (Rome: Institut oriental, 1930) and *La guerre antireligieuse en Russie sovietique* (Paris, 1930); Maynard, *op. cit.,* p. 363.

36. For detailed information on the persecution of the Orthodox Church and other major religious groups, consult the following: Paul B. Anderson, *People, Church, and State in Modern Russia* (New York: The Macmillan Co., 1944); Matthew Spinka, *The Church in Soviet Russia* (New York: Oxford University Press, 1956); Matthew Spinka, *The Church and the Russian Revolution* (New York: The Macmillan Co., 1927); Nikita Struve, *Les chretiens en U.R.S.S.* (Paris: Editions du Seuil, 1963); Nicholas Timasheff, *Religion in Soviet Russia, 1917-1942* (New York: Sheed and Ward, 1942); Kolarz, *op. cit.;* Curtiss, *op. cit.;* Marshall, *op. cit.;* Conquest, *op. cit.;* William C. Fletcher, *A Study in Survival: The Church in Russia, 1927-1943* (New York: Macmillan, 1965); William C. Fletcher, *Russian Orthodox Church Underground 1917-1970* (London: Oxford University Press, 1971).

37. Obviously if Stalin feared war he would have never launched the economically disruptive First Five Year Plan.

38. The Left wing of the Party was criticizing Stalin's conduct of foreign affairs, especially in view of the Shanghai massacre in 1927.

39. *Annuario Pontificio Per L'Anno 1946* (Rome: Tipografia Poliglotta Vaticana), pp. 225-26 (hereinafter cited as *A.P.*); Galter, *op. cit.,* pp. 47-49.

40. M. Chudnovtsev, *Politecheskaia rol tserkovnikov i sektantov v SSSR* (Political role of church-people and sectarians in the USSR) (Moscow, 1930), pp. 78-79.

41. Kolarz, *op. cit.,* pp. 201-02.

42. *Ibid.,* p. 200; for the resolution see *KPSS v resoliusiiakh sezdov, konferentsii i plenumov tseka* (CPSU in the resolutions and decisions of congresses, conferences and plenary sessions of the central committee) (Moscow, 1953), Vol. I, p. 742.

43. Kolarz, *ibid.,* pp. 200-201.

44. Chudnovtsev, *op. cit.,* p. 76.

45. For a good survey of the antireligious propaganda, see S. Tyszkiewicz (Tyshkevich), "Litterature antireligieuse en U.R.S.S.," *Bulletin de l'association d'etudes et d'informations politiques internationales,* No. 105 (mars 1-15, 1954), 1-15.

46. See S. N. Savelev, "Em Iaroslavskii i preodolenie anarkhistskikh vliiany v antireligioznoi rabote v SSSR," (E. Iaroslavskii and the overcoming of anarchistic influences in antireligious work in the USSR), *Ezhegodnik muzeia istorii religii i ateizma* (Yearbook of the museum of history of religion

and atheism), Vol. VII (1963), 37-49.

47. Kolarz, *op. cit.,* pp. 182-84.

48. *Ibid.,* p. 202; see also *Antireligioznik,* No. 5, 1930; *Bezbozhnik,* August 25, 1930.

49. *A.P. 1946,* pp. 225-26; Galter, *op. cit.,* pp. 47-49.

50. On the Ukrainian Autocephalous Orthodox Church, see I. Vlaskovs-'kyi, *Narys Istorii Ukrains'koi Pravoslavnoi Tserkvy,* IV, Parts I & II (New York-Bound Brook, N.J., 1961, 1966); Kolarz, *op. cit.,* pp. 106-15; J. S. Reshetar, "Ukrainian Nationalism and the Orthodox Church," *The American Slavic and East European Review,* No. 1 (1951), pp. 38-49; Bohdan R. Bociurkiw, "The Autocephalous Church Movement in the Ukraine: The Formative State (1917-1921)," *The Ukrainian Quarterly* (Autumn, 1960), pp. 211-23; J. A. Armstrong, *Ukrainian Nationalism* (New York: Columbia University Press, 1963), pp. 188-210; Heyer, *op. cit.,* 172-223 and *passim.* On other institutions see the recent study based on Soviet documents by Boris Levytsky, *The Stalinist Terror in the Thirties* (Stanford: Hoover Institution Press, 1974).

51. Nikolai Orleanskii, ed., *Zakov o religioznykh ob'edineniiakh RSFSR (Law on religious associations of the RSFSR (Moscow: Izdatel'stvo Bezbozhnik, 1930),* p. 47.

52. *Mourin, op. cit.,* pp. 56-62; P. P. Pius XI, "Allocutio," *A.A.S.,* XV (1923), 251, 605-608; XVI (1924), 494ff; XII (1930), 89-93; *L'Osservatore Romano,* April 7, 1929; Galter, *op. cit.,* p. 47.

53. Mourin, *ibid.,* p. 59.

54. PP. Pius XI, "Ad Enum P.D. Basilium Episcopum Vleternum S.R.E. Card. Pompilj, Vice Scara in Urbe Antistitem: De Divinis Iuribus In Ditione Russica Dire Laesis Reparandis," *A.A.S.,* XXII (1930), 89-93; also see Tyshkevich, *Sovetskoe bezbozhie,* p. 1; Pontificia Commissio Pro Russia, "De Precibus pro Russia in Liturgia no latina," *A.A.S.,* XXII (1930), 366.

55. Kolarz, *op. cit.,* pp. 185 and M. A. Zaborov, *Krestovye pokhody* (The Crusades) (Moscow: Izd-vo. Akademii Nauk SSSR, 1956), p. 276 and Tyskiewicz, "Litterature antireligieuse," p. 4 and E. Iaroslavskii, *Bor'ba za predelenie religii* (Struggle to overcome religion) (Moscow: Ogiz, 1935), p. 168.

56. Kolarz, *ibid.,* pp. 185-86.

57. *Izvestiia,* March 27, 1930.

58. Kolarz, *op. cit.,* pp. 199-200; *A.P. 1946,* pp. 225-26, 319; Galter, *op. cit.,* pp. 47-49.

59. Kolarz, *ibid.,* p. 186.

60. *Ibid.,* p. 187.

61. *Ibid.,* p. 188.

62. Braun, Memoirs, appendix: "Roosevelt-Litvinov Agreement"; also

see Donald C. Bishop, *The Roosevelt-Litvinov Agreement: The American View* (Syracuse: Syracuse University Press, 1965).

63. Kolarz, *op. cit.,* p. 203.

64. *Ibid.,* pp. 202-203; also see Ia. Koval'chuk, *Ks'ondzy na Ukraini* (Kharkov: Derzh. vid-vo Ukraini, 1929) (Priests in the Ukraine); E. Iaroslavskii, *Protiv religii i tserkvi* (Against Religion and Church) (Moscow-: Ogiz, 1932). For a useful collection on the antireligious campaigns, see F. Garkavenko, ed., *O religii i tserkvi. Sbornik documnetov* (Religion and the church. Collection of documents) (Moscow: Izd-vo. politcheskoi literatury, 1965); N. Teodorovich, "The Roman Catholics," *Genocide in the USSR* (New York: The Scarecrow Press for the Institute for the Study of the USSR in Munich, 1958), p. 214.

65. Kolarz, *ibid.,* pp. 188-89.

66. *Ibid.,* pp. 189-90.

67. *Oeuvres de Maurice Thorez* (Paris, 1954), Vol. XII, pp. 165-69, as cited in Kolarz, *ibid.,* pp. 190-91.

68. Kolarz, *ibid.,* p. 191.

69. *Antireligioznik,* no. 7, 1937.

70. On the earlier propaganda see Tyskiewicz, "Litterature antireligieuse," pp. 4-7.

71. Braun, *Memoirs,* p. 54. Bishop Neveu has been the recent subject of an unpublished biography by an American Assumptionist, Rev. Patrick A. Croghan.

72. See Leopold Braun, *Religion in Russia From Lenin to Khrushchev: An Uncensored Account* (Patterson, N.J.: St. Anthony Press, 1959).

73. *A.P. 1946,* p. 319; Galter, *op. cit.,* pp. 47-49.

74. F. Oleshchuk, *Bor'ba tserkvi protiv naroda* (Struggle of the church against the people) (Moscow: Gos. izd-vo. polit. lit-ry, 1939), p. 55.

75. PP. Pius XI, *Divini Redemptoris, A.A.S.,* XXIX (1937), 65-106.

76. PP. Pius XI, *Mit Brennender Sorge, A.A.S.,* XXIX (1937), 145-67.

77. *Antireligioznik,* no. 7, 1937.

78. *Ibid.* and 1938, no. 8-9, 1938.

79. *Ibid.,* nos. 5, 7, 1938; also see Kolarz, *op. cit.,* p. 192.

80. *Antireligioznik,* nos. 5, 7, 1938; Kolarz, *ibid; Bezbozhnik,* Illustrated edition, no. 12, 1938.

81. *Bezbozhnik,* Illustrated edition, nos. 4, 6, 1939; also see Timasheff, *Religion in Soviet Russia,* pp. 112ff and Nicholas Timasheff, *The Great Retreat* (New York: E. P. Dutton, 1946), pp. 228-39.

82. Ulam, *op. cit.,* p. 259ff.

NOTES TO CHAPTER IV

1. Braun, *Memoirs,* pp. 50, 130, 254; Leopold Braun au Père Gervais Quenard, A. A., Moscou, 4 mars 1946, *Documents divers 1946-1949,* Archivio, Padri Assunzionisti, Roma, 2ET, N. 74 (hereinafter cited as *Doc. 1946-1949*).

2. The desire of the Allies and Nazis for an accord with the USSR was clearly revealed in the spring of 1939. See: *New York Times,* March 19, April 15, April 16, 1939. Germany and Britain also revealed their willingness for detente with the USSR directly to the Vatican: *Actes et documents du Saint Siège relatifs à la seconde guerre mondiale,* Vol. I: *Saint Siège et la guerre en Europe (mars 1939-aout 1940)* (Citta del Vaticano: Libreria Editrice Vatican, 1970), nrs. 47, 52, 55, 56 (hereinafter cited as *Actes et documents*).

3. Pius XI had already denounced the extremities of National Socialism in *Mit Brennender Sorge.* Pius XII's private correspondence also clearly indicated that he was abhorred by Nazism. See: *Actes et documents,* Vol. II: *Lettres de Pie XII aux évêques allemands (1939-1944)* (Citta del Vaticano: Lebreria Editrice Vatican, 1967), nrs. 20, 23, 24, 28, 32, 35, 36, 45, 53. Also see Anthony Rhodes, *The Vatican in the Age of the Dictators* (London: Hodder and Stoughton, 1973), p. 223.

4. *Actes et documents,* I, nrs. 18-20.

5. *Ibid.,* nrs. 22, 23, 25-27.

6. *Ibid.,* nr. 47.

7. *Ibid.,* nrs. 53, 81. See also the writings of the former French and British ambassadors to Germany: Andre Francois-Poncet, *Souvenirs d'une ambassade à Berlin, Septembre 1931-October 1938* (Paris: 1946), p. 340; Sir Neville Henderson, *Failure of a Mission: Berlin 1937-1939* (New York: G. P. Putnam's Sons, 1940), pp. 170-71. *Actes et documents,* I, nrs. 58, 81, 143, 148, 151.

8. *Documents on German Foreign Policy 1918-1945* (Washington, D.C.: Department of State, 1954), Series D, VIII, No. 504, 608.

9. *Actes et documents,* I, nrs. 83, 85.

10. *Documents on German Foreign Policy 1918-1945* (Washington, D.C.: Department of State, 1956), Series D, VII, No. 320, 326. Also see John Wheeler-Bennett, *The Nemesis of Power* (London: Macmillan and Co., Ltd., 1964), pp. 447, 452, 460.

11. *Actes et documents,* I, nrs. 47, 83, 85. Also see *Documents on British Foreign Policy 1919-1939,* Third Series, 9 Vols. (London: His Majesty's Stationery Office, 1949-1955), VI, no. 275, 304 note 2.

12. *Actes et documents,* I, nrs, 47, 115; *Documents on British Foreign Policy,*

Third Series, VII, no. 284, 229-31; Henderson *op. cit.,* pp. 270-72.

13. *Actes et documents,* I, nrs. 67, 69.

14. *Izvestiia,* January 23, 1940.

15. *Actes et documents,* I, nrs. 151-53, 132-34, 127-28. The Papacy continued to work for peace, even to the point of secretly collaborating with the anti-Nazi Germans. See John S. Conway, "The Vatican, Great Britain, and Relations with Germany, 1938-1940," *Historical Journal,* Vol. XVI, No. 1 (1973), 146-47.

16. *Actes et documents,* Vol. III, part 1: *Le Saint Siège et la situation religieuse en Pologne et dans les Pays Baltes 1939-1941* (Citta del Vaticano: Libreria Editrice Vatican, 1967), nrs. 13, 21, 26, 33, 63, 64. Also see Guenter Lewy, *The Catholic Church and Nazi Germany* (New York: McGraw-Hill Paperbacks, 1964), p. 227.

17. *L'Osservatore Romano,* September 20, October 14, 1939; *Actes et documents,* III, part 1, nrs. 15, 21, 45. Pius XII's encyclical, *Summi pontificatus,* also indirectly deplored the war and attacks upon religion in Poland: *Actes et documents,* I, nr. 213. The fact that the encyclical was directed against German atrocities in Poland was revealed by Cardinal Hlond's reaction to it: *Actes et documents,* III, part. 1, nrs. 21, 36.

18. *Actes et documents,* III, part. 1, pp. 3-4; Radio Vatican, *Daily Digest of Foreign Broadcasts:* British Broadcasting Corporation, Part I, February 28, 1940, 3C, ii (hereinafter cited as BBC). The original Molotov-Ribbentrop agreement was amended on September 28 when the USSR gave ethnic Poland to Germany in exchange for Lithuania. See Degras, *Soviet Documents on Foreign Policy,* III, 377-78, 380-82.

19. By the term "official," I refer to reports issued by bishops, nuncios, apostolic delegates, and apostolic administrators in or near the occupied zones. "Unofficial," on the other hand, relates to such news sources as *L'Osservatore Romano, Bezbozhnik,* etc.

20. *Actes et documents,* III, nrs. 40, 54.

21. Radio Moscow, BBC, October 27, 1939, 4B, ii.

22. This was also the case in the Latin diocese of Lviv. See *Actes et documents,* III, part. 1, nr. 297.

23. *Ibid.,* nr. 48.

24. *Ibid.,* nrs. 41, 43, 44. The Vatican, to the dismay of the Lithuanians agreed to a Polish concordat in 1925 which recognized Vilnius as a Polish diocese. See *The Royal Institute of International Affairs, The Baltic States* (London, 1938), p. 57.

25. *Actes et documents,* III, part 1, nr. 48.

26. *Ibid.,* nr. 73.

27. *Ibid.,* nrs. 50, 105. For some examples of the Soviets' attempts to

exploit the anti-Polonism of the Ukrainians see Radio Moscow, BBC, October 10, 4B, ii; October 17, 4A, i; October 27, 4B, i (1939); January 11, 4A, i; January 2, 4B, i; January 3, 4B, i; January 10, 4B, ii; January 24, 4B, ii; January 25, 4B, iii; February 11, 4B, xi; February 21, 4B, iv; February 28, 4A, i; March 31, 4A, iii; April 8, 4B, iv; April 17, 4A, ii; April 25, 4B, iii; June 26, 4A, i; September 17, 4A, iv; September 17, 4B, ii-iii; October 14, 4B, iv (1940); Radio Vatican, January 8, 2C, January 10, 2C, i (1940). Also see Molotov's speech to the Fifth Session of the Supreme Soviet on the Partition of Poland and Soviet Foreign Relations, Degras, *Soviet Documents on Foreign Policy*, III, 388-400.

28. *Actes et documents*, III, part 1, nr. 79.

29. *Ibid.*, nr. 297.

30. Volodymyr Kobijovyč, *Ukraine: A Concise Encyclopedia*, 2 vols. (Toronto: University of Toronto Press, 1971), II, 189-90.

31. *Actes et documents*, III, part 1, nr. 50.

32. *Ibid.*, nr. 52 and note 3, p. 135. Bishop Slipyi thanked Pius XII on August 5, 1941. See *Actes et documents*, III, part. 2, nr. 288.

33. Metropolitan Sheptyts'kyi also named, between September 17, 1939, and September 17, 1940, four exarchs. See pp. 134-35.

34. *Actes et documents*, III, part. 1, nr. 79.

35. Radio Vatican, BBC, January 3, 2C, i; January 4, 2C, i; February 28, 3C, ii (1940); *L'Osservatore Romano*, January 3, 25, 1940.

36. There was a significant increase in antireligious publications between 1939 and 1941 and, obviously, if the Soviets did not think it beneficial, they would not have wasted the resources—human and financial—to run the atheistic campaign. See Curtiss, *Russian Church and Soviet State*, pp. 279-89, and Chukovenkov, "Sovetskaia antireligioznaia rechat' v 1937-1941 gg.," pp. 76-90.

37. Donald A. Lowrie and William Fletcher, "Khrushchev's Religious Policy 1959-1964," *Aspects of Religion*, pp. 131-55; also see David E. Powell, *Antireligious Propaganda in the Soviet Union* (Cambridge: The MIT Press, 1975).

38. Papal encyclical, *Summi pontificatus*, issued on October 20, 1939, blamed the war, in part, on "anti-Christian movements." See *Actes et documents*, I, nr. 213; *L'Osservatore Romano*, December 1, 1939.

39. *L'Osservatore Romano*, December 1, 1939.

40. *New York Times*, December 25, 1939.

41. See Wilfred Strik-Strikfeldt, *Against Stalin &Hitler, 1941-1945* (New York: John Day Co., 1970); Solzhenitsyn, *Gulag Archipelago*, pp. 251-62. Anthony Rhodes makes it quite clear that the Papacy had little sympathy with Nazism except as a temporary foil to Communism. See Rhodes, *Vatican*, pp. 238-41.

42. *Actes et documents,* I, nrs. 235, 257.

43. Ulam, *Expansion & Coexistence,* p. 291.

44. *Actes et documents,* I, nr. 284.

45. *Ibid.,* nrs. 206, 212.

46. See footnote eight above.

47. *Actes et documents,* I, nr. 235. For a survey of Papal peace efforts, see Paul Duclos, *Le Vatican et la seconde guerre mondiale. Action doctrinale et diplomatique en faveur de la paix* (Paris, 1955).

48. Radio Vatican, BBC, July 3, 1940, 3C, ii; *Kommunist,* October 9, 1939; *Antireligioznik,* November, 1939, pp. 21-26; *Antireligioznik,* October, 1939, pp. 56-57.

49. Myron C. Taylor was named U.S. envoy at the end of December, 1939. See *Actes et documents,* I, nr. 233; *Foreign Relations of the United States, 1939,* III (Washington, United States Government Printing Office, 1956), 871-82, and 1940, I (1959), 123-25.

50. *Actes et documents,* III, part. 1, nr. 94.

51. *Ibid.,* nr. 105.

52. Radio Vatican, BBC, January 22, 2C, I; January 24, 2C, i (1940); January 25, 2C, i; February 4, 2C, ii; February 13, 2C, i; February 28, 3C, ii; March 4, 3C, i; March 11, 3C, ii; March 12, 3C, i; March 18, 3C, ii (1940). *L'Osservatore Romano,* January 25, 1940.

53. Radio Moscow, BBC, January 22, 1940, 4B, i.

54. *New York Times,* April 28, 1940.

55. Other events cited were implemented with the advent of Soviet control.

56. *Actes et documents,* III, part. 1, nr. 144.

57. Radio Vatican, BBC, May 4, 1940, 3C, i.

58. *Actes et documents,* III, part. 1, nr. 134.

59. *Pravda,* March 11, March 20, May 9, May 15, 1940; *Bezbozhnik,* May 18, 1940; Radio Moscow, BBC, March 26, 4A, v; May 17, 4A, ii (1940).

60. Braun, *Memoirs,* pp. 312-24; *Foreign Relations of the United States,* 1941 (7 Vols.) (Washington: United States Government Printing Office, 1958-1962), I, 995.

61. See footnote 36 above; on the revival of atheistic literature and on the Church, see Timasheff, *Religion in Soviet Russia,* pp. 112ff.

62. Kobijovyc, *Ukraine,* p. 174.

63. See Bociurkiw, "The Unite Church," pp. 92-93.

64. Radio Vatican, BBC, May 13, 3C, i; May 14, 3C, i (1940).

65. *Actes et documents,* III, part. 1, nr. 144.

66. A reference to Stalin's speech at the Eighteenth Congress of the C.P.S.U. in which he revealed his uneasiness about Ukrainian irredentism

and, specifically, about the Carpatho-Ukraine by ridiculing the notion of a "merger of an elephant (Soviet Ukraine) with a gnat (Carpatho-Ukraine)." I. V. Stalin, *Sochineniia,* ed. Robert H. McNeal (Stanford: Hoover Institution on War, Revolution, and Peace, 1967), I (XIV), 340.

67. Galter, *op. cit.,* p. 64; Vittorio Vignieri, "Soviet Policy Toward Religion in Lithuania: The Case of Roman Catholicism," *Lithuania Under the Soviets,* ed. V. Stanley Vardys (New York: Praeger Publishers, 1965), pp. 215-16. For a good picture of general politics and history in Lithuania on the eve of the war, see V. Stanley Vardys, "Independent Lithuania: A Profile," *Lithuania Under the Soviets,* pp. 21-46; also see Henry de Chambon. *La Lithuanie moderne* (Paris, 1933); Owen J. C. Norem, *Timeless Lithuania* (Chicago, 1943); Alfred E. Senn, *The Emergence of Modern Lithuania* (New York, 1959); Aleksandras Merkelis, *Anatanas Smetona, jo visuomenine Kulturine in politine veikla* (New York, 1964); Romuald J. Misiunas, "Fascist Tendencies in Lithuania," *The Slavic and East European Review,* XLVIII, No. 110 (January, 1970), 88-109.

68. Galter, *op. cit.,* pp. 56-57; Kolarz, *op. cit.,* p. 206.

69. Galter, *ibid.,* p. 53.

70. Romania, however, did have diplomatic relations with the Vatican. For an excellent study of Romania's pivotal position in the Balkans before the Soviet advance, see Frank Marzari, "The Bessarabian Microcosm, September 1939-February 1940," *Canadian Slavonic Papers,* XII, No. 2 (1970), 128-41.

71. *Actes et documents,* III, part. 1, nr. 153 and note 1, p. 257.

72. *Ibid.,* nrs. 159, 160.

73. *Ibid.,* nr. 165.

74. *Ibid.,* nr. 166.

75. Radio Moscow, BBC, July 1, 1940, 4B, iii-v.

76. *Ibid.,* July 1, 4B, iii-v; July 2, 4B, v; July 7, 4A, v; July 12, 4A, v (1940). Also see Degras, *Soviet Documents,* III, 458-69.

77. *Actes et documents,* III, part. 1, nrs. 167, 170, 179.

78. *Ibid.,* nr. 174.

79. There were demonstrations against the Soviet incorporation of Lithuania. See *Actes et documents,* III, part. 1, nr. 187.

80. *Ibid.,* nr. 177.

81. Radio Vatican, BBC, July 29, 1940, 3C, i.

82. Radio Moscow, BBC, August 4, 1940, 4A, iii.

83. *Actes et documents,* III, part. 1, nr. 187.

84. Radio Vatican, BBC, August 13, 1940, 3C, ii.

85. *Actes et documents,* III, part. 1, nr. 191.

86. *Ibid.,* Vol. IV: *Le Saint Siège et la guerre en Europe (juin 1940-juin 1941)*

(Citta del Vaticano: Libreria Editrice Vaticana, 1967), nrs. 43, 44.

87. *Ibid.*, nrs. 46, 47.

88. Galter, *op. cit.*, p. 57. Mgr. Centoz went directly to Rome where he was placed in charge of a newly founded commission for combating Communism. See *New York Times,* October 3, 1940.

89. Radio Vatican, BBC, August 21, 1940, 3C, ii.

90. *Actes et documents,* III, part. 1, nr. 199.

91. Radio Vatican, BBC, September 17, 1940, 3C, ii.

92. *Actes et documents,* III, part. 1, nr. 208.

93. *Ibid.*, nr. 214. He was imprisoned at Maryompole until June 23, 1941, when the German liberated him. See *ibid., p. 314, note 3.*

94. *Ibid.*, nr. 208.

95. Ibid., nr. 297.

96. *Ibid.*, p. 565, note 1.

97. *Ibid.*, nr. 208.

98. Radio Vatican, BBC, October 9, 1940, 3C, ii.

99. *Ibid.*, October 25, 1940, 3C, i.

100. *Actes et documents,* III, part. 1, nr. 217.

101. *Ibid.*, nr. 226.

102. *Ibid.*, nr. 219.

103. Radio Vatican, BBC, December 12, 1940, 3C, i.

104. Since the Vatican almost daily castigated Communism, just a few representative attacks will be cited: Radio Vatican, BBC, January 3, 2C, i; January 4, 2C, i; January 6, 2C, i; January 9, 2C, i; January 11, 2C, i; January 19, 3C, i; February 19, 3C, i; March 28, 3C, i; April 16, 3C, i; May 15, 3C, i; June 8, 3C, i; July 22, 3C, i; August 21, 3C, i; September 17, 3C, ii; October 25, 3C, i-ii; November 22, 3C, i (1940). *L'Osservatore Romano,* January 3, 1940.

105. *Actes et documents,* IV, nrs. 257, 283.

106. Again because of the commonness of this reproach in Papal media, only representative examples will be listed: Radio Vatican, BBC, January 31, 3C, i; February 27, 3C, iii; February 28, 3C, i; March 27, 3C, i; July 9, 3C, i; July 29, 3C, i; September 16, 3C, i-ii; November 11, 3C, i; December 18, 3C, i-ii (1940).

107. *Actes et documents,* I, nr. 257.

108. *Ibid.*, nrs. 257, 258.

109. Cardinal Maglione to Myron Taylor, April 26, 1940, PSF 43, FDR Library; Cordell Hull to Commission for Polish Relief, Inc., June 18, 1940, PSF 43, FDR Library; *Actes et documents,* I, nrs. 286, 292, 317, 324, 329; *Foreign Relations of the United States,* 1940, Vol. II, 686-93, 705-706.

110. Radio Vatican, BBC, January 9, 2C, i; January 17, 2C, ii (1940).

111. *Ibid.*, January 17, 1940, 2C, ii.

112. *Ibid.,* July 12, 3C, i; July 29, 3C, i (1940).

113. *Actes et documents,* I, nr. 360.

114. *Ibid.,* nr. 365.

115. *Ibid.,* IV, nrs. 116, 117, 216.

116. *Ibid.,* I, nr. 363. *Izvestiia,* on June 23, 1940, denied rumors of Soviet-German disagreement.

117. *Actes et documents,* IV, nr. 39.

118. *Ibid.,* nr. 114.

119. *New York Times,* October 3, 1940.

120. *Actes et documents,* IV, nr. 239.

121. Cardinal Godfrey had reported, throughout the latter part of 1940, that Britain was attempting to find an accommodation with the Soviet Union. See *Actes et documents,* IV, nrs. 123, 142, 165, 171, 230. No doubt to avoid antagonizing Hitler, Stalin eschewed the British overtures.

122. Through most of 1940, Stalin, as in 1939, seemed oblivious to the Vatican's anti-Soviet efforts. Communist news media continued to portray the Catholic Church as a tool of the capitalists or, as *Izvestiia,* on January 23, phrased it, "a living corpse." For some examples of the anti-Catholic propaganda, see Radio Moscow, BBC, February 15, 4A, ii; March 17, 4A, ii; April 28, 4A, i (1940); *Izvestiia,* February 24, 1940; *Pravda,* January 13, March 20, May 9, 1940; *Bezbozhnik,* July 28, August 11, 1940.

123. It is generally assumed that Stalin did not prepare or was caught off guard by the Nazi invasion. That charge, however, must be modified in light of two facts. One, he did take more housing from the Catholic Church in Eastern Europe and it is logical to assume he needed more quarters because additional troops had been moved into the west. Secondly, he did strengthen his border defenses, in a negative sense, by removing *en masse* those people whom he considered untrustworthy. Obviously he could not dramatically improve his military posture by deploying large numbers of troops in the west for that in itself could have irritated the Germans and stimulated an immediate Nazi invasion.

124. *Actes et documents,* IV, nr. 257; also p. 378, note 1.

125. *Ibid.,* nr. 227.

126. Radio Vatican, BBC, January 7, 3C, i; April 2, 3C, ii (1941); Religious Situation in Russia, September 20, 1941, PSF 43, FDR Library.

127. *Actes et documents,* III, part. 1, nr. 288.

128. *Ibid.,* nr. 289.

129. Religious Situation in Russia, September 20, 1941, PSF 43, FDR Library.

130. *Actes et documents,* III, part. 1, nr. 297.

131. *Ibid.,* nr. 324.

132. *Ibid.,* part. 2, nr. 482. Also see nr. 529 and part. 1, nr. 297.

133. *Ibid.,* part. 1, nr. 265.

134. *Ibid.,* nr. 270.

135. *Ibid.,* nr. 307.

136. *Ibid.,* nr. 310.

137. Religious Situation in Russia, September 20, 1941, PSF 43, FDR Library.

138. *Actes et documents,* III, part. 1, nr. 316.

139. *Ibid.,* part. 2, nr. 355.

140. *Ibid.,* nr. 365.

141. *Ibid.,* nr. 400.

142. *Ibid.,* nr. 425.

143. *Ibid.,* IV, nr. 309.

144. Kubijovyc, *Ukraine,* p. 174; Bociurkiw, "The Uniate Church," p. 93.

145. *Actes et documents,* III, part. 1, nr. 191 note 3.

146. For some good studies on the details of the first Soviet occupation and deportations in Eastern Europe, see Irina Saburova, "The Soviet Occupation of the Baltic States," *The Russian Review,* XIV, No. 1 (January, 1955), 36-49; V. Stanley Vardys, "Aggression, Soviet Style, 1939-1940," *Lithuania Under the Soviets,* pp. 47-60; V. Stanley Vardys, "The Partisan Movement in Postwar Lithuania," *Lithuania Under the Soviets,* pp. 87-91; Zenonas Ivinskis, "Lithuania During the War: Resistance Against the Soviet and Nazi Occupants," *Lithuania Under the Soviets,* pp. 61-84; Eugen Glowinskyi, "The Western Ukrainians," pp. 149-51 and Simon Kabysh, "The Belorussians," pp. 84-85 in *Genocide in the USSR.*

147. Braun, *Memoirs,* pp. 371-81; Religious Situation in Russia, September 20, 1941, PSF 43, FDR Library; *Foreign Relations of the United States,* 1941, I, 995-98.

148. See above, pp. 115-18, 137-41. And for representative examples in 1941, see Radio Vatican, BBC, January 10, 3C, i; February 5, 3C, i; April 2, 3C, ii; June 21, 3C, i (1940).

149. *Actes et documents,* IV, nr. 258.

150. *Ibid.,* nr. 331.

151. *Ibid.,* nr. 403.

152. *Ibid.,* nr. 411.

1. *Actes et documents,* V: *Le Saint Siège et la guerre mondiale juillet 1941-octobre 1942* (Citta del Vaticano: Libreria Editrice Vaticana, 1969), 4.

2. Winston S. Churchill, *The Grand Alliance* (Boston: Houghton Mifflin Company, 1950), pp. 371-73.

3. *Russkaia Pravoslavnaia Tserkov* (The Russian Orthodox Church) (Moscow, 1958), pp. 211-17; *Russkaia Pravoslavnaia Tserkov i verlikaia otechestvennaia voina: Sbornik* (The Russian Orthodox Church and the Great Fatherland War: A Symposium), Epistle of November 24, 1941, pp. 8-10; W. Alexeev, *The Foreign Policy of the Moscow Patriarchate, 1939-1953* (New York: Research Program on the USSR, 1955), pp. 220-221; Moscow Patriarchate, *The Truth About Religion in Russia* (Moscow, 1942), pp. 5-8; *Pravda,* November 7, 1942; George Kennan to Myron Taylor, October 2, 1942, PSF 43, FDR Library; Leopold Braun to Myron Taylor, October 1, 1941, PSF 43, FDR Library; Fireside, *Icon & Swastika,* pp. 166-92; Braun, *Memoirs,* pp. 83, 376-85; Conquest, *op. cit.,* pp. 34-35.

4. *The Truth About Religion In Russia,* pp. 5-6, 8-9. The government and the Church did not admit that the new policy was a reversal but simply allowed that what had changed was the Church's adoption of a patriotic attitude toward the Soviet government. Cf. A. Kolosov, "Religiia i tserkov v SSSR" (Religion and church in the USSR), *Bolshaia Sovietskaia Entsiklopediia* (Large Soviet Encyclopedia), Vol. L,SSSR (The USSR) (Moscow, 1948), pp. 1775-90; Metropolitan Nikolai, ed., *The Russian Orthodox Church and the War Against Fascism* (Moscow, 1943), pp. 5-6; Moskovskaia Patriarkhiia, *Russkaia Pravoslavnaia Tserkov: Ustoroistvo, polozhenie, deiatelnost* (The Russian Orthodox Church: Organization, situation, activity (Moscow, 1958), p. 14; Moskovakaia Patriarkhiia, *Patriarkh Sergii i ego dukhovnoe nasledstvo* (Patriarch Sergii and his spiritual heritage) (Moscow, 1947), pp. 308-9. For an excellent analysis, see Bociurkiw, "Church-State Relations in the USSR," pp. 93-94.

5. Bociurkiw, *ibid.,* p. 90. The regime now showed a preference for working with the conservative ecclesiastical leadership rather than the "progressive" heads of the Living Church. In 1943, in fact, the Renovationist Church was dissolved. Cf. L. I. Yemelyakh, ed., *Pravda o religii* (The Truth About Religion) (Moscow, 1959), p. 414.

6. Bociurkiw, *ibid.,* pp. 90-91; also see N. Teodorovich, "The Political Role of the Moscow Patriarchate," *Studies on The Soviet Union,* Vol. IV, No. 4 (1965), 241-47. For a recent study on religion and foreign policy, see William C. Fletcher, *Religion and Soviet Foreign Policy* (London: Oxford University Press, 1973).

7. Bociurkiw, *ibid.,* p. 91.

8. Tyszkiewicz, "La litterature antireligieuse," p. 10; Curtiss, *Russian Church and Soviet State,* p. 292; Braun, *Memoirs,* pp. 381-82.

9. *Actes et documents*, V, nrs. 62, 105, 151, p. 9.

10. *Ibid.*, III, part. 1, nrs. 292, 299, 314.

11. *Ibid.*, V, nr. 119; *Foreign Relations of the United States*, 1941, I, 253-54.

12. See J. K. Zawodny, *Death in the Forest* (Notre Dame: University of Notre Dame Press, 1962).

13. *Actes et documents*, V, nrs. 5, 8, 30, 91; *The Times* (London), July 1, 1941.

14. *The Times* (London), July 16, 18, 1941; also see June 30, August 21, 22; October 24, 1941; *Actes et documents*, V. nrs. 5, 8, 30, 129, 150.

15. *Actes et documents*, V. nr. 57. The American Catholic hierarchy was divided on the issue of aid to the USSR. See *ibid.*, nrs. 56, 67, 72; *New York Times*, October 1, 2, 4, 5, 6, 1941; Braun, *Memoirs*, p. 384. It was reported that ninety percent of American's Catholic clergy opposed aid to the USSR.

16. *Actes et documents*, V, nr. 61.

17. *Ibid.*, nr. 69.

18. *Foreign Relations of the United States*, 1941, I, 832, 999 note 28.

19. *Ibid.*, pp. 1000-1; *Actes et documents*, V, nr. 113. The American hierarchy objected to this assertion. See *New York Times*, footnote 15 above.

20. *Foreign Relations of the United States*, 1941, I, pp. 1001-2; *Actes et documents*, V, nr. 137.

21. Myron C. Taylor, *Wartime Correspondence between President Roosevelt and Pope Pius XII* (New York: The Macmillan Company, 1947), p. 58.

22. Radio Moscow, BBC, 4B, July 17, 1941, p. i; August 12, 1941, p. ii.

23. *Actes et documents*, III, part. 2, nr. 391; Extract of Speech Delivered by Ivan M. Maisky, September 23, 1941, PSF 43, FDR Library, Taylor to FDR, January 2, 1943, PSF 43, FDR Library.

24. Extract of Speech Delivered by Ivan M. Maisky, September 23, 1941, PSF 43, FDR Library.

25. *Actes et documents*, V, nr. 137.

26. *Foreign Relations of the United States*, 1941, I, 1002-3; Radio Moscow, BBC, October 5, 1941, 4A, p. iii.

27. Leopold Braun to Myron Taylor, October 1, 1941, PSF 43, FDR Library; Leopold Braun, "Father Braun From Moscow," *Newsweek*, XXVII (January 14, 1946), 83; "One Catholic Priest in Russia," *The Catholic World* (March, 1945), pp. 562-63; Braun, *Memoirs*, pp. 299, 406-7.

28. *Actes et documents*, V, nrs. 132; *The Times* (London), October 4, 1941.

29. See pp. 191-93 below.

30. Vatican organs suddenly fell silent about Communism, although *Civilta Cattolica* published two anti-Communist articles in the fall of 1941 which had been prepared before the Nazi invasion. See Francesco Pellegrino, S. J., "Lattacco a fondo dell'ateismo sovietico," *Civilta Cattolica*, 1941, III, 181-96; Francesco Pellegrino, S. J., "Sopravvivenza religioisa nella

Russia soveitica," *Civiltà Cattolica*, 1941, IV, 25-34. The Axis powers, of course, were quite perturbed that the Vatican did not support their anti-Communist crusade to the point where Hitler considered Pius XII his personal enemy. See *Actes et documents*, V, nrs. 62, 84, 111, 106, 271, 280, 410, 417. The Papacy chose to allow *Divini Redemptoris* to be interpreted by Mgr. McNicholas, Archbishop of Cincinnati, in such a way that it would be possible for Catholics to ally with the Soviets against Nazism. See Rhodes, *Vatican*, p. 263; *Actes et documents*, V, pp. 24-26.

31. *Actes et documents*, V, nrs. 69, 72, 79.

32. *Ibid.*, nr. 79.

33. *Actes et documents*, VII: *Le Saint Siège et la guerre mondiale (novembre 1942-decembre 1943)* (Citta del Vaticano: Libreria Editrice Vaticana, 1973), nr. 499. Taylor to FDR, June 23, 1944, PSF 44, FDR Library; Memorandum on interview between Pius XII, Admiral Standley and Hugh Wilson, August 12, 1944, PSF 44, FDR Library; Telegram from Taylor to Secretary of State, August 23, 1944, PSF 44, FDR Library; Telegram from Taylor to Secretary of State, December 28, 1944; PSF 44, FDR Library; *New York Times,* June 25, 1944. To be sure, the Vatican continued to pray for peace, but it issued no public declarations as in December of the preceding year. See Radio Vatican, BBC, August 12, 1941, 3C, p. i; April 12, 1943, p. iii; May 3, 1943, p. i.

34. Taylor to Secretary of State, (July 7), 1944, PSF 43, FDR Library.

35. *Actes et documents*, V, 82; Personal Memorandum, Tardini to Taylor, September 30, 1941, PSF 43, FDR Library; Memorandum, Conversation between Salazar and Taylor, October 7, 1942, PSF 43, FDR Library. The German ambassador to the Holy See, Baron Weizsacker claimed that hostility to Bolshevism was the most stable component of Papal foreign policy and that the Vatican detested the Anglo-American alliance with the USSR and considered it short-sighted of the Western Allies to persist in that arrangement. See Telegram from Weizsacker to Berlin, October 7, 1943, Staatssekretar: Vatikan, Auswartiges Amt, Bonn, Manuskript, cited in Saul Friedlander, *Pius XII and the Third Reich: A Documentation* (New York: Alfred A. Knopf, 1966), p. 195. Pius informed Taylor in late 1944 that Weizsacker was not a Nazi. See Telegram from Taylor to Secretary of State, December 28, 1944, PSF 44, FDR Library.

36. *Actes et documents*, V, nr. 82.

37. *Ibid.*, nr. 94, 83; Personal Memorandum on the Religious Situation in Russia, September 20, 1941, PSF 43, FDR Library.

38. This was clear not only from the Vatican's unwillingness to specifically denounce the Fascists, but also from the fact that it established ties with such Hitlerite puppets as Mgr. Tiso in Slovakia, Ante Pavelic in

Croatia, Bogdan Filoff in Bulgaria and, yet, refused to have relations with Eduard Beneš, the leader of the Czechoslovakian government-in-exile in London. See *Actes et documents,* V, nrs. 13, 20, 21, 36, 26, 123, 140, 242. Soviet propagandists, of course, made much of this, claiming among other things that the Church supported the Fascist persecution of the Balkan Orthodox Christians. See M. M. Sheinman, *Vatikan, vrag mira i demokratii* (Vatican, enemy of peace and democracy) (Moscow, 1950), p. 30; M. M. Sheinman, *Vatikan vo vtoroi mirovoi voine* (Vatikan during the second world war) (Moscow, 1951), p. 147; M. M. Sheinman, *Kratkie ocherki istorii papstva* (Short outline of the history of the papacy) (Moscow, 1952), p. 169.

39. Taylor was representative of the Anglo-American point of view which was to blunt Vatican criticism of the USSR and, simultaneously, to convince the Papacy that the Soviets no longer attacked religion. See *Actes et documents,* V, nrs. 5, 8, 30, 56, 59, 67, 72, 87, 113, 129, 150; Taylor, *Wartime Correspondence between President Roosevelt and Pope Pius XII,* p. 61; PP. Pius XII, "Sermo," *A.A.S.,* XXXIV (1941), 5-14; Personal Memorandum, Myron C. Taylor's summary of Cardinal Tardini's opinions on the wartime conditions, September 20, 1941, PSF 43, FDR Library.

40. *Actes et documents,* V, nr. 481.

41. *Ibid.,* nr. 137.

42. *Ibid.,* III, part. 2, nrs. 524, 543, 567.

43. *Ibid.,* nr. 425.

44. *Ibid.,* nrs. 366, 382, 387, 402, 458, 524, 543, 567.

45. *Ibid.,* nr. 388.

46. *Ibid.,* nrs. 400, 533.

47. *Ibid.,* nr. 448.

48. For Lutsk, Peremyshl, and Pinsk, see *ibid.,* nrs. 549, 555, 563, 605; on Lviv, see nrs. 529, 530.

49. Stepan Baran, *Mytropolyt Andrei Sheptyts'kyi* (Metropolitan Andrei Sheptyts'kyi) (Munich: Vernyhora Ukrains'ke Vydavnyche Tovarystvo, 1947), pp. 123-32; also see *Actes et documents,* III, part. 2, nr. 367.

50. *Actes et documents, ibid.,* nr. 375, 503; Beran, *ibid.;* Fireside, *op. cit.,* p. 140; Armstrong, *op. cit.,* pp. 197-98.

51. *Actes et documents, ibid.,* nr. 406.

52. *Ibid.,* IV, nr. 433; V, nr. 4.

53. *Ibid.,* V, nrs. 122, 125, 151; III, part. 2, nr. 355.

54. *Ibid.,* V, nrs. 122, 125, 151; III, part. 2, nr. 355. Alexander Dallin adds the often overlooked fact that Nazism was inherently antireligious and, thus, opposed to Catholicism and Orthodoxy. *German Rule In Russia 1941-1945* (New York: St. Martin's Press; London: Macmillan and Co., Ltd., 1947) pp. 472-75.

55. *Actes et documents*, V, nrs. 209, 294, 298; Moscou, 16 mars 1945, *Doc. div. 1940-1945*, 2ET, N. 114; also see Walter J. Ciszek, S. J. with Daniel L. Flaherty, S. J., *With God in Russia* (New York-Toronto-London: McGraw-Hill Book Company; New York: The American Press, 1964) and Aldo Valori, *La Campagna di Russia* (Rome: Grafica Nazionale Editrice, 1951); also see Armstrong, *op. cit.*, pp. 199-200; Kolarz, *op. cit.*, p. 215.

56. *Actes et documents*, V, nrs. 74, 75.

57. *Ibid.*, nrs. 229, 230.

58. *The Truth About Religion In Russia*, pp. 122-24.

59. *Actes et documents*, V, nrs. 189, 216, 218.

60. *Ibid.*, nr. 453. The Soviets paid close heed to Taylor's visitations. See Halan, *Tvory*, II, 424-28; H. M. Segal', *Vatikan na sluzhbe u amerikanskoi reaktsii* (Vatican in the service of american reaction) (Moscow, 1948), p. 14.

61. *Actes et documents*, V, nrs. 222, 227; Churchill, *The Grand Alliance*, pp. 476-86.

62. *Actes et documents*, V, nr. 430.

63. *Ibid.*, nrs. 232, 237, 256, 281, 305, 312, 309, 313, 316, 318, 319, 342, 357, 376, 378, 392, 403, 430.

64. *Ibid.*, nr. 204.

65. *The Truth About Religion In Russia*, pp. 122-24; anti-Vatican literature did not begin until near the war's end.

66. Braun had problems in 1942, but they were with Ambassador Steinhardt not the Soviet Government. See Braun, *Memoirs*, p. 416.

67. *Actes et documents*, V, nrs. 254, 358.

68. *Ibid.*, III, part. 2, nr. 391.

69 .*Ibid.*, nrs. 421, 422.

70. *Ibid.*, V, nr. 430 note 1.

71. *Ibid.*

72. *Ibid.*, III, part. 2, nr. 375 note 2.

73. *Ibid.*, V, nrs. 62, 84, 111, 126, 271, 280, 343, 355, 417.

74. *Ibid.*, III, part. 2, nr. 375 note 2; V, nr. 275.

75. *Ibid.*, III, part. 2, nr. 375.

76. *Ibid.*, nr. 406.

77. *Ibid.*, V, nr. 274; *New York Times*, March 8, April 22, 1942; February 18, May 6, May 27, May 28, 1943.

78. *Actes et documents*, V, nrs. 489, 490.

79. *Ibid.*, nr. 487.

80. *Ibid.*, nr. 364.

81. *Ibid.*, nr. 284.

82. *Ibid.*, III, part. 2, nr. 418.

83. *Ibid.*, V, nr. 207.

84. *Ibid.,* nr. 206. There is mounting evidence indicating that Stalin was prepared to come to terms with the Nazis, but it still is preposterous to think he would have told the British of his plans in his critical position. See Vojtech Mastny, *"Stalin and the Prospects of a Separate Peace in World War II,"* *The American Historical Review,* Vol. LXXVII, No. 5 (December, 1972), 365-88.

85. *Actes et documents,* V, nr. 209, 238; also see Taylor to Secretary of State (July 7), 1941, PSF 43, FDR Library.

86. *Actes et documents,* V, nr. 246.

87. *Ibid.,* nr. 240.

88. *Ibid.,* nr. 237.

89. *Ibid.,* nrs. 272, 292, 293; *Foreign Relations of the United States,* 1942, III, 784-85.

90. *Actes et documents,* V, nrs. 255, 261.

91. *Ibid.,* nr. 262.

92. *Foreign Relations of the United States,* 1942, III, 779-86.

93. *Actes et documents,* V, nr. 285.

94. *Ibid.,* nr. 303.

95. *Ibid.,* nr. 299; *Foreign Relations of the United States,* 1942, III, 785-87.

96. *Actes et documents,* V, nrs. 303, 316.

97. *Foreign Relations of the United States,* 1942, III, 778-79.

98. *Ibid.,* pp. 783, 786-87.

99. *Actes et documents,* V, nrs. 413, 421, 423; VII, nrs. 10, 90, 98, 183.

100. *Ibid.,* V, nrs. 472, 490, 374; *Foreign Relations of the United States,* 1942, III, 775-76.

101. Memorandum, Conversation Between Maglione and Taylor, September 25, 1942, PSF 43, FDR Library; Sumner Welles to Taylor, October 21, 1942, PSF 43, FDR Library.

102. Memorandum, Conversation Between Maglione and Taylor, September 25, 1942, PSF 43, FDR Library; American Legation in Bern to Secretary of State, September 4, 1942, PSF 43, FDR Library. The Church actually did a great deal for refugees. See Actes et documents, VI: *Le Saint Siège et les victimes de la guerre (mars 1939-decembre 1940)* and VIII: *Le Saint Siege et les vitimes de la guerre (janvier 1941-de\u0107embre 1942)* (Citta Del Vaticano: Libreria Editrice Vaticana, 1973, 1974).

103. Memorandum, Conversation Between Pope Pius, Cardinals Maglione, Montini, and Tardini and Taylor, September 19, 22, 26, 1942, PSF 43, FDR Library; Memorandum, Conference Between Maglione and Taylor, September 25, 1942, PSF 43, FDR Library; Cerejeira to Taylor, October 3, 1942, PSF 43, FDR Library.

104. Memorandum, Conversation Between Pope Pius, Cardinals Maglione, Montini, and Tardini and Taylor, September 19, 22, 26, 1942, PSF 43,

FDR Library; Memorandum, Conference Between Maglione and Taylor, September 25, 1942, PSF 43, FDR Library.

105. *Actes et documents,* V, nrs. 477, 487.

106. *Ibid.,* nrs. 477, 480, 481.

107. *Ibid.,* nrs. 480, 484, 486; Personal Memorandum, Taylor's Summary of Conversation with Cardinal Tardini, September 26, 1942, PSF 43, FDR Library; Memorandum, Conversation Between Salazar and Taylor, October 7, 1942, PSF 43, FDR Library; Memorandum on Italy, Reported to Taylor by an undisclosed source, September 7, 1942, PSF 43, FDR Library; Memorandum reported to Taylor by an undisclosed source, September 24, 1942, PSF 43, FDR Library (internal evidence indicates that the source was Count Dalla Torre, director of *L'Osservatore Romano*: Personal Memorandum, Taylor's Summary of Conversation with Cardinal Tardini, September 26, 1942, PSF 43, FDR Library).

108. *Actes et documents,* V, nrs. 481, 484, 486.

109. Personal Memorandum, Taylor's Summary of Conversation with Cardinal Tardini, September 26, 1942, PSF 43, FDR Library.

110. *Actes et documents,* V, nr. 480.

111. *Ibid.,* nrs. 484, 486; VII, nr. 60.

112. Personal Memorandum, Taylor's Summary of Conversation with Cardinal Tardini, September 26, 1942, PSF 43, FDR Library; Personal Memorandum, Conversation Between Pius XII and Taylor, September 9, 1942, PSF 43, FDR Library; Memorandum, Conversation Between Franco and Taylor, September 30, 1942, PSF 43, FDR Library; Memorandum, Conversation Between Salazar and Taylor, October 7, 1942, PSF 43, FDR Library; M. Papee to Tittmann, October 2, 1942, PSF 43, FDR Library; Lozoraitis to Taylor, September 25, 1942, PSF 43, FDR Library.

113. Actes et documents, V, nrs. 52, 236; VII, nrs. 38-58, 63, 65, 73, 75-80 *passim; Foreign Relations of the United States,* 1943, II, 910; 1944, II, 1274-1314.

114. Mooney to Taylor, November 30, 1942, PSF 43, FDR Library; Gawlina to Stritch, September 17, 1942, PSF 43, FDR Library; Personal Memorandum, Taylor's Summary of Conversation with Cardinal Tardini, September 26, 1942, PSF 43, FDR Library; U.S. Bishops' Statement on Victory and Peace to Taylor, November 14, 1942, PSF 43, FDR Library; Taylor to FDR, May 6, 1943, PSF 43, FDR Library; *Actes et documents,* VII, nrs. 60, 71, 135, 138, 150, 154, 162, 173, 216, 256, 505; Rhodes, *Vatican,* p. 272.

115. *Personal Memorandum, Taylor's Summary of Conversation with Cardinal Tardini, September 26, 1942, PSF 43, FDR Library.*

116. *Gawlina to Stritch, September 17, 1942, PSF 43, FDR Library; Memorandum from Polish Embassy at Iran to Wendell Wilkie, September 16, 1942, PSF 43, FDR Library.*

117. *Mooney to Taylor, November 30, 1942, PSF 43, FDR Library; Taylor to FDR, July 17, 1944, PSF 44, FDR Library.*

118. *Russkaia Pravoslavnaia Tserkov i velikaia otechestvennaia voina: Sbornik, op. cit.,* Epistle of December 30, 1942, pp. 41-42. For details on the religious movement in the German controlled regions of the Soviet Union, see Heyer, *Die Orthodoxe Kirche in der Ukraine von 1917 bis 1945,* pp. 172-223 and *passim;* Armstrong, *op. cit.,* pp. 188-210. Both of these authors feel the Ukrainian Autocephalous Orthodox Church was "separatist," that is, a product of Ukrainian nationalism. Cf. Fireside, *op. cit.,* pp. 131-65 and Wassilij Alexeev, *Russian Orthodox Bishops in the USSR* (New York: Research Program on the USSR, 1954).

119. Until 1943, religious activities were controlled at the Union Republic level. In the Russian Republic, religious administration was handled by the Commission for the Affairs of Cults, a branch of the RSFSR's Supreme Soviet Presidium. See V. D. Bonch-Bruevich, *Izbrannye sochineniia* (Selected Works', Vol. I: *O religii, religioznom sektanstve i tserkvi* (On religion, religious sectarianism, and the churches) (Moscow, 1959), p. 86. For details on Karpov, see N. Yeremin, ed., *Za boevuiu antireligioznuiu propagandu* (For a militant, antireligious propaganda) (Leningrad, 1937), pp. 246-51. Also see Bociurkiw, "Church-State Relations," p. 92.

120. Soviet antireligious writers later condemned the Vatican's crusade. See E. Vinter, "papskoi politike ob'edeneniia tserkvei," pp. 25-26; D. E. Mikhnevich, *Ocherki iz istorii katolicheskoi reaktsii* (Outline of the history of catholic reaction) (Moscow, 1955), p. 359.

121. *Actes et documents,* III, part. 2, nr. 503.

122. *Ibid.,* nr. 485.

123. Memorandum Correspondence between Pope Pius, Cardinal Tardini, and Taylor, July 17, 1944, PSF 44, FDR Library.

NOTES TO CHAPTER VI

1. See Bociurkiw, "Uniate Church," pp. 89-90; Kolarz, *op. cit.,* p. 226; Baran, *Mytroplyt Sheptyts'kyi,* p. 144.

2. See, for example, M. M. Sheinman, *Vatikan i katolitsizym na sluzhbe mezhdunarodnoi reaktsii* (Vatican and catholicism in the service of international reaction) (Moscow, 1954), p. 19; M. M. Sheinman, *Sovremennyi Vatikan* (Contemporary Vatican) (Moscow, 1955), p. 25; M. M. Sheinman, *Kratkie ocherki istorii papstva* (Short outline of the history of the papacy) (Moscow,

1952), pp. 127-28; D. E. Mikhnevich, *Ocerki iz istorii katolicheskoi reaktsii* (Outline of the history of catholic reaction) (Moscow, 1955), p. 359; Halan, *Tvory,* II, 79-82, 360-61.

3. Soviet authors, it is interesting to note, have contended that the Uniates were forced into the Union in accordance with a policy that has been described as "Catholic Pan-Slavism." See P. N. Dovgaluk, "Ukrainskie pisateli o vatikane," *Ezhegodnik museia istorii religii i ateizma* (Yearbook of the museum of religion and atheism), Vol. II (1958), 188; Sheinman, *Kratkie ocherki istorii papstva,* pp. 111-18; Halan, *Tvory,* II, 276-78, 288-330.

4. Bociurkiw, "Uniate Church," p. 95.

5. It is significant that the Soviets allowed an elaborate funeral for the metropolitan and, once the "reunion" was formalized, claimed that the archbishop was a "precursor of reunion." See *Diiannia Soboru Hreko-Katolyts'koi Tserkvy, 8-10 bereznia 1946, u L'vovi* (Proceedings of the Sobor of the Greek-Catholic Church) (Lviv, 1946), pp. 136-37; *First Victims,* p. 32; *Pravda,* November 4, 1944.

6. Armstrong, *op. cit.,* p. 297; Bociurkiw, "Uniate Church," pp. 95-96.

7. See M. M. Persits, *Otdelenie tserkvi ot gosudarsvta i shkoly ot tserkvi v SSSR 1917-1919 gg.* (Separation of the church from the state and the school from the church in the USSR, 1917-1919) (Moscow, 1958), p. 120. Cf. Bociurkiw, "Church-State Relations," p. 91 n. 43.

8. For the best analysis of the Soviet suppression of the Ukrainian Uniate Church, see Bociurkiw, *ibid.,* pp. 96-97. In addition, see Denis Dirscherl, S. J., "The Soviet Destruction of the Greek Catholic Church," *Journal of Church and State,* Vol. XII, N. 3 (Autumn, 1970), 421-39; Ivan Hrynioch, "The Destruction of the Ukrainian Catholic Church in the Soviet Union," *Prologue,* Vol. IV, No. 1-2 (Spring-Summer, 1960), 1-15; Roman Reynarowych, "The Catholic Church in the West Ukraine After World War II," *Diakonia,* N. 4 (1970), pp. 372-87; Walter Dushnyck, *Martyrdom in Ukraine: Russia Denies Religious Freedom* (New York, The American Press, n.d.); this author's "The Disappearance of the Ukrainian Uniate Church: How and Why?" *Ukrainskyi Istoryk,* 1-2 (33-34), Rik IX (New York-Munich, 1972), 57-65.

9. This was the first indication following the turn in the tide of battle against the Germans. Actually, as indicated earlier, there were concrete manifestations of a Soviet policy to assimilate the Uniate Church during the first Russian occupation, 1939-1941.

10. *Actes et documents,* II, nr. 503.

11. *Izvestiia,* February 1, 1944; February 3, 1945; March 10, 1945; *Zhurnal Moskovskoi Patriarkhii,* No. 2, 1944, pp. 13-18; No. 4, 1945, pp. 7-9, 19-21; No. 5, 1945, pp. 36-43; *Pravda,* March 25, August 3, 1945; February 28, 1946.

12. Dirscherl, "Soviet Destruction of the Greek Church," p. 428; Galter, *op. cit.,* p. 91.

13. Moscou, 16 mars 1945, *Doc. div. 1940-1945,* 2ET, N. 114. This particular reference is to a letter written by Fr. Anthony Leoni, the Jesuit who resided in Odessa for most of the German-Romanian occupation of the Ukraine. He strongly intimated that the *Sobor* had made a decision to persecute the Uniates and absorb the Ukrainian Uniate Church.

14. *First Victims,* pp. 32, 103; Halan, *Tvory,* II, 285.

15. *First Victims,* pp. 32-33, 107; see also V. Beliaev, *Nauka i religiia,* No. 11, 1960, pp. 66-67.

16. *First Victims,* p. 33; cf. Halan, *Tvory,* II, 285, 381-82.

17. Bociurkiw, "Uniate Church," p. 98.

18. *Ibid.,* p. 99; Reynarowych, "The Church in the West Ukraine," p. 376.

19. Halan, *Tvory,* II, 360-61, 363.

20. *First Victims,* p. 33; Bolshakoff, *Nonconformity,* p. 140; Bociurkiw, "Uniate Church," pp. 99-100; Reynarowych, "The Church in the West Ukraine," p. 376; Galter, *op. cit.,* p. 92. The diocesan archives were also evidently seized. See Halan, *Tvory,* II, 382.

21. Bolshakoff, *Nonconformity,* p. 140, claims 500 clerics were arrested but this has yet to be authoritatively confirmed. In June, 1945, Soviet police in Berlin arrested Mgr. Petro Verhun, another member of the Ukrainian Greek hierarchy. See Baran, *Mytropolyt Andrei Sheptyts'kyi,* p. 139 and Bociurkiw, "Uniate Church," pp. 99-100.

22. *Tablet* (London), January 12, 1946, p. 18 (The *Tablet* was and is a highly respected Catholic weekly with close ties to the Vatican; see A. Cardinal Hinsley to Taylor, October 6, 1942, PSF 43, FDR Library); for Vatican reaction see *Il Quotidiano,* June 6, 1945 and *New York Times,* June 7, 1945; Dushnyck, *Martyrdom,* pp. 33-35.

23. Bociurkiw, "Uniate Church," pp. 100-101.

24. *Zh. M. P.,* No. 4, 1946, p. 36; *First Victims,* pp. 33-34; Bociurkiw, "Uniate Church," p. 100; Halan, *Tvory,* II, 379-82.

25. Bociurkiw, *ibid.,* pp. 100, 110; *First Victims,* pp. 34-36; Galter, *op. cit.,* pp. 92-93; Reynarowych, "The Church in the West Ukraine," p. 376.

26. Bociurkiw, "The Uniate Church in the Soviet Ukraine," pp. 100, 110; Reynarowych, "The Church in the West Ukraine," pp. 381-82; Conquest, *Religion in the U.S.S.R.,* p. 96.

27. *Zh. M. P.,* No. 10, 1948, p. 12; Bociurkiw, "Uniate Church," p. 101; Galter, *op. cit.,* p. 93; Hrynioch, "Destruction of the Ukrainian Church," pp. 20-22; *First Victims,* p. 106; G. W. Schuster, *Religion Behind the Iron Curtain* (New York: The Macmillan Company, 1954), pp. 138-40.

28. *First Victims*, p. 108; Galter, *op. cit.*, p. 93; Bociurkiw, "Uniate Church," p. 101.

29. Bociurkiw, *ibid.*, p. 102.

30. *First Victims*, p. 38.

31. Bociurkiw, "Uniate Church," p. 101; Galter, *op. cit.*, p. 94.

32. Bociurkiw, *ibid.; First Victims*, pp. 39–40; Dushnyck, *op. cit.*, p. 27.

33. *Diiannia Soboru*, pp. 15, 23; documents also in *Tablet* (London), January 12, 1946, pp. 18-19; Bociurkiw, *ibid.*

34. *Diiannia Soboru*, p. 125; *First Victims*, p. 38; Bociurkiw, *ibid.*, pp. 101-104; Galter, *op. cit.*, pp. 94-95.

35. *First Victims*, pp. 40, 42; Bociurkiw, *ibid.*, pp. 103-104; Galter, *op. cit.*, p. 95; *Diiannia Soboru*, pp. 61, 53-58.

36. *Zh. M. P.*, No. 4, 1946, p. 5.

37. *Ibid.*

38. Bociurkiw, "Uniate Church," p. 104; also note the Vatican's reaction: *New York Times*, March 19, 1946.

39. *Diiannia Soboru*, pp. 42-43.

40. *Zh. M. P.*, No. 4, 1946, p. 5; *Diiannia Soboru*, pp. 127-28.

41. *Zh. M. P.*, No. 4, 1946, p. 9; *Diiannia Soboru*, pp. 127-28.

42. *Diiannia Soboru*, pp. 127-28; See Bociurkiw, "Uniate Church," pp. 104-107 for an excellent analysis of the *Sobor.*

43. *Diiannia Soboru*, pp. 127-28.

44. *Ibid.; Zh. M. P.*, No. 4, 1946, pp. 22-23.

45. Bociurkiw, "Uniate Church," p. 106.

46. *Diiannia Soboru*, pp. 136-37; *Zh. M. P.*, No. 4, 1946, p. 24; Bociurkiw, *ibid.;* Reynarowych, "The Catholic Church in the West Ukraine," p. 378.

47. *Diiannia Soboru*, p. 147.

48. *Ibid.*, pp. 141-42; *Zh. M. P.*, No. 4, 1946, p. 24; the letter to Stalin also appeared in *Pravda*, March 17, 1946; Bociurkiw, *ibid.*; Reynarowych, *op. cit.*

49. *Diiannia Soboru*, pp. 129-30.

50. *Zh. M. P.*, No. 4, 1946, pp. 35-36.

51. *Ibid.*, No. 10, 1948, pp. 9-10; Bociurkiw, "Uniate Church," pp. 108-109; *First Victims*, p. 106.

52. Bociurkiw, *ibid.*, pp. 107-108; Reynarowych, *op. cit.*, p. 384; Galter, *op. cit.*, p. 107.

53. For the best to date account of the "reunion" process in Transcarpathia, see Vasyl Markus, *Nyshchennia Hreko-Katolyts'koi Tserkvy v Mukachivs'kii Ieparkhii v 1945-1950 rr.* (Paris, 1962); see also *First Victims*, pp. 48-58; *Zh. M. P.*, No. 10, 1949, pp. 5-11.

54. Boshakoff, *Nonconformity*, pp. 140-41.

55. Metropolitan Sheptyts'kyi named Reverend Anto Nemancevic, S.J.,

the Exarch of Belorussia, but, in October, 1942, when he assumed his post in Minsk, he was arrested and presumably executed by the Germans. See *Actes et documents*, III, part. 2, nr. 375 note 1; cf. Nicholas P. Vakar, *Belorussia* (Cambridge: Harvard University Press, 1956), p. 278.

56. Kolarz, *op. cit.*, pp. 226-27; cf. Fireside, *op. cit.*, p. 140.

57. *Izvestiia*, February 1, 1944; February 10, 1945; March 10, 1945; Pravda, March 25, 1945; August 3, 1945; February 28, 1946; Zh. M. P., No. 2, 1944, pp. 13-18; No. 2, 1945, p. 11; No. 4, 1945, pp. 7-9, 19-21; No. 5, 1945, pp. 36-43; Radio Moscow, BBC, February 1, 1944, 4A, pp. viii-ix. Also see Tyszkiewicz, "La litterature antireligieuse"; "L'Ateismo Militante Sovietico E Il Papato," II, 600-603, III, 19-27, 1949, *Civilta Cattolica; Foreign Relations of the United States*, 1945, V, 112-1121, 1120 note 75.

58. See footnote thirteen above.

59. *Zh. M. P.*, No. 2, 1945, p. 11; *Izvestiia*, February 10, 1945.

60. Tyszkiewicz, "Lat Litterature antireligieuse," pp. 10-11; Tyszkiewicz, "L'Ateismo Militante Sovietico E Il Papato," II, 600-603 and III, 19-27; Halan, *Tvory*, II, 360-61, 363.

61. M. M. Sheinman, *Vatikan vo vtoroi mirovoi voine* (The Vatican during the second world war) (Moscow, 1951), p. 157; M. M. Sheinman, *Vatikan, vrag mira i demokratii* (The Vatican, enemy of peace and democracy) (Moscow, 1950), p. 30; Iaroslav Halan, *Vatikan bez maski* (The Vatican unmasked) (Moscow, 1952), p. 139.

62. *New York Times*, February 2, 1944; February 13, March 11, March 22, March 27, 1945; *Il Quotidiano*, February 12, 1945; March 26, 1945; *L'Osservatore Romano*, February 2, 1945; February 10, 1945; May 10, 1945; March 4, 1946; *Foreign Relations of the United States*, 1945, V, 1120 note 75.

63. *L'Osservatore Romano*, March 4, 1946.

64. Taylor to FDR, August 26, 1944, Map Room File 12, FDR Library; Taylor to FDR, Jund 23, 1944, PSF 44, FDR Library; Telegram from Taylor to Secretary of State, December 12, 1944, PSF 44, FDR Library; Telegram from Taylor to Secretary of State, February 28, 1945, PSF 44, FDR Library; Telegram from Taylor to Secretary of State, March 21, 1945, PSF 44, FDR Library; Taylor to FDR, July 17, 1944, PSF 44, FDR Library.

65. Taylor to FDR, June 23, 1944, PSF 44, FDR Library; Memorandum on interview between Pius XII, Admiral Standley and Hugh Wilson, August 12, 1944, PSF 44, FDR Library; Telegram from Taylor to Secretary of State, August 23, 1944, PSF 44, FDR Library; Memorandum on Taylor's audience with Pius XII, August 11, 1944, PSF 44, FDR Library; Taylor to FDR, August 26, 1944, Map Room Rile 12, FDR Library; Telegram from Taylor to Secretary of State, December 12, 1944, PSF 44, FDR Library; Telegram from Taylor to Secretary of State, December 13, 1944, PSF 44, FDR Library;

Telegram from Taylor to Secretary of State, February 28, 1944, PSF 44, FDR Library; Telegram from Taylor to Secretary of State, March 21, 1945, PSF 44, FDR Library; *Foreign Relations of the United States,* 1945, V, 1120 note 75.

66. Taylor to FDR, June 23, 1944, PSF 44, FDR Library; Taylor to Secretary of State, August 9, 1944, PSF 44, FDR Library; Memorandum on interview between Pius XII, Admiral Standley and Hugh Wilson, August 12, 1944, PSF 44, FDR Library; Telegram from Taylor to Secretary of State, August 23, 1944, PSF 44, FDR Library; Telegram from Taylor to Secretary of State, December 28, 1944, PSF 44, FDR Library; *New York Times,* June 25, 1944.

67. Taylor to FDR, June 23, 1944, PSF 44, FDR Library; Telegram from Taylor to Secretary of State, August 23, 1944, PSF 44, FDR Library.

68. Taylor to FDR, June 23, 1944, PSF 44, FDR Library; Memorandum on interview between Pius XII, Admiral Standley and Hugh Wilson, August 12, 1944, PSF 44, FDR Library; Telegram from Taylor to Secretary of State, August 23, 1944, PSF 44, FDR Library.

69. Taylor to Secretary of State, August 9, 1944, PSF 44, FDR Library; Memorandum on interview between Pius XII, Admiral Standley and Hugh Wilson, August 12, 1944, PSF 44, FDR Library; Telegram from Taylor to Secretary of State, August 23, 1944, PSF 44, FDR Library; Telegram from Taylor to Secretary of State, December 28, 1944, FDR Library; *L'Osservatore Romano,* May 10, 1945.

70. Taylor to FDR, June 23, 1944, PSF 44, FDR Library; Telegram from Taylor to Secretary of State, December 12, 1944, PSF 44, FDR Library; Memorandum, Stettinius to FDR, December 13, 1944, PSF 44, FDR Library; Telegram from Taylor to Secretary of State, December 13, 1944, PSF 44, FDR Library; Telegram from Taylor to Secretary of State, February 28, 1945, PSF 44, FDR Library; Telegram from Taylor to FDR, March 5, 1945, PSF 44, FDR Library; Telegram from Taylor to Secretary of State, March 21, 1945, PSF 44, FDR Library.

71. Memorandum on Taylor' audience with Pius XII, August 11, 1944, PSF 44, FDR Library.

72. Pius XII, *Orientales Omnes Ecclesias, A.A.S.,* XXXVIII (1946), 33-63. This encyclical was interpreted by the Soviets as an anti-Russian decree. See E. Vinter, "O papskoi politike ob'edineniia tserkvei," *Ezhegodnik,* VI (1962), 26.

1. For an excellent study of Eastern Europe under the Soviets, see Hugh Seton-Watson, *The East European Revolution* (New York: Praeger Publishers, 7th Printing, 1971); for recent assessments, see Chalmers Johnson, ed., *Change in Communist Systems* (Stanford: Stanford University Press, 1970); William E. Griffith, ed., *Communism in Europe,* 2 Vols. (Cambridge: M.I.T. Press, 1964, 1966); Samuel P. Huntington and Clement H. Moore, eds., *Authoritarian Politics in Modern Society* (New York: Praeger Publishers, 1970); R. V. Burks, *The Dynamics of Communism in Eastern Europe* (Princeton: Princeton University Press, 1961). Also see the recent discussion on the prospects for change in Eastern Europe in the *Slavic Review,* Vol. XXXIII, No. 2 (June, 1974), 219-58.

2. Frank Dinka, "Sources of Conflict Between Church and State in Poland," *Review of Politics,* Vol. XXVIII, No. 3 (July, 1966), 323-34.

3. Cf. Michael J. Lazna, "Causes of the Communist Victory in the 1946 Czechoslovak Election," (Unpublished dissertation, The George Washington University, 1971).

4. *Foreign Relations of the United States,* 1944, III, 1398-1399, 1402; *New York Times,* May 13, 1944; Radio Moscow, BBC, May 15, 1944, 4A, pp. iv-v.

5. *New York Times,* May 13, 1944; Radio Moscow, BBC, April 28, 1944, 4A, p. ii. The other obvious purpose of the invitation was Stalin's attempts to convince the Polish Catholics and Polish Americans that they had nothing to fear from the USSR. Possibly Stalin was attempting to help FDR out with the Polish voters since the President had expressed, at Teheran, concern that the recognition of Soviet wishes regarding the Polish-Russian border might embitter the American Poles against FDR. Stalin specifically requested that the American Government grant Orlemanski and Professor Oscar Lange passports. The Polish-Government-in exile objected to the visit. See *Foreign Relations of the United States,* 1944, III, 1402, 1406-1407; Radio Moscow, BBC, April 29, 1944, 4B, p. iv.

6. *New York Times,* May 13, 1944; Radio Moscow, BBC May 14, 1944, 4A, pp. iv-v.

7. *Foreign Relations of the United States,* 1944, III, 1407-1409; *New York Times,* May 13, 1944; Radio Moscow, BBC, May 14, 1944, 4A, pp. iv-v.

8. *New York Times,* May 13, 1944; Radio Moscow, BBC, May 14, 1944, 4A, pp. iv-v.

9. *New York Times,* May 13, 1944; Radio Moscow, *ibid.*

10. *Foreign Relations of the United States,* 1944, IV, 868-869; *New York Times, ibid.;* Radio Moscow, *ibid.*

11. *Foreign Relations of the United States, ibid.; New York Times, ibid.;* Radio Moscow, *ibid.*

12. *Foreign Relations of the United States, ibid.; New York Times, ibid.;* Radio Moscow, *ibid.*

13. *Foreign Relations of the United States, ibid.; New York Times, ibid.;* Radio Moscow, *ibid.*

14. *Foreign Relations of the United States, ibid., New York Times, ibid.;* Radio Moscow, *ibid.*

15. *Foreign Relations of the United States, ibid.; New York Times, ibid.;* Radio Moscow, *ibid.*

16. *Pravda,* May 14, 1944.

17. R. C. Lauterbach, *These Are the Russians* (New York-London: Harper and Brothers, 1945), p. 277.

18. *New York Times,* May 14, 15, 1944; Manhattan, *The Vatican in World Politics,* pp. 355-56; Leopold Braun explained, in part, the Vatican's reaction when he declared that Orlemanski's mission was a Stalinist ploy and that a concordat with Stalin would be "very difficult" since he "protects in a special fashion the old Orthodox Church which . . . favors Pan-Slavism and . . . looks upon Catholics with traditional distrust." See P. Quenard au Nonce Apostolique, Paris, 26 fevrier 1945, *Doc. div. 1940-1945,* 2ET, N. 38. The U.S. Embassy in Moscow, on the other hand, interpreted it as a genuine effort on Stalin's part to improve Soviet-Catholic relations. See *Foreign Relations of the United States,* 1944, IV, 869.

19. Radio Moscow, BBC, May 22, 1944, 4A, pp. ii-iii.

20. Edward Dolan, "Post-War Poland and the Church," *American Slavic and East European Review* (1955), p. 84.

21. Dinka, *op. cit.,* p. 333; also see Frank Dinka, "Church and State in Poland: Political Conflict Between the Catholic Church and the Communist Regime," (Published Ph.D. dissertation, Washington University, 1963), chapters 1 & 2. Also see Gary MacEoin, *The Communist War on Religion* (New York: The Devin-Adair Co., 1951), p. 195.

22. Haroška, *op. cit.,* pp. 99-100.

23. *Ibid.,* p. 99.

24. *New York Times,* January 11, 1945.

25. *Ibid.*

26. *Ibid.*

27. *Actes et documents,* III, part. 2, nr. 598.

28. Elizabeth Valkenier, "The Catholic Church in Communist Poland, 1945-1955," *Review of Politics,* XVIII (July, 1956), 306.

29. *Ibid.*

30. Marion Dziewanowski, "Communist Poland and the Catholic Church," *Problems of Communism,* III, No. 5 (Sept.-Oct., 1954), 1-2.

31. Dinka, "Sources of Conflict," p. 335.

32. Valkenier, *op. cit.*, p. 306.

33. *Ibid.*, pp. 306-307; for a good study of the government's infringement on the legal rights of the Church, see Marion S. Mazgaj, J. C. D., "The Communist Government of Poland as Affecting the Rights of the Church from 1944 to 1960," (Unpublished Ph.D. dissertation, The Catholic University of America, 1970).

34. Dolan makes a good case against this charge, *op. cit.*, p. 85.

35. Valkenier, *op. cit.*, p. 307.

36. *Ibid.*

37. *Ibid.*, p. 308.

38. *Ibid.*

39. *Ibid.*, pp. 308-309.

40. *Tablet* (London), November 16, 1946.

41. Dolan, *op. cit.*, p. 85.

42. Valkenier, *op. cit.*, pp. 310-11; *New York Times*, October 21, November 24, 1946; "Communist Offenses Against the Integrity of Education, Science, and Culture," *Collected Intelligence Research Reports on Communism: United States Government 1949-1954* (on microfilm at Kent State University), p. 97, 102-5 (hereinafter cited as *CIRRCUS Materials*); Dziewanowski, "Communist Poland and the Catholic Church," p. 1.

43. Valkenier, *ibid.*

44. *Ibid.*, p. 311.

45. *Ibid.*, pp. 311-12.

46. *Ibid.*, p. 311.

47. Stephen Kertesz, "Church and State in Hungary," *Review of Politics,* XI (April, 1949), 209-10; Galter, *op. cit.*, pp. 195-96; MacEoin, *Communist War on Religion,* pp. 114-15; Camille Cianfarra, *The Vatican and the Kremlin* (New York: E. P. Dutton & Co., Inc., 1950), p. 149; George N. Shuster, *In Silence I Speak* (New York: Farrar, Straus, and Cudahy, 1956), p. 8.

48. Shuster, *ibid.;* Galter, *op. cit.*, pp. 196-97; "Communist Offenses Against the Integrity of Education, Science, and Culture," *CIRRCUS Materials,* p. 80.

49. Schuster, *Religion Behind the Iron Curtain,* pp. 166-68, 173-74; also see Robert Tobias, *Communist-Christian Encounter in East Europe* (Indianapolis, Ind.: School of Religion Press, 1956), p. 24; Free Europe Committee, *The Red and the Black* (New York: The National Committee for a Free Europe, 1953), pp. 51, 73-74.

50. For an excellent study of the Catholic Church as well as other Churches' role in Hungarian history from 1919 to 1945, see Leslie Laszlo, "Church and State in Hungary, 1919-1945," (Unpublished Ph.D Dissertation, Columbia University, 1973).

51. Taylor to FDR, March 3, 1946, PSF 44, FDR Library. Taylor quoted at length a report on the Church in Hungary that had been prepared by Dr. K. Jonas Toth who was a Vatican official in Hungary.

52. *Ibid.*

53. *Ibid.;* Kertesz, *op. cit.,* p. 215. The papers had to contend with censorship and a chronic shortage of newsprint.

54. Shuster, *In Silence,* p. 8; MacEoin, *Communist War on Religion,* pp. 113-14; Galter, *op. cit.,* pp. 196, 212; "Communist Offenses Against the Integrity of Education, Science, and Culture," *CIRRCUS Materials,* p. 80. For background on Mindszenty, see Kertesz, *ibid.,* pp. 213-14.

55. Taylor to FDR, March 3, 1946, PSF 44, FDR Library; Galter, *op. cit.,* pp. 200-1; Cianfarra, *op. cit.,* p. 152; MacEoin, *op. cit.,* p. 118; Mourin, *op. cit.,* p. 167.

56. József Cardinal Mindszenty, *Memoirs* (London: Weidenfeld and Nicolson, 1974), pp. 31, 41; *New York Times,* February 18, 1946; Galter, *ibid.,* p. 210; Schuster, *Religion Behind the Iron Curtain,* pp. 166-68, 176-79; Shuster, *In Silence,* p. 18; Cianfarra, *ibid.,* p. 154; Seton-Watson, *op. cit.,* p. 192; Kertesz, *op. cit.,* p. 214.

57. Seton-Watson, *ibid.,* p. 196; Kertesz, *ibid.,* p. 215.

58. Galter, *op. cit.,* pp. 200-1.

59. See the recent, balanced account of Tiso's regime by John Conway, "The Churches, the Slovak State and the Jews 1939-1945," *The Slavonic and East European Review,* LII, No. 126 (January, 1974), 85-112.

60. Galter, *op. cit.,* p. 342; Ludvik Nemec, *Church and State in Czechoslovakia* (New York: Vintage Press, Inc., 1955), see Chapter V "John Hus and the Reformation" and Chapter VI "The 'Away From Rome' Movement"; Vratislav Busek and Nicholas Spulber, eds., *Czechoslovakia* (New York: Frederick A. Praeger, 1957), pp. 136-37.

61. Theodore Zubek, *The Church of Silence in Slovakia* (Whiting, Ind.: John Lach, 1956), pp. 29-30; MacEoin, *op. cit.,* pp. 23-24.

62. Zubek, *ibid.,* p. 40; Nemec, *op. cit.,* p. 202; MacEoin, *op. cit.,* pp. 23-24; Shuster, *Religion Behind the Iron Curtain,* pp. 68-69. Eduard Benes wrote the Vatican in 1941 and again in 1943 and warned the Church that the Czech government, when restored, would suppress the Catholic Party and Tiso in Slovakia and that the Vatican was exacerbating Czechoslovak-Catholic relations by allowing the German-controlled Slovak regime and not the Czech government-in-exile to maintain a representative in Vatican City. See Memorandum for the Holy See from Eduard Benes, May 12, 1943, PSF 44, FDR Library.

63. Nemec, *op. cit.,* pp. 206-18; MacEoin, *op. cit.,* pp. 24-25; Zubek, *op. cit.,* pp. 29-30, 36-43.

64. PP. Pius XII, "Ad Excum Virum Arthurum Maixner, novum Reipublicae Cecoslovachiae Legatum exta ordinme liberis cum mandatis," *A.A.S.*, XXXVIII (1946), 323-4; *New York Times*, May 15, 1946; Galter, *op. cit.*, pp. 342-43.

65. Radio Prague, *Daily Reports*, March 1, 1948, p. DD4; *Tablet* (London), May 22, 1948; Nemec, *op. cit.*, p. 232.

NOTES TO CHAPTER VIII

1. *Actes et documents*, III, part 2, nr. 598.

2. See Yevhen Glovinsky, "The Ukrainian Catholic Church," *Religion in the USSR*, p. 91; Vardys, "The Partisan Movement in Postwar Lithuania," pp. 102-103; also see Institute for the Study of the USSR, *Genocide in the USSR, passim*.

3. Forced resettlement and migration were major tools used by the Soviets to destroy nationalist minority centers throughout the Soviet Union. See Andrei Lebed, "Destruction of National Groups Through Compulsory Migration and Resettlement," *Genocide in the USSR*, pp. 6-7.

4. Leŭ Haroška, "The Roman Catholic Church in the Belorussian SSR," *Religion in the USSR*, p. 99; also see Vakar, *op. cit.*, p. 159.

5. Haroška, *ibid.*

6. *Ibid.*, pp. 99-100.

7. *Ibid.*, p. 100; Kolarz, *op. cit.*, p. 206.

8. Eugen Glowinskyi (Glovinsky), "The Western Ukrainians," *Genocide in the USSR*, pp. 151-53.

9. Haroška, *op. cit.*, p. 100.

10. Vardys, "Partisan Movement," pp. 85-87.

11. *Ibid.*, p. 103; also see Vittorio Vignieri, "Soviet Policy Toward Religion," p. 221; anonymous, "Communism's Struggle with Religion in Lithuania," *Lituanus*, IX, No. 1 (March, 1963), pp. 4-5.

12. Vignieri, *ibid.*; "Communism's Struggle with Religion," p. 5; Kolarz, *op. cit.*, p. 207; *Baltic States Investigation, Hearings Before the Select Committee to Investigate the Incorporation of the Baltic States into the USSR*, Part I (House of Representatives, 83rd Congress, First Session) (Washington, D.C.: U.S. Government Printing Office). The other three bishops active in Lithuania in 1944, Msgrs. J. Skvireckas, V. Padolskis, and V. Brizgys were taken away on July 26, 1944, by the Gestapo. See Casimir Gecys, "The Roman Catholic Church in the Lithuanian SSR," *Religion in the USSR*, p. 110.

13. Vignieri, *op. cit.*, p. 221; Vytautas Vaiteikunas, "Genocide Against the Roman Catholic Church in Lithuania," *Baltic Review*, No. 2/3 (June, 1954), p. 62.

14. Kolarz, *op. cit.*, p. 209; cf. Gecys, *op. cit.*, p. 111 and Vaiteikunas, *op. cit.*, p. 62.

15. Kolarz, *ibid.*; *Tablet* (London), September 6, 1947; Radio Vatican, *Daily Reports*, August 10, 1948, p. NN2; cf. Gecys, *op. cit.*, p. 111.

16. Vignieri, *op. cit.*, p. 222; "Communism's Struggle with Religion," p. 6; Vaiteikunas, *op. cit.*, p. 62.

17. Vaiteikunas, *ibid.*; Vignieri, *ibid.*, p. 221; "Communism's Struggle with Religion," p. 6.

18. Gecys, *op. cit.*, p. 111; Vignieri, *ibid.*; "Communism's Struggle with Religion," p. 6.

19. Radio Vatican, August 17, 1948, p. NN2; and November 19, 1948, p. NN4; Jean de Malta au Père Général, Moscou, *Correspondance 1944-1950*, Archivio, Padri Assunzionisti, Roma, 2DZ, 25 janvier 1949, N. 221, 13 juillet 1949, N. 228 (hereinafter cited as *Corr. 1944-1950*).

21. Gecys, *op. cit.*, p. 110; Radio Vatican, November 19, 1948, p. NN4.

22. Radio Vatican, March 16, p. NN2; March 17, 1949, p. NN3.

23. *Soviet Monitor*, October 20, 1950.

24. Kolarz, *op. cit.*, p. 208.

25. *Ibid.*

26. *Ibid.*, p. 209; also see Nikolaus Valter, "The Roman Catholic Church in Latvia and Estonia," *Religion in the USSR*, p. 118.

27. Radio Vatican, December 6, 1948, p. NN3.

28. Kolarz, *op. cit.*, p. 209; Valter, *op. cit.*, p. 118.

29. *Soviet Monitor*, October 3, 1951.

30. Valters, *op. cit.*, p. 117.

31. Braun, *Memoirs*, pp. 157-59, 172, 195, 198-200, 202-203, 340, 354-56, 367, 415-19, 428, 430, 436, 443, 455, 460-61, 476; Leopold Braun au Mr. Doyle, Moscou, 8 juillet 1945, *Documents divers 1940-1945*, Archivio, Padri Assunzionisti, Roma, 2ET, N. 51 (hereinafter cited as *Doc. div. 1940-1945*); Cresent, A.A. au Père Général, New York, April 27, 1945, *Doc. div. 1940-1945*, 2ET, N. 41. The Russians also refused to recognize Braun as the Vatican's Apostolic Administrator. See *Foreign Relations of the United States*, 1944, IV, 1211-12116, 1222-1223.

32. Braun, *Memoirs*, pp. 436-38.

33. *Ibid.*, pp. 435-38, 442, 449; Leopold Braun au Mr. Doyle, Moscou, 8 juillet 1945, *Doc. div. 1940-1945*, 2ET, N. 59; *Foreign Relations of the United States*, 1944, IV, 1222-1223. Ambassador Harriman felt Braun's health had deteriorated and that he should be replaced. See *Foreign Relations of the United*

States, 1945, V, 1125.

34. Braun, *Memoirs*, p. 441; *Foreign Relations of the United States,* 1945, V. 1126. It is, of course, quite likely that Braun was set up for this altercation for the Soviets were aware of the American Embassy's opinion of Braun and could have used such an event as concrete evidence of Braun's deteriorating condition and, thus, of the necessity of his recall. This interpretation of the affair is reinforced by the fact that the Soviets delayed Braun's trial until July to give the American government and the Vatican an opportunity to remove Braun. *Foreign Relations of the United States,* 1945, V, 1128.

35. Braun, *Memoirs*, p. 442; *Foreign Relations of the United States,* 1945, V, 1126 note 94.

36. Braun, *Memoirs*, pp. 446-48; *New York Times,* May 31, 1941; July 3, 1945; August 1, 1945; Leopold Braun, A. A.: Formal Declaration, Moscow, May 17, 1945, *Doc. div. 1940-1945,* 2ET, N. 44; *Foreign Relations of the United States,* 1945, V, 1126 note 94.

37. Crescent, A. A. au Père Général, New York, April 27, 1945, *Doc. div. 1940-1945,* 2ET, N. 41; 22 mai 1945, Doc. div. 1940-1945, 2ET, N. 51.

38. Crescent, A. A. au Père Général, New York, April 27, 1945, *Doc. div. 1940-1945,* 2ET, N. 41; *Foreign Relations of the United States,* 1945, V, 1125. Ambassador Harriman agreed with Flynn. See *Foreign Relations of the United States,* 1945, V, 1125 note 90.

39. Crescent, A. A. au Père Général, New York, April 27, 1945, *Doc. div. 1940-1945,* 2ET, N. 41; Telegram from Taylor to Secretary of State, March 21, 1945, PSF 44, FDR Library.

40. *New York Times,* March 6, March 13, March 15, March 22, March 23, March 29, 1945. The *New York Times* also reported that the attack upon the Uniates quashed any possibility of a *modus vivendi* between Rome and Moscow: January 26, 1946.

41. Crescent, A. A. au Père Général, New York, April 27, 1945, *Doc. div. 1940-1945,* 2ET, N. 41; Taylor to Secretary of State, March 21, 1945, PSF 44, FDR Library; *Foreign Relations of the United States,* 1945, V, 1129-1131.

42. Braun, *Memoirs*, pp. 469-70; *New York Times,* December 28, 1945; *Foreign Relations of the United States,* 1945, V, 1131 note 10.

43. Michael Francis Doyle au Rev. Wilfrid J. DuFault, 14, 17 juillet 1947, *Documents divers 1946-1949,* Archivio, Padri Assunzionisti, Roma, 2ET, N. 96 (hereinafter cited as *Doc. divers* 1946-1949); Jean de Malta a la Sr. Agathe, Moscou, 22 septembre 1948, Corr. 1944-1950, 2DZ, N. 213; Pere Jean Marie Thomas sur l'eglise francaise St. Louis a Moscou, mai 1949, *Doc. divers* 1946-1949, 2ET, N. 113; Jean de Malta a la Chere Tante, Moscou, 13 janvier 1949, Corr. 1944-1950, 2DZ, N. 237; Moscou, avril 1948, Doc. 1946-1949, 2ET, N. 109. Laberge was also under pressure from the French Embassy which, for

matters of "prestige," wanted to replace him at St. Louis Church with a French priest. Undoubtedly the Communist make-up of the French government was also influential in the Embassy's hostile attitude. See *Foreign Relations of the United States*, 1946, VI, 674-76; 1947, IV, 560-61; also see Walter Bedell Smith, *My Three Years in Moscow* (Philadelphia: Lippincott, 1950), pp. 277-79.

44. Smith, *ibid.*

45. Gervais Quenard sur Francais de Russie, Paris, mai 1949, *Doc. 1946-1949*, 2ET, N. 115; La note sur l'église française St. Louis remise a l'Ambassade, Paris, 7 mai 1949, *Doc. 1946-1949*, 2ET, N. 114; Pere Gervais Quenard (Memorandum), Paris, 3 mai 1949, Doc. 1946-1949, 2ET, N. 112; P. Gervais Quenard au Mgr. Tardini, Paris, 31 mai 1949, Doc. 1946-1949, 2ET, N. 116; Père Jean Marie Thomas sur l'église française St. Louis a Moscou, mai 1949, Doc. 1946-1949, 2ET, N. 113.

46. Kolarz, *op. cit.,* p. 194.

47. M. M. Sheinman, *Vatikan mezhda dvumia mirovymi voinami* (The Vatican between the two world wars) (Moscow, 1948), p. 31.

48. *Ibid.,* p. 34.

49. *Ibid.,* 36.

50. *Ibid.*

51. *Ibid.,* p. 198ff.

52. M. M. Sheinman, *Idiologiia i politika Vatikana na sluzhbe imperializma* (The Ideology and politics of the Vatican in the service of imperialism) (Moscow, 1950).

53. M. M. Sheinman, *Vatikan, vrag mira i demokratti* (The Vatican, enemy of peace and democracy) (Moscow, 1950), p. 30.

54. M. S. Vozchikov, *Sovremennii Vatikan, ego ideologiia i politika* (The Contemporary Vatican, its ideology and politics) (Moscow, 1957), pp. 254-59.

55. M. M. Sheinman, *Vatikan i kotolitsizm na sluzhbe imperializma* (The Vatican and catholicism in the service of imperialism) (Moscow, 1950).

56. *Ibid.,* p. 346.

57. *Ibid.*

58. M. M. Sheinman, *Vatikan vo vtoroi mirovoi voine* (The Vatikan in the second world war) (Moscow, 1951), p. 147.

59. *Ibid.,* p. 11.

60. M. M. Sheinman, *Sokrashchenie istorii papstva* (An Abridgement of the history of the papacy) (Moscow, 1952), p. 108.

61. *Ibid.,* p. 18.

62. *Bol'shaia sovetskaia entsiklopediia* (The Great soviet encyclopedia), Second Edition, 51 Vols. (Moscow, 1950), Vol. III, 353.

63. P. Pavelkin, *Religiozne sueveriia i ikh vred* (Religious superstitions and their harmfulness) (Moscow, 1951), p. 81.

64. I. Halan, *Vatikan bez maski* (The Vatican unmasked) (Moscow, 1952), p. 139.

65. *Ibid.,* pp. 14, 44.

66. Radio Moscow, *Daily Reports,* June 28, 1948, p. AA15.

67. *Ibid.,* July 30, 1948, pp. CC7-8; August 3, 1948, pp. BB4-5.

68. *Ibid.,* July 30, 1948, pp. CC7-8.

69. Radio Vatican, *Daily Reports,* August 19, 1948, p. NN2.

70. Radio Moscow, *Daily Reports,* August 23, 1948, p. AA8.

71. *Ibid.,* August 26, 1948, pp. BB6-7.

72. *Ibid.,* September 28, 1948, p. CC12; Radio Vatican, September 24, 1948, p. NN2.

73. Radio Moscow, *ibid.,* October 4, 1948, p. AA11; October 11, 1948, p. BB3.

74. *Ibid.,* October 21, 1948, pp. BB9-10; December 3, 1948, p. AA3.

75. *Ibid.,* January 4, 1949, pp. BB1-2; January 12, 1949, pp. BB11-13; February 4, 1949, pp. BB7-8; February 7, 1949, p. BB1.

76. *Ibid.,* January 26, 1949, pp. AA10-11.

77. *Ibid.*

78. *Ibid.*

79. *Ibid.,* February 14, 1949, pp. BB2-3; February 25, 1949, pp. BB14-15; June 16, 1949, pp. BB2-3.

80. *Ibid.,* January 11, 1949, pp. BB5-6; January 18, 1949, pp. BB1-3; January 19, 1949, pp. BB9-10.

81. Radio Vatican, *Daily Reports,* March 7, 1949, pp. NN3-4; June 6, 1949, p. VV2; *Il Quotidiano,* February 15, 1949.

82. *Il Quotidiano,* April 5, 1949.

83. Curtiss, *Russian Church and Soviet State,* p. 308.

84. *Soveshchanie glav i predslavitelei avtokefalynkh pravoslavnykh tserkvei* (Moscow, 1948). *Actes de la Conference des chefs et des representants des eglises orthodoxes autocephales* (Moscow, Moscow Patriarchate, 1950-1952, 2 vols.), I, 95-96.

85. *Ibid.,* pp. 97-99.

86. *Ibid.*

87. *Ibid.,* p. 130.

88. *Ibid.,* p. 133.

89. *Ibid.,* II, 211ff.

90. *Ibid.,* pp. 218-22.

91. *Ibid.,* p. 218.

92. *Ibid.,* p. 228.

93. *Ibid.,* pp. 236-37.

94. *Ibid.,* pp. 440-41; *Zh. M. P.,* Special Number, 1948, pp. 23-25.

95. *Actes de la Conference des chefs et des representants des eglises orthodoxes autocephales,* II, 441-43.

96. *Ibid.,* p. 443.

97. *Ibid.,* pp. 443-44.

98. *Ibid.,* p. 444.

99. *Ibid.*

100. *Ibid.*

101. *Ibid.*

102. Radio Vatican, *Daily Reports,* August 19, 1949, p. NN2. Apparently some of the outstanding delegates whose signatures appeared on these resolutions had neither signed nor given their assent to the contents thereof. See: Tobias, *Communist-Christian Encounter,* p. 267.

103. *Zh. M. P.,* No. 6, 1949, pp. 7-18.

104. *Ibid.,* No. 9, 1949, pp. 43-51.

105. *Ibid.,* p. 52-57.

106. *Ibid.,* No. 5, 1950, pp. 32-33.

107. *Ibid.*

108. See William C. Fletcher, *Religion and Soviet Foreign Policy 1945-1970,* pp. 33-34, 106-116.

NOTES TO CHAPTER IX

1. Ulam, *Expansion & Coexistence,* pp. 432-50.

2. *Ibid.,* pp. 440-48.

3. Many observers felt the Communists had victory secured. See *New York Times,* February 17, 1948, January 7, 31, February 3, 1948; Pravda, April 15, 1948; Radio Moscow, *Daily Reports,* January 13, 1948, pp. BB-19-20; February 9, 1948, p. AA21; April 15, 1948, pp. BB11-12; April 16, 1948, pp. BB5-6; Radio Rome, January 13, 1948, pp. NN4-5; February 26, 1948, p. NN3; Radio Leipzig, April 16, 1948, pp. FF1-6; *Tablet* (London), March 13, 1948. The Italian Communist Party, under Palmiro Togliatti, was totally loyal to Stalin. See Giulio Seniga, *Togliatti e Stalin* (Milan: Sugar editore, 1961), pp. 121-22.

4. Vatican warned Catholics not to vote for the Communists on pain of mortal sin and the United States stationed part of the 6th Fleet off the Italian coast. See PP. Pius XII, "Ad parochos urbis et concionatores sacri temporis quadrage-similis," *A.A.S.,* XL (1948), 119; *Tablet* (London), April 17, 1948;

224 NOTES

Cianfarra, *Vatican and Kremlin,* pp. 235–40; *New York Times,* April 22, May 6, 1948. For the Soviet point of view, see Sheinman, Sovremennii Vatikan (Contemporary Vatican) (Moscow, 1955), p. 64; Sheinmann, *Vatikan katolitsizm na sluzhbe mezhdunarodnoi reaktsii* (Vatican and catholicism in the service of international reaction) (Moscow, 1954), pp. 30, 32, 43, 47; M. S. Vozchikov, *Vatikan na sluzhbe amerikanskogo imperializma* (Vatican in the service of american imperialism) (Moscow, 1952), p. 9; H. M. Segal', *Vatikan na sluzhbe u amerikanskoi reaktsii* (Vatican in the service of american reaction) (Moscow, 1948), p. 17; Halan, *Tvory,* II, 429–30; Radio Moscow, *Daily Reports,* April 20, 1948, p. CC1; April 21, p. BB1; April 22, pp. AA3–4, C1–4; Radio Warsaw, April 21, pp. DD3; Radio Leipzig, April 21, p. FF1; Radio Budapest, April 22, pp. DD2–3; Radio Prague, April 22, pp. DD3–4; Sheinman, *Kratkie ocherki istorii papstva* (Short outline of the history of the papacy) (Moscow, 1952), p. 174.

5. Sheinman, *Kratkie ocherki istorii papstva,* p. 174–76; Sheinman, *Vatikan i katolitsizm na sluzhbe mezhdunarodnoi reaktsii,* pp. 14, 30, 32, 38, 43; Sheinman, *Religiia v period imperializma,* pp. 7–12, 22–27; Vozchikov, *Vatikan na sluzhbe amerikanskogo imperializma,* pp. 1–10, 14, 19, 21ff; Segal', *Vatikan na sluzhbe u amerikanskoi reaktsii,* pp. 5–7, 14, 17; Halan, *Tvory,* II, pp. 429–30.

6. See Adam B. Ulam, *Titoism and the Cominform* (Cambridge: Harvard University Press, 1952).

7. Valkenier, *op. cit.,* p. 312.

8. Galter, *op. cit.,* pp. 262–63; Radio Vatican, *Daily Reports,* May 17, 1948, p. NN3.

9. Galter, *ibid.,* p. 263.

10. Dinka, *op. cit.,* p. 336.

11. *Ibid.*; J. Szuldrzynski, *The Pattern of Life in Poland: The Situation of the Catholic Church* (Paris, 1953), p. 47.

12. MacEoin, *Communist War on Religion,* p. 198; Dziewanowski, "Communist Poland and the Catholic Church," p. 2; Galter, *op. cit.,* p. 263.

13. Galter, *ibid.,* p. 261; *Tablet* (London), January 22, 1949; Radio Warsaw, *Daily Reports,* May 13, 1948, p. DD5; May 14, 1948, p. DD3; Radio Vatican, June 1, 1948, p. NN4; June 16, 1948, P. NN1; July 7, 1948, pp. NN-1-2; *New York Times,* January 20, 1950.

14. Dolan, *op. cit.,* p. 88.

15. Radio Warsaw, *Daily Reports,* May 13, 1948, p. DD5; May 14, 1948, p. DD3.

16. Radio Warsaw, *ibid.,* May 14, 1948, p. DD3.

17. Radio Vatican, *Ibid.,* June 1, 1948, p. NN4; June 16, 1948, p. NN1; July 7, 1948, pp. NN1-2.

18. Radio Vatican, *ibid.,* July 29, 1948, p. NN1.

9.*Ibid.,* August 24, 1948, p. NN1.

20. MacEoin, *Communist War on Religion,* p. 198; *Tablet* (London), November 20, 1948.

21. MacEoin, *ibid.,* pp. 199-200.

22. *Ibid.*

23. Radio Vatican, *Daily Reports,* September 23, 1948, p. NN4; October 26, 1948, p. NN4; *New York Times,* September 1, 3, 1948.

24. *Tablet* (London), November 20, 1948, p. 333; Warsaw Radio, *Daily Reports,* October 5, 1948, p. DD6; Radio Vatican, October 26, 1948, p. NN4.

25. Valkenier, *op. cit.,* p. 312.

26 MacEoin, *Communist War on Religion,* p. 200.

27. Radio Vatican, *Daily Reports,* November 5, 1948, p. NN3; November 23, 1948, pp. NN1-2.

28. MacEoin, *op. cit.,* p. 200.

29. Valkenier, *op cit.,* p. 313.

30. Dziewanowski, "Communist Poland and the Catholic Church," p. 2.

31. *Ibid.; Tablet* (London), June 19, 1948, pp. 289-90; July 17, 1948, p. 42; November 20, 1948, p. 332.

32. Radio Warsaw, *Daily Reports,* December 6, 1948, p. DD6.

33. Valkenier, *op. cit.,* p. 313.

34. Radio Vatican, *Daily Reports,* December 8, 1948, p. NN3.

35. *New York Times,* January 12, 1949; MacEoin, *Communist War on Religion,* pp. 201-202.

36. *New York Times,* January 28, 30, 1949.

37. *Ibid.,* February 3, 1949.

38. *Ibid.,* February 7, 1949.

39. *Ibid.,* February 9, 10, 1949.

40. *Ibid.,* February 19, 27, 28, 1949; Radio Warsaw, *Daily Reports,* February 9, 1949, pp. DD5-6.

41. *New York Times,* March 1, 2, 3, 1949.

42. *Ibid.,* March 12, 1949.

43. Radio Vatican, *Daily Reports,* March 2, 1949, p. NN3.

44. *Ibid.,* March 31, 1949, p. NN3; Valkenier, *op. cit.,* p. 313.

45. MacEoin, *Communist War on Religion,* p. 200; Dinka, *op. cit.,* p. 336; Valkenier, *op. cit.,* p. 318.

46. MacEoin, *ibid.;* Dinka, *ibid.;* Valkenier, *ibid.*

47. Radio Vatican, March 21, *Daily Reports,* 1949, p. NN3.

48. *Ibid.,* March 22, 1949, p. NN3.

49. *Ibid.,* March 25, 1949, p. NN2; March 29, 1949, p. NN2; March 31, 1949, p. NN2.

50. Radio Warsaw, *Daily Reports,* April 4, 1949, pp. DD2-3.

51. Galter, *op. cit.,* pp. 264-65; R. H. Markham, *Communists Crush Churches in Eastern Europe* (Boston: Maeder Publishing Co., 1950), p. 104; *Tablet* (London), April 30, 1949.

52. Galter, *op. cit.,* p. 265; Valkenier, *op. cit.,* pp. 313-14.

53. MacEoin, *Communist War on Religion,* p. 202; *Tablet* (London), April 16, 1949, p. 254; Radio Vatican, *Daily Reports,* April 7, 1949, pp. NN1-2.

54. MacEoin, *Communist War on Religion,* p. 202.

55. *Ibid.*

56. Radio Vatican, *Daily Reports,* April 22, 1949, p. NN1; *Tablet* (London), April 30, 1949, p. 293; September 3, 1949, p. 157, April 16, 1949, pp. 253-54; *New York Times,* March 26, 30, April 3, 25, 1949.

57. Radio Vatican, *Daily Reports,* April 11, 1949, p. NN3.

58. *Ibid.,* April 22, 1949, p. NN1.

59. Personal Interview with Joseph Cardinal Slipyi, June 16, 1969, Vatican City.

60. Radio Warsaw, *Daily Reports,* April 25, 1949, pp. DD2-3.

61. Galter, *op. cit.,* p. 265; *New York Times,* June 20, 1929.

62. Radio Warsaw, *Daily Reports,* May 24, 1949, pp. FF3-4; Radio Vatican, June 2, 1949, p. VV2.

63. PP. Pius XII, "Ad Emum Adamum Stephanum Tit. S. Mariae Novae S.R.E. Presbyterum Cardinalem Saphieha, Archiepiscopum Cracoviensem, Atque Ceteros Excmos PP. DD. Poloniae Archiepiscopos, Episcopos Locorumque Orindarios," *A.A.S.,* XLI (1949), 450-53; Tobias, *Communist-Christian Encounter,* pp. 418-19.

64. Tobias, *ibid.,* p. 394.

65. Valkenier, *op. cit.,* p. 314; Dolan, *op. cit.,* p. 88.

66. Valkenier, *ibid.*

67. Dinka, *op. cit.,* p. 342; Szuldrzynski, *op. cit.,* p. 39; National Committee For a Free Europe, *Poland in the Year 1951,* p. 73.

68. Dinka, *ibid.;* National Committee For a Free Europe, *ibid.,* p. 74; *News From Behind the Iron Curtain,* XII (September, 1953), 47.

69. National Committee For a Free Europe, *ibid.,* p. 73.

70. Dolan, *op. cit.,* pp. 86-88; Dinka, *op. cit.,* p. 341; Valkenier, *op. cit.,* p. 314.

71. Valkenier, *ibid.*

72. MacEoin, *Communist War on Religion,* p. 202.

73. Valkenier, *op. cit.,* p. 314; Dolan, *op. cit.,* p. 87; M. Leveque, *Persecution en Pologne* (Paris: Chez Leveque, 1954), pp. 27-28.

74. Valkenier, *ibid.;* for text see B. Wierzbianski, ed., *White Paper on the Persecution of the Church in Poland* (London, n.d.), pp. 34-41.

75. Valkenier, *ibid.,* p. 315; Dolan, *op. cit.,* p. 88; Dinka, *op. cit.,* pp. 335,

337.

76. Bociurkiw, "The Uniate Church," p. 110; *First Victims*, pp. 46-47.

77. Bociurkiw, *ibid.*, pp. 110-111.

NOTES TO CHAPTER X

1. Galter, *op. cit.*, p. 212.

2. Kurt Hutten, *Iron Curtain Christians*, trans. Walter G. Tillmanns (Minneapolis, Minn.: Augsburg Publishing House, 1967), pp. 178-79; MacEoin, *Communist War on Religion*, p. 127; Shuster, *In Silence*, p. 176.

3. Radio Budapest, *Daily Reports*, April 26, 1948, p. DD5; April 27, 1948, p. DD3; May 4, 1949, pp. DD2-3.

4. *Ibid.*, May 2, 1948, p. DD5; May 4, 1948, pp. DD2-3; Radio Vatican, *Daily Reports*, May 14, 1948, pp. NN1-2; Galter, *The Red Book*, p. 213; Gsovski, *Church and State Behind the Iron Curtain*, pp. 77; Barron Waddams, *Communism and the Churches*, pp. 62-63.

5. Cardinal Mindszenty, *Four Years' Struggle of the Church in Hungary*, ed. C. Hollis (London: Longmans, Green and Co., 1949), pp. 138-39, 143, 146; *New York Times*, May 16, 17, 1948.

6. Radio Vatican, *Daily Reports*, May 14, 1948, pp. NN1-2.

7. *Ibid.*

8. Mindszenty, *Four Years'*, pp. 137-39, 148-48; *New York Times*, May 24, 1948.

9. Radio Vatican, *Daily Reports*, May 17, 1948, p. NN4.

10. Mindszenty, *Four Years'*, p. 136; *New York Times*, May 31, 1948; Vatican Radio, *Daily Reports*, June 14, 1948, p. NN1.

11. Radio Vatican, *Daily Reports*, May 13, 1948, p. NN4; May 28, 1948, p. NN1.

12. Radio Budapest, *Daily Reports*, May 19, 1948, p. DD4; May 24, 1948, pp. DD7-8; May 26, 1948, p. DD5; June 14, 1948, p. DD5.

13. Tobias, *Communist-Christian Encounter*, p. 441.

14. Mindszenty, *Four Years'*, pp. 152-53.

15. *Times* (London), May 22, 1948.

16. Mindszenty, *Four Years'*, pp. 140-47.

17. *Ibid.*, p. 149.

18. Galter, *op. cit.*, pp. 214-16.

19. *Radio Vatican, Daily Reports*, June 1, 1948, p. NN5; June 14, 1948, p. NN1.

20. *Ibid.*, May 24, 1948, p. NN3.

21. *New York Times,* June 7, 1948; Cianfarra, *The Vatican and the Kremlin,* p. 164; Kertsz, *op. cit.,* p. 216.

22. Radio Budapest, *Daily Reports,* June 7, 1948, p. DD3; *New York Times,* June 15, 1948; *Tablet* (London), June 19, 1948, p. 338.

23. Radio Budapest, *Daily Reports,* June 7, 1948, p. DD3; June 21, 1948, pp. DD3-4; June 8, 1948, p. DD5; June 14, 1948, p. DD5; Radio Vatican *Daily Reports,* June 17, 1948, p. NN3.

24. Radio Budapest, *Daily Reports,* June 7, 1948, p. DD3.

25. Barron and Waddams, *Communism and the Churches,* p. 65.

26. "Communist Offenses Against the Integrity of Education, Science, and Culture," pp. 90-91; MacEoin, *Communist War on Religion,* p. 127; Shuster, *In Silence,* p. 77.

27. Radio Budapest, *Daily Reports,* June 15, 1948, p. DD5; *New York Times,* June 12, 1948.

28. Radio Budapest, *Daily Reports,* June 15, 1948, pp. DD4-5; June 18, 1948, p. DD8; Radio Prague, *Daily Reports,* June 16, 1948, p. DD2; *New York Times,* June 11, 12, 13, 1948; *Times* (London), June 14, 1948.

29. *Times* (London), June 14, 1948.

30. *New York Times,* June 14, 1948; *Tablet* (London), June 19, 1948, p. 388.

31. Radio Budapest, *Daily Reports,* June 18, 1948, p. DD8; "Communist Offenses Against the Integrity of Education, Science, and Culture," p. 80; Barron and Waddams, *Communism and the Churches,* p. 64; MacEoin, *Communist War on Religion,* pp. 125-26; for figures see: Free Europe Committee, *The Red and the Black,* p. 11.

32. Radio Budapest, *Daily Reports,* June 28, 1948, p. DD4; Barron and Waddams, *Communism and the Churches,* p. 64.

33. Radio Budapest, *Daily Reports,* July 6, 1948, pp. DD6-7.

34. Mindszenty, *Four Years,* p. 155.

35. *New York Times,* June 25, 1948; Kertesz, *op. cit.,* p. 216.

36. Radio Vatican, *Daily Reports,* August 28, 1948, p. NN2; Tobias, *Communist-Christian Encounter,* pp. 44.

37. Radio Vatican *Daily Reports,* August 28, 1948, p. NN2; Barron and Waddams, *Communist-Christian Encounter,* p. 66.

38. Radio Vatican, *Daily Reports,* September 7, 1948, p. NN2.

39. *Ibid.,* July 16, 1948, p. NN3; Radio Budapest, Daily Reports, July 2, 1948, p. DD4; *New York Times,* July 3, 1948; also arrested were Revs. Ral Nemeth, Antal Olesszo, and Loas Harsanyi.

40. Radio Vatican, *Daily Reports,* July 17, 1948, p. NN3.

41. *New York Times,* July 3, 1948.

42. Radio Vatican, *Daily Reports,* July 19, 1948, p. NN1.

43. *New York Times,* July 12, 1948.

44. Radio Vatican, *Daily Reports,* July 14, 1948, p. NN1; *New York Times,* July 14, 24, 1948; Free Europe Committee, *The Red and the Black,* pp. 12-13.

45. Galter, *The Red Book,* p. 218.

46. Mindszenty, *Four Years,* pp. 160-63.

47. Radio Vatican, *Daily Reports,* July 19, 1949, p. NN1; *New York Times,* July 18, 1949.

48. Radio Vatican, *Daily Reports,* August 19, 1948, p. NN3; September 27, 1948, p. NN3; MacEoin, *Communist War on Religion,* p. 215; Galter, *The Red Book,* p. 219ff.

49. Radio Vatican, *Daily Reports,* September 27, 1948, p. NN3; Kertesz, *op. cit.,* p. 216.

50. *L'Osservatore Romano,* October 10, 1948.

51. *Ibid.*

52. *Ibid.,* October 22, 1948.

53. *New York Times,* October 23, 1948.

54. Radio Budapest, *Daily Reports,* November 24, 1948, p. DD5; November 29, 1948, pp. DD15-16; *Il Quotidiano,* November 26, 1948, Galter, *op. cit.,* pp. 225-26.

55. *Il Quotidiano,* November 26, 1948.

56. Radio Vatican, *Daily Reports,* November 5, 1948, p. NN5.

57. Mindszenty, *Four Years',* pp. 180-81; *Il Quotidano,* November 26, 1948.

58. Mindszenty, *Four Years',* pp. 182-84; Budapest Radio, *Daily Reports,* December 1, 1948, p. DD7.

59. Radio Budapest, *Daily Reports,* November 29, 1948, pp. DD15-16; *New York Times,* November 28, 1948; *Tablet* (London), December 4, 1948, p. 358; Barron and Waddams, *Communism and the Churches,* p. 66.

60. Schuster, *Religion Behind the Iron Curtain,* pp. 175-76.

61. Hungarian Government, *Documents on the Mindszenty Case* (Budapest: Athenaeum, 1949), p. 3; Radio Budapest, *Daily Reports,* December 29, 1948, p. DD4.

62. Radio Budapest, *Daily Reports,* November 25, 1948, pp. DD4-5.

63. Radio Vatican, *Daily Reports,* December 9, 1948, p. NN2; December 15, 1948, p. NN3; Galter, *The Red Book,* p. 226.

64. Radio Budapest, *Daily Reports,* December 15, 1948, p. DD4; December 16, 1948, pp. DD11-12.

65. Mindszenty, *Four Years',* p. 185.

66. *Ibid.;* Galter, *op. cit.,* p. 236; *New York Times,* January 7, 1949.

67. Radio Budapest, *Daily Reports,* December 27, 1948, p. DD5; December 28, 1948, p. DD3; December 30, 1948, pp. DD1-2; Hungarian Government, *Documents,* p. 3; Mindszenty, *Four Years',* p. 188.

68. Radio Budapest, *Daily Reports,* December 29, 1948, pp. DD1-7;

Hungarian Government, *Documents,* p. 3; *New York Times,* December 28, 1948; Galter, *op. cit.,* p. 227; the Government listed the arrested clerical leaders in its broadcast over Budapest Radio. See: Radio Budapest, *Daily Reports,* December 29, 1948, p. DD4.

69. Sacra Congregatio Consistorialis, "Declaratio," *A.A.S.,* XLI (1948); *Il Quotidiano,* December 28, 1948; Radio Vatican, *Daily Reports,* December 28, 1948, p. NN1; December 30, 1948, pp. NN1-3; December 31, 1948, p. NN1; Radio Rome, *Daily Reports, December 28, 1948, p. NN1; La Documentation Catholique,* January 1949, cols. 131-161, 210-228; *La Civilta Catholica,* Vol. L (1949), 465-72, 585-600. The Vatican was extremely upset and perturbed at the Hungarian Government's arrest of Cardinal Mindszenty. The Catholic press around the world condemned the action and attempted to arouse indignation in the West. For the most part, the western press also denounced the arrest of Mindszenty.

70. PP. Pius XII, "Ad Excmos P.P. DD. Archiepiscopos et episcopos Hungariae," *A.A.S.,* XLI (1949), 29-30.

71. Radio Vatican, *Daily Reports,* January 3, 1949, p. NN4; January 11, 1949, p. NN2.

72. *Ibid.,* January 5, 1949, p. NN3; January 17, 1949, p. NN5; *L'Osservatore Romano,* January 16, 1949.

73. Radio Vatican, *Daily Reports,* January 6, 1949, p. NN2.

74. Radio Budapest, *Daily Reports,* January 3, 1949, pp. DD4-7; January 10, 1949, p. DD11; January 17, 1949, p. DD5.

75. *Ibid.,* January 5, 1949, p. DD7; January 10, 1949, p. DD10.

76. Radio Vatican, *Daily Reports,* January 13, 1949, p. NN2.

77. Radio Budapest, *Daily Reports,* January 18, 1949, p. DD13; Jan7ary 26, 1949, p. DD2; Hungarian Government, *Documents,* p. 4.

78. The *Yellow Book* is the work, cited above, entitled *Documents on the Mindszenty Case.* Also see: Radio Budapest, *Daily Reports,* January 24, 1949, pp. DD1-6; January 25, 1949, p. DD5; February 4, 1949, p. DD3; Radio Moscow, *Daily Reports,* April 27, 1949, pp. CC8-10; *New York Times,* January 20, February 5, 1949; *Tablet* (London), February 5, 1949.

79. *L'Osservatore Romano,* January 21, 1949.

80. Radio Budapest, *Daily Reports,* January 24, 1949, pp. DD6-10.

81. For details see: Hungarian Government, *The Trial of Jozsef Mindszenty* (Budapest: Hungarian State Publishing House, 1949); Radio Budapest, *Daily Reports,* February 7, 1949, pp. DD1-13.

82. Hungarian Government, *Trial of Mindszenty,* pp. 162-63; *New York Times,* February 5, 1949; Radio Budapest, *Daily Reports,* February 7, 1949, pp. DD1-13; February 8, 1949, pp. DD1-3; February 9, 1949, p. DD1; *Tablet* (London), January 15, 1949, pp. 38-39; February 12, 1949, pp. 100-103. Many

claimed that the Government used drugs on Mindszenty; see: *New York Times,* January 26, 1949; Galter, *op. cit.,* pp. 226ff; Bela Just, *Un Process Prefabrique: L'Affaire Mindszenty* (Paris: Editions du Temoignag Chretien, 1949), p. 125; MacEoin, *Communist War on Religion,* pp. 110-11, 127-29; Schuster, *Religion Behind the Iron Curtain,* p. 186.

83. Hungarian Government, *Trial of Mindszenty,* p. 165; Galter, *The Red Book,* p. 226. Cardinal Mindszenty was freed during the Hungarian Revolution in 1956 and, after the rebellion was crushed, he received asylum in the American Embassy in Budapest where he remained until 1972 when the Vatican arranged his release into its custody at Rome. He eventually took up residence in Vienna where he died on May 6, 1975.

184. Radio Vatican *Daily Reports,* February 10, 1949, pp. NN1-3; February 14, 1949, p. NN4.

85. *Ibid.,* February 15, 1949, p. NN4.

86. Gerhard Simon, "The Catholic Church and the Communist State in the Soviet Union and Eastern Europe," in Bohdan R. Bociurkiw and John W. Strong, eds., *Religion and Atheism in the USSR and Eastern Europe* (Toronto: University of Toronto Press, 1975), p. 198.

87. Leslie Laszlo, "Towards Normalisation of Church-State Relations in Hungary," in Bociurkiw and Strong, eds., *ibid.,* p. 292.

88. *New From Behind the Iron Curtain,* Vol. I, No. 8 (August, 1952), 35.

89. Jean de Mala à la Chère Tante, Moscou, 13 janvier 1949, *Corr. 1944-1950,* 2DZ, N. 237.

90. *L'Osservatore Romano,* July 11, 1949.

NOTES TO CHAPTER XI

1. *Tablet* (London), May 22, 1948.

2. *Ibid.*

3. Radio Prague, *Daily Reports,* May 24, 1948, p. DD7.

4. Radio Vatican, *Daily Reports,* June 4, 1948, p. NN4.

5. Galter, *op. cit.,* p. 353.

6. *New York Times,* June 15, 1948; MacEoin, *Communist War on Religion,* pp. 30-31; Nemec, *op. cit.,* p. 288.

7. Radio Prague, *Daily Reports,* June 10, 1948, p. GG3; F. Cavalli, "Chiesa Cattolica E. Governo Cominista In Cecoslovacchia," *Civilta Cattolica,* Vol. III (1949), 243-44; MacEoin, *ibid.;* Galter *op. cit.;* "Communist Offenses Against the Integrity of Education, Science, and Culture," *CIRRCUS*

Materials, p. 123.

8. MacEoin, *ibid.,* pp. 29-30; Barron and Waddams, *op. cit.,* pp. 48-49.

9. Zapotocky replaced Gottwald who moved up to the Presidency. Gottwald succeeded Eduard Benes who "resigned" in June, 1948, four months after the Communist coup.

10. Radio Prague, *Daily Reports,* July 6, 1948, p. DD1.

11. Radio Vatican, *Daily Reports,* July 13, 1948, p. NN5.

12. *Ibid.,* July 30, 1948, p. NN1.

13. *New York Times,* August 30, 1948; Galter, *op. cit.,* p. 357.

14. Radio Prague, *Daily Reports,* August 6, 1948, pp. DD1-2; Radio Vatican, *Daily Reports,* August 31, 1949, pp. NN1-3.

15. Radio Vatican, *Daily Reports,* August 31, 1949, pp. NN1-3.

16. *New York Times,* September 23, 1948; Radio Vatican, *Daily Reports,* August 31, 1948, pp. NN1-3; *Tablet* (London), June 12, 1948, p. 372; Nemec, *op. cit.,* pp. 254-55; Archbishop Beran was admitted into this union in late 1947.

17. Radio Vatican, *Daily Reports,* May 26, 1948, p. NN1; June 2, 1948, pp. NN6-7; *New York Times,* May 20, 1948; MacEoin, *op. cit.,* p. 28; Nemec, *ibid.,* pp. 247-55.

18. Radio Vatican, *Daily Reports,* September 27, 1948, p. NN2.

19. *Ibid.,* October 4, 1948, p. NN3; *Tablet* (London), October 16, 1948, p. 252; Nemec, *op. cit.,* p. 255.

20. Radio Vatican, *Daily Reports,* December 31, 1948, p. NN2; January 10, 1949, p. NN3; Galter, *op. cit.,* pp. 349ff; Nemec, *ibid.,* p. 257; Free Europe Committee, *The Red and the Black,* pp. 21-24.

21. Radio Vatican, *Daily Reports,* November 5, 1948, p. NN2; December 31, 1948, p. NN2; January 10, 1949, p. NN3.

22. Radio Prague, *Daily Reports,* November 30, 1948, pp. DD1-3; Barron and Waddams, *op. cit.,* p. 47.

23. Radio Prague, *ibid.,* pp. DD2-3 and December 8, 1948, p. DD4.

24. Galter, *op. cit.,* p. 356.

25. *Ibid.;* Free Europe Committee, *The Red and the Black,* pp. 21-24.

26. Free Europe Committee, *ibid.*

27. Nemec, *op. cit.,* p. 256; Galter, *op. cit.,* p. 357; MacEoin, *op. cit.,* pp. 34-36.

28. Galter, *ibid.*

29. Radio Vatican, *Daily Reports,* December 9, 1948, p. NN2.

30. Radio Prague, *Daily Reports,* December 30, 1948, p. DD2.

31. *Manchester Guardian,* December 30, 1948.

32. Galter, *op. cit.,* pp. 359-60.

33. *Ibid.,* p. 360.

34. *New York Times,* January 8, 1949.

35. *Ibid.*

36. Radio Vatican, *Daily Reports,* January 10, 1949, pp. NN2-3.

37. Galter, *op. cit.,* p. 362.

38. *New York Times,* February 10, 1949.

39. Radio Prague, *Daily Reports,* February 28, 1949, p. DD1.

40. *New York Times,* March 17, 1949.

41. Nemec, *op. cit.,* pp. 257-58; MacEoin, *op. cit.,* pp. 30-31.

42. Galter, *op. cit.,* p. 361; *Tablet* (London), May 28, 1949; Nemec, *ibid.,* pp. 260-65.

43. Nemec, *ibid.*

44. Galter, *op. cit.,* p. 362; Nemec, *ibid.,* p. 267; *Tablet* (London), May 21, 1949.

45. Galter, *ibid.;* Nemec, *ibid.,* pp. 270-72.

46. Galter, *ibid.,* p. 352.

47. *Ibid.,* p. 362; Nemec, *op. cit.,* p. 275.

48. *New York Times,* May 21, 1949.

49. *Ibid.*

50. *Il Quotidiano,* May 30, 1949.

51. MacEoin, *op. cit.,* p. 31.

52. *Ibid.; Tablet* (London), August 6, 1949.

53. *New York Times,* June 11, 1949.

54. Radio Prague, *Daily Reports,* June 10, 1949, pp. GG3-4.

55. Nemec, *op. cit.,* pp. 272-78; Galter, *op. cit.,* p. 364.

56. Galter, *ibid.*

57. *Ibid.*

58. Radio Prague, *Daily Reports,* June 14, 1949, p. GG1; June 16, 1949, p. GG3; June 20, 1949, pp. GG1-2; June 23, 1949, pp. GG3-4; Galter, *op. cit.,* p. 365.

59. *Tablet* (London), June 11, 1949; Markham, *op. cit.,* p. 23.

60. *Tablet* (London), June 18, 1949, p. 404.

61. Nemec, *op. cit.,* pp. 279-80; Barron and Waddams, *op. cit.,* p. 54; Galter, *op. cit;* Free Europe Committee, *The Red and the Black,* pp. 21-24; *Tablet* (London), June 11, 1949.

62. Radio Vatican, *Daily Reports,* June 14, 1949, p. VV3.

63. Galter, *op. cit.,* pp. 365-66; *New York Times,* June 17, 1949.

64. Radio Prague, *Daily Reports,* June 20, 1949, pp. GG2-3.

65. Galter, *op. cit.,* pp. 366-68; *New York Times,* June 20, July 11, 1949; *Tablet* (London), August 27, 1949; Nemec, *op. cit.,* pp. 281-82.

66. Nemec, *ibid.*

67. Suprema Sacra Congregation Sancti Offici, "Decretum: Schismatica

'Action Catholica' in Cecoslovachia damnatur," *A.A.S.*, XLI (1949), 333; *L'Osservatore Romano*, June 20, 1949; Nemec, *ibid.*, pp. 285-286.

68. Radio Prague, *Daily Reports*, June 27, 1949, pp. GG1-3.

69. MacEoin, *op. cit.*, p. 40.

70. *Ibid.*

71. *Ibid.*

72. *Ibid.*, p. 41; *New York Times*, July 12, 1949; Nemec, *op. cit.*, p. 306.

73. Nemec, *ibid.*, pp. 306-7; MacEoin, op. cit., p. 41.

74. Jean de Malta au Pere General, Moscou, 13 juillet 1949, *Corr. 1944-1950*, 2DZ, N. 228.

75. *New York Herald Tribune*, October 18, 1949.

76. *New York Times*, April 18, 19, 20, 1950; A. Michel, *Religious Problems in a Country under Communist Rule* (Rome: Pnt. Greg University Press, 1954), pp. 24, 52.

77. *New York Times*, December 20, 1950.

78. Nemec, *op. cit.*, p. 364.

79. Bociurkiw, "The Uniate Church," p. 111; *First Victims*, pp. 58-59; *Svetlo Pravoslavia*, No. 1-2 (1950), pp. 1-27; *Zh. M. P.*, No. 7, 1950, pp. 40-53.

80. For a useful study of this event see P. Cârnatiu and M. Toderiniu, "Calvarul Bisericii Unite" in *Biserica Română Unită Două Sute Ani de Istorie* (Madrid, 1952), pp. 275-365; Radu Florescu places the Romanian Uniate Church in its historical context in an excellent article: "The Uniate Church: Catalyst of Rumanian National Consciousness," *The Slavonic and East European Review,"* (July, 1967), pp. 324-.

81. Bociurkiw, "The Uniate Church," p. 111.

NOTES TO CHAPTER XII

1. Acta SS. Congregationum, *Decretum: responsa ad dubia de communismo*, *A.A.S.*, Vol. XLI (1949), 334.

2. *Soviet Monitor*, July 22, 1949.

3. *Ibid.*

4. *Ibid.*

5. *Ibid.*

6. *Izvestiia*, July 29, 1949.

7. *Pravda*, July 30, 1949.

8. *Ibid.*

9. *Izvestiia*, August 6, 1949.

10. *Ibid.*

11. *New York Times,* July 14, 15, 16, 17, 18, 20, 22, 27, 29, 30, 1949; August 3, 4, 5, 13, 1949; Radio Budapest, *Daily Reports,* July 18, 1949, p. HH1; Radio Prague, *Daily Reports,* July 18, 1949, p. GG1; Radio Warsaw, July 19, 1949, pp. EE1-3; Radio East Berlin, July 19, 1949, pp. DD1-3.

12. *New York Times,* July 14, August 7, 1949.

13. See Ulam, *Expansion & Coexistence.* Marshall Shulman has recently been commissioned by the Research Committee of the American Association for the Advancement of Slavic Studies to research the relationship between domestic and foreign policy.

14. *Actes et documents,* III, part. 2, nrs. 543, 580, 590, 594.

BIBLIOGRAPHY

Archives and Manuscript Collections

Correspondance 1935-1936, Moscou, Archivio, Padri Assunzionisti, Roma, 2DZ, Ns. 1-76.

Correspondance 1937-1941, Moscou, Archivio, Padri Assunzionisti, Roma, 2DZ, Ns. 77-159.

Correspondance 1944-1950, Moscou, Archivio, Padri Assunzionisti, Roma, 2DZ, Ns. 160-257.

Documents divers 1940-1945, Moscou, Archivio, Padre Assunzionisti, Roma, 2ET, Ns. 1-70.

Documents divers 1946-1949, Moscou, Archivio, Padri Assunzionisti, Roma, 2ET, Ns. 71-121.

    The correspondence and documents in the Assumptionist Archives represent a major source of eye-witness accounts of Moscow's attitude toward the Catholic Church. Much of the material deals with the internal affairs of the Assumptionist Order, but a significant portion treats the impressions left upon these "representatives" of the Vatican by the Soviet system. The greater part of the material is in French, but there are entries in both Russian and English.

Roosevelt, Franklin D., Papers, Franklin D. Roosevelt Library, Hyde Park, New York. Documents are cited as PSF (President's Secretary's File), PPF (President's Personal File), OF (Official File) and Map Room File.

Taylor, Myron C., Papers, Frankling D. Roosevelt Library, Hyde Park, New York.

Personal Interviews

Personal interviews with Josyf Cardinal Slipyi, Metropolitan and Archbishop Major of the Ukrainian Uniate Church, Vatican City, June 16, 1969, and Bishop Vincent Brizgys, exiled Lithuanian Bishop, Chicago, Illinois, May 18, 1974.

Books, Articles, and Individual Manuscripts

——, "Communism's Struggle with Religion in Lithuania," *Lituanus,* Vol. IX, No. 1 (March, 1963), 1-17.

Acta SS. Congregationum, *Decretum: Responsa ad dubia de communismo, Acta Apostolicae Sedis,* Vol. XLI (1949), 334. All the official acts of the Holy See are conveniently recorded in the *Acta Apostolicae Sedis* (cited as *A.A.S.*).

Adler, Erwin, "Lenin's Views on Religion," *Studies on the Soviet Union,* Vol. X, No. 1 (1970), 61-69.

Afanasev, V. L., "Katolitsizm-avangard kolonializma," (Catholicism—the avant-garde of colonialism), *Ezhegodnik muzeia istorii religii i ateizma* (Yearbook of the museum of the history of religion and atheism), Vol. VI (Moscow, 1962), 424-49.

Alef, Gustave, "The Adoption of the Muscovite Two-Headed Eagle: A Discordant View," *Speculum,* Vol. XLI (January, 1966), 1-21.

Alexeev, W. *The Foreign Policy of the Moscow Patriarchate, 1939-1953.* New York: Research Program on the USSR, 1955.

—— *Russian Orthodox Bishops in the Soviet Union, 1941-1953; materials for the history of the Russian Orthodox Church in the U.S.S.R.* New York: Research Program on the U.S.S.R., 1954 (text in Russian).

Allen, W. E. D. *The Ukraine.* New York: Russel and Russell, Inc., 1963.

Anicas, J., "Klerikalinis antikomunizmas Lieturoje Hitlerines okupacijos met ais (1941-1944)," (Clerical anti-Communism in Lithuania during the Hitlerite occupation (1941-1944), *Lietuvos TSR Moksly adademijos darbai* (USSR), Vol. XXXIX (1972), 49-62.

Anderson, Paul B. *People, Church, and State in Modern Russia.* New York: The Macmillan Company, 1944.

Annuario Pontifico, Official Yearbook. Rome: Tipografia Poliglotta Vaticana.

The *Annuario Pontifico* details such facts as the names and numbers of the Catholic bishops throughout the world, where these men are assigned, the names of dioceses, the size of the Catholic populations in a particular diocese, etc. (cited as *A.P.*).

Armstrong, Benjamin L., "The Attitude of the Soviet State to Religion, 1959-1965 as Expressed in Official Russian Periodicals." New York University, Unpublished Ph.D. dissertation, 1967.

Armstrong, John A. *Ukrainian Nationalism.* New York and London: Columbia University Press, 1963.

Bach, Marxus, *God and the Soviets*. New York: Thomas Crowell Company, 1958.

Barmine, Alexander. *One Who Survived: The Life Story of a Russian Under the Soviets*. New York: G. P. Putnam's Sons, 1945.

Barron, J. B. and H. M. Waddams, eds. *Communism and the Churches: A Documentary*. London: SCM Press, 1950.

Baran, Stepan. *Metropolyt Andrei Sheptyts'kyi* (Metropolitan Andrei Sheptyst-'kyi). Munich: Vernyhora Ukrains'ke Vydaryche Tovary Stvo, 1947.

Beeson, Trevor. *Discretion and Valour*. London: Collins, 1974.

Bello, Nino L. *The Vatican Empire*. New York: Trident Press, 1968.

Berdyaev, Nicholas. *The Origin of Russian Communism*. Ann Arbor, Michigan: The University of Michigan Press, 1966.

Billington, James. *The Icon and the Axe: An Interpretive History of Russian Culture*. New York: Alfred A. Knopf, 1966.

Bishop, Donald. *The Roosevelt-Litvinov Agreement: The American View*. Syracuse, N.Y.: Syracuse University Press, 1965.

Bissonnette, Geroges. *Moscow Was My Parish*. New York-London-Boston: Beacon Press, 1951.

Blet, Pierre *et alii*. *Actes et documents du Saint Siège relatifs à la seconde guerre mondiale*. Vol. I: *Le Saint Siège et la guerre en Europe (mars 1939-juin 1940)*. Vol. II: *Lettres de Pie XII aux évêques allemands (1939-1944)*. Vol. III: *Le Saint Siège et la situation religieuse en Pologne et dans les Pays Baltes (1939-1945)*, 2 parts. Vol. IV: *Le Saint Siège et la guerre en Europe (juin 1940-juin 1941)*. Vol. V: *Le Saint Siège et la guerre mondiale (juillet 1941-octobre 1942)*. Vol. VI: *Le Saint Siège et les victimes de la guerre (mars 1939-décembre 1940)*. Vol. VII: *Le Saint Siège et la guerre mondiale (novembre 1942-décembre 1943)*. Vol. VIII: *Le Saint Siège et les victimes de la guerre (janvier 1941-décembre 1942)*. Citta Del Vaticano: Libreria Editrice Vaticana, 1967-1974. (Cited as *Actes et documents*).

Bober, M. M. *Karl Marx's Interpretation of History*. New York: W. W. Norton and Company, Inc., 1965.

Bociurkiw, Bohdan R., "The Autocephalous Church Movement in the Ukraine," *The Ukrainian Quarterly* (Autumn, 1960), pp. 211-23.

_____, "Church-State Relations in the USSR," in William C. Fletcher and Max Haywood, eds., *Religion and the Soviet State: A Dilemma of Power*. New York: Praeger, 1969, pp. 71-104.

_____, "De-Stalinization and Religion in the U.S.S.R.," *International Journal*, Vol. XX, No. 3 (Summer, 1965), 312-30.

_____, "Lenin and Religion," in Leonard Schapiro and Peter Reddaway, eds., *Lenin: The Man, The Theorist, The Leader. A Reappraisal*. New York: Praeger, 1967, pp. 107-34.

———, "Religious Dissent and the Soviet State," in Bohdan R. Bociurkiw and John W. Strong, eds., *Religion and Atheism in the USSR and Eastern Europe.* Toronto: University of Toronto Press, 1975, pp. 58-90.

———, "Religious Dissent in the USSR: Lithuanian Catholics," in James Scanlan and Richard DeGeorge, eds., *Marxism and Religion.* Dordrecht: Reidel, 1976, pp. 147-75.

———, "The Renovationist Church in the Soviet Ukraine, 1922-1939," *Annals of Ukrainian Academy of Arts and Science,* Vol. IX, No. 1-2 (1961), 41-74.

———, "The Orthodox Church and the Soviet Regime in the Ukraine, 1953-1971," *Canadian Slavonic Papers,* Vol. XIV, No. 2 (1972), 191-211.

———, "Religion and Atheism in Soviet Societ," in Richard H. Marshall, Jr., *et alii, Aspects of Religion in the Soviet Union 1917-1967.* Chicago: University of Chicago Press, 1971, pp. 45-60.

———, "Soviet Religious Policy," *Problems of Communism* (May-June, 1973), pp. 37-51.

———, "The Uniate Church in the Soviet Ukraine: A Case Study in Soviet Church Policy," *Canadian Slavonic Papers,* Vol. VII (1965), 89-113.

Bonch-Breuvich, V. D. *Izbrannye sochineniia.* Vol. I: *O religii religioznon sektanstve i tserkvi.* Moscow: 1959.

Bolshaia sovetskaia entsiklopediia (Large Soviet Encyclopedia). 1st Edition, 65 volumes with supplementary volume on "Soiuz Sovetskikh Sotsialisticheskikh Respublik (USSR)." Moscow: Sovetskaia entsiklopediia, 1926-1947; 2nd Edition, 51 volumes, Izd-vo bolshaia sovetskaia entsiklopediia, 1950-1958.

Bolshakoff, Serge. *Russian Nonconformity.* Philadelphia: The Westminster Press, 1950.

Bourdeaux, Michael, "Dissent in the Russian Orthodox Church," *The Russian Review,* Vol. XXVIII, No. 4 (October, 1969), 416-27.

——— *Opium of the People: The Christian Religion in the USSR.* London: Faber and Faber, 1965.

——— *Patriarch and Prophets: Persecution of the Russian Orthodox Church Today.* New York: Macmillan, 1970.

———, "Reform and Schism," *Problems of Communism* (Sept.-Oct., 1967), pp. 108-118.

——— *Religion Ferment in Russia.* New York: St. Martin's Press, 1968.

Bourgeois, Charles. *A Priest in Russia and the Baltic.* Dublin-London: Burns, Oates, and Washbourne, 1953.

Braun, Leopold, "Father Braun From Moscow," *Newsweek,* Vol. XXVII (January 14, 1946), 83.

——— *Memoirs* (My Title). Unpublished manuscript, 1961, located in the Assumptionist Archives, Assumptionist Provincial House, New York,

New York.
This manuscript records Braun's experiences and recollections in Moscow from 1934 to 1946.

———, "One Catholic Priest in Russia," *The Catholic World* (March, 1945), 562-63.

——— *Religion in Russia From Lenin to Krushchev: An Uncensored Account.* Paterson, N.J.: St. Anthony Guild Press, 1959.

———, "Russian Youth Wants Religion," *The American Mercury,* Vol. LXXX-VI, No. 408 (January, 1958).

British Broadcasting Corporation. *Daily Digest of Foreign Broadcasts.* Part I & II. 1939-1950. (cited as BBC).

Bromke, Adam, "From 'Falanga' to Pax," *Survey,* No. 39 (Dec., 1961), 29-40.

Brzezinski, Zbigniew K. *Ideology and Power in Soviet Politics.* New York: Praeger, 1962.

——— *The Soviet Bloc, Unity and Conflict.* Cambridge: Harvard University Press, revised edition, 1967.

Burks, R. V. *The Dynamics of Communism in Eastern Europe.* Princeton: Princeton University Press, 1961.

Burns, James MacGregor. *Roosevelt The Soldier of Freedom 1940-1945.* New York: Harcourt, Brace, Jovanovich, Inc., 1970.

Busek, Vratislav and Nicholas Spulber, eds. *Czechoslovakia.* New York: Praeger, 1957.

Carnatiu, P. and M. Toderiniu, "Câlvarul Bisericii Unite" in *Biserica Română Unită Două Sute Ani de Istori.* Madrid: 1952, pp. 275-365.

Carr, E. H. *Socialism in One Country, 1924-1926.* New York: The Macmillan Company, 1958.

Cassidy, Henry. *Moscow Dateline 1941-1943.* Boston: Houghton Mifflin Company, 1943.

Chambon, Henry de. *La Lithuanie moderne.* Paris: Editions de la Revue parlementaire, 1933.

Chambre, Henri. *Christianisme et communisme.* Paris: 1949.

Charles-Roux, Francois. *Huit ans au Vatican.* Flammarion: 1949.

Cherniavsky, Michael, "Holy Russia: A Study in the History of an Idea," *The American Historical Review,* Vol. LXIII, No. 3 (April, 1958), 617-37.

Chew, Allen F. *An Atlas of Russian History.* New Haven and London: Yale University Press, 1967.

Chukovenkov, Iu. A., "Sovetskaia antireligioznaia pechat v 1937-1941 gg.," *Ezhegodnik muzeia istorii religii i ateizma* (Soviet antireligious press from 1937 to 1941), Vol. V (Moscow, 1961), 76-90.

Churchill, Winston S. *The Second World War.* 5 Vols. Boston: Houghton

Mifflin Company, 1948-1953.

Cianfarra, Camille. *The Vatican and the Kremlin.* New York: E. P. Dutton and Company, Inc., 1950.

Ciano, Galeazzo. *The Ciano Diaries.* Hugh Gibson, ed. Garden City, New York: Doubleday & Company, 1946.

Ciszek, Walter S. with Daniel L. Flaherty. *With God In Russia.* New York-Toronto-London: McGraw-Hill and New York: The American Press, 1964.

Claudia, M. *Guide to the Documents of Pius XII.* Westminster, Md.: The Newman Press, 1955.

Conquest, Robert. *Religion in the U.S.S.R.* New York and Washington: Praeger, 1966.

Conway, John, "The Churches, the Slovak State and the Jews 1939-1945," *The Slavonic and East European Review,* Vol. LII, No. 126 (January, 1974), 85-112.

———, "The Vatican, Great Britain, and Relations with Germany, 1938-1940," *Historical Journal,* Vol. XVI, No. 1 (1973), 146-67.

Croghan, Patrick. *Bishop Neveu* (My Title). Unpublished biography of Eugene Neveu, 1969, located in the Assumptionist Archives, Assumptionist Provincial House, New York, New York.

Cross, Samuel H. (trans.). *The Russian Primary Chronicle. Harvard Studies and Notes in Philology and Literature.* Vol. XII. Cambridge: Harvard University Press, 1930.

Curtiss, John S. *Church and State in Russia 1900-1917.* New York: Columbia University Press, 1940.

——— *The Russian Church and the Soviet State 1917-1950. Boston: Little, Brown, 1953.*

Denisoff, E., *"Aux origines de l'église russe autocephale,"* Revue des Etudes Slaves, Vol. XXIII (1947), 89-99.

Dallin, Alexander. *German Rule in Russia 1941-1945.* New York: St. Martin's Press; London: Macmillan, 1947.

Degras, Jane, ed. *Soviet Documents on Foreign Policy.* 3 Vols. London-New York-Toronto: Oxford University Press, 1953.

Delaney, Joan, "The Origins of Soviet Antireligious Organizations," in *Aspects of Religion 1917-1967,* Richard H. Marshall, Jr. Chicago: University of Chicago Press, 1971, pp. 103-29.

Deutscher, Isaac. *Stalin: A Political Biography.* New York: Oxford University Press, 1949; second edition, 1967.

Diiannia Soboru Hreko-Katolyts'koi Tserkvy, 8-10 bereznia 1946, u L'vovi (Proceedings of the Council of the Greek-Catholic Church in Lviv, 8-10 March 1946. Lviv, 1946.

Dinka, Frank, "Church and State in Poland: Political Conflict Between the Catholic Church and the Communist Regime." Unpublished Ph.D. dissertation, Washington University, 1963.

———, "Sources of Conflict Between Church and State in Poland," *Review of Politics,* Vol. XXVIII, No. 3 (July, 1966), 322-49.

Dirscherl, Denis, S. J., "The Soviet Destruction of the Greek Catholic Church," *Journal of Church and State,* Vol. XII, No. 3 (Autumn, 1970) 421-39.

Djilas, Milovan. *Conversations with Stalin.* New York: Harcourt, Brace, and World, Inc., 1962.

Documenta Pontificium Romanorum Historiam Ucrainae Illustantia 1075-1953. 2 Vols. Rome, 1954.

Documents on British Foreign Policy 1919-1939. London: His Majesty's Stantionery Office, 1947.

Documents on German Foreign Policy 1918-1945. Washington: Department of State, 1947.

Dolan, Edward, "Post-War Poland and the Church," *American Slavic and East European Review* (1955), pp. 84-92.

Dovgaliuk, P. N., "Ukrainskie pisateli o Vatikane," *Ezhegodnik muzeia istorii religii i ateizma* (Ukrainian writers on the Vatican), Vol. II (Moscow, 1958), 183-97.

Duclos, Paul. *Le Vatican et la seconde guerre mondiale. Action doctrinale et diplomatique en faveur de la paix.* Paris: Pedone, 1955.

Dufault, Wilfrid *et alii,* "Notre mission d'orient: echos du centenaire, valpre 31 mars 1963," *Pages d'archives,* No. 6 (mars 1965), 417-74.

Dunn, Dennis J., "The Catholic Church and the Soviet Government in Soviet Occupied East Europe, 1939-1940," in James P. Scanlan and Richard DeGeorge, eds., *Marxism and Religion.* Dordrecht: Reidel, 1976, pp. 107-18.

———, "The Disappearance of the Ukrainian Uniate Church: How and Why?" *Ukrains'kyi Istoryk,* 1-2 (33-34) (Munich-New York, 1972), 57-65.

———, "The Kremlin and the Vatican: *Ostopolitik,*" *Religion in Communist Lands* (London), No. 4 (Winter 1976), pp. 16-19.

———, "Papal-Communist Detente: Motivation," *Survey: A Journal of East & West Studies,* No. 99 (Spring 1976), 140-54.

———, "The Papal-Communist Détente, 1963-73: Its Evolution and Causes," in Bernard Eissenstat, ed., *The Soviet Union: The Seventies and Beyond.* Lexington, Mass.: Lexington, 1975, pp. 121-40.

———, "Pre-World War II Relations Between Stalin and the Catholic Church," *Journal of Church and State,* Vol. XV, No. 2 (Spring, 1973), 193-

204.

_____, "Stalinism and the Catholic Church During the Era of WWII," *The Catholic Historical Review*, VOl. LIX, No. 3 (October, 1973), 404-28.

Dushnyck, Walter. *Martyrdom in Ukraine: Russia Denies Religious Freedom*. New York: The American Press, n.d.

Dvornik, Francis. *The Making of Central and Eastern Europe*. London: The Polish Research Centre, Ltd., 1949.

_____ *The Slavs: Their Early History and Civilization*. Boston: Little, Brown, Inc., 1959.

Dziewanowski, Marian K. *The Communist Party of Poland. An Outline History*. Cambridge, Mass.: Harvard University Press, 1959. 2nd Edition, 1976.

_____, "Communist Poland and the Catholic Church," *Problems of Communism*, Vol. III, No. 5 (September-October, 1954), 1-2.

Engels, Friedrich. *Anti-Duhring*. New York: International Publishers, New World Paperbacks, 1939, new printing, 1966.

Enisherlov, M., ed. *Voinstvuiushchee bezbozhie v SSSR za 15 let 1917-1932* (Fifteen years of militant godlessness in the USSR). Moscow: Gos. antireligioznoe izd-vo., 1932.

Evans, Stanley. *The Churches in the USSR*. London: Cobbett Publishing Co., Ltd., 1943.

Falconi, Carlo. *The Silence of Pius XII*. London: Faber and Faber, 1970.

Feis, Herbert. *Churchill, Roosevelt, Stalin*. Princeton, N.J.: Princeton University Press, 1957.

Feuer, Lewis, ed. *Marx and Engels: Basic Writings on Politics and Philosophy*. Garden City, New York: Anchor Books, 1959 (cited as B.W.).

Fireside, Harvey. *Icon & Swastika: The Russian Orthodox Church Under Nazi and Soviet Control*. Cambridge: Harvard University Press, 1971.

Fletcher, William C. *Religion and Soviet Foreign Policy 1945-1970*. London: The Royal Institute of International Affairs by Oxford University Press, 1973.

_____, "Religious Dissent in the USSR in the 1960s," *Slavic Review*, Vol. XXX, No. 2 (June, 1971), 298-316.

_____ *Russian Orthodox Church Underground 1917-1970*. London: Oxford University Press, 1971.

_____ *A Study in Survival: The Church in Russia, 1927-1943*. New York: Macmillan, 1965.

_____ and Max Haywood, eds. *Religion and the Soviet State: A Dilemma of Power*. New York: Praeger, 1969.

Florescu, Radu, "The Uniate Church: Catalyst of Rumanian National Consciousness," *The Slavonic and East European Review* (July, 1967), pp. 324-42.

Floridi, Ulisse A. *Mosca e il Vaticano*. Milan: La Casa di Matriona, 1976.

Florinsky, Michael T. *Russia: A History and an Interpretation.* 2 Vols. New York: Macmillan, 1953.

Foreign Relations of the United States, 1939-1949. Washington: United States Government Printing Office, 1956-75.

François-Poncet, André. *Souvenirs d'une ambassade à Berlin, septembre 1931-octobre 1938.* Paris: Flammarion, 1946.

Free Europe Committee. *The Red and the Black.* New York: The National Committee For a Free Europe, 1953.

―――― *Religious Persecution in the Baltic Countries, 1940-1952.* New York: 1952.

Friedlander, Saul. *Pius XII and the Third Reich: A Documentation.* New York: Alfred A. Knopf, 1966.

Galter, Albert. *The Red Book of the Persecuted Church.* Westminster, Md.: The Newman Press, 1957.

Garkavenko, F., ed. *O religii i tserkvi. Sbornik dokumentov* (Religion and the church. Collection of documents). Moscow: Izd-vo Politicheskoi Literatury, 1965.

Geanakopolos, Deno J. *Byzantine East and Latin West: Two Worlds of Christendom in Middle Ages and Renaissance.* New York and Evanston: Harper Torchbooks, 1966.

Gecys, Casimir C., "The Roman Catholic Church in the Lithuanian SSR," *Religion in the USSR.* Munich: Institute for the Study of the USSR, 1960, pp. 103-16.

Gidulianov, P. V., ed. *Otdelenie tserkvi ot gosudarstva; polny sbornik dekretov RSFSR i SSSR, instruktsii, tsirkuliarov i.t.d.* (The Separation of the church from the state; complete collection of decrees of the RSFSR and USSR, instructions, circulars, etc.). Moscow: Iurid. izd-vo, 1924; revised edition, 1926.

Gill, Joseph. *The Council of Florence.* Cambridge: Cambridge University Press, 1959.

Gripenberg, G. A. *Finland and the Great Powers.* Lincoln: University of Nebraska Press, 1965.

Giordani, Igino. *Vita contro morte. La Santa Sede per le vittime della seconda guerra mondiale.* Milano: 1956.

Glovinsky, Yevhen, "The Ukrainian Catholic Church," *Religion in the USSR,* pp. 90-92.

Glowinsky, Eugen, "The Western Ukrainians," *Genocide in the USSR.* New York: The Scarecrow Press for the Institute for the Study of the USSR, Munich, 1958, pp. 149-51.

Golubinsky, Eugenii E. *Istoriia Russkoi Tserkvi.* 2 Vols. (History of the Russian Church) Moscow: 1901-1917.

Graham, Robert A. *Vatican Diplomacy.* Princeton: Princeton University

Press, 1959.

Griffith, William, ed. *Communism in Europe.* 2 Vols. Cambridge, Mass.: MIT Press, 1964, 1966.

Grunwald, Constantine de. *The Churches and the Soviet Union.* New York: The Macmillan Co., 1962.

Gsovski, Vladimir. *Church and State Behind the Iron Curtain.* New York: Praeger, 1955.

Halan, Iaroslav. *Izbrannoe. Perevod s ukrainskogo.* (Selections. Translations from ukrainian writings). Moscow: Sovetskii pisatel, 1952.

———. *Svet s vostoka.* (Light from the east). Moscow: Molodai gvardiia, 1954.

———. *Tvory* (Works). 2 Vols. Kiev: Derzh. vid-vo kudozh. lit-ry, 1953.

———. *Vatikan bez maski* (The Vatican unmasked). Moscow: Literaturnaiia gazeta, 1952.

Halecki, Oscar. *Borderlands of Western Civilization.* New York: The Ronald Press, 1952.

———. *From Florence to Brest (1439-1596).* New York: Fordham University Press, 1958.

——— and John Murphy. *Pius XII: Eugenio Pacelli.* New York: Farrar, Straus & Young, Inc., 1954.

Haroška, Leŭ, "The Roman Catholic Church in the Belorussian SSR," *Religion in the USSR,* pp. 93-102.

Hazard, John N. *Communists and Their Law.* Chicago: University of Chicago Press, 1969.

Henderson, Sir Neville. *Failure of a Mission: Berlin 1937-1939.* New York: G. P. Putnam's Sons, 1940.

d'Herbigny, Michel. *Évêques russes en exil.* Rome: Institut oriental, 1930.

———. *La guerre antireligieuse en Russie soviétique.* Paris: Bussière, 1930.

Heyer, Friedrich. *Die orthodoxe Kirche in der Ukraine von 1917 bis 1945.* Colgne: Rudolf Muller, 1953.

Hrynioch, Ivan, "The Destruction of the Ukrainian Catholic Church in the Soviet Union," *Prologue,* Vol. IV, No. 1-2 (Spring-Summer, 1960).

(Hungarian Government). *Documents on the Mindszenty Case.* Budapest: Athenaeum, 1949.

———. *The Trial of József Mindszenty.* Budapest: Hungarian State Publishing House, 1949.

Huntington, Samuel P. and Clement H. Moore, eds. *Authoritarian Politics in Modern Society.* New York: Praeger, 1970.

Hutten, Kurt. *Iron Curtain Christians.* Trans. Walter C. Tillmanns. Minneapolis: Augsburg Publishing House, 1967.

Iaroslavskii, E. *Borba za predelenie religii* (Struggle for religious predestination). Moscow: Ogiz, 1935.

——— *Protiv religii i tserkvi* (Against religion and church). Moscow: Ogiz, 1932.

——— *Religion in the USSR*. New York: International Publishers, 1934.

Institute for the Study of the USSR. *Genocide in the USSR*. New York: The Scarecrow Press, 1958.

——— *Religion in the USSR*. Munich: Institute for the Study of the USSR, 1960.

Ivinskis, Zenonas, "Lithuania During the War: Resistance Against the Soviet and Nazi Occupants," in V. Stanley Vardys, ed. *Lithuania Under the Soviets: Portrait of a Nation*. New York: Praeger, 1965, pp. 61-84.

Johnson, Chalmers, ed. *Change in Communist Systems*. Stanford: Stanford University Press, 1970.

Just, Bela. *Un process prefabrique, l'affaire Mindszenty*. Paris: 1949.

Kabysh, Simon, "The Belorussians," *Genocide in the USSR*, pp. 84-85.

Kandelero, D. Sh. *Katolicheskoe divizhenie v Italii* (Catholic action in Italy). Moscow: Izd-vo Akademii nauk SSSR, a955.

Kennan, George F. *Russia and the West Under Lenin and Stalin*. Boston: Little, Brown, 1960.

Kent, G. O., "Pius XII and Germany. Some Aspects of German-Vatican Relations, 1933-1943," *American Historical Review*, Vol. LXX (1964), pp. 59-78.

Kertesz, Stephen, "Church and State in Hungary," *Review of Politics*, Vol. XI (April, 1949), 208-19.

Khrushchev, Nikita. *The Crimes of the Stalin Era: Special Report to the 20th Congress of the C.P.S.U. The New Leader*, 1962.

Kliuchevsky, V. O. *Kurs russkoi istorii* (Course in russian history). 5 Vols. Petrograd: 1918-21.

Kolarz, Walter. *Religion in the Soviet Union*. New York: St. Martin's Press, 1962.

Kolosov, A., "Religii i tserkov v SSR," *Bolshaia soveitskaia entsiklopediia*. Vol. L, SSSR. Moscow: 1948, pp. 1775-90.

Korolevski, Cyrille. *Metropolite Andre Szeptyskyj, 1865-1944*. Rome: Opera Theologicae Societatis Scientificae Ucrainorum, Vols. XVI-XVII, 1964.

KPSS v rezoliutsiiakh i resheniiakh s'ezdov, konferentsii i plenumov TsK (The CPSU in resolutions and decisions of congresses, conferences and plenums of the CC). 7th edition. 4 Vols. Moscow: Gos. izd-vo polit. lit. ri., 1954-60.

Kohn, Hans, "Eastern Europe, 1948," *Current History*, Vol. XVI, No. 92 (April, 1949), 193-98.

Koval'chuk, Ia. *Ks'ondzy na Ukraini* (Priests in the Ukraine). Kharkov: Derzh. vid-vo. ukraini, 1929.

Krylenko, N. V. *Sudebnye rechi, 1922-1930* (Court speeches, 1922-1930). Moscow: Gosiurizdat, 1931.

Kryton, Constantine, "Secret Religious Organizations in the U.S.S.R., *The Russian Review,* Vol. XIV, No. 2 (April, 1955), 121-27.

Kubijovyc, Volodymyr. *Ukraine: A Concise Encyclopedia.* 2 Vols. Toronton: University of Toronto Press, 1971.

Kuroedov, Vladimir A. *Religiia i zakon* (Religion and law). Moscow: Znanie, 1970.

———— and A. S. Pankratov, eds. *Zakonodal'stvo o religioznykh kultakh: Sbornik materialov i dokumentov.* Moscow: 1971.

Langer, William L. and Everette Gleason. *The Undeclared War 1940-1941.* New York: 1953.

Laszlo, Leslie, "Church and State in Hungary, 1919-1945." Unpublished Ph.D. dissertation, Columbia University, 1973.

————, "Towards Normalisation of Church-State Relations in Hungary," in Bociurkiw and Strong, eds., *Religion,* pp. 292-313.

Latreille, Andre, *La seconde guerre mondiale 1939-1945.* Paris: 1966.

Lauterback, R. E. *These are the Russians.* New York and London: Harper and Bros., 1945.

Lazna, Michael J., "Causes of the Communist Victory in 1946 Czechoslovak Election." Unpublished Ph.D. dissertation, The George Washington University, 1971.

Lebed, Andrei, "Destruction of National Groups Through Compulsory Migration and Resettlement," *Genocide in the USSR,* pp. 6-7.

Ledit, Joseph, S. J. *Archbishop John Baptist Cieplak.* Montreal: Palm Publishers, 1964.

Lencyk, Wasyl. *The Eastern Catholic Church and Czar Nicholas I.* Rome-New York: Ukrainian Catholic University Press, 1966.

Lenin, V. I. *Religion.* New York: International Publishers, 1933.

———— *Sochineniia* (Works). 4th Edition, 35 Vols. Moscow: Institut Marksa-Engelsa-Lenina, 1941-50.

———— *V. I. Lenin ob ateizme religii i tserkvi* (V. I. Lenin on atheism, religion and churches). Moscow: Misl, 1969.

Leveque, M. *Persecution en Pologne.* Paris: Chez Leveque, 1954.

Levytsky, Boris. *The Stalinist Terror in the Thirties.* Stanford: Hoover Institution Press, 1974.

Lewy, Guenter. *The Catholic Church and Nazi Germany.* New York: McGraw-Hill Book Co., 1964.

Lichtheim, George. *Marxism: An Historical and Critical Study.* New York: Praeger, 1964.

Lowrie, Donald A. and William C. Fletcher, "Khrushchev's Religious

Policy, 1959-1964," in *Aspects of Religion*, pp. 131-55.

Lowry, Charles W. *Communism and Christianity*. New York: Collier Books, 1962.

MacEoin, Gary. *The Communist War on Religion*. New York: Devin-Adair Co., 1951.

McLellan, David. *Karl Marx: His Life and Thought*. New York: Harper, 1973.

Mailleux, Paul, S. J., "The Catholic Church in Russia and Exarch Fedorov," *Religion in Russia: A Collection of Essays Read at the Cambridge Summer School of Russian Studies, 1939*. Ed. George Bennigsen. London: Burnes, Oates and Washbourne, Ltd., 1940, pp. 31-48.

_____ *Exarch Leonid Fedorov: Bridgebuilder Between Rome and Moscow*. New York: P. J. Kenedy & Sons, 1964.

_____, "The Roman Catholics," *Aspects of Religion*, pp. 359-78.

Makarski, Stefan, "Campaign Against the Church," *Polish Affairs*, Vol. XII, 1/2 (February, 1965), 5-9.

Manhattan, Avro. *The Vatican in World Politics*. New York: Gaer Associates, 1949.

Marin, Y., "The Moscow Patriarchate in Soviet Foreign and Domestic Policy," *Bulletin*, Vol. III, No. 2 (February, 1961).

Markham, R. H. *Communists Crush Churches in Eastern Europe*. Boston: Meader Publishing Co., 1950.

Markus, Vasyl. *Nyshchennia Hreko-Katolyts'koi Tserkvy v Mukachivs'kii Ieparkhii v 1945-1950*. (Destruction of the Greek-Catholic Church in the Muchachiv Diocese in 1945-1950). Paris: 1962.

_____, "Religion and Nationality: The Uniates of the Ukraine," in Bociurkiw and Strong, *Religion*, pp. 101-22.

Marshall, Richard H., Jr. *et alii*, eds. *Aspects of Religion in the Soviet Union 1917-1967*. Chicago: The University of Chicago Press, 1971.

Marx, Karl. *Das Kapital*. Edited by Friedrich Engels and condensed by Serge L. Levitsky. Vol. I. Chicago: Henry Regnery Co., Gateway Edition, 1961.

_____ and Friedrich Engles. *Harold J. Laski on the Communist Manifesto*. New York: Random House, Vintage Books, 1967.

Marzari, Frank, "The Bessarabian Microcosm, September 1939-February 1940," *Canadian Slavonic Papers*, Vol. XII, No. 2 (1970), 128-41.

Mastny, Vojtech, "Stalin and the Prospect of a Separate Peace in World War II," *The American Historical Review*, Vol. LXXVII, No. 5 (December, 1972), 365-88.

Maynard, Sir John. *The Russian Peasants and Other Studies*. London: Victor Gollancz, Ltd., 1943.

Mazgaj, Marion S., J. C. D., "The Communist Government of Poland as

Affecting the Rights of the Church from 1944 to 1960." Unpublished Ph.D. dissertation, The Catholic University of America, 1970.

McCullagh, Capt. Francis. *The Bolshevik Persecution of Christianity*. London: E. P. Dutton, 1924.

McNeal, Robert, ed. *Stalin's Works*. Stanford: The Hoover Institution on War, Revolution and Peace, Bibliographical Series: XXVI, 1967.

Medvedev, Roy A. *Let History Judge: The Origins and Consequences of Stalinism*. New York: Alfred A. Knopf, 1972.

Metropolitan Nikolai, ed. *The Russian Orthodox Church and the War Against Fascism*. Moscow: 1943.

Michel, A. *Religious Problems in a Country Under Communist Rule*. Rome: Pont. Greg. Univ. Press, 1954.

Mikhnevich, D. E. *Ocherki iz istorii katolicheskoi reaktsii* (Outlines of the history of catholic reaction). Moscow: Izd-vo Akademii nauk SSSR, 1953.

Mindszenty, Cardinal Jozsef. *Four Years' Struggle of the Church in Hungary*. London: Longmans, Green Co., 1949.

———. *Memoirs*. London: Weidenfeld and Nicolson, 1974.

Mirtchuk, J., "The Ukrainian Uniate Church." *Slavonic Review*, Vol. X, No. 29 (December, 1931), 377-85.

Misiunas, Romuald J., "Fascist Tendencies in Lithuania," *The Slavonic and East European Review*, Vol. XLVIII, No. 110 (January, 1970), 88-109.

Monticone, Ronald C., "The Catholic Church in Poland, 1945-1946," *Polish Review*, Vol. XI, No. 4 (1966), 75-100.

Moskovskaia Patriarkhiia. *Patriarch Sergii i ego dukovnoe nasledstvo* (Patriarch Sergii and his spiritual legacy). Moscow: Izd- Moskovskoi patriarkhii, 1947.

———. *Russkaia Pravoslavnaia Tserkov; ustovoistvo, polozhenie, deiatelnost* (Russian Orthodox Church; decrees, statutes, activities). Moscow: Izd. Moskovskoi Patriarkhii, 1958.

———. *The Truth About Religion in Russia*. Moscow: Moscow Patrarchate, 1942.

Mourin, Maxime. *Le Vatican et l'URSS*. Paris: Editions du Seuil, 1963.

National Committee For a Free Europe. *Poland in the Year 1951*. New York: 1953.

Nemec, Ludwig. *Church and State in Czechoslovakia*. New York: Vantage Press, 1955.

Nicholas, J., "L'Assomption en Russie," *Pages d'archives*, No. 3 (decembre, 1955), 37-52.

Norem, Owen J. C. *Timeless Lithuania*. Chicago: Amerlith Press, 1943.

Nowicki, Donald, "Mosce e Solowski." Unpublished manuscript at the Pontifical Institute of Oriental Studies, Rome.

Obolensky, Dmitri, "Russia's Byzantine Heritage," *Oxford Slavonic Papers*,

Vol. I (1950). Oxford: Clarendon Press, pp. 37-63.

Ogden, Georgine L., "Russian Imperialism as a Cause of Permanent War," *The Ukrainian Quarterly*, Vol. XXVIII, No. 2 (1972), 166-77.

Oleshchuk, F. *Borba tserkvi protiv naroda* (The Struggle of the Church against the people). Moscow: Gos. izd-vo. polit. lit-ry, 1939.

Orleanskii, Nikolai, ed. *Zakon o religioznych ob'edineniiakh* RSFSR (Law on religious unification RSFSR). Moscow: Izdatelstvo Bezbozhnik, 1930.

Orlov, Alexander. *The Secret History of Stalin's Crimes*. London-New York: Jarrolds, Publishers, 1957.

Ostrogorsky, George. *History of the Byzantine State*. New Brunswich, N.J.: Rutgers University Press, 1957.

Pacelli, Eugenio Cardinale et Franz von Papen, "Inter Sanctam Sedem et Germanicam Respublicam Sollemnis Conventio," *Acta Apostolicae Sedis*, Vol. XXV (1933), 389-408.

Pavelkin, P. *Religioznye sueveriia i ikh vred* (Religious superstitions and their harmfulness). Moscow: Gos. izd-vo. polit. lit-ry., 1951.

Pellegrino, Francesco, S. J., "L'attacco a fondo dell'ateismo sovietico," *Civiltà Cattolica*, III (1941), 181-96.

———, "Sopvavvivenza religiosa nella Russia sovietica," *Civiltà Cattolica*, IV (1941), 25-34.

Persits, M. M. *Otdelenie tserkvi ot gosudarsvta i shkoly ot tserkvi v SSSR (1917-1919 gg.)* (Separation of the church from the state and the schools from the church in the USSR (1917-1919 gg.). Moscow: Izd-vo. Akademii nauk SSR, 1958.

Pontificia Commissio Pro Russia, "De precibus pro Russia in Liturgia non latina," *Acta Apostolicae Sedis*, Vol. XXII (1930), 366.

Powell, David E. *Antireligious Propaganda in the Soviet Union*. Cambridge, Mass.: The MIT Press, 1975.

PP. Pius XI, *Acta Apostolicae Sedis*, 1923-1937.

PP. Pius XII, *Acta Apostolicae Sedis*, 1937-1949.

Quénard, G., "L'Assomption en Russie: Les premiers pionniers avant la guerre de 1941," *Pages d'archives*, No. 11 (octobre 1959), 369-84.

Reshetar, J. S., "Ukrainian Nationalism and the Orthodox Church," *The American Slavic and East European Review*, No. 1 (1951), 38-49.

"The Results of the Nineteenth Congress of the Communist Party of the USSR and the Death of Stalin," *Proceedings of the Conference of the Institute for the Study of the History and Culture of the USSR*, New York, March 20, 22, 1953. Munich: 1953.

Reynarowych, Roman, "The Catholic Church in the West Ukraine after World War II," *Diakonia*, No. 4 (1970), 372-87.

Rigby, T. H., ed. *Stalin*. Englewood Cliffs, N.J.: Prentice-Hall, Inc., Great

Lives Observed Series, 1966.

Rhodes, Anthony. *The Vatican in the Age of the Dictators 1922-1945*. London: Hodder and Stoughton, 1973.

The Royal Institute of International Affairs. *The Baltic States*. London: 1938.

Russkaia Pravoslavnaia Tserkov. *Velikaia Otechestvennaia voina: Sbornik* (Great Fatherland war: Collection). Moscow: Obraztsovaia tipografiia ogiza, 1944.

Saburova, Irina, "The Soviet Occupation of the Baltic States," *The Russian Review*, Vol. XIV, No. 1 (January, 1955), 36-49.

Sacra Congregation Consistorialis, "Declaration," *Acta Apostolicae Sedis*, Vol. XLI (1948), 31.

Sacra Congregazione Per La Chiesa Orientale, "Communicato," *Acta Apostolicae Sedis*, Vol. XVIII (1926), 62.

Savelev, S. N., "Em. Iaroslavsky i preodolenie anarkhistskikh vliiany v antireligioznoi rabote v SSSR," (E. Iaroslavsky and the overcoming of anarchistic influence in antireligious work in the USSR), *Ezhegodnik*, Vol. VII (1963), pp. 37-49.

Savasis, Jonas. *The War Against God in Lithuania*. New York: Manyland Books, 1966.

Segal', H. M. *Vatikan na sluzhbe u amerikanskoi reaktsii* (The Vatican in the service of american reaction). Moscow: 1948.

Schuster, G. W. *Religion Behind the Iron Curtain*. New York: Macmillan Co., 1954.

Seniga, Guill. *Togliatti e Stalin*. Milano: Sugar editore, 1961.

Senn, Alfred E. *The Emergence of Modern Lithuania*. New York: Columbia University Press, 1959.

Seton-Watson, Hugh. *The East European Revolution*. 3rd Edition. New York: Praeger, 1954.

Shakhnovich, M. I. *Lenin i problemy ateizma* (Lenin and the problem of atheism). Leningrad: Izd-vo Akademii Nauk SSSR, 1961.

Sheinman, M. M. *Idiologia i politika Vatikana na sluzhbe imperializma* (The Ideology and politics of the Vatican in the service of imperialism). Moscow: Gos. izd-vo. polit. lit-ry., 1950.

———. *Kratkie ocherki istorii papstva* (Short outline of the history of the papacy). Moscow: Akademiia nauk SSSR, 1952.

———, "Modernizm i modernizatsiia v katolitsizme," *Ezhegodnik muzeia istorii religii i ateizma* (Modernism and modernization in catholicism). Vol. II (Moscow, 1958), 230-51.

———, *Papstvo* (Papacy). Moscow: Izd-vo. Akademii nauk SSSR, 1959.

———. *Religiia v period imperializma* (Religion in the period of imperialism). Moscow: Znanie, 1955.

_____ *Sokrashchenie istorii papstva* (An Abridgement of history of the papacy). Moscow: Izd-vo. Akademii nauk SSSR, 1952.

_____ *Sovremennyi Vatikan* (Contemporary Vatican). Moscow: Izd-vo. Akademii nauk SSSR, 1955.

_____ *Vatikan i katolitsizm na sluzhbe imperializma (The Vatican and catholicism in the service of imperialism).* Moscow: Pravda, 1950.

_____ *Vatikan i katolitsizm na sluzhbe mezhdunarodnoi reaktsii* (Vatican and catholicism in the service of international reaction). Moscow: Gos. izdvo. kulturno-prosvetitelnoi lit-ry, 1954.

_____, "Vatikan i Rossiia v period mezhdu Fevralem i Octiabrem 1917g.," (Vatican and Russia in the period between February and October 1917), *Voprosy istorii religii i ateisma,* V (Moscow, 1958), 72-89.

_____ *Vatikan mezhdu dvumia morivymi voinami* (The Vatican between two world wars). Moscow: Izd-vo. Akademii nauk SSSR, 1948.

_____ *Vatikan vo Vtoroi Mirovoi voine* (The Vatican during the Second World War). Moscow: Izd-vo Akademii nauk SSSR, 1951.

_____ *Vatikan, vrag mira i demokratii* (The Vatican, enemy of peace and democracy). Moscow: Molodaia gvardiia, 1950.

Shub, David. *Lenin.* New York: Doubleday, 1949.

Shuster, George N. *In Silence I Speak.* New York: Farrar, Straus, & Cudahy, 1956.

Simon, Gerhard, "The Catholic Church and the Communist State in the Soviet Union and Eastern Europe," in Bociurkiw and Strong, *Religion,* pp. 190-221.

_____ *Church, State and Opposition in the U.S.S.R.* Berkeley and Los Angeles: University of California Press, 1974.

Slipyi, Josyf. *Tvory* (Works). Rome: 1968-69.

Sloskans, Mgr. Boleslas, "Diario di S. E. Mons. Boleslao Sloskan." Unpublished manuscript at the Pontifical Institute of Oriental Studies, Rome.

Smith, Walter Bedell. *My Three Years in Moscow.* Philadelphia: Lippincott, 1950.

Solzhenitsyn, Alexander. *Gulag Archipelago.* New York: Harper and Row, 1973-74.

Somerville, John. *The Philosophy of Marxism: An Exposition.* New York: Random House, 1967.

Sourvarine, Boris. *Stalin: A Critical Survey of Bolshevism.* Trans. C. L. R. James. New York: Alliance Book Corporation; London: Martin Secker & Warburg, Ltd., 1939.

Soveshchanie glav i predstavitelei avtokefal'nykh pravoslavnykh tserkvei, Moscow, 1948. *Actes de la Conferences des chefs et des representants des eglises orthodoxes autocephales.* 2 Vols. Moscow: Moscow Patriarchate, 1952.

Spasov, G. *Freedom of Religion in the USSR.* London: Soviet News, 1951.

Spinka, Matthew. *Christianity Confronts Communism.* New York-London: Harper, 1936.

———. *The Church and the Russian Revolution.* New York: Macmillan, 1927.

———. *The Church in Soviet Russia.* New York: Oxford University Press, 1956.

Spreaight, Robert. *Voice of the Vatican. The Vatican Radio in Wartime.* London: (1942).

Stalin, J. V. *Sochineniia* (Works). 3 Vols. Edited by Robert H. McNeal. Stanford: Hoover Institute for War, Revolution, and Peace, 1967.

———. *Works.* 13 volumes published (see Robert McNeal, *Stalin's Works,* above, for vols. 14-16). Moscow: 1952-55.

Standley, William H. and Arthur A. Ageton. *Admiral Ambassador to Russia.* Chicago: Henry Regnery, 1955.

Staron, Stanislaw, "State-Church Relations in Poland," *World Politics,* Vol. XXI, No. 4 (July, 1969), 575-601.

Stehle, Hansjacob. *Die Ostpolitik des Vatikans.* Munich: 1975.

Stremooukhoff, Dimitri, "Moscow, the Third Rome: Sources of the Doctrine," *Speculum,* Vol. XXVIII, No. 1 (January, 1953), 84-101.

Strik-Strikfeldt, Wilfried. *Against Stalin & Hitler, 1941-1945.* New York: John Day, 1970.

Stroyen, William B. *Communist Russia and the Russian Orthodox Church 1943-1962.* Washington, D.C.: The Catholic University of American Press, 1967.

Struve, Nikita. *Les Chretians en URSS.* Paris: Editions du Seuil, 1963.

Suprema Sacra Congregation Sancti Officii, "Decretum: Schismatica 'Action Catholica' in Cecoslovachia damnatur," *Acta Apostolicae Sedis,* Vol. XLI (1949), 333.

Swan, Jane. *A Biography of Patriarch Tikhon.* Jordanville, New York: Holy Trinity Russian Orthodox Monastery, 1964.

Szczesniak, Boleslaw. *The Russian Revolution and Religion.* Notre Dame: University of Notre Dame Press, 1959.

Szuldrzynski, Jan. *The Patterns of Life in Poland: The Situation of the Catholic Church.* Paris: 1953.

Taborsky, Edward. *Communism in Czechoslovakia 1948-1960.* Princeton: Princeton University Press, 1961.

Taylor, Myron C. (intro. and explanatory notes). *Wartime Correspondence Between President Roosevelt and Pope Pius XII.* New York: Macmillan, 1947.

Teodorovich, N., "The Political Role of the Moscow Patriarchate," *Studies on the Soviet Union,* Vol. IV, No. 4 (1965), 241-47.

———, "The Roman Catholics," *Genocide in the USSR,* pp. 214-18.

Timasheff, N. S. *The Great Retreat.* New York: E. P. Dutton, 1946.

———. *Religion in Soviet Russia 1917-1942.* New York: Sheed and Ward, 1942.

Tobias, Robert. *Communist-Christian Encounter in East Europe.* Indianapolis, Ind.: School of Religion Press, 1956.

Togliatti, Palmiro. *Per La Salvezza de Nostra Paese.* Rome: 1946.

Toma, Peter A. and Milan J. Reban, "Church-State Schism in Czechoslovakia," in Bociurkiw and Strong, *Religion,* pp. 273-91.

Torma, A. and H. Perlitz. *The Church in Estonia: The Fate of Religion and Church Under Soviet Rule in Estonia, 1940-1941.* New York: World Association of Estonians, 1944.

Toumanoff, Cyril, "Moscow the Third Rome: Gensis and Significance of a Politico-Religious Idea," *The Catholic Historical Review,* Vol. XL (1955), pp. 411-47.

Trakiskis, A. *The Situation of the Church and Religion Practices in Occupied Lithuania* pt. 1: "Under Soviet Occupation, 1940-1941," New York: Lithuanian Bulletin, 1944.

Treadgold, Donald W. *Twentieth Century Russia.* Chicago: Rand McNally & Co., 3rd Edition, 1972.

———. *The West in Russia and China.* Vol. I: *Russia, 1472-1917.* Cambridge: Cambridge University Press, 1973.

Tucker, Robert C. *The Soviet Political Mind.* New York-London: Praeger, 1963.

———. *Stalin as Revolutionary, 1879-1929.* New York: Norton, 1973.

Tyshkevich, S. *Sovetskoi bezbozhie i papstvo* (Soviet godless and the papacy). Rome: 1950.

Tyszkiewicz, S., S. J. (Tyshkevich), "L'Ateismo Militante Sovietico e Il Papato," *Civiltà Cattolica,* II (1949), 593-603; III (1949), 16-27.

"Litterature antireligieuse en U.R.S.S.," *Bulletin de l'association d'etudes et d'informations politiques internationales,* No. 105 (mars 1-15, 1954), 1-15.

Ulam, Adam B. *The Bolsheviks.* New York: Macmillan, 1965.

———. *Expansion & Coexistence: The History of Soviet Foreign Policy 1917-1973.* New York: Praeger, 1974.

———. *Stalin.* New York: Harper, 1973.

———. *Titoism and the Cominform.* Cambridge: Harvard University Press, 1952.

———. *The Unfinished Revolution: An Essay on the Sources of Influence of Marxism and Communism.* New York: Random House, 1960.

U.S., "Communist Offenses Against the Integrity of Education, Science, and Culture," *Collected Intelligence Research Reports on Communism: United States Government, 1949-1954* (cited as CIRRCUS Materials). On microfilm at Kent State University, Kent, Ohio.

———. Foreign Broadcast Information Service. *Daily Reports, Foreign Radio*

Broadcasts, 1947-1951 (cited as *Daily Reports*).

——— House of Representatives, Committee on Foreign Affairs, *Antireligious Activities in the Soviet Union and Eastern Europe, May 10-12, 1965.* (89th Cong. 1st Sess.). Washington, D.C.: U.S. Government Printing Office, 1965.

——— House of Representatives. *Hearings Before the Select Committee to Investigate the Incorporation of the Baltic States into the USSR,* Part I (83rd Cong. 1st Sess). Washington, D.C.: U.S. Government Printing Office, 1953.

——— Library of Congress, Legislative Reference Service, *World Communist Movement, Selective Chronology 1818-1957,* Vol. II: 1946-50, Vol. III: 1951-53. 4 Vols. (88th Cong. 1st Sess.). Washington, D.C.: U.S. Government Printing Office, 1963.

——— Senate, Committee on the Judiciary, *Communist Controls on Religious Activity:* Hearing Before the Subcommittee . . . May 5, 1959. (86th Cong. 1st Sess.). Washington, D.C.: U.S. Government Printing Office, 1959.

——— Committee on the Judiciary, *Communist Exploitation of Religion:* Hearing before the Subcommittee . . . May 6 1966. (89th Cong. 2d Sess.). Washington, D.C.: U.S. Government Printing Office, 1966.

——— Committee on the Judiciary, *The Church and State Under Communism:* A Special Study of the Subcommittee, Vol. I, Parts 1-3: *The USSR,* Vol. IV: *Lithuania, Latvia, and Estonia,* Vol. V: *Poland,* Vol. VI: *Hungary, Czechoslovakia, German Democratic Republic.* (89th Cong. 1st Sess.). Washington, D.C.: U.S. Government Printing Office, 1965.

——— Committee on the Judiciary, *A Study of the Anatomy of Communist Takeovers.* (89th Cong. 2d Sess.). Washington, D.C.: U.S. Government Printing Office, 1966.

Vahter, Leonard, "Aspects of Life in Estonia: Religious Persecution," *Baltic Review,* No. 28 (December, 1964), 39-56.

Vakar, Nicholas P. *Belorussia: The Making of a Nation.* Cambridge: Harvard University Press, 1956.

Valentinov, A. A. *The Assault of Heaven: A Collection of Facts and Documents Relating to the Persecution of Religion and Church in Russia Baed Mainly Upon Official Sources.* London: Boswell Printing and Publishing Co., 1929. Trans. of Russian work published in 1925.

Valkenier, Elizabeth, "The Catholic Church in Communist Poland, 1945-1955," *Review of Politics,* Vol. XVIII (July, 1956), 305-26.

Valters, Nikolaus, "The Roman Catholic Church in Latvia and Estonia," *Religion in the USSR,* pp. 117-20.

Vardys, V. Stanley, "Catholicism in Lithuania," *Aspects of Religion,* pp. 379-

403.

———, ed. *Lithuania Under the Soviets: Portrait of a Nation.* New York: Praeger, 1965.

———, "Modernization and Baltic Nationalism," *Problems of Communism* (Sept.-Oct., 1975), pp. 32-48.

———, "Modernization and Latin Rite Catholics," in Dennis J. Dunn, ed. *Religion and Modernization in the Soviet Union,* forthcoming.

Vasiliev, A. A. *History of the Byzantine Empire 324-1453.* Madison: The University of Wisconsin Press, 1952.

Vasilii, Diakon, OSBM. *Leonid Fedorov. Zhizn' i deiatel'nost'.* (Leonid Fedorov. Life and Works). Rome: "Studion" Publications, III-IV, 1966.

Vernadsky, George. *A History of Russia.* New Haven and London: Yale University Press, 12th Printing, 1968.

Vignieri, Vittorio, "Soviet Policy Toward Religion in Lithuania: The Case of Roman Catholicism," *Lithuania Under the Soviets,* pp. 215-27.

Vlasovs'kyi, I. *Narys istorii ukrains'koi pravoslavnoi tserkvy.* Vol. IV, Parts I & II. New York-Bound Brook, N.J.: 1961, 1966.

Von Rauch, Georg. *The Baltic States.* Berkeley and Los Angeles: University of California Press, 1974.

Vozchikov, M. S. *Sovremenii Vatikan, ego ideologiia i politika* (Contemporary Vatican, its ideology and politics). Moscow: Znanie, 1957.

——— *Podryvnaia deiatelnost katolicheskoi reaktsii* (Damaging activities of catholic reaction). Moscow: Znanie, 1954.

——— *Vatkian na sluzhbe amerikanskogo imperializma* (Vatican in the service of American imperialism). Moscow: Znanie, 1952.

Walsh, Edmund A. *The Last Stand: An Interpretation of the Soviet Five-Year Plan.* Boston: Little, Brown, 1931.

Ware, Timothy. *The Orthodox Church.* Baltimore: Penguin Books, 1963.

Weidle, Vladimir. *Russia: Absent and Present.* Trans. A. Gordon Smith. New York: Vintage Books, 1961.

Weingartner, Erich, ed. *Church Within Socialism: Based on the Work of Giovanni Barberini.* Rome: IDOC International, 1976.

Werth, Alexander. *Russia at War, 1941-1945.* New York: E. P. Dutton and Co., 1964.

Wetter, Gustav A. *Dialectical Materialism: A Historical and Systematic Survey of Philosophy in the Soviet Union.* Trans. Peter Heath. New York: Praeger, 1958.

Wheeler-Bennett, John W. *The Nemesis of Power.* London: Macmillan, 1964.

Wierbianski, B., ed. *White Paper on the Persecution of the Church in Poland.* London: n.d.

Wilmot, Chester. *The Struggle for Europe.* New York: Harper and Brothers, 1952.

Winter, E., "O papskoi politike ob'edineniia tserkvei," (On papal politics of
    church unification), *Ezhegodnik muzeia istorii religii i ateizma,* Vol. VI
    (Moscow, 1962), 18-28.
Wolff, Robert Lee, "The Three Romes: The Migration of an Ideology and
    the Making of an Autocrat," *Daedalus,* Vol. LXXXVIII (1959), 291-311.
Yemeliakh, L. I., ed. *Pravda o religii; sbornik* (Truth on religion; documents).
    Moscow: Gos. izd-vo. polit. lit-ry., 1959.
Zaborov, M. A. *Krestovye pokhody* (The Crusades). Moscow: Izd-vo. Akade-
    mii nauk SSSR, 1956.
Zatko, James J. *Descent into Darkness.* Notre Dame: The University of Notre
    Dame Press, 1965.
Zawodny, J. K. *Death in the Forest.* Notre Dame: The University of Notre
    Dame Press, 1962.
Zenkovsky, Serge. *Medieval Russia's Epics, Chronicles, and Tales.* New York: E.
    P. Dutton, 1963.
Zubek, T. *The Church of Silence in Slovakia.* Whiting, Ind.: John Lach, 1956.

Newspapers and Periodicals

Antireligioznik (The Antireligious), periodical, organ (1924-1941) of the
    League of Militant Atheists.
Bezbozhnik (The Godless), Periodical, organ (1923, 1932-41) of the League of
    Militant Atheists.
Bezbozhnik (The Godless), newspaper, organ (1922-1934, 1938-1941) of the
    League of Militant Atheists.
Bolshevik, former political and economic journal of the Soviet Communist
    Party.
Civiltà Cattolica, organ of the Society of Jesus, Rome.
Current Digest of the Soviet Press, weekly. 1949. Published at Ohio State
    University under auspices of the American Association for the Ad-
    vancement of Slavic Studies.
East Europe, periodical issued by the Free Europe Committee.
La documentation catholique, French Catholic weekly.
Il Quotidiano, newspaper, organ of Italian Catholic Action.
Izvestiia (News), newspaper, organ of the Presidium of the Supreme Soviet
    of the USSR.
Kommunist (The Communist), formerly *Bolshevik,* periodical, organ of the
    Central Committee of the CPSU.
Komsomolskaia Pravda (Young Communist Truth), newspaper, organ of the
    Central and Moscow Komsomol Committees.

Laboro, newspaper, organ of the Italian Socialist Party.

Manchester Guardian.

Molodoi bolshevik (Young bolshevik', now *Molodoi kommunist* (Young communist), periodical, organ of the Komsomol Central Committee.

Nauka i religiia (Science and religion), monthly, Znanie Society.

Nauka i zhisn (Science and life), periodical, Znanie Society.

Newsletter from Behind the Iron Curtain, periodical, Free Europe Committee.

New York Herald Tribune.

New York Times.

L'Osservatore Romano, newspaper, semi-official organ of the Vatican.

Polish Facts and Figures, issued by Polish Embassy, London.

Pravda (Truth), newspaper, organ of the Central Committee of the CPSU.

Revoliutsiia i tserkov (Revolution and church), journal, first national antireligious periodical of Bolsheviks.

Soviet Monitor, issued by Tass, London.

Tablet (London), Catholic newspaper, weekly.

The Times (London).

Unita, newspaper, organ of the Italian Communist Party.

Voiovnychyi ateist (Militant atheist), now *Liudyna i svit* (Man and the world), antireligious monthly in Ukrainian language.

Voprosy nauchnogo ateizma (Problems of scientific atheism), biannual issued by Institute of Scientific Atheism of the Academy of Social Science of Central Committee of the CPSU.

Zhurnal Moskovskoi Patriarkhii (Journal of the Moscow Patriarchate), periodical, organ of the Moscow Patriarchate.

INDEX

EAST EUROPEAN MONOGRAPHS